WALK
THRU THE
BIBLE
TAKE A WALK. CHANGE THE WORLD.

The ONE YEAR walk with GOD
DEVOTIONAL

365 daily Bible readings
to transform your mind

chris tiegreen

TYNDALE HOUSE PUBLISHERS, INC.
Carol Stream, Illinois

Visit Tyndale's exciting Web site at www.tyndale.com.

TYNDALE and Tyndale's quill logo are registered trademarks of Tyndale House Publishers, Inc.

The One Year is a registered trademark of Tyndale House Publishers, Inc.

LeatherLike is a registered trademark of Tyndale House Publishers, Inc.

The Walk Thru the Bible logo is a registered trademark of Walk Thru the Bible Ministries, Inc.

The One Year Walk with God Devotional: 365 Daily Bible Readings to Transform Your Mind

Designed by Jennifer Ghionzoli

ISBN 978-1-4143-1661-1 (lthrlike)
ISBN 978-1-4143-0056-6 (sc)

Printed in China

16   15   14   13   12   11
13   12   11   10   9   8

DEDICATION

With grateful appreciation to Paul and Marilyn Johnson whose faith, leadership, generosity, and service in ministry have advanced the Kingdom of God and blessed innumerable lives.

INTRODUCTION

We are told in Romans 12:2 to be transformed by the renewing of our minds. As every Christian knows, that's a process. We did not come into this world with a clear perception about God and His Kingdom—or about our own selves, for that matter. We began with distorted views, and part of our task as Christians is to let God change our views to accurately reflect His character and His Kingdom. In other words, we need wisdom.

That's what these daily readings are about. They are aimed at redirecting our thinking so that we understand ourselves, our world, and our God accurately. They are designed to move us further along that path of having our minds renewed and our lives transformed.

Although the focus in these devotionals is biblical wisdom, the readings are not limited to what we normally consider the Bible's "wisdom literature"— Job, Psalms, Proverbs, Ecclesiastes, and Song of Songs. These books are the core of biblical wisdom, but God's mind is found everywhere throughout the Scriptures. You will find that about half of these devotionals come from the wisdom books, and about half come from other parts of the Bible. In every case, however, the daily reading is meant to help you reflect on how your mind works.

As you read these wisdom devotionals, remember that the Word of God expresses the mind of God. His thoughts are available to us. Let these devotionals help you dig deeper into His revelation. Let His Spirit change your thinking. Most of all, let your mind be renewed and your life be transformed.

Where Wisdom Begins

The fear of the Lord is the beginning of wisdom.
PROVERBS 9:10

JANUARY 1
Proverbs 9:10-12

IN WORD   We're uncomfortable with the idea of fearing God. We defend Him as One whose love is so great He needs not be feared. As 1 John 4:18 says: "Perfect love drives out fear." So we redefine fear as "awe" and "reverence." Yet the Scriptures use the term "fear of God" frequently enough to give us the impression that something more than awe is appropriate. It is the kind of fear that terrified the disciples when they heard God's voice at the Transfiguration (Matthew 17:6); that overwhelmed Isaiah when he cried out: "Woe to me! . . . I am ruined!" in God's presence (Isaiah 6:5); and that drove John facedown at the sight of the glorified Son (Revelation 1:17).

True wisdom is gazing at God.

—the Syrian

Why does a God of love tell us that wisdom begins when we fear Him? Because when we approach the Holy One with a casual familiarity, we are not living in reality. We do not take Him as seriously as we ought, and we do not take our sin as seriously as we ought. Fear—not of punishment but of the overwhelming greatness of God—sees Him correctly. When we stand on the edge of the vast, bottomless chasm that separates us from Him, and we behold the immeasurable expense He paid to bridge that chasm, we experience fear. Fear of what would have been if we had never known the gospel. Fear of our own unworthiness. Fear of the absolute dedication to Him that is now required of us. When this fear grips us, we begin to understand the enormity of the gospel and of our God. That understanding begins to rearrange our lives. And that is what wisdom is all about.

IN DEED   It is vital that we know God's love and rest comfortably in it. But a true understanding of God's love begins with an overwhelming awareness of His greatness, holiness, and power as they contrast our own sinful nature. There is nothing more fear-inducing than that. But this is where we must begin. This will shape our self-awareness, our relationships, our work, our prayers—*everything* we think and do. It will make us wise.

1

Wise Worship

I urge you, brothers, in view of God's mercy, to offer your bodies as living sacrifices, holy and pleasing to God—this is your spiritual act of worship. ROMANS 12:1

JANUARY 2
Romans 12:1-2

Worship . . . is not part of the Christian life; it is the Christian life.

—Gerald Vann

IN WORD Wisdom begins with basing one's life on reality. "The fear of the LORD is the beginning of wisdom" (Proverbs 9:10). Why? Because fear of the Lord is based on a true understanding of who we really are and who God really is. But there is a next step. Wisdom doesn't begin and end with fear; it continues into worship. When we really understand who God is, the natural response is to offer Him whatever we can get our hands on—and all we have is ourselves.

All of those in the Bible who encountered the living God in His glory fell on their face in worship. Like Isaiah, they would offer themselves (Isaiah 6:8). If we have not yet gotten to that point of laying ourselves on the altar before Him—*without reservation*—we have not yet encountered the living God. His glory prompts sacrifice. It is the only wise, intelligent, reasonable response to the magnitude of His goodness.

IN DEED We often think of worship as words and songs that come out of our mouths. It is so much more. It is a lifestyle, a sacrificial way of living that acknowledges every moment of every day that there is One far more worthy of our allegiance than ourselves. When His interests consistently supercede ours, and we act accordingly, we are worshiping.

Imagine yourself in the throne room of God. See the altar at His feet. Get on it. Lay yourself out before Him and say to Him: "I am Yours. Do with me as You will. I give up my right to govern myself, because You are far more worthy to do it, and You will never do me harm. I exist for Your purposes, and for Yours alone." Do this every morning, then live out your day mindful of whose you are. In light of who He is, this is true worship. And true worship is the wisest thing we can do.

A Higher Mind

We have the mind of Christ.
1 CORINTHIANS 2:16

IN WORD At first glance, Paul's claim is boastful. It would not go over well in our "politically correct" culture of today. It probably did not go over well in the Corinthian culture then, except within the church. There, it would have been a treasured truth and an amazing revelation.

So it is with us. It is almost unthinkable: the mind of the One through whom the entire universe was created, the fount of all wisdom, is available to us. We are not limited to human reasoning. We are not bound by the limitations of history's greatest thinkers, who, while often exceeding human standards of intelligence, have all fallen drastically short of discovering eternal truth by natural means. No, we have a supernatural access to ultimate reality from an eternal perspective. We know the direction of history and where it is leading; we know how to escape this fallen world; and we know who holds all power in the palm of His right hand. This vast, incomprehensible treasure is ours—if we will accept it.

That's our problem. We often resort to lesser means of wisdom because we're unaware that the mind of Christ is accessible, or we're unable to believe such an extravagant promise. But if we can't believe it, we can't have it. The mind of Christ is ours through the Spirit of God, who comes to us only through faith. The Spirit searches the deep things of God (v. 10) and reveals them to His people. Such things are foolish to the world, but they are truth nonetheless—truth that we can know and base our lives on.

IN DEED You have your own mind. You also have Christ's. Which would you rather depend on? Begin each day by disavowing your own wisdom. We must acknowledge that we do not have the understanding to make the decisions we will face each day. We do not know all the details or future implications of any decision. But God does, and He makes His wisdom available. Acknowledge your utter dependence on the mind of Christ, ask for His wisdom, and believe.

JANUARY 3
1 Corinthians 2:6-16

The truly wise are those whose souls are in Christ.

—St. Ambrose

3

Driven by Instinct

In the last times there will be scoffers who will
follow their own ungodly desires.   JUDE 18

JANUARY 4
Jude 17-21

Let temporal things
serve your use,
but the eternal
be the object of
your desire.

—Thomas à Kempis

IN WORD   Guidance is always a pressing issue for the Christian. Pick a moment in your life—any moment at all—and it is likely that you have needed guidance on some critical area at that particular moment. We are *always* in need of direction, and most of us are acutely aware of that need.

The unbeliever, as this passage says, is a slave to instinct and self. Those who do not follow God must follow their own internal logic. And that logic is a mess of distorted perspectives, most often driven by self. The self-guided person will make decisions based on emotional needs, cravings for self-esteem, physical impulses, and present-life planning. There is nothing eternal about their choices, no urge to submit to their Creator, no consistent willingness to put others' needs ahead of their own desires. Even in their highest moral behavior, they are driven from within, where the Spirit does not dwell.

We, too, often lapse into instinctual decision making. Though we want God's guidance and ask for it, we often do not wait for it. We make decisions based on what our internal logic tells us. Is that logic guided by the Spirit? Or do we serve our own emotional needs, self-esteem cravings, physical impulses, and present-life interests? We are inhabited by God's wise, eternal Spirit. But are we driven by Him?

IN DEED   When we are driven by our own internal impulses and reasoning, we are settling for second best. Even when those instincts are shaped by years of discipleship, they are still subject to sin and deception. We can use them to God's glory, but we can't trust them. They must always be submitted to the guiding mind of God.

We do not need to follow the patterns of this world. We are not left to figure things out on our own. We are not ruled by our base desires, or even by our noble ones. We have not been abandoned to our own moral codes and higher philosophies. We are called to follow our Leader. We must submit our instincts to Him and follow Him diligently.

Guided by God

*If my people would but listen to me, . . . how quickly would I
subdue their enemies and turn my hand against their foes!*

PSALM 81:13-14

IN WORD   The hardest aspect of the Christian life is to
learn to submit to God in all things. His yoke is easy, but
remembering to be bound by it is difficult. We worship Him
for His goodness, we thank Him for His love, we pledge
to be His disciples, and we ask Him for His wisdom. All
the while, the nuts and bolts of following Him are hard to
grasp. When it comes to making decisions, we still like our
independence.

What is it about our independence that so intrigues us?
Why are we so captivated with our decision-making powers? Why, even when we know that a sense of autonomy
is Satan's specialty and the root of our sin, do we insist on
maintaining little pieces of it in various corners of our lives?
Why, when God tells us one thing and our internal compulsions tell us another, do we often choose the compulsions?
What does that say about our trust in God?

That's what the fall of man in the Garden of Eden was
all about: mistrusting God and seeking our own interests.
And that's still what sin is all about. When we choose our
own will over God's, we're mistrusting Him and trusting
ourselves. What an absurdity! We forget the most basic of all
biblical teaching: God's will is in our best interest.

IN DEED   Are you convinced of that? The Christian life
will be a struggle until we know deep down in our hearts
that His commands—even the hard ones—are ultimately for
our benefit. We can be sure that the best way to seek our own
self-centered interests is to be entirely God-centered. In this
paradox, godliness and the self-life meet. Or, as Jesus said,
"Whoever loses his life will preserve it" (Luke 17:33). Our
happiness is deeper and richer when we listen to Him.

In that sense, it is a self-fulfilling act to forsake our own
will and submit to His. Submission seems so noble, but we
have a lot at stake in it. When we serve Him, we serve ourselves. Believe that wholeheartedly, and see what happens.

JANUARY 5
Psalm 81:11-16

If God's will is
your will and if
He always has
His way [with
you], then you
always have
your way also.

—Hannah Whitall
Smith

Not Your Own

You are not your own; you were bought at a price.
1 CORINTHIANS 6:19-20

The condition for gaining God's full blessing is absolute surrender to Him.

—Andrew Murray

IN WORD Life is a series of decisions. Some of them are relatively minor, others have lasting impact. We often act on the minor decisions—what to eat, what to wear, whom to talk to—out of our natural behavior patterns, giving them little thought. With the serious choices—which job to take, where to live, and the like—we weigh pros and cons and try to determine the right course of action. In any case, we are likely to forget an important backdrop to our decision making: We are not our own. We belong to God.

Isn't this easy to forget? We tend to approach life with a certain autonomy, as though we are independent individuals with a responsibility to acknowledge God in worship and sacrifice. But God wants a deeper worship in our lives. Rather than living independently of Him while giving Him our respect, we honor Him by living dependently on Him with awareness that every action, every thought, every impulse is to fit into His purposes. We must not act—or even breathe—without this awareness. We have been bought. We are His.

Some might consider this the equivalent of slavery or servitude. Paul always did (Romans 1:1; Galatians 1:10; Philippians 1:1; Titus 1:1), regardless of whether he was free or in prison. But it is a joyful service that carries with it no sense of oppression. How could it? Our Master is the epitome of benevolence. He knows our innermost being and is zealously intent on fulfilling us. The key for us is living with the knowledge that we are owned and operated by the most loving and qualified Owner possible.

IN DEED The Christian who lives with this wisdom— that we are owned by Another—is a Christian profoundly changed. Our decisions are affected, our character is reformed, and our load is lightened. We lose the right to ourselves, but we also lose the burden of self-rule. It is a wonderfully freeing truth. Everything about us is the concern of Someone else.

The Available Mind of God

If any of you lacks wisdom, he should ask God, who gives generously to all without finding fault. JAMES 1:5

IN WORD Why would God set up a process for us to gain wisdom? Why would He not just give it to us? Because asking for His wisdom and receiving it brings us into relationship with Him. The wisdom we receive is not information imparted, but character learned. We observe who He is and we learn to behave like Him. We come to know Him better in the process. His wisdom is readily available, but we must ask.

Have you found yourself needing guidance in a given situation? Our usual tendency is to pray for direction. But God has a better way. Pray for wisdom, and the direction will become clear. If we were to pray for direction, God could only answer by giving us information. But if we pray for wisdom, God answers by giving us His own mind.

We are prone to call upon God for wisdom only when we find ourselves in a difficulty. But far from being a one-time request in a moment of need, this verse hints at an ongoing process. It isn't that we ask for wisdom one day when we're at our wit's end; we are to ask for wisdom daily because we will find ourselves at wit's end sooner or later. God's provision of His mind is often given in advance. It is more than instructions for a way to go; it is training for a way of life.

IN DEED Do you need direction? Guidance? Wisdom from above? The crucial step, often neglected, is to ask. How often we try to figure things out on our own! How often we ask others for advice before we ask God! Ask Him now. Ask often. Make the asking a regular part of your life. Don't wait until trouble comes; learn the mind of God now. He offers it generously.

JANUARY 7
James 1:2-7

There is a deep wisdom inaccessible to the wise and prudent, but disclosed to babes.

—Christopher Bryant

The Obedient Mind of Man

When he asks, he must believe and not doubt, because he who doubts is like a wave of the sea, blown and tossed by the wind.
JAMES 1:6

JANUARY 8
James 1:2-7

God will never reveal more truth about Himself till you obey what you know already.

—Oswald Chambers

IN WORD We easily forget the requirement before the promise. God's extravagant gift of His wisdom is only given when a prior condition is met. When we ask we must believe. Otherwise, His wisdom will not come.

What does God mean by requiring our belief? Is it only that we must believe He will answer us? It is that, but it is more. We must believe—ahead of time—that what He tells us is wisdom to be followed. We must be committed to heed His instructions before He gives them. If we are not committed, He will not answer. If we do not purpose in our hearts to do His will, we will never discover it.

Many Christians ask for God's wisdom as an option to throw into the mix. It becomes one possibility among a range of many. If we are only requesting His advice, He will not give it. He only gives solutions to be implemented, not suggestions to consider. The commitment to follow comes first. The mind of God is generously granted to us, but only for us to obey. It is not a shopping item. It does not come with a return policy.

To ask for God's will as an option to consider rather than a command to obey is to place our intellect above His. We put ourselves in the position of authority, with Him submitting His proposals. But He will not relate to us that way. He is the authority. When He speaks, there is no better option. The omniscient Creator does not offer us a second-rate plan. His first direction is always the right one.

IN DEED Do you ask God for His wisdom with a resolve to obey it? If not, do not expect it to come. Expect rather to be tossed around like a wave in a storm. But if your heart will commit to His way, His way will be easily found. God gives us His mind in response to our faith.

In Defense of Truth

The LORD detests lying lips, but he delights in men who are truthful. PROVERBS 12:22

IN WORD Dishonesty is epidemic in our culture. Court records, academic surveys, and common observation confirm it. Truth and integrity are expendable in our society.

Why do people lie? Or, to put it more subtly and inclusively, why do virtually all of us sometimes try to create an impression that isn't entirely accurate? The reasons are many and varied. They include a desire to stay out of trouble, a drive to get ahead, and an obsession about our image. In any case, a person's dishonesty indicates a lack of trust in God for the consequences of integrity. When we lie—even in a seemingly insignificant way—it is because we are avoiding the results of not lying. We take matters into our own hands because we're afraid of what will happen if we tell the truth. We do not trust God to honor our integrity.

But our God is a God of integrity. It is in His character. He never lies, and He is not silent when the truth needs to be revealed. It is His nature to be absolutely reliable. There is no hint of pretense in Him. He is who He says He is, He does what He says He will do, and He honors those who follow His lead. Always.

IN DEED This is both comforting and convicting. It is comforting because we know that God's promises in His Word are reliable. When He inspires prophecy, it is accurate. When He promises blessing, it will come. When He says He will defend His people, He will. We can read His Word with unwavering assurance that it is pure truth with no fine print hidden away from our trusting eyes.

But the purity of God's character is also convicting. We know that though we are called to be like Him, our integrity falls short of His. He is shaping us to reflect His glory, but when we give a false impression, we interfere with His work.

Trust God with the truth. Tell it and display His integrity. Know that He will always defend truth—and those who tell it.

JANUARY 9
Proverbs 12:22

Where truth is, there is God.

—Miguel de Cervantes

9

Perfect Timing

I waited patiently for the LORD; *he turned to me and heard my cry.* PSALM 40:1

JANUARY 10
Psalm 40:1

Simply wait upon Him. So doing, we shall be directed, supplied, protected, corrected, and rewarded.

—Vance Havner

IN WORD Patience is one of the hardest virtues for us to understand. We pray to an omnipotent God. We know He is able to help us at any moment. We know that He who defines Himself as "love" and gave His Son for us is not reluctant to help us. So when we ask such a God to intervene in our circumstances, why is there so often a delay?

Nowhere in the Bible does God promise us instant answers to our prayers. His promises for answered prayer are amazing and reassuring, but none of them includes a timetable. He only assures us that He is never too late. Yet in our impatience, we don't want an answer that is simply "not too late." We want an answer now. We have needs, and we do not understand why those needs must be prolonged.

But God has His reasons. Perhaps our needs are being prolonged because they are accomplishing something in us that nothing else will. Perhaps they are being prolonged because God is doing a necessary work in the life of someone else who is involved in our situation. Perhaps He is teaching us about prayer or perfecting our faith. Maybe He is even letting us identify with Jesus in the fellowship of His sufferings—it is, after all, His overarching purpose to conform us to the image of Christ. How can we be conformed if we have no identification with His pain?

IN DEED Sometimes God will make clear that our answer is delayed because the delay will further His work in our own hearts or in another area. Sometimes He gives us no reason at all. The Christian's wise response, in either case, is to know that if we are waiting on God, there must be a very good reason. And if we wait in faith and expectancy, the wait will be amply rewarded. His timing is always perfect.

The Renewed Mind

Do not conform any longer to the pattern of this world, but be transformed by the renewing of your mind. ROMANS 12:2

IN WORD How will we see things when God's wisdom has become a part of our own thinking? What should this renewed, transformed mind of the believer look like? There are three radical reorientations that we must undergo. We will begin to understand our time, our treasures, and our talents differently. We will stand in a dramatically different place than we once stood, and our perspective will reflect the change. Our eyes will gaze on new heights and our desires will lean in new directions. We are a new creation; we will learn to live as one.

How do we get there? Do we change suddenly or little by little? Is it by the diligence of our effort or by the merciful gift of God? Is it a matter of hard study or spiritual osmosis? The answer is "all of the above." God will give us His mind—we can be sure of that. It comes from Him out of the mercies of His good will, and He is generous with all of His children. But it also requires a diligence that will search His Word, seek His guidance, cooperate with His plan, receive His correction, and wait patiently for His providence. We are to boldly persevere in our ambitious drive to receive the completely free gift of God's wisdom.

IN DEED If you became a Christian as a child and do not remember well the difference between your new life and your old, you may have lost sight of the radical nature of the new mind. Or, if you once knew the power of transformation but have since let it slide into a hybrid life of the new and the old, you may have lost sight of the constant call of the new creation. In either case, let your mind be transformed and your life renewed again and again. It is a lifelong process for the believer, a work that God will complete the day He takes you into His presence. Never settle for the status quo. Never grow complacent or stale. Never lose sight of the upward call of God out of the ways of this world and into the heart of His will.

JANUARY 11
Romans 12:1-2

The difference between worldliness and godliness is a renewed mind.

—Erwin Lutzer

The City with Foundations

He was looking forward to the city with foundations, whose architect and builder is God. HEBREWS 11:10

The only way to get our values right is . . . to see things not in the light of time, but in the light of eternity.

—William Barclay

IN WORD Those who sit in God's fellowship often, meditating on His mind and accepting His love, will begin to view time in terms of eternity rather than the brief life we live on this broken planet. Rather than trying to build heaven in our few decades here, we will be freed to make sacrifices now, knowing that an everlasting heaven awaits. We will make decisions not with present security and future retirement in mind, but with "forever" in full view. The Spirit of the eternal God will fill us with eternal thoughts.

What stands in the way of this perspective? Fear. We are often afraid that we will not have enough to take care of our families and ourselves if we live "all out" for God. We wonder if God will lead us to hard fields and violent crosses as He did our Savior and His disciples. We fear the consequences of a completely Godward life. And so we build houses for now and hope for the eternal mansion down the road.

God's promises allow us to go ahead and consider the mansion down the road as ours. We don't have to obsess about our security now when we are assured of an everlasting home that cannot be taken away. We can put up with a few years of sacrifice, toil, pain, and service with the calm confidence that our citizenship is elsewhere. We are free to serve God at whatever cost, because nothing can cost us our inheritance. We know where this life will lead us and that it will never end.

IN DEED Forsake fear. Every Christian has in the back of his or her mind, from time to time, a little voice that cautions against a completely sacrificial life. That's not God's voice! His mind, which He shares with us, will overcome such thoughts. His Spirit, if we trust Him, will assure us that His promises are certain and that this present abode is a place of joyful sacrifice. How do we receive such assurance? With an eternal perspective. We know what counts, and we can live with our gaze on the city with eternal foundations.

Rich toward God

I'll say to myself, "You have plenty of good things laid up
for many years. Take life easy; eat, drink and be merry."
LUKE 12:19

IN WORD When we sit in God's presence and seek His mind, His Spirit will convince us of the treasure we have in His name. Ephesians 1, one of the great chapters on what it means to be "in Christ," tells us that we have "every spiritual blessing in Christ" (v. 3)—redemption, forgiveness, knowledge, hope, the Holy Spirit, security, and an incorruptible inheritance. God has lavished such imperishable gifts on us. They cannot be taken away, they are immediately accessible, and they could not possibly be any greater. We are indeed highly favored.

Yet the problem from our present perspective is this: We don't know how to access these precious gifts. We see our physical needs as much more urgent and our heavenly riches as much more distant. We're happy about the salvation we've been given, but it won't help us take that much-needed vacation today. We're excited about the prospect of heaven, but it won't pay the mortgage this month. We're thrilled to be seated with Jesus by God's throne, but that doesn't secure the position we need to advance our career. Or does it?

It all depends on how we see our mortgages and careers. Are they tools for godly living? Or are they a means to secure our heaven now? Do we leverage the goods of this world for eternal purposes? Or do we spend them on our momentary satisfaction? Where are we really investing? Does our full portfolio major on spiritual realities? Have we learned that current investments can have everlasting returns? If so, our income and expenses are really very spiritual. They build God's Kingdom.

IN DEED Materialism is deceptive. We are encouraged at every turn to live the high life, go for the gusto, grab life by the horns, and hang on to what we've got. We are obsessive about our upward mobility. Our problem is that we've forgotten how to define "upward."

Know your citizenship in heaven and invest in it. Take care of your physical needs and the needs of others, and then live in the Kingdom of God. It will forever pay dividends.

JANUARY 13
Luke 12:13-21

A man there was, though some did count him mad; the more he cast away, the more he had.

—John Bunyan

Heavenly Sacrifice

*Whoever wants to become great among you
must be your servant.*   MARK 10:43

JANUARY 14

Mark 10:42-45

The only life that
counts is the
life that costs.

—Frederick P. Wood

IN WORD   When we have the mind of Christ, we have a servant mind. "Even the Son of Man did not come to be served, but to serve," Jesus proclaimed (v. 45). Even Him. That's what His Kingdom is all about—sacrifice and service, giving and sharing, considering the needs of others at least equal to, if not greater than, the needs of ourselves.

It's a pleasant thought, isn't it? But it's a difficult process. Why? Because we are used to thinking of our talents and gifts in terms of what they can accomplish for us. Deep down inside, we want to get ahead. We are driven with an ambition to accomplish something, and sin has distorted that drive to make it self-serving. Like the architects of the Tower of Babel, we want to "build ourselves a city" and "make a name for ourselves" (Genesis 11:4). Our desired "city" is often an impressive reputation and the praise of those who will recognize it. Such a drive does not naturally lead us into service.

But Jesus never asked us to do what comes naturally. The mind that He cultivates within us will have nothing to do with self-serving accomplishment. It will have drive and ambition, to be sure, but not in the direction we once pursued. No, we will be consumed with a vision for heavenly unity, and we will realize that the only way to have it is to serve. We will not care for our own reputations nearly as much as we care for the reputation of the Kingdom of God. Instead of making a name for ourselves, we will make a name for His Kingdom. And it will be a humble, sacrificial name.

IN DEED   God Almighty clothed Himself in human flesh and served sinful people. We could learn from His example. In fact, we must. It is a command. But it is a command with an unexpected promise: This service is greatness in God's Kingdom. As surely as self-interest drives us away from Him and others, self-sacrifice draws us in. Our gifts and our talents become useful tools for the benefit of others.

Guarded Lives

Do not let them out of your sight, keep them within your heart; for they are life to those who find them and health to a man's whole body.   PROVERBS 4:21-22

IN WORD   The godly life is not lived passively. It is not random, and it is not a life of wandering. Those who wait for God's Word to change them will only find it so doing when they actively feed themselves with it. Those who expect the sermons they hear and the words they read to make them godly will be entirely frustrated unless they are diligent in meditating on the truth and applying it to their lives. Simply sitting in a pew week after week will do nothing radical in a believer's life. Wisdom is not gained by passive absorption. It must be consumed and savored. It must become the focal point of our thinking.

Those who hear words of wisdom and do not apply them are like the receivers of the seed in Jesus' parable of the four soils (Matthew 13:20-22). They hear the truth. They understand it. They even agree with it. But it has no benefit for them. It isn't real faith. James concurs (James 1:22-24): Hearing, understanding, and agreeing without application is a self-deceptive dynamic. It appears to be faith, but it effects no change in the life of the hearer. Something more is needed—diligence, for example. And action. God and His truth are to be treasured more than any other affection of our heart.

IN DEED   Where do your affections lie? Do you hear the truth and then turn your heart to other things? We will not retain what we've heard or read unless we dwell on it for a while, turning it over in our minds and locking it within our hearts. We will not be changed and we will not grow by passive hearing. We must set our affections on God's wisdom, act on it, and beat away any philosophical or material rivals. The promise for doing that is amazing: life and health. Truth and righteousness are powerful; they are the substance of our lives.

JANUARY 15
Proverbs 4:20-27

One gem from that ocean [the Bible] is worth all the pebbles from earthly streams.

—Robert Murray M'Cheyne

15

Guarded Hearts

Above all else, guard your heart, for it is the wellspring of life.
PROVERBS 4:23

JANUARY 16
Proverbs 4:20-27

Oh, study your
hearts, watch
your hearts, keep
your hearts!

—John Flavel

IN WORD Our hearts, the wellsprings of our lives, are given free reign by most of us. We're under the illusion that we can't help how we feel; our emotions are considered the foundation of who we are. And as our feelings rise and fall as often as the wind changes direction, so does our life. We are guided by feelings far more often than we'd like to think. We make decisions based on feelings and then rationalize them, rather than making decisions based on rationality and then letting the feelings fall in behind. We let our emotions define us. It is a dangerous way to live.

David could testify to that. His extraordinarily Godward heart usually led him into the Father's will. But it also led him into temptation and a sin with catastrophic results. Even his heart, so often in sync with God's, was fickle. And fickle hearts produce misdirected people.

We think, when we turn our hearts over to God, that He governs us and shapes us automatically. That's not what inspired Scripture says in Proverbs 4:23, however. This is a command. We are to guard our hearts. We are to be careful about what we let into them. Our hearts cannot be an open door to unbiblical and ungodly influences. We are not to be captive to them; they are to be captive to the Word of God. We are given the responsibility of being vigilant about their content.

IN DEED Does your heart ride along with your feelings like an anchorless ship on the waves? Is it subject to deep swells and rapidly changing courses? If so, finding direction from God may be a challenge. You may be waiting for Him to shape your heart, while He is waiting for you to guard it. He will do His part, but only you can do yours. The wisdom of Proverbs makes your vigilance the highest priority: "above all else." That is the attention we are to give to our emotional swells. It is paramount. Be on guard.

Guarded Eyes

*Let your eyes look straight ahead, fix your gaze
directly before you.*   PROVERBS 4:25

IN WORD   Many sins begin with the eyes. What the eyes gaze upon, the heart begins to crave. They are like personal advertisers letting us know all the options available to us. Their range is great, but they are not naturally discerning. They take in everything, and in our weakness we let them make too many demands. They can lead us to holy cravings for God and truth, but they also lead us in paths of coveting and lust.

Jesus shocked His disciples with a warning about our eyes. If one of them causes us to sin, we should gouge it out and throw it away (Matthew 5:29). Is the eye really that corrupt? No, but sin is that serious. It must be dealt with. And the first practical way to deal with it is to guard the eyes.

Just as we are responsible for the things that fill our hearts and the words that roll off our tongues, we are also responsible for the gaze of our eyes. Too many lives on a straight course in God's will have been turned aside by an irrelevant stare. A glimpse turns into a gaze, a gaze turns into a craving, a craving turns the heart to the side, and a misdirected heart wreaks havoc on godliness and service. Glances can quickly become compulsions, and compulsions quickly become idols.

IN DEED   Take an inventory of what you stare at. The results will tell you a lot about what is important to you. In all likelihood, you will find some things that are inappropriately significant to you—a hobby too time-consuming, an unholy desire, a passion contrary to God's revealed direction for your life. All fall short of God's good will for us.

A tendency to look aside indicates a dissatisfaction with what you already have. If you are dissatisfied, the answer is not in looking in new directions; it is in strengthening your gaze on the Savior and His ways. Fix your eyes on what is ultimately worthy of your attention. Gaze at Jesus.

JANUARY 17
Proverbs 4:20-27

God is most glorified in us when we are most satisfied in Him.

—John Piper

Guarded Feet

Make level paths for your feet and take only ways that are firm.
PROVERBS 4:26

JANUARY 18
Proverbs 4:20-27

The center of
God's will is
our only safety.

—Betsie ten Boom

IN WORD   The advice in this verse is not unusual wisdom; it could be heard from the mouth of almost any father, from any military training camp, or from any advice column. The issue for us as believers is how to define its terms. What does "level" mean? Which ways are firm?

We will find a vast disagreement between what the world considers level or firm and the directions God leads us in. Take Abraham, for example. He thought he was choosing the level and firm path when he had a son through Hagar, trying to fulfill God's promise (Genesis 16). It seemed like the only rational way. But God's way, though not rational by man's standards, was a far surer path. Or look at Jesus for another example. Which of His disciples would have told Him that the way of the Cross was the way of wisdom? By their standards, it was foolishness and disaster. By God's, it was the ultimate expression of faithfulness and truth.

When this verse commands us to make level paths and to take firm ways, it is not telling us to follow conventional wisdom. This is not a suggestion to play it safe. It is an order to follow God, to heed His wisdom and trust His guidance, no matter how foolish it looks to a skeptical and watching world. It is a call to base our lives in the ultimate reality of Scripture rather than the finite understanding of human logic. We must understand that the level and firm paths are the ones that are level and firm in God's sight—not ours, not anyone else's.

IN DEED   When you seek a direction for your life, give no attention to whether your path is safe or risky, conventional or unconventional. Consider only whether it is based in God's truth, sensitive to His voice, and reflecting His purposes as revealed in His Word. This is ultimately the only safe, level, firm way there is.

Guarded Tongues

Put away perversity from your mouth; keep corrupt talk far from your lips.   PROVERBS 4:24

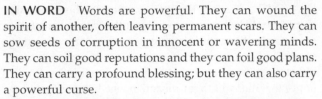

IN WORD   Words are powerful. They can wound the spirit of another, often leaving permanent scars. They can sow seeds of corruption in innocent or wavering minds. They can soil good reputations and they can foil good plans. They can carry a profound blessing; but they can also carry a powerful curse.

Peter learned about the power of words one day. "You are the Christ, the Son of the living God," he told Jesus (Matthew 16:16). Those were potent words. The church would be built on that declaration. But moments later, Peter contradicted the will of God with a thoughtless rebuke of the Lord. His words were a stumbling block, a product of the kingdom of darkness. They were corrupt in a way not many of us consider; they did not reflect God's reality.

Is Proverbs telling us simply to avoid vulgarities in our speech? Probably not. There are many forms of corruption and perversity in addition to coarse vulgarities: gossip, deception, mindless chatter, rumors, negativity, bitterness, insults, and more. All of these contradict the revealed truth of God. They run against the current of His will. In a very real sense, they slander and misrepresent the reality and beauty of His Kingdom and His character.

IN DEED   Scripture tells us to do away with irrelevant and improper speech. Our words will carry a certain amount of power with them, whether for good or for bad. It is our responsibility to make sure they carry power that builds up rather than tears down; that reflects glory rather than corrupts the image of God; that honors truth rather than falsehood.

Do you guard your mouth? Many passages of Scripture warn us of the importance of doing so. The tongue is no small weapon. It wields a power few of us realize. Use it honorably and with extreme care.

JANUARY 19
Proverbs 4:20-27

Wisdom is knowing when to speak your mind and when to mind your speech.

—Anonymous

19

A Heart and a Song

My heart is steadfast, O God, my heart is steadfast;
I will sing and make music.   PSALM 57:7

JANUARY 20
Psalm 57

Streams of mercy,
never ceasing,
call for songs of
loudest praise.

—Robert Robinson

IN WORD   Reading the Psalms, one gets the impression that life for its writers, especially David, was one tumultuous episode after another. There are psalms of praise and joy, of grief and defeat, of deep meditation and inspiring victory. But regardless of the focus of each psalm, it is hard not to notice that many of them—most, in fact—are written in the context of crisis (see v. 1, for example). Cries to God come out of the crucible, and God's response comes into it.

One thing God looks for when we are in the crucible is a steadfast heart—a heart that will not, under any circumstances, fall away. No matter what uproar is going on around us, no matter how much pressure is applied, God will wait to answer us until it is clear to Him, to us, and to those who observe us, that our heart is resolutely fixed on Him. And more than just steadfastness of hope is required; it is a steadfastness of worship, too. The heart that learns to make music in its darkest moments is the heart that is delivered.

The deliverance usually comes twice. First, a worshipful heart has risen above oppressive circumstances, even when the circumstances remain. It is an inward liberation that can find deep joy regardless of what's happening on the outside. But a resolved, singing heart then finds deliverance in a God who responds. He frequently invades circumstances and scatters our enemies, sometimes dramatically. The wait may be long, but the victory is sure. God does not remain silent in His love when we do not remain silent in our worship.

IN DEED   When circumstances oppress, the battle rages, and the heat of the crucible rises, where is your heart? Is it steadfast in its worship? Does it sing of the God who reigns above every cloud? If so, expect deliverance. Expect it within and without. You can sing your song of victory before victory even comes. In the most important sense, it already has.

Ascribe Glory

*Ascribe to the L*ORD *the glory due his name.*

PSALM 96:8

IN WORD   Have you ever seen someone take credit for something you've done? If so, you can relate to God. He sees us do it all the time.

When someone is sick, we pray. When God heals, we give credit to the medical care our friend has received, or to natural healing processes. Both may have played a significant part, but if they are all that's needed, why did we pray? No intervention of God was needed if healing could have been obtained through less than supernatural means. Or we pray for a job. When God gives it, we credit our good fortune, our résumé, or our connections, never acknowledging publicly the God behind them all. In our age of political correctness, we do not attribute successes to God's power. We know that many will not share our faith. Inwardly, we give quiet thanks. Outwardly, we let the misconception lie. We keep our speech God-free. Meanwhile, the Giver of all good things is silent.

Why do our words not give Him the glory due His name? Why do we not verbally credit Him with every blessing? Perhaps we don't want to sound overly pious. Perhaps we've noticed how obnoxious our society perceives people who constantly speak of God. We've let our culture intimidate us into never mentioning His name. In many of our circumstances, He remains unglorified.

IN DEED   One of God's purposes behind His great works, aside from the simple fact that He loves us, is His zeal for the glory of His name. When we credit Him for what He has done, we are aligning ourselves with the zeal of the Lord Himself. We are fulfilling our created purpose: to glorify Him.

Have you subverted God's purpose in your blessings by not acknowledging Him as the source? Repent from that and ascribe to Him the glory due His name. As a result, the Giver of all good things will be even more ready to give to you.

JANUARY 21
Psalm 96

Men . . . praise God in such a manner that He scarcely obtains the tenth part of His due.

—John Calvin

Unfailing Love

Whoever is wise, let him heed these things and consider the great love of the LORD.   PSALM 107:43

God does not love us because we are valuable. We are valuable because He loves us.

—Fulton John Sheen

IN WORD   In a secular society, depression statistics rise dramatically. Suicide rates soar. Anger, bitterness, and hopelessness are evident in the cultural expressions of our times. Why? There is often a missing ingredient in the psyche of modern man: the love of God.

Whenever we take retribution into our own hands; seek to feed ourselves with substances or ideas that only soothe bruised egos; become envious, strive to get ahead, or lose hope; we have forgotten this missing ingredient. The love of God renders all of our false emotions pointless.

Think about your emotional tendencies. Don't most of our behavioral problems and psychological flaws come from an insecurity deep within? But if we, the redeemed, were thoroughly convinced of God's love—the unflinching goodness which He has shown us since the dawn of creation—then we would lose the basis of nearly every one of our insecurities. Those who have immersed themselves in the immeasurable love of God are wise indeed—and extremely secure. They have no need to envy; no desire for revenge; no reason to fear; no time for pettiness; and no cause for self-promotion.

Read Psalm 107. Are you wandering in a wasteland (v. 4)? Are you suffering in chains (v. 10)? Have you been rebellious (v. 17)? Has the tempest threatened your safety (v. 25)? The wise response is found in verses 6, 13, 19, and 28: "They cried out to the LORD in their trouble." The result is always deliverance, at least by His definition if not ours. Why? Because God's love is unfailing. This psalm alone says so five times. The Word could not be more emphatic.

IN DEED   Human nature tells us to hide when we're in trouble. God's Word tells us to cry out to Him. Following God's Word is infinitely wiser than following fallen human nature. The next time you're in distress, cling to one unalterable fact: the unfailing love of God for His redeemed.

The Art of Worship

*Blessed are those who have learned to acclaim you, who walk
in the light of your presence, O LORD.*   PSALM 89:15

IN WORD   Worship is a learned art. It is an attitude of
the heart that continually acknowledges God and values His
character. It is the ultimate reflection of reality in the mind
of the believer. And it is the key to blessing.

JANUARY 23
Psalm 89:14-18

To worship God
is to realize the
purpose for which
God created us.

—Herbert M. Carson

Observe any Christian who is perpetually struggling
with personal flaws or overwhelming circumstances, and
you will likely see a Christian whose eyes are on himself. It
is a natural human tendency, but it is rarely fruitful. Worship
changes that. It gives us a new perspective, taking us out of
the realm of oppression—an unnecessary state for anyone
who takes the Bible's promises seriously—and placing us in
the realm of God's power, wisdom, and love—the realm of
eternal truth. It opens the eyes to what is real.

With natural eyes, we often see our struggles as huge
obstacles and our chances of overcoming them as slim. We
are easily overwhelmed. We know our limitations, and
God's omnipotence seems distant. When we acclaim Him,
as the psalm says, we shed those earthbound illusions. Our
worship brings us into the light of His presence and reminds
us of who He really is. It radically alters our perspective.
Where we once thought our struggles were real and our
God might be illusory, we realize that our God is real and
our struggles are illusory.

IN DEED   There is profound blessing in knowing who
God is and claiming His presence in your life. His greatness
makes all other things—especially the hard things—seem
small. It allows you to pray with confidence and faith that
you, through Him, will overcome. When He fills your heart
with His presence, no burden can fill your heart with its
weight. Learn the art of worship, and be blessed.

The Discipline of Acclaim

Blessed are those who have learned to acclaim you, who walk in the light of your presence, O LORD. PSALM 89:15

Psalm 89:14-18

If worship does not change us, it has not been worship.

—Richard Foster

IN WORD Many of us are pessimistic by nature. The glass is always half empty—*at least* half, if not more. We see our areas of need far more easily than we see how God has met them. We know He has blessed us, of course. We just don't dwell on those blessings. We dwell on what is yet lacking in our contentment.

Those of us for whom this pessimism is true rarely see it for the sin that it is. We consider it one of the eccentricities of our human nature, a personality trait rather than a spiritual problem. But it is, in fact, deeply spiritual. And it is quite a problem. It fails to acknowledge God's goodness as often as it ought to be acknowledged. It is the root of the same sin of complaining that so angered God about the Israelites in the wilderness.

This psalm gives us the wisdom to change our attitudes. It shows the way out of the wilderness of discontent. Instead of affirming our areas of need, it turns our focus to our blessings. It tells us to acclaim Him, to verbally acknowledge who He is. When we do, His presence becomes a greater reality to us—greater than it once was, and greater than all of the sources of our dissatisfaction. Those who learn to acclaim Him learn the reality of the God of all sufficiency. In short, we become joyful creatures. Or, as the psalm says, we are blessed.

IN DEED Human beings tend to be caught in one of two cycles: a downward cycle of disappointment, or an upward cycle of blessing. When we focus on unmet needs, we lose sight of God's goodness and we are unprepared to receive more of it. When we focus on our blessings, not only do we feel more content, we actually receive the greater blessing of knowing God. We expect to receive more, and He is happy to give it to those who acknowledge Him faithfully.

The Depth of Mercy

Answer me, O L<small>ORD</small>, out of the goodness of your love;
in your great mercy turn to me.   PSALM 69:16

IN WORD   On what basis do we call upon God? What right do we have to approach His throne and appeal for help? If we don't know the answer—if it isn't deeply rooted in our souls—we may have a barren prayer life. And if we're spiritually hungry, the lack of fruitfulness will bother us. We'll ask why.

One hindrance to a fruitful life of prayer is approaching God on the wrong basis. He is often, in our minds, our debtor—a Father who is obligated to care for us regardless of our attitude. It's true that He will care for us, but not according to our specifications. He will straighten us out. He will teach us to approach Him with His true nature—love and mercy—in the forefront of our minds.

Though we know His grace, we often get confused. We come to view Him as lenient rather than merciful. The difference is monumental. He does not casually dismiss our sin— see the Cross as exhibit A. No, He forgives it. Knowing the difference has huge implications for us. When we see Him as lenient, we will be casual about our sin, just as we assume He is. We will take Him for granted and never know the depth of His love. We will pray with sinful, distorted hearts. When we understand mercy, we will grieve and repent. And we will never again approach Him with a sense of entitlement.

IN DEED   David's cry is a model for prayer. Children who act entitled to the favors of their parents are annoying, both to their parents and other observers. Worse than that, they never come to appreciate their parents' generosity. They take it for granted. God will not let us relate to Him that way for long. He is not lenient toward us; He is merciful. He sees the ugliness of sin and loves us anyway. He has dealt with our rebellion painfully. And then He blesses us with answered prayer. When you pray, know the depth of His mercy. It is behind every answer.

JANUARY 25
Psalm 69:13-18

The heavenly Father has no spoiled children. He loves them too much for that.

—Fred Mitchell

Surrounded with Favor

Surely, O LORD, you bless the righteous; you surround them with your favor as with a shield. PSALM 5:12

God's investment in us is so great He could not possibly abandon us.

—Erwin Lutzer

IN WORD When we observe the world around us, it's easy to become negative. We often see righteous people suffer, and we see the wicked prosper. But what we see are the circumstances that surround someone. What we don't usually see is God's attitude toward that person. They are not always the same. Sometimes His favor results in visible blessing; sometimes it doesn't.

As in so many other psalms, David cried out to God for help in Psalm 5:2. His conclusion at the end of the psalm is that he will be blessed. Why? He knows who God is. Though he is suffering at the hands of evil, he knows that this will not always be his situation. We, too, may not see justice at a given moment, but over the course of time we will see two unalterable trends: the blessing of those who pursue righteousness and the destruction of those who pursue evil.

IN DEED We need to know this when we wonder whether our pursuit of godliness is worth the cost. It always is. We may not see it right away, but we will see it eventually. God has never withheld blessing from anyone whose heart was right toward Him. Never. That would contradict His character and it would violate His promise. He blesses the righteous and He surrounds them with favor.

Do you wonder about your future? Are you afraid for your welfare? Don't be, not if your heart belongs to God and you live for Him. It is not in His nature to forsake His faithful ones. He may let you experience a hard time, but never without abundant grace and never indefinitely. There will be relief. His favor already surrounds you like a shield. Sooner or later you will see it.

Our Greatest Need

O LORD my God, I take refuge in you.
PSALM 7:1

IN WORD Why are so many of the psalms about help and deliverance? Why is it so important to know God as our refuge? Because this is our greatest need.

We might not think so. We think we need more fruit of the Spirit or more character; more possessions or power; more wisdom or talent. But God's assessment in the Bible is that we are sheep in need of a Shepherd, the oppressed in need of a Deliverer, the lost in need of a Savior. The other needs are important, too; but our first and foremost deficiency is our helplessness. It simply is not within us to be able to help ourselves.

This is a direct contradiction to humanistic philosophies and other religious doctrines. Most belief systems place a lot of faith in the self's ability to do good works, attain enlightenment, obey precepts, or acquire wisdom. The solution, they say, is within. Not so, says God. The solution is outside of us, above and beyond our own abilities. Whatever our need is, it is met by looking away from ourselves and casting ourselves with abandon on our Savior. We must run to Him. He is the source of everything we need. He is the solution.

Perhaps this is why biblical faith is so offensive to some. There is a certain amount of pride in being able to work out one's own solution. We want to win victories, not be rescued. But the Bible's assessment of our ability is clear: We need rescuing, and we cannot do it ourselves.

IN DEED We learned this lesson with regard to our salvation, if in fact we know Jesus as our Savior. But many of us forget along the way that this vulnerability is characteristic of the entire Christian life. In *everything* we are completely dependent on God. There is a reason God allowed David's desperate psalms so much space in His Word. His desperation is like ours. Need provision? It comes from Him. Protection? Also Him. Holiness? Again, from Him. You name the need, He is the source of supply. Learn to run to your Refuge.

JANUARY 27
Psalm 7

Is it not wonderful news to believe that salvation lies outside of ourselves?

—Martin Luther

Our Shield

I will not fear the tens of thousands drawn up against me on every side.   PSALM 3:6

JANUARY 28
Psalm 3

The cure for
fear is faith.

—Norman Vincent
Peale

IN WORD   We read a verse like this in the psalms and we marvel at the beauty of David's faith. Cast him in a modern-day environment, however—without the historical and spiritual reverence in which his writings are held—and we would consider this statement dangerously irrational. Those who are surrounded by tens of thousands of hostile forces on every side *should* be afraid. Only the mentally ill would say they aren't. We would label such folly as escapism, denial, or delusion. We would tell David to be realistic.

But David knows something many of us don't consider. The invisible God is more real than the visible enemy. Tens of thousands are hopelessly powerless in the face of His power. With spiritual eyes, David can say with Elisha: "Those who are with us are more than those who are with them" (see 2 Kings 6:15-17). Those who only see the many enemies are not focused on reality. They are only focused on the visible. They have forgotten a foundational principle of the spiritual life: The "visible" and the "real" are two vastly different things.

IN DEED   Are you bogged down in the burdens of life? Do you have a multitude of enemies? Are you overwhelmed by the spiritual battles you are in? Are you losing hope? Do not forget this principle: What you see is not all there is. Above and beyond your problems are: (1) the power of the Lord of Hosts; (2) all of His obedient servants ready to do warfare on your behalf; and (3) your prayers and your faith—the clear lines of communication between you and your Deliverer.

Like David, we can refuse to be intimidated by the tens of thousands drawn up against us. Why? Because we know a Savior infinitely stronger than tens of thousands. This is not an irrational hope. It is not escapism. It is reality. We have no reason to fear.

Revealing Choices

The righteousness of the upright delivers them, but the
unfaithful are trapped by evil desires.   PROVERBS 11:6

IN WORD   Choices. Every one of them, in a sense, is a
test. Why? Because they reveal our desires. Sometimes
the desires they reveal have no moral or spiritual consequences—our taste in food or clothes, for example. Other
times, the desires revealed by our choices have a profound
spiritual result: Our taste for obedience is exposed. We may
find out if we treasure expedience or righteousness. We may
display whether we prefer physical or spiritual satisfaction.
Our deepest loves come to the surface in the choices we
make. Even when we deny our strong desires, we demonstrate that we must have had even stronger ones directing
our choices.

Anyone who has ever struggled with repeating bad
choices—in other words, virtually all of us—knows the ability of desires to trap us. They can compel us to act contrary
to our own conscience. Like Paul in Romans 7, we often do
what we don't want to do, and don't do what we actually
want to do. We have a deep-rooted inability to live according
to the law of God within us.

Only Jesus can set us free from this inability. It is not
always a matter of simple obedience. But even as He begins
to set us free, we must be reminded of the gravity of our
choices. Obedience counts. In our most tempting and repeat-
able sins, we must realize that we give God clear answers to
our tests. We prefer to satisfy wrong desires over obeying
Him.

IN DEED   Have you struggled with an addictive behavior?
Have you repeated the same sin over and over? Understand
the statement you are making when you indulge in it: You
prefer the passing pleasure of a sinful desire to the fellowship that comes from obedience. It's a revealing choice.
Refuse to be trapped by it. Let righteousness—an unrivaled
desire for God—deliver you.

JANUARY 29
Proverbs 11:6

Holy obedience
puts to shame
all natural and
selfish desires.

—St. Francis of Assisi

Commitment and Success

Commit to the LORD whatever you do, and your plans will succeed. PROVERBS 16:3

JANUARY 30
Proverbs 16:3

It is not your business to succeed, but to do right; when you have done so, the rest lies with God.

—C. S. Lewis

IN WORD The promise of this verse is extravagant, and the condition seems to be straightforward. If we commit our plans to the Lord—and it really does seem to focus on *our* plans—then we will find success. The doubter in our soul wants to say, "Yes, but . . . ," yet the inspired Word doesn't give us that option. It does, however, call us to look a little closer. There are two keys to understanding this wonderful promise of success: We must first understand what it means to commit to the Lord whatever we do, and we must also understand how God defines success.

What does it mean to commit to the Lord whatever we do? It doesn't mean that we come up with our own plans and then ask God to bless them, expecting that He will unconditionally honor the whims of our hearts. It means that if we have made a commitment to honor God with our lives, and that commitment has shaped our whole manner of living, then He will ensure success. It means that a life dedicated to God will experience a God dedicated to life.

How does God define success? The perfect case study is Jesus. Did God consider His life successful? We know He did. Yet at the time, the world did not. He was an utter failure, a failed revolutionary who could not live up to His claims of messiah-hood at the most critical time to prove them. Yes, in God's eyes, crucifixion is a success. So is persecution, hardship, and sacrifice. The issue is not status, achievements, reputation, or profit. It is godly character and eternal fruit.

IN DEED Know what it means to commit your ways to God and understand how He defines success, and the result will be a highly successful life. It may or may not appear that way to others, but appearance seems to matter little to God. Never look to blind guides to find out if you're successful. The One who sees is the One who makes the final judgment on how well you've lived. Commit to Him, and the blessing of success is assured.

Bound by Debt

*The rich rule over the poor, and the borrower is
servant to the lender.*   PROVERBS 22:7

IN WORD   A recent survey indicated that the bulk of debt in the United States is credit card debt. That is one of many signs that modern societies, particularly in the western hemisphere, are driven to acquire at all costs. We accumulate the stuff of our material world at alarming rates. One of the prevailing shortfalls of our generation is that we are always "spending" more than we earn. We are called "consumers" because we consume—a lot.

Biblical wisdom orders us to be extremely careful with our indebtedness. Why? Because "the borrower is servant to the lender." We are held captive—or at least restrained—by the debts we are obligated to pay. When those debts mount, we are limited in our choices. If God tells us to pick up and move somewhere else, we may not be in a position to do so. If He tells us to embark on a different career path, we may not have the resources. We put ourselves in a position to limit His work in our lives.

We are bound by the laws of our governments and by the morals of our faith to pay what we've promised to pay. God would have us do that faithfully and zealously. But He would prefer that we never find ourselves in such a limited position. When we do, we may have made some inaccurate assumptions. We have assumed that tomorrow's income will be at least as high as today's, if not higher. We've tried to lock God into His bounty as though it were our right to receive rather than His right to give. We assume too much about tomorrow.

IN DEED   The Bible does not absolutely forbid indebtedness. Each believer must determine as a matter of conscience and of the Spirit who works within us which debts are scripturally sound and which ones are not. But we are given strong warnings. God wants His people to be free from the world and bound only to Him. We must be careful: We should serve others because we are called by His name, not because we are obligated by our frequent signatures.

JANUARY 31
*Proverbs 22:7;
Romans 13:8*

Are we as willing to go into debt for the work of God as we are for a vacation to Hawaii?

—Erwin Lutzer

God's Value System

When a man's ways are pleasing to the Lord, he makes even his enemies live at peace with him. PROVERBS 16:7

FEBRUARY 1

Proverbs 16:7;
2 Timothy 3:12

God's promises
are like the stars;
the darker the
night, the brighter
they shine.

—David Nicholas

IN WORD The wisdom literature of the Scriptures contains certain principles of life that we do not always see in our experience. Consider this verse, for example: "When a man's ways are pleasing to the Lord, he makes even his enemies live at peace with him." Yet we know that the ways of Jesus, and even of Stephen, Paul, Peter, and many other victims of aggression, were pleasing to the Lord—and their enemies did not live at peace with them. What are we to do when we find principles like this that are overwhelmingly affirmed in Scripture and so often not affirmed in experience? Shall we deny the truth of the Bible?

Obviously not. The Bible is our Word of life. It has never proven false. What we see in the wisdom books of Psalms, Proverbs, and Ecclesiastes, among others, is a description of the way life is supposed to work. They are not always absolute statements of cause and effect; they are often guiding principles of God's value system. If they contain promises, the promises will be fulfilled. How could it be otherwise? They come from the Faithful One. But they may not be fulfilled today. You may first have adversaries. Your good may be repaid with evil. You may live the principles of God and see the aggression of the enemy—for a time.

IN DEED The wisdom of Scripture is deeper than we think. These are not superficial platitudes. They are truths to be mined like precious jewels. We need to explore the truths of God's wisdom deeply and let it be written into our hearts. We must know His value system inside and out.

Do not be discouraged when you encounter verses that have not been realized in your own life. Trust that they will be. Be patient, and have constant faith in God, and you will eventually see the promise as facts. God's value system will prevail, and His light will penetrate all darkness. Those who hold to His Word will be vindicated in the end.

In Sync with God

*If anyone turns a deaf ear to the law, even his
prayers are detestable.* PROVERBS 28:9

IN WORD No one wants detestable prayers. The very
thought is strong enough warning to keep us faithful to
God. But the prescription for acceptable prayers is hard for
us to live with. Legalism? Is that really what God wants
from us?

Scripture never tells us that God only hears our prayers
when we keep His law perfectly. It does, however, exhort
us to have our hearts turned toward Him and to be zealous about our obedience. We often learn the negatives by
heart—"Your iniquities have separated you from your God;
your sins have hidden his face from you, so that he will not
hear" (Isaiah 59:2), for example—but positive encouragement is stressed in Scripture at least as often, if not more so.
A heart inclined toward God opens the way for Him to have
ears inclined toward us. He can answer our prayers a lot
more frequently when He's not disciplining us for ungodly
behavior.

Any time the Old Testament Law is stressed in Scripture,
we get uptight about legalism, as though obedience in order
to earn righteousness might be confused with obedience as
a result of faith. They may look the same on the surface,
but their motivations are poles apart. So we can relax: God
never tells us that legalism is the means to a vibrant prayer
life. He only tells us that those who accept the order and
standards woven into His creation are qualified to ask Him
to intervene in it. A heart in sync with God's heart results in
prayers in sync with His plan.

IN DEED Have you struggled with unanswered prayer?
There are numerous possible reasons that God may withhold His answers, but consider this one: Have you submitted to His authority? It only makes sense that if we are going
to appeal to His authority that we would be expected to live
under it. When we rebel against His will and then ask Him
to accomplish His will, we are contradicting ourselves. But
when we submit to His will, we are lining ourselves up with
the flowing current of creation. We are ready to experience
the power of prayer.

FEBRUARY 2
*Proverbs 28:9;
Isaiah 59:2*

He who runs from
God in the morn-
ing will scarcely
find Him the
rest of the day.

—John Bunyan

Representing Jesus

Whatever you do, work at it with all your heart, as working for the Lord, not for men. COLOSSIANS 3:23

A dairy maid can milk cows to the glory of God.

—Martin Luther

IN WORD We see our lives in terms of activity and achievement. We interpret our success in terms of what we've accomplished. So it only makes sense that when we work, we define its quality by externals—what we've done, whom we've done it for, and what results it will have.

God has His eye on other criteria. He sees our lives in terms of fruit, which may include activities and achievements but encompasses so much more. Fruit involves those qualities the Holy Spirit cultivates in us—love, joy, peace, patience, kindness, goodness, faithfulness, gentleness, and self-control (Galatians 5:22-23). So when God sees us at work, He is more interested in how the work is being done than in what it accomplishes. He looks at motives and attitudes. Most of all, He looks to see if our motivation is derived from Him or if He is peripheral to what we do. And if He is peripheral, He is grieved.

Ultimately, every inch of our lives is God's, even our work. If He wants to be Lord of our thoughts and our relationships, He clearly would also want to be Lord of our employment, or whatever vocation occupies our time. We do not cease being His disciples when we punch a time clock. If He is truly our Lord, then everything we do is for Him.

IN DEED Do you work for an employer? Perhaps so, but the impression you make on him or her is entirely God's business. He is zealous for the reputation of His name. If you have claimed His name, He is therefore zealous for your reputation. Your character and His go hand in hand. If other people—believers and nonbelievers alike—observe godly qualities in you, then God is glorified. If they don't, He isn't. We literally represent Jesus wherever we are, including the workplace. Represent Him with all your heart.

Displaying Jesus

Whatever you do, work at it with all your heart, as working for the Lord, not for men.   COLOSSIANS 3:23

IN WORD   There is a deeper issue here than working with the right attitude. It is a question of life orientation. Whom do you belong to? Who is sovereign over your circumstances? Who is really in control?

Multitudes of people do not enjoy their jobs. The unbelieving would simply rather be doing something else. As believers, we often see our work as an interference in our lives of faith. We would enjoy our lives more without it. We would have time to study God's Word more if we didn't have to put in our forty-hour weeks. We would have more time to build important relationships. We easily feel as if we are in the wrong place when we are working at the things we have to do. At the bottom of that feeling is a questioning of God's sovereignty in our lives. We wonder why He has put us where He has.

God has not placed us where we are simply for the output we can produce, whether it is at a factory, at a desk, at school, or at home with children. He has put us there because that is a context in which He wants to display Himself. Our work is about Him, even if it's entirely secular in our minds. We are there because God wants to put godliness on display for others to see. He wants to infiltrate the culture we work in.

IN DEED   Is godliness at work in your preoccupation? If you're like many people, you may be preoccupied by the unpleasantness of being there. You may feel like your work is pointless, your boss is unfair, or your coworkers are petty. Never mind. None of those things are the point. The point is for the Holy Spirit to dwell in you there, wherever you happen to be. And in that sense, you are working for God, not for the one who signs your paycheck. Whatever you do, have this in mind: You are doing it not just because God wants you to be there, but because He wants to be there too.

FEBRUARY 4
Colossians 3:23-25

Work without a love relationship spells burnout.

—Lloyd John Ogilvie

A Selfish View of God

*A man's own folly ruins his life, yet his heart rages
against the LORD.*   PROVERBS 19:3

FEBRUARY 5
Proverbs 19:3

Some folks treat
God like a lawyer.
They go to him
only when they
are in trouble.

—Anonymous

IN WORD   The problem is almost universal. As partici-
pants in the human rebellion, we have all acted foolishly.
Any time we have lived without thought of the Lord's will
in a matter, any time we have not stirred up our love for
Him, and any time we have intentionally acted in our own
best interests without concern for the consequences to others, we have welcomed a sense of separation between us
and our Creator. It is part and parcel of fallen human nature
to put distance between God and ourselves. We can serve
ourselves better that way. In our times of independence, we
don't want Him getting too close.

But when trouble comes, we cry out to God as though
we're the most helpless of victims. What's worse, we often
cry out with a hint of accusation: "Why are You doing this to
me?" We frequently fail to make a vital connection between
our willful independence in our times of self-sufficiency and
the seeming absence of God in our times of need. It doesn't
occur to us that when we keep God on the periphery of
our lives, we have no business accusing Him of not "being
there" for us when we need Him.

Proverbs calls this "folly." It is utter foolishness to
set ourselves up as self-directed people when times are
easy, get ourselves into trouble, and then appeal to God's
fatherly obligations. But we inherited foolishness in the Fall.
We are genetically prone to want a convenient God who is
there when we need Him and will leave us alone when we
don't.

IN DEED   What is the solution to this selfish view of God?
It isn't to stop calling on Him in times of trouble. He welcomes that—even commands it. The solution is to let Him be
the integral and intimate foundation of our lives now, before
trouble comes. Then our cries to Him will be the pleasing
voice of a treasured child, and when we need Him, He will
show Himself strong on our behalf.

New Clothes

You were taught, with regard to your former way of life,
to put off your old self . . . and to put on the new self.
EPHESIANS 4:22, 24

IN WORD   Living the Christian life should become as
natural to us as changing clothes. We take off the old and we
put on the new. The old may have been comfortable, but it is
dirty and horribly out of fashion in our new kingdom. The
new is the permanent style of the Kingdom of Heaven, and it
will cause us to resemble God increasingly. Our responsibility is to continually shed what is no longer appropriate and
put on the clothes we have been given.

But many of us walk an unwise path. We claim citizenship in the new kingdom but continue to wear the fashions
of the old. In trying to fit in everywhere, we find that we fit
in nowhere. We may blend into the old kingdom, but we no
longer have proper ID there. We have the proper ID for the
new kingdom, but we're slow to fit in. Either way, it's an
awkward situation to be in.

What is our reluctance? Why do we hesitate to put on
our new clothes? Because we know we will experience rejection, and no one likes rejection. But rejection will come to
everyone, either from the world or from the Kingdom of
Heaven. The question is not whether we can avoid it, but
whose we most want to avoid. Wisdom calls for a choice.
Trying to dress for both kingdoms is not a viable option.

IN DEED   Are you reluctant to place both feet firmly in the
Kingdom of God? Do you try to hang on to remnants of your
former citizenship? Let them go. Shed them like an old set
of ragged clothes. The way to settle into your new kingdom
and advance in it is to be reclothed. It's a daily process. We
deny deceitful desires (v. 22) and saturate ourselves in a new
attitude (v. 23). We become like God in righteousness and
holiness (v. 24). There is no greater wisdom than this.

FEBRUARY 6
Ephesians 4:17-24

We cannot
help conform-
ing ourselves to
what we love.

—St. Francis de Sales

37

The Opinion That Matters

Fear of man will prove to be a snare, but whoever trusts in the LORD is kept safe.   PROVERBS 29:25

I'd rather be a fool in the eyes of men than a fool in the eyes of God.

—Anonymous

IN WORD   The need to impress. The desire to stay out of trouble. The tendency to compare ourselves to others. The urge to maneuver and manipulate. All of these are products of our natural fear of man. If "the fear of the LORD is the beginning of wisdom" (Proverbs 9:10), the fear of man is the end of it. We cannot serve Him well with our eyes on popular opinion.

We do all sorts of strange things because of an inbred dependence on the approval of others. We may not actually be afraid of others, but every person alive tends to be concerned with how others think of us. When we are, our welfare rises and falls with the trends of our culture, the vagaries of human opinion, and the moods of the people closest to us. We have no firm footing in such an uncertain world. Our human-centered living proves to be a snare. We find ourselves trapped in a sinful society's norms.

God's desire is to remove us entirely from this no-win situation. He does not want us in a futile search for popular approval or an obsessive fear of rejection. He never asks us to compare ourselves to others. No, God wants His opinion alone to matter to us. He calls us to place our identity entirely in Him. When we do, our behavior will be godly because we have an audience of One, and we know our audience is forgiving, strengthening, and gentle. We have nothing to lose when we approach Him in humility and honesty.

IN DEED   God commands us to resist the urge to run with the crowd. It's an urge based on insecurity, rooted in our former alienation from our Creator. But once reconciled to our Creator, we have no need for human approval. There is no crowd to please, no culture to accommodate, no hoops to jump through for the momentary applause of a fickle audience. Best of all, there is no snare to fall into. Living Godward lives, we are kept safe from the false values of this world.

An All-the-Time God

Shall we accept good from God, and not trouble?

JOB 2:10

IN WORD   The casual relationship with God takes Him to be a good-luck charm. The world is full of people who will pray to God, praise His goodness, speak of His plans, and call themselves His children. Yet when trouble comes, they complain that He is not treating them well. They wonder what they have done to deserve His disfavor. He isn't serving them as they expected.

God is not a good-luck charm. He is not the amulet we hold in our hands as we play the roulette wheel or the stock market. He is not the great coach in the sky who was on our side when our team won but was not when we lost. Our prayers are not the mantras we chant so that we won't have any trouble this day. He is not the big Santa Claus upstairs who keeps track of all our wishes in case we're good. And His Word is not our horoscope, telling us all the tricks we must do to be successful in our ventures.

No, all of these approaches to God have elements of truth but end up as lies. He is more than a dispensable "blesser," available when we want to use Him and irrelevant when we don't. He is the Governor of our lives, the Sovereign who directs us in every way we should go, the Blesser who measures His blessings by the depths of His grace, the Shepherd who will lead us through both comfortable plains and difficult valleys. He is the God of real life.

IN DEED   Real life has troubles. God will protect us from many of them, but He will also walk us through many of them. He will do what is best for us, not what our shallow hearts dictate to Him. Like Job's wife, we have a hard time understanding that. We worship Him more desperately in a storm than in a calm.

It's good for us to know, when times are tough, that God is sovereign over our circumstances. He has allowed them, because there was something good in them to allow. We have a lesson to learn and a Savior to lean on. Trust that He has you there for just those reasons.

FEBRUARY 8
Job 2:7-10

Oh, for a spirit that bows always before the sovereignty of God.

—Charles Spurgeon

Deep Guidance

He reveals deep and hidden things.
DANIEL 2:22

FEBRUARY 9
Daniel 2:19-23

Deep in your heart
it is not guidance
you want so much
as a guide.

—John White

IN WORD Sometimes we think God has given us a bare minimum of information. We want to know the answers to all of our deep questions, but because wise philosophers struggle with the meaning of life as much as we do, we assume that we are confined in ignorance for the length of our lives. And aside from the mysteries of the ages, we'd even settle for guidance in today's choices. Our finite minds need help.

God does not leave us in darkness; He makes that very clear. He spoke light into our world on page one of the Old Testament, and He sent the Light of the World to us on page one of the New. The mysteries of life—and today's guidance—are revealed in Him. Our God is more than willing to direct us.

So why do we so often struggle to find our way? Perhaps our struggle is not so much a matter of knowledge as it is a matter of will. We often know the right thing to do, but we search for reasons not to do it. Or perhaps we want our fortunes told. We just want direction, not God. We don't want to put in the time and the effort for a life-changing relationship with Him. The mind of Christ takes a while to grow in us, and it has radical implications. We just want a little direction today.

God won't usually work that way. He offers us deep and hidden things, but to find them we must have a deep and hidden relationship with Him—deep in faith and hidden in Christ (Colossians 3:3). Everything we want to know is there, but it involves a heavy cost on our end: a sacrificial life, a thirst for truth, a love for our Savior, and a promise to follow Him wherever He leads. Daniel demonstrated such qualities long before God gave him the understanding revealed in this passage. The revealer of mysteries asks no less of us.

IN DEED Do you want wisdom from above? It is far-reaching and powerful, deep and true. But asking for the light of His wisdom demands a pledge to *live* in the light of His wisdom. That's often our missing ingredient. He won't let us settle for superficial direction. Visions of truth come to those who will follow it.

Righteous Hunger

The LORD does not let the righteous go hungry but he thwarts the craving of the wicked. PROVERBS 10:3

IN WORD We are, in a sense, defined by our hunger. Think about it: Our cravings are descriptive, to a large degree, of the spirit within us. Our personality, our preferences, our problems are all revealed in and through the things we strive for.

God's Word affirms this—it often defines us by our hunger. Jesus said those who hunger and thirst for righteousness would be filled (Matthew 5:6). They are His. It pleases Him when we crave His righteousness and seek it as a treasure. He delights in that desire. And when we have it, He never mentions our sin—it no longer defines us. He mentions only our future—the fullness we will receive from Him. The craving, by His description, is who we are.

This is why Proverbs can tell us that the righteous will not go hungry. The righteous will not go hungry because they hunger for righteousness. God gives such treasures to all who seek them. The wicked, however, crave wickedness. If they are filled, it will only be for a moment. It will not last.

God promises daily bread to those who trust Him for it with a right spirit. This verse affirms that, but it goes far beyond food. It describes matters of the heart, not matters of the stomach. The heart that is fixed on God will find itself in sync with the purpose of creation itself. The heart that has more inclination toward wickedness than toward God will find itself horribly out of step with the rest of the universe.

IN DEED Does contentment elude you? Check your desires. They are an accurate description of who you are and the kingdom you'd rather live in. What do you hunger for? If your cravings lead you to God, you will never go hungry. If they do not, you always will. God's Kingdom is always about righteousness. Never forget that, and be filled.

FEBRUARY 10
Proverbs 10:3

Man finds it hard to get what he wants because he does not want the best.

—George MacDonald

Internal Law

*His delight is in the law of the LORD, and on his law
he meditates day and night.*   PSALM 1:2

Law says 'Do';
grace says 'Done.'

—John Henry Jowett

IN WORD   Many Christians get confused about the Law of the Old Testament, even with Paul's lengthy teachings on its role for believers in Jesus. We don't want to be legalists, trying to earn righteousness through our works, as other religions teach. Our righteousness is found exclusively in Christ—why would we seek it in our own efforts? On the other hand, we don't want to be lawless. The Bible—even the New Testament—condemns lawless behavior. God is holy, and so must we be (Leviticus 11:44; 1 Peter 1:16). Somehow, we are to have holiness and liberty all at the same time. How?

The Law that was written on stone tablets—i.e., the Ten Commandments, the sum of God's moral standard—was once an agenda for how sinful humans could be godly. No one ever fulfilled it, of course, except for Jesus. But it was the right standard. It is now not our agenda, but a description of what God does in us to make us godly. There is no difference in the godliness of the Old Testament and the New, per se. The difference is in how it is obtained. It was once an external objective; it is now an internal work of the Spirit of God. But it is the same Law.

IN DEED   It is as appropriate in New Testament faith to meditate on God's Law as it was for the psalmist hundreds of years before Christ. The trick for the Christian is never to put it outside of ourselves as something to strive for. Instead, we are to see it as a measure of what God has already done and will continue to do in our hearts.

Suppose you have failed one of the commandments. Meditate on it, but do not strive to fulfill it in your strength alone. Pray to have it fulfilled in you. Confess your transgression of it, but know that its fulfillment is an act of God. It comes with your prayers and full cooperation, of course, but it is His work. The perfect Son of God lives in you. Why attempt the life He has already lived? Delight in His holiness and let Him write it on your heart.

External Fruit

He is like a tree planted by streams of water, which yields its fruit in season and whose leaf does not wither. Whatever he does prospers. PSALM 1:3

IN WORD   God plants His Spirit within us—we have the eternal Son of God in our being by faith. When nonbelievers read the Gospels, the stories of Jesus ought to remind them of those of us who believe. The fact that there is sometimes little visible resemblance between the biblical Jesus and the Spirit dwelling in our flesh today is a tragedy. There should be in our character and lifestyle a clear correspondence to one controversial Galilean of ancient history.

God's character is expressed in His works. What He does emanates from His personality. He expects the same of us—our faith will result in works. The fruit of the Spirit is not just internally received but externally expressed. God meets us in deep, inward places, but He always leads us outward. His Spirit does not invade our being to remain hidden. We are the display of His glory, not its best-kept secret.

The one who realizes this—who has meditated on the life and law of God inscribed upon his heart—will be firmly established. He will be like a tree planted by streams of water. And there *will* be fruit. There's no doubt about it: When the season is right, fruit will come, and the fruit will be good. Why? Because there is an infinitely rich, ever-flowing stream of water that nourishes this tree. It is not a tree that establishes itself; it is planted and tended by the living God.

IN DEED   God calls us to be like Himself. His eternal character produced the purity of the Law, words of wisdom, the voice of the prophets, the saving work of Jesus, and the life of the church. What does our character produce? If it comes from God, it produces reflections of the very same themes. It produces the kind of prosperity that glorifies God and keeps us in His extravagant grace. It produces fruit that lasts forever.

FEBRUARY 12
Psalm 1

Our actions disclose what goes on within us, just as its fruit makes known a tree otherwise unknown to us.

—Thalassios the Libyan

43

Life in the Spirit

After beginning with the Spirit, are you now trying to attain your goal by human effort?   GALATIANS 3:3

FEBRUARY 13

Galatians 3:1-5

The Father in heaven loves to fill His children with His Holy Spirit.

—Andrew Murray

IN WORD   The Galatians had diverted from the right path. They had become "religious." It's a trap any of us can fall into, and we often do. We follow a law—any law, even a good one like Jesus' words—trying to live the Christian life apart from Christ. We try to accomplish the work of God in the strength of the flesh. It can't be done.

Jesus was very clear: "Apart from me you can do nothing" (John 15:5). We may have thought that being a Christian meant being better, improving ourselves, and having a profound reason to obey God and do good works. If so, we set our eyes on the result of the Christian life and forgot the means to get there. We cannot become mature disciples except by supernatural means. Jesus did not come into this world to make us better; He came into this world to make us new. There's a significant difference.

We know what a mature Christian looks like. He or she will have the fruit of the Spirit: love, joy, peace, patience, kindness, goodness, faithfulness, gentleness, and self-control (Galatians 5:22-23). What we don't seem to know—or we forget easily—is that we don't grow these attributes by doing our best at them. We get them by realizing how foreign they are to our human nature, how futile our attempts at achieving them are, and how dependent on God we are for His life within us. It's a supernatural means to a supernatural life.

IN DEED   Are you frustrated with your Christian growth? Are you strong in religion but weak in faith? Understand the difference between the two. Avoid the foolishness of the Galatians. No amount of human effort can fulfill God's laws. You were born of the Spirit when you believed. Now live by the Spirit. Cry out to God for Him to live His life in you, and He will accomplish your righteousness.

Understanding Weakness

My grace is sufficient for you, for my power is made perfect in weakness. 2 CORINTHIANS 12:9

IN WORD Why does human reasoning run so contrary to God's ways? It seems only logical that if we want to be strong, we should strive to be strong. If we want victory, we should exert power. If we want success, we should learn strategies for success. This makes sense in any line of reasoning—except God's. His methods don't fit our logic because His purposes do not match ours. He will not divert His glory to His creatures. Our victories must come from His hands. And for Him to be glorified in them, His hands must be visible.

That is why God has us fighting our battles from a state of weakness. We fight from a position of strength—in Him—but in a natural state of weakness so that His demonstration of power will not be clouded by our own resources and feeble self-efforts. It is a hard lesson for a Christian to learn. We are strongest when we are weakest.

Paul was tormented by a messenger of Satan. We don't know how that messenger manifested itself, though theories abound. What we do know is that God, in His wisdom, did not remove the thorn in Paul's flesh. He used it as an occasion to demonstrate His powerful grace. And Paul, in wisdom that can only come from God, learned to accept his hardship for the greater good of displaying God's strength.

IN DEED When you find yourself in the heat of a battle—and any Christian living a godly life often will—resist the urge to muster up strength. Call on His. Acknowledge your natural impotence. It only stands to reason that fallen, finite beings will always be outmatched in a life-or-death spiritual struggle. Let no pride talk you out of accepting that truth. Embrace it and lean on His grace, understanding that the key to your battle today is His power—a power that will only be revealed when you stop trying to rival it. Your sufficiency is in what He brings to the situation: Himself.

FEBRUARY 14
2 Corinthians
12:7-10

We have no power
from God unless
we live in the
persuasion that
we have none
of our own.

—John Owen

45

The Exchange of Grace

Shall we go on sinning so that grace may increase?
ROMANS 6:1

FEBRUARY 15

Romans 6:1-14

Free grace can go into the gutter and bring up a jewel!

—Charles Spurgeon

IN WORD   It seems so unreal. This gospel of grace, the thought that *everything* we have ever done and will ever do is covered by the sacrifice of Jesus, seems so unlikely. The world we live in has not conditioned us to believe that anything truly valuable is free. The knowledge deep within us that we are spiritually and morally corrupt has not conditioned us to accept mercy so easily. We're trained to understand that people get what they deserve, not that a something-for-nothing transaction is worth anything. Especially when the "something" is so huge and the "nothing" so clearly devoid of merit.

So Paul asked this question: Shall we go on sinning? If none of this gospel is based on merit, should we just give up trying to behave ourselves? It's a question that, if we have to ask it, unmasks our motives. We really just wanted salvation. We'd prefer not to have much to do with God.

The answer to this question of sinning in the face of grace, according to Paul, is a horrified "Of course not!" Paul is clear on one thing we frequently forget: We did not simply sign a contract for our salvation; we exchanged lives with a Redeemer. He took our sinful selves into the grave with Him and brought us a resurrected life instead. And that life can never be comfortable with sin. Never.

IN DEED   Do you view your salvation simply as a contractual agreement that will guarantee you a pleasant eternity? Then you will have epic struggles with sin. You will find it much too easy to justify your indiscretions because, after all, a merciful God will overlook them. But if you view your salvation as a life-exchange—a once-profane existence now traded for a Holy Substitute—then the very thought of sin will seem ludicrous. Yes, there will still be struggles, but not from any attempt to justify disobedience. The struggle will only be with the power of the flesh, which Jesus is ready and willing to subdue. With that kind of Savior, is there any reason at all to go on sinning?

46

Resurrection Life

Just as Christ was raised from the dead through the glory of the Father, we too may live a new life. ROMANS 6:4

IN WORD If new life is ours in Christ, why does life often seem so old? Why do we struggle with sin and death when we're united with the One who overcame both? Perhaps the answer lies within us. Perhaps it's all a matter of perspective. Perhaps when the Bible says we've died and been raised up again, we haven't really believed it. We're reminded of our old nature often, and we let it speak louder than the promise of God.

Effective discipleship, the fruitful Christian walk, begins with death and resurrection. This is foundational. If we see ourselves as people in a process of reform, trying to make the bad habits good and sinful tendencies weak, we will fail. But if we see ourselves as dead and then raised, then we have the basis for a new way of life, and in fact, a new life that isn't really ours. It's His, and only He knows how to live it.

It's critical for us to understand: Jesus doesn't offer to improve us. He offers to let us die and then to inhabit our personalities with His presence. That's why discipleship can hurt; there's a cross. But it's the key to the glory that follows.

IN DEED Are you living the resurrected life? Many Christians are striving in the flesh to do the works of the Spirit, and they are frustrated and tired. Wouldn't you rather rest in the Resurrection than try to overhaul the old nature that was—and should continually be—crucified with Jesus? New life is an eternal blessing, but it has no short-term benefit if we refuse to live in it.

How do you get there? Not by straining for it, not by reading about it, and not by frantically immersing yourself in church life. No, just by asking. Ask often, trust deeply, let yourself be convinced of the promise, think about it often, and most of all give Jesus free reign in your heart. The power of His resurrection is available when the power of your self is exhausted. Live in His power. Or better yet, let His power live in you.

FEBRUARY 16
Roman 6:1-14

The characteristic of the new birth is that I yield myself so completely to God that Christ is formed in me.

—Oswald Chambers

A Life of Belief

If we died with Christ, we believe that we will also live with him.
ROMANS 6:8

Christ has turned all our sunsets into dawns.

—Clement of Alexandria

IN WORD It is strange to our ears: "We died with Christ." It doesn't seem much like we died. Most days, we seem all too alive—we have responsibilities that clamor for our attention, people who get on our very sensitive nerves, battles to fight, and habits to lose. If this is life, we're not sure we want it to be like this. And if we've died with Christ and been raised with Him, we're more than a little confused. This doesn't seem much like resurrection.

One of our problems is a matter of timing. We live between the Cross and the final Resurrection. While the death and resurrection of Jesus are legal facts for us, they are both growing experiences. In a sense we died, but in another sense, we are dying. Jesus told His disciples so; their cross would be a daily fact of their walk. And in a sense we've been raised, but in another sense, we will be raised. We're just learning what it means to live in Christ and for Him to live in us. This new life comes on the heels of a very persistent old one, and sometimes the boundaries between the two are not all that clear to us. They're very real; they just aren't that clear.

IN DEED Many Christians are disenchanted with the Christian life. It isn't the experience of spiritual power and holy discipleship they felt it would be. The joy of following Jesus seems to be lacking.

Don't despair. That life is available. It can be experienced in glimpses and even long seasons for now. And it will be experienced ultimately and finally, forever and ever.

Meanwhile, though our status with God is complete and incorruptible, in practice we linger somewhere between corruption and holiness, between old and new, between death and life, and between Spirit and flesh. God is calling us ever forward, while sin and Satan grab the heels of their lost possession. Keep fleeing from them, right into the arms of God. Paul's prescription is belief. Don't lose heart. We must know whose we are and where we belong. We must believe in the life we've been given.

Count Yourself

Count yourselves dead to sin but alive to God in Christ Jesus.

ROMANS 6:11

IN WORD   Nowhere is there a clearer connection between wisdom—the renewed mind that God gives us in Christ—and our life in the Spirit than in this verse. Our encounter with life in Christ, according to Paul, stems from what we *know* to be true. The truth of our life is a matter of what Jesus did for us on the Cross and the third day; our experience of it is a matter of our mental grasp of this truth. We are to count ourselves dead but also alive. Other translations also make it an issue of our thought-life. We are to consider, to reckon, to count on the truth: We died with Jesus and we are raised with Him.

Many Christians miss out on experiencing the victorious, joy-filled life, not because they aren't in fact crucified and raised in Jesus, but because they don't know it. Perhaps it is only a theological belief or a matter of creed. Perhaps it is misunderstood as something to strive for rather than to accept. Perhaps it is seen as a future possibility rather than an established position. None of that is enough. A Christian will really experience the joy and power and victory of the Christian life when he or she believes its foundation: We were crucified with Jesus, and now we are raised in His life. And it must be more than belief; we must know it, count on it, cling to it as a rock-solid event as certain as the day we graduated, got married, or signed a contract.

IN DEED   Too many Christians are trying to make the Christian experience true for them. They have put the cart before the horse. Experience doesn't lead to truth, truth leads to experience. Instead of praying for the resurrected life, accept it and live it. Instead of hoping you will die to sin, count on the fact that you already have. Our struggles are often only a product of how we see ourselves. If we see ourselves as sinners trying to be better Christians, that is how we'll live. If we see ourselves as sinners who were buried with Christ and raised to new life, that too is how we'll live. Romans 6:11 tells us what to see. Count on it, and watch your experience line up with truth.

FEBRUARY 18
Romans 6:11

You do not need to wait . . . before beginning to live eternally.

—James S. Stewart

Naked Faith

Blessed is the man who makes the LORD his trust.
PSALM 40:4

FEBRUARY 19
Psalm 40:1-5

A little faith will
bring your soul
to heaven, but a
lot of faith will
bring heaven
to your soul.

—D. L. Moody

IN WORD Those of us who claim a relationship with God have placed our trust in Him. But when it comes to daily living, we tend to trust a lot of other sources of help as well. Few of us have learned to trust the Lord *alone*. We usually trust the Lord *and* financial resources, medical research, counselors' advice, popular opinion, or any number of other avenues of assistance. None of these in themselves are necessarily false helps. The issue is our heart attitude of trust. Do we know in our hearts where our help really comes from? It comes from God.

David claims that the person who makes the Lord his trust will be "blessed"—utterly happy, spiritually prosperous, envied, and honored. God's "shalom"—His peace and wellness—will be upon him. The picture is of someone who has forsaken all confidence in other things and cast himself without reservation—even recklessly—on God. It is a naked faith, with no human props to fall back on. It is a spiritual placing of all eggs in one basket.

This kind of trust requires a certain amount of courage. It hangs everything on an invisible God. It does not hedge its bets but believes that God, as He is revealed in His Word, will act toward us as we have been told He will. But in the end, it is the safest trust there is. God has never failed anyone who has invested all hopes in Him.

IN DEED How pure is your trust? Are you using God to fill in the gaps around your other sources of help? Do you have a plan B if God doesn't intervene the way you want Him to? If so, do not expect the blessedness of being abandoned to Him. That only comes with a pure, unbridled faith in God alone. No false idols, no confidence in the flesh, no backup plans, no pride. Make the Lord your exclusive trust, and expect to be blessed.

Handling Rebuke

*If you had responded to my rebuke, I would have poured out
my heart to you and made my thoughts known to you.*

PROVERBS 1:23

IN WORD We don't have to try long to apply God's
Word to our lives before we realize that we often violate it.
When we come up against His Word, we have essentially
two choices: We can seek change in ourselves; or we can
try to change the Word. We can't *really* change God's Word,
of course. Nevertheless, we try often, don't we? We have a
range of methods: "That verse doesn't really mean what it
says on the surface." "That principle applied to the culture
in which it was written, but not ours." "That must mean
something else in context, or in the original language, or . . ."
You know the routines. We've all rationalized our behavior
at one time or another.

But the better option—the only really rational one—is
to adapt ourselves to God's unchanging Word. When we
do, God offers an amazing promise: His wisdom will pour
out His heart to us and make His thoughts known to us.
Responsiveness begets wisdom, and greater responsiveness
begets greater wisdom. Ignoring God's rebukes, however
painful they may be at times, leads in the opposite direction—toward utter folly.

IN DEED We often think that God's rebuke will only
carry negative consequences if we reject it. That's true, but
in this particular verse, God promises a positive reward for
a submissive response. It's enough to blow our minds, if we
think about it: The wisdom of the God of the universe—the
Almighty's innermost thoughts, the passionate heart of the
Creator—rushes upon us like a rapidly flowing fountain.

People have sought true wisdom their whole lives and
never found such a treasure. Why? They didn't understand
God's rebuke. Listen for His call and receive the abundance
of eternal wisdom. Let Him pour His heart out to you.

FEBRUARY 20
Proverbs 1:20-33

The Bible is not
meant merely
to inform, but
to transform.

—Anonymous

Waiting for Humility

*The LORD longs to be gracious to you; he rises
to show you compassion.*   ISAIAH 30:18

FEBRUARY 21
Isaiah 30:15-18

The door of God
is humility.

—John the Short

IN WORD   We ask a common question in times of difficulty: "Where is God?" We don't raise such questions when all is well. But there are times when all is not well, and we grow suspicious of our Creator. If the difficulty is prolonged, the question grows more accusing. We wonder why answers to our pleas for help are not immediate.

God's answer is here in Isaiah: He longs to be gracious. That is His nature. Regardless of what our circumstances tell us, we must know beyond the shadow of a doubt that He is, at His very core, a gracious, compassionate God. Whatever other questions may come to mind, we must never doubt that compassion directs Him. Even when He is angry, as when Isaiah prophesied to His covenant people, it is an anger backed by redemption. There is a caring purpose in it.

Knowing this, we are stuck with one nagging question: Why does He have to "long" to be gracious? If He is so ready to show us His compassion, why does He wait? Two related reasons: (1) There is a purging purpose that only time can accomplish in our hearts; and (2) His compassion only becomes visible when we're repentant (v. 15). Humility is the key. Most of God's blessings are promised to the humble—those who acknowledge their bankrupt condition before Him. None are promised to the proud.

IN DEED   Are you wondering where the presence of God is in your life? If He is waiting, there may be a lack of humility that, when corrected, will open the door for Him to act. You may be going through a purging process that will not be lifted until His work in your heart is complete. His compassion is too great to relieve your circumstances while leaving your heart in the same condition as before. He is too merciful to solve your problems without imparting His character to you. Let your waiting accomplish His work. Then you will see His compassion.

The Promise of Warfare

One of you routs a thousand, because the LORD your God
fights for you, just as he promised. JOSHUA 23:10

IN WORD Few of us knew that the day we became a Christian was the day we enlisted in the armed forces. We might have hoped for a serene, pastoral way of life, with the Lord as our Shepherd and a scarcity of wolves in the pasture. But we soon found that the Christian life was not like that at all. To be a citizen of the Kingdom of God is to be a soldier in its military. There is no area of our kingdom not targeted by the enemy. There is no peacetime service—not yet.

The battle is worth the cost, of course. There are great victories to be won and an eternity to celebrate them. And the warfare, though intense, is backed by an unlimited source of power on our side. Joshua's observation in verse 10 does not just apply to Israel's conquest of Canaan; it applies to the nature of God. He fights for His people. There are no odds great enough to overwhelm a true servant of God. Any one of us can rout a thousand of the enemy. Why? Because of a warrior God and a promise. Those who have forsaken sin and devoted themselves to Him will lack no strength for the battle.

Victory belongs to those whose heart is completely God's. We may wonder, in this fallen world, why it often seems to elude us; but the problem is likely in our definition of victory. Yes, we will be wounded at times, and eventually death comes to all. But for the faithful, never at the wrong time, and never without a promise. God's Kingdom purposes will be established through us. Victory is certain.

IN DEED A wise assessment of our struggles will always include this glorious fact: Almighty God fights on behalf of those whose hearts are His. When we look at a problem with a sense of defeat, we are not wise to the reality of God's power or His promise. We must always know who holds victory in His hand, and we must never lose heart.

FEBRUARY 22
Joshua 23:6-11

Christianity is a warfare, and Christians are spiritual soldiers.

—Robert Southwell

A Discipline of Thanks

Enter his gates with thanksgiving.
PSALM 100:4

FEBRUARY 23
Psalm 100

A life of thankfulness releases the glory of God.

—Bengt Sundberg

IN WORD   The distance of God is an all-too-common malady among believers. It isn't that God is really distant, but we go through waves of feeling that He is. Sometimes the waves are prolonged—circumstances batter us, discouragement plagues us, and God seems far, far away.

God's prescription for entering His presence is to give thanks. This verse doesn't just tell us the right attitude with which we are to enter His gates; it also tells us the means by which we enter them. Thanksgiving coupled with praise will bring us to where He is; or it will bring Him to where we are. Either way, we find that worshipful gratitude is the right place to be. God lives where He is acknowledged.

If God does not seem to be living near you, perhaps there is something lacking in your acknowledgment. You rarely see gratitude in someone who thinks negatively about life. Why? Pessimistic thoughts remove the glory of His presence. Negative thinking is not faith; it is the antithesis of reality from God's point of view. Reality, as He defines it, is all about who He is and what He does. Negativity isn't. It assumes the worst. It feeds—and is fed by—the enemy of God.

IN DEED   Paul told believers to give thanks in every circumstance (1 Thessalonians 5:18). He didn't tell them to give thanks only when the clear evidence of God's blessing is visible. He told them to give thanks always—in every situation. How can we do this? On the basis of who God is. If we always see the downside, we are doubting something about God—that He is good, or able, or wise. But if we know that He is good, and that He is sovereign, and that He is wise, we can give thanks that He is working out His plan even in the difficult circumstances of life.

Establish in your mind a discipline of thanks. Enumerate every aspect of your life and thank God for it. In every circumstance, choose to see it from an angle that will cultivate gratitude. God will be honored. And His presence will be real.

Your Account

A man's ways are in full view of the Lord, and he examines all his paths.   PROVERBS 5:21

IN WORD   Have you sought dramatic change in your life? Consider the fact of Proverbs 5:21. Nothing will so radically alter your perspective as the knowledge of this truth. It is an older version of Paul's sobering observation: "Each of us will give an account of himself to God" (Romans 14:12).

Jesus illustrated the principle with several parables (Matthew 25:31-46; Luke 16:1-12; 19:11-27). We are not left on this planet as unobserved, unaccountable masters of our own selves. We are seen. We are accountable to our Creator. And one day we will stand before Him to explain what we have done and what we have left undone. We will have to own up to every thoughtless comment (Matthew 12:36). We will have to explain the discrepancy between the resources we've been given and the resources we've used.

This can be a frightening thought, but it is not meant to frighten us. Before our accounting we have already been given assurance of forgiveness in Christ. Those who are not in Christ have reason to fear indeed, but we who believe have been covered by the sacrifice of Jesus. What meaning, then, does this verse have for us? It is sobering in spite of our salvation. One day at the end of our earthly lives, we will stand before God with a full understanding that we had the power of Jesus Himself working within us, and an acute awareness that we did so little with it.

IN DEED   These words are not for judgment, they are for encouragement. God gives them to stir us up. They prompt us to live with an understanding of whose we are and why we were made. Let the truth of God's ownership sink in. When it does, it changes everything. Your life will never be the same.

As long as I see anything to be done for God, life is worth having.

—David Brainerd

Protective Wisdom

Do not forsake wisdom, and she will protect you; love her, and she will watch over you. PROVERBS 4:6

FEBRUARY 25
Proverbs 4:1-9

Time is short. Eternity is long. It is only reasonable that this short life be lived in the light of eternity.

—Charles Spurgeon

IN WORD Godly wisdom protects. This verse is clear. But from what does it protect us? Disease? Calamity? Conflict? Perhaps not always, but sometimes these are the results of unwise choices. Most of all, godly wisdom protects us from the self-inflicted disaster of superficial decisions. It keeps us from sacrificing ourselves to the deity of self-will.

Samson is one of the Bible's most tragic heroes (Judges 13–16). Dedicated from before his birth to the service of God and endowed with superhuman strength, the man was captive to his own fleeting impulses. This deliverer was bound because he developed an early pattern of satisfying his passing urges at the expense of long-term goals. Lack of wisdom held as a helpless captive the strongest man on earth.

So it is with us. We are called to make life-changing decisions—whom to marry, what career to pursue—at an early age, when we are barely equipped to make them. Many have made mindless choices and devastated their future because of a simple lack of wisdom. With all the resources of the eternal God at our fingertips, we often decide things with our own finite minds. And as we age, we must make repeated choices that will affect our own lives and the lives of those around us profoundly. The sooner we learn godly wisdom, the safer we will be. Wisdom protects us from futility.

IN DEED We are given a very brief amount of time on this planet. But what we do here can have eternal impact on ourselves and others. We must invest our time. We must invest our resources. We must direct everything at our disposal toward an eternal Kingdom. Without God's wisdom, years are wasted. We make self-defeating decisions. We squander opportunities to serve God and bear eternal fruit. Why should we never forsake wisdom? It's a matter of self-defense. It protects us from a world of evil, and it protects us from ourselves.

Supreme Wisdom

*Wisdom is supreme; therefore get wisdom. Though it cost
all you have, get understanding.* PROVERBS 4:7

IN WORD Wisdom is a rare commodity in our world.
We have plenty of smart people—geniuses, in fact—but
few who are wise. And our culture hardly knows the difference. We value status, fame, wealth, a good reputation, companionship, and achievement—not all bad in themselves.
But none of them satisfy unless handled with wisdom. We
should seek true understanding first and foremost, or all of
the rest become mere idols.

Wisdom is a right understanding of the world and
our role in it. It knows who God is, it knows who we are,
and it sees the relative importance of all things. It is a correct ordering of priorities, majoring on truth and character
before superficial pleasures. It is the only way, in the long
run, to be truly satisfied.

History is littered with kings and celebrities who seemingly had it all. But in the end they had nothing. They did not
know God and built their lives on superficialities. Abundant
are the stories of people on their deathbeds, wishing they
could do it all over again. They are often envied by everyone
but themselves, because they know the emptiness and lies of
worldly fulfillment. They learn that everything they thought
would satisfy eventually did not.

IN DEED Are you satisfied with life? Do you think that
the next achievement, the next salary range, the next job, the
next relationship, the next "whatever" will finally make you
content? Stop where you are and seek wisdom above all else.
Make it your overarching priority to learn who God is, what
He is like, how He relates to us, and what He is doing in this
world. Then invest your entire life in what you've learned.
Even if it costs you all you have, it is well worth it. Only a life
based on this kind of understanding will satisfy. Only godly
wisdom can make everything else meaningful.

FEBRUARY 26
Proverbs 4:1-9

He is truly wise
who looks upon
all earthly things
as folly that he
may gain Christ.

—Thomas à Kempis

Exalting Wisdom

Esteem her, and she will exalt you; embrace her,
and she will honor you.   PROVERBS 4:8

FEBRUARY 27
Proverbs 4:1-9

If I take care of my character, my reputation will take care of itself.

—D. L. Moody

IN WORD   We all long for glory and honor. It is a longing built into us by a Creator whose image we bear and who Himself is worthy of all glory and honor. And there is, in fact, a way in this world that we can live to receive a crown. But it is not the way most people think.

Human instinct tells us to seek a crown by exalting ourselves. It prompts us to climb to the top of the ladder—socially, professionally, emotionally, and even spiritually. It is all about attainment. Godly wisdom, on the other hand, tells us to seek a crown by embracing understanding. It prompts us to become humble and self-aware, submitting to a higher Authority and becoming like Him. It has little to do with achieving; it is all about character.

Human striving is an interesting dynamic. When we seek self, we lose self. When we seek God, we gain God *and* self. And with God, all of His blessings are included. Jesus said it well: "Whoever wants to save his life will lose it, but whoever loses his life for me and for the gospel will save it" (Mark 8:35).

A substantial part of seeking God is seeking His wisdom. Those who want to benefit from His blessings but do not care to build their lives on His truth are fooling themselves. They are asking for an impossibility, like the benefit of good health without the wisdom of a good diet and exercise, or the benefit of passing a course without doing the homework. God has not constructed life to work that way. There is blessing in building on His truth.

IN DEED   Whose wisdom forms the foundation of your life? Is it your own? A family member or friend? The collective voice of our culture? If so, why? With all of God's wisdom available to us, why build on lesser material? Seek God's wisdom. Esteem it and embrace it, and you will be crowned with honor by the only One whose opinion matters.

Lord of All

In your hearts set apart Christ as Lord.
1 PETER 3:15

IN WORD When we became Christians, we confessed Jesus as Lord. When we pray, we call Him Lord. But as we live, is He really Lord in our hearts? The words of our mouths do not tell the whole story. There is a depth in most of our hearts to which Jesus' Lordship does not go. As much as we call Him Lord, most of us have held back a corner of our heart to ourselves. His Lordship extends only so far.

The work of the Holy Spirit in bringing us to maturity in Christ—i.e., sanctification—is this: to extend the Lordship of Jesus to every inch of our lives. It is a contentious process. We want the benefits of being a Christian—such as salvation, peace, joy, and the like—but we want to retain a little autonomy as well. We have internal struggles that our friends and family do not see. There are places in our hearts that we guard, holding the Holy Spirit at a distance. We like to control the tempo of our discipleship.

To the extent that we do this, we base our lives on a false supposition—that we have the right to govern ourselves, even after we've supposedly laid our all on the altar. It is an unwise position to try to manage Jesus' Lordship over us. In fact, it isn't His Lordship at all when we control even a portion of ourselves. It's just an illusion.

IN DEED Is Jesus Lord of 100 percent of your heart? Your thoughts, your behaviors, your dreams—are they yours or His? What corners of your being have you retained for yourself? Whatever they are, they are footholds for the enemy and shelters for the sinful flesh. Jesus desires more of you than you have given Him to this point. He wants it all. This seems like painful surrender to us, but from His perspective, it is a happy day when one of His people lays it all on the altar. Blessing is the result. He is trustworthy with everything we give Him, and He will manage our lives better than we ever have. At no point resist Him; set Him apart as Lord.

FEBRUARY 28
1 Peter 3:15-16

Christ is either Lord of all or He is not Lord at all.

—Hudson Taylor

59

A Personal Walk

He whose walk is upright fears the LORD, but he whose ways are devious despises him. PROVERBS 14:2

MARCH 1
Proverbs 14:2

Only he who believes is obedient, and only he who is obedient believes.

—Dietrich Bonhoeffer

IN WORD In our individualistic culture, we tend to think that our behavior is our own domain. "It's my life," "It's my body," "It's nobody's business but my own," are all common declarations of independence that most of us have heard—or even said—often. We see ourselves as isolated actors on a crowded stage. People do their own thing.

That was the philosophy in the period of the judges too. "Everyone did as he saw fit" (Judges 21:25). They used their own standards of morality not only because they had no king, but also because they disregarded God. In our era of tolerance, we are immersed in a philosophy of "to each his own." Anyone claiming an absolute standard of behavior is sure to hear the mantra of the age: "As long as it's not hurting anyone else, it doesn't matter what a person does." God has a direct response: It matters.

Why does it matter? Because those who are upright in heart and behavior show a respect for God and His ways. Those who are not—who are devious in their plans and destructive in their ways—show that they couldn't care less that God exists. His standards are irrelevant to them. Ideas, behaviors, and lifestyles are not just personal decisions affecting only ourselves; they are personal statements about the God who created us. What we think and what we do says a lot about the One we serve.

IN DEED Have you made that connection between your lifestyle and your opinion of God? The two are intimately linked. Those who fear God with respect and awe will reflect it in their lives. Those who don't believe God exists—or don't care that He does—will also reflect that in their lives.

In an independent age, that's a foreign thought. We who believe the Word can no longer say, "My life is my business." Our lives are statements of who He is. Consider your thoughts, your words, and your actions well. Understand the statement you are making.

Fit for Glory

May the words of my mouth and the meditation
of my heart be pleasing in your sight, O LORD,
my Rock and my Redeemer.   PSALM 19:14

IN WORD   Psalm 19 is all about the glory of God and the perfection of the things He has ordained. It ends with David's desire to live consistently with God's ordinances. In such a glorious creation that proclaims God's goodness from the rising of the sun to its setting, David knows how tragic it would be not to fit in. He prays for forgiveness and for protection from willful sins (verses 12-13). And then he gets to the heart of the matter: the purity of words and thoughts. Most of us can maintain righteous behavior most of the time. Our deepest struggles are in our thought life and the words that proceed from it. James even goes so far as to tell us that anyone who has mastered the tongue has become perfect (James 3:2). Why? Because the tongue is a barometer for the mind. It measures what is going on inside our heads. Sooner or later, it will tell the truth about us—that we have pride, prejudices, impurities, petty agendas, and a strong self-will. If we can keep ourselves pure within, we will be pure in our speech and in our actions as well.

IN DEED   Are you fit for glory? Do your thoughts and your words reflect the truth of who God is? Do they admire His ordinances? Anyone who is honest will have to admit that, many times, our inward thoughts lie to us about God—His love, His purity, His care for us, the goodness of His plan. And, many times, those thoughts slander His ordinances. We want to violate them in ways that will be pleasing to us or that will satisfy our personal agendas. We constantly need to ask ourselves whether our words and even our thoughts fit with the God of glory and truth.

Follow David's example. Marvel at the glory of God's creation. Praise the wisdom of His statutes. Count on His forgiveness. And then ask that He might grant you the blessing of having meditations and speech that is pleasing to Him.

MARCH 2
Psalm 19

Holy Spirit, think through me till your ideas are my ideas.

—Amy Carmichael

A Kingdom Pursuit

Blessed is the man who finds wisdom, the man who gains understanding, for she is more profitable than silver and yields better returns than gold. PROVERBS 3:13-14

MARCH 3

Proverbs 3:13-18

There is a deep wisdom inaccessible to the wise and prudent, but disclosed to babes.

—Christopher Bryant

IN WORD Solomon speaks from experience. One night early in his reign, God appeared to Solomon and asked him what divine favor he would want. Solomon asked for wisdom and knowledge, and because his heart's desire was not material but godly, God gave it all: wisdom and knowledge, plus riches, honor, victory, and more. When Solomon says wisdom and understanding are more profitable than silver and gold, he knows. This is not hypothetical, and it is not simply to impress others with his godliness. It is truth based on real life.

In a sense, we have the same choice available to us. No, God hasn't appeared to us in the dark of night to ask us what favor we would seek. But we do choose what things in life we will pursue. Do we value understanding more than wealth? If so, we are in the minority. Most people believe more money is the key to more happiness. More money means—in theory only—less work, more vacation time, more time-saving technology, hired help, more conveniences, more luxury. The opposite is actually true. More money means more maintenance, more details, more uncertain investments, more to manage, more headaches. Understanding, however, has the opposite dynamic. More is better. Always.

IN DEED Isn't the choice God presents Solomon with remarkably similar to what Jesus taught His disciples? "Seek first [God's] kingdom and his righteousness, and all these things will be given to you as well" (Matthew 6:33). Solomon sought a kingdom commodity, and all the rest was added. We would be fools not to seek the same agreement with our Lord. He offers it; why would we not accept it? Examine the things you pursue. Make sure they are ultimately worth it.

Seize the Kingdom

If the dead are not raised, "Let us eat and drink, for tomorrow we die." 1 CORINTHIANS 15:32

IN WORD The *carpe diem* philosophy—"seize the day"—is as old as humanity. It is written of in Ecclesiastes, Isaiah, and a parable of Jesus, but its practitioners have an older history than that. They assume that human life is short and that our capacity for enjoyment is limited to our physical life span. Pleasure is a god in itself—a god with a very short reign.

This is probably the prevailing Western philosophy of our day. We hear it whenever someone remarks, "Well, as long as he's happy and not hurting anyone, what does it matter what he does?" We see it in our arts and entertainment. And, like it or not, we in the faith often act as if it's our philosophy too. Ours is not a culture that often denies short-term pleasure for long-term gain. The question for us is how much of our culture we'll absorb.

Paul's indictment against this philosophy, whether it's full-fledged hedonism or simple shortsightedness, is based on the Resurrection. Because we now know that life is eternal, seizing the day for immediate gain is folly. It exchanges eternal blessings for temporal satisfaction. It forfeits the truly meaningful for the truly mundane. It's like trading away a Rembrandt for a drawing in the sand, or forsaking life in a mansion for a weekend trip. It's dumb.

IN DEED As Christians, we must frequently take an inventory of our life. Are we living in light of eternity? Or are we offering up our most valuable resources for a momentary benefit? To know the difference, we must be sensitive to the motivations behind our actions. Are our morals based on eternal considerations? Why do we spend our money the way we do? Is it for today alone or for the Kingdom of God? What about our time? Our energy? Our talents? Know yourself well, and rearrange your life, if you must. Seize the Kingdom. It lasts.

MARCH 4
1 Corinthians 15:32

He who provides for this life, but takes no care for eternity, is wise for a moment, but a fool forever.

—John Tillotson

Gold That Remains

When he has tested me, I will come forth as gold.

JOB 23:10

MARCH 5

Job 23:1-12

In shunning a trial, we are seeking to avoid a blessing.

—Charles Spurgeon

IN WORD   Few of us would have the confidence Job did. We might rather assume that when God has tested us in the same manner that gold is refined, many impurities will be consumed. Eventually, perhaps, we will come forth as gold, but not immediately. Sin runs too deep and the refining takes so excruciatingly long.

Perhaps it is overconfidence that leads Job to say such a thing, or perhaps he really was that much more righteous than the rest of us. Either way, whether he is right about himself or not, he has hit on a foundational spiritual principle: God tries His servants, and the intended result is pure gold.

Just as the Cross of Jesus revealed the character of God within Him, so does the fire of trial reveal the character of God within us. Are we patient? We and the world will only know it if our patience is tested. Are we loving? It will not be seen until we are confronted with hatred. Are we full of faith? There's no evidence until circumstances dictate against it. Every fruit of the Spirit is latent within us until its antithesis appears. Superficial joy and real joy look exactly the same until the storm comes and blows one of them away. Peace isn't really peace unless it can survive when attacked. And deeper still: Your life in the Spirit isn't life at all if it melts away when death threatens.

IN DEED   We want all the fruits of the Spirit and all of the blessings of Christlikeness, but we rarely realize the cost. Nothing God gives us is proven genuine until it is assaulted by the troubles of this world and the wiles of the enemy. It is the only way God reveals Himself through His saints. It is the only way the authentic is distinguished from the superficial. It is the only way to come forth as gold.

Are you running from tests? Don't. Stand firm in them. Let God do His purifying work. Get ready to shine.

Necessary Perseverance

You have heard of Job's perseverance and have seen what the Lord finally brought about. JAMES 5:11

IN WORD Staying power. It's a rare commodity in a microwave society. Technological advancement has made travel, communication, and daily chores incredibly time-efficient, if not instantaneous. The result is that we're not trained in perseverance. We're not accustomed to pains that can't be relieved and problems that can't be corrected. When they come, we send up prayers with almost the same expectation as when we press the buttons on our microwave. A few seconds, we think, and we should be done with it.

God doesn't usually work that way. He is thorough and precise, and He will not be rushed. When He tries us in the fire, as He did Job, nothing can get us out. The time cannot be shortened and our growth cannot come more quickly. We must learn perseverance.

James began his letter by telling about the results of perseverance—maturity and completeness (1:4). There is no way to become a mature Christian without trials. We may pray for Christlike character and hope that it will come by spiritual osmosis, but it will not. God's plan for all of His people is trial by fire. It is the only way to burn away the flesh and reveal the Spirit. It is the only way to grow. No one has ever become a true disciple without perseverance, and no one has ever persevered without pain.

IN DEED What is your reaction to trials? Do you expect instantaneous answers to your prayers for deliverance? More often than not, you will be disappointed. Change your perspective. Rather than looking for escape, look for the benefit of the trial. Let endurance have its perfect result. Ask God what He's accomplishing and then participate in it willingly. If you can learn perseverance, you will be a rarity in this world and well fit for the Kingdom of God.

MARCH 6
James 5:7-11

When a train goes through a tunnel and it gets dark, you don't throw away your ticket and jump off. You sit still and trust the engineer.

—Corrie ten Boom

Constant Growth

Many a man claims to have unfailing love, but
a faithful man who can find?   PROVERBS 20:6

By persever-
ance the snail
reached the ark.

—Charles Spurgeon

IN WORD   Nearly everyone has a spiritual mountain-top experience on occasion. For most of us, this is how we measure our spiritual maturity. We assume that the heights we've reached indicate the level to which we've grown.

But God has a different measure of our maturity. It's not about the peaks we've scaled but our consistency between them. The peaks are great; we need them for an occasional boost. But they do not define us. Learning the mind of God is not a roller-coaster experience. It's a steady climb.

This is where many Christians go astray. We let our spiritual highs determine our self-image, and we live off of their memory while neglecting daily growth. We think we've stocked up on our Godward obligations and that He must be satisfied with us as long as we are satisfied with ourselves. A peak experience will indeed give us a satisfy-ing feeling for a while, and we'll gladly dwell on it as long as we can. But while we dwell there, we can lose sight of today's needs.

Think of the inconsistency of that. Do we feast one day and then decide that we need no more nutrition for a few weeks? No, our bodies pester us with their need for daily sustenance, no matter how well we ate the day before. Our souls are more subtle. We respond to their hunger pangs with memories of past meals and expect them to be satisfied. But sporadic love isn't love at all, and occasional obedience is an oxymoron. True discipleship is consistent.

IN DEED   Our God is not One to be appeased periodically and ignored in the interims. His love for us is constant and persistent. His character never changes. His mercy is new every morning, and His compassion does not fail. If our minds are being renewed to be like His, isn't consistency a logical result? The blessings of discipleship and worship are found only in their constancy. Measure yourself not by your highs or lows, but by who you are in between them.

When Distress Reigns

*Evening, morning and noon I cry out in distress,
and he hears my voice.*   PSALM 55:17

IN WORD   Problems can consume us. When trials strike, we can find ourselves completely preoccupied with how to deal with them. We obsess about their outcomes, and we strategize ways to flee them. We go to sleep thinking about them, and we wake up thinking about them still. We think we cannot rest until they are resolved.

The context of this psalm of David is the treachery of a friend. Someone had betrayed him, and the betrayal incited others to oppose him. David felt surrounded, overwhelmed, discouraged, and defeated. We can relate. We have exactly the same reaction when life gets tough.

God hears. That's comforting. It's even more comforting when we consider other translations of this passage. "I will complain and murmur, and He will hear my voice" (NASB). Or "I utter my complaint and moan and sigh, and He will hear my voice" (AMP). The implication is that even when we whine and grumble, God still hears. He doesn't like our complaining, perhaps, but He knows our pain. Grace tolerates our attitudes. We don't have a trial that God isn't concerned with. We cannot stumble without evoking His compassion. We can't be overwhelmed without His knowledge and without His appeal to cast it all on Him. Whatever we're going through, God hears.

IN DEED   We've all heard that before. For some of us it's a reality; for others, just words. Some of us have heard that promise as often as we've heard that Jesus loves us, and though we know these things are true, we have grown numb to them. They just don't sink in, and we aren't affected.

Wake up to the fact that the almighty, overwhelming God is listening. Even when you complain, He cares. More than that, He hears with a plan to act. He is not passively listening, He is preparing to answer. Wouldn't you love for Him to step into your situation? According to the Bible, He will. Watch and wait. Your distress is His concern.

MARCH 8
Psalm 55:16-23

God will never permit any troubles to come upon us unless He has a specific plan by which great blessing can come out of the difficulty.

—Peter Marshall

67

When the Battle Rages

*He ransoms me unharmed from the battle waged against
me, even though many oppose me.*   PSALM 55:18

MARCH 9
Psalm 55:16-23

Christianity is a
battle, not a dream.

—Wendell Phillips

IN WORD   You have enemies. Perhaps you are aware of
them, perhaps not. Either way, they are there, even if they are
covertly operating underground without your knowledge.
They may manifest themselves in people who have a grudge
against you. Or they may simply be hidden in the systems of
this corrupt world, with all of its false philosophies, ideologies, and temptations. And then there are the principalities
of God's archenemy who will harass, tempt, and discourage
you. Sometimes your opponent is even your own flesh, the
desires that compete with your allegiance to God.

If life has been a struggle, there's a reason. The Kingdom
of God that you crave is in conflict with the fallen world that
you live in. You have welcomed the new while surrounded
by the old. That does not make for a peaceful life.

Were you aware of this battle? If you've been a Christian
for any length of time, you've probably noticed that the
Christian life, being supernatural, is not naturally easy. In
fact, it's impossible unless there's a new birth, a constant
faith, a learned dependence, and a holy ambition. Knowing
the Holy Spirit is essential. Otherwise we are simply fallen
creatures striving and wishing for something better.

IN DEED   Don't be discouraged by the fact that there is
a battle in your life. There always will be until the day you
pass from this earthen vessel into an incorruptible, heavenly
dwelling place (2 Corinthians 5:1-4). The battle, in fact—if it
is between the new and the old, the true and the false, or the
gospel and the world—is evidence that you are a citizen of
the Kingdom of God.

The battle comes with a promise: We are ransomed
unharmed. It may not seem like we're unharmed, but by
God's definition, we most certainly are. There is no enemy
stronger than Him "who is enthroned forever" (Psalm 55:19).
Your Savior reigns. Remember that when the battle rages.

The Art of Casting

Cast your cares on the LORD and he will sustain you;
he will never let the righteous fall. PSALM 55:22

IN WORD What does it mean to cast your cares on the Lord? We really need to know. It's the difference between being sustained and faltering, between faith and fear. If we're confused on this point, we will be riddled with anxieties and phobias, afraid to face the future and far from the will of God. If we understand, we can go through anything with peace in our hearts. Our circumstances may not be easy, but we can be brought through in the safety of His hand—if we learn what it means to cast our cares on Him.

Does it mean to offer up a prayer? Not necessarily. Many prayers have been uttered without a sense of peace. Praying does not guarantee internal rest. Our requests of God can be acts of anxiety rather than acts of faith. When we're stressed, our prayers often even accuse Him of not keeping His Word. There's more to casting cares than asking Him to help.

Does it mean to abandon any sense of responsibility because, after all, God will take care of it? Not at all. Casting cares on Him does not imply that we cease to care. It does not involve apathy in the least, and it is not an invitation to be irresponsible. No, casting our cares on God is much more purposeful than that. It is the most proactive thing we can do.

IN DEED It makes no sense to cast our cares on God and then take them up again. When we trust Him with our concerns, we ask Him to manage them. We acknowledge our own futility, and we rely on His power to resolve them. We actively watch, not ignorantly wait. We expectantly believe, not aggressively intervene. We act when He says to act and sit still when He says to sit. We obey His instructions because we know He's in charge—and we're comfortable with that. We can go to sleep at night knowing we can do nothing more effective than acknowledging His wisdom, power, love, and Lordship. We can wake up without a single burden, because our burdens are on His shoulders. We refuse to micromanage. We will hope only in Him, because He is where our cares have been cast.

MARCH 10
Psalm 55:16-23

Worry is an intrusion into God's providence.

—John Haggai

The Priority to Pursue

Let love and faithfulness never leave you; bind them around your neck, write them on the tablet of your heart.
PROVERBS 3:3

MARCH 11

Proverbs 3:1-12

Put everything
you have into
the care of your
heart, for it deter-
mines what your
life amounts to.

—Dallas Willard

IN WORD Solomon's words would have had familiar connotations for a faithful Jew. In Deuteronomy 6, a landmark chapter in Old Testament theology, God told the Israelites first to love Him with all their heart, soul, and strength. Then He told them to take the words of the Law, divinely inscribed on tablets of stone, and inscribe them into the fabric of their souls. Let them be always on your hearts, He commanded. Work them into your children's hearts. Talk about them always. Tie them as symbols on your hands and foreheads. Never be away from them (see Deuteronomy 6:4-9).

The interesting connection between Deuteronomy and Proverbs is that the Law is defined as "love and faithfulness." It is also interesting that Deuteronomy is specific in where our love and faithfulness are first to be directed: toward God. The foremost element of a believer's life is not obedience, not service, and not doctrine. These are important—indispensable, in fact. But they are not the priority. Love is. A passionate, vital, all-encompassing love that reaches to the depths of our being. When that is there, the rest is easy.

IN DEED Do you consider your heart to be a tablet? What is written on it? Do you realize that some things can be erased by the power of God and others inscribed by that same power? It requires your full cooperation, but the junk that we've inscribed there—through all of the media and entertainment we absorb, the relationships we've had, the information we consume—can be rewritten. It can be replaced with love and faithfulness. In fact, it *must* be replaced with love and faithfulness if we are to learn the mind of our God at all. This is who He is, and He insists that we become like Him. Love and faithfulness define Him. Do they define you? Let them saturate your heart.

The Key to Favor

You will win favor and a good name in the sight of God and man. PROVERBS 3:4

IN WORD God's promise of favor is a little suspicious to us. We've known of many faithful servants who did not have a good name, at least in the eyes of their peers. Sometimes they were burned at the stake, sometimes they were tarnished with false accusations, sometimes they faced firing squads. In fact, Jesus assured His disciples they would be hated by many. How, then, can Solomon, if he is at all inspired by God, promise a good name to those who write love and faithfulness on their hearts?

We do not read God's promises with enough faith or patience. We must first know that the promise of favor with God is immediate. He never withholds His affection from those who love Him faithfully. It's the second part of this promise we struggle with. He promises favor in the sight of man. Can this be true? Yes, if we'll read it with eternity in view. Those who love God will have remarkable reputations in the Kingdom. Men *will* know that God has favored His faithful ones. They may not know it now or even soon. They may not know it before they die. But they will eventually know it. God has promised.

IN DEED We often get off track because we are determined to have a good reputation among our peers right now. Many a believer has compromised his or her faith because of a desire to be respected by other people more than by God. But love and faithfulness are selective. They cannot be directed toward God and toward our own present reputation at the same time. Compromise is deadly. We must be content—even thrilled—with the idea that God's favor is ours right now, and man's will come later—maybe even much later, when eternity is revealed to all. Hearts filled with love and faithfulness will not care. They will be patient. They will know the promise of the One they love.

MARCH 12
Proverbs 3:1-12

Faith in God will always be crowned.

—William S. Plummer

The Direction to Lean

Trust in the Lord with all your heart and lean not on your own understanding. PROVERBS 3:5

MARCH 13
Proverbs 3:1-12

O Lord, in Thee
have I trusted;
let me never be
confounded.

—Book of Common
Prayer

IN WORD In order to learn the mind of God, we have to face up to a sobering fact: Our own understanding is fundamentally flawed. The human mind is never dependable, and it cannot be given free reign to choose its own direction. Why? Because our knowledge is limited and our motives are not pure. In our original condition, we do not desire above all else to glorify God at any cost. Even when we've come into a relationship with Him, our motives can be awfully mixed. We want His glory, but we want to seek our own good—in our own way—as well. We cannot be wise in this world without realizing we need the wisdom of Another. Desperately.

Think about it. Would you prefer to depend on the logic of a finite mind tainted with sinful motives? Or on the vast intellectual resources of the Omniscient—the One who knows the fabric of our souls and holds the future in His hands? The answer ought to be clear. Yet, at a practical level, we are often ambivalent about the choice. In principle, we want God's wisdom. In practice, we follow our own.

IN DEED The best advice we can find in Proverbs repeatedly points us to a wisdom beyond our own. God is worthy of all of our trust. We are worthy of suspicion. Yet we often struggle between His wisdom and ours. His can seem so hard. We forget that ours is harder. There are ominous consequences for depending on our own limited resources.

Trust is not natural to the fallen human heart. The redeemed heart has to learn it. We must make a conscious decision to forsake our own understanding and lean on His. Crises confront us all the time. Use them as opportunities to drink in the wisdom of the Source of all wisdom. Are you faced with a choice today? Make up your mind not to act on it until you have sought God's wisdom diligently, persistently, and patiently. Ask Him for it. Follow it, no matter how hard it is. Let His mind become yours.

The Path to a Straight Path

*In all your ways acknowledge him, and he will
make your paths straight.* PROVERBS 3:6

IN WORD We are starved for direction. We live in a world
that presents us with a multitude of options. Some can be
ruled out easily, but many of them seem good. What will we
do? Whom should we relate to? Where will we go? When
should we move forward? We don't know enough about the
future to make such decisions well. We try to make sound
choices and hope for the best. We want more information;
but we hesitate when we find that God's plan for us first
requires casting our all on Him.

That's why horoscopes are so appealing to so many.
They offer direction without making any demands on our
character. They promise information without requiring the
hard work of submission to God and acceptance of His work
on our fallen hearts. But God loves us too much for that.
Getting direction from Him means, first and foremost, getting Him. His Spirit shapes us, His wisdom becomes a part
of us, and the substance of godliness molds us into a form
of godliness.

IN DEED God is not usually an oracle-giver; He's a life-
transformer. He usually directs us not by passing on information about what we're to do, but by fundamentally altering
us from within. He changes our character, our outlook, our
priorities. Then we are directed by the person God has made
us into—a new creation governed by the indwelling Jesus.

This is a shock to our system, but it's essential. That is
why this proverb does not simply start with: "He will make
your paths straight." There are conditions. We trust Him
with all our heart. We refuse to lean on our own understanding. We acknowledge His sufficiency—implying our
own insufficiency—in everything. Then He makes our paths
straight. Why? Because He is present. We have not simply
used Him for His vast information, we have invited Him to
come along on the journey.

MARCH 14
Proverbs 3:1-12

God always gives
His very best
to those who
leave the choice
with Him.

—Hudson Taylor

The Escape from Self

Do not be wise in your own eyes; fear the LORD
and shun evil.   PROVERBS 3:7

All the graces
of a Christian
spring from the
death of self.

—Madame Guyon

IN WORD   If we ever take hold of the idea that we are
innately wise, we are destined for failure. In fact, Proverbs
16:18 says as much: "Pride goes before destruction, a
haughty spirit before a fall." Placing any faith in our own
wisdom is a form of pride. It is also self-delusion. We do
not know anything about the future for certain; we don't
know the intricacies of our own hearts; we don't see all the
motives and moods of other people; we don't have an infallible understanding of human psychology; and we don't
fully grasp the spiritual realities of God's Kingdom. God
has a handle on all of these things; we have a handle on
none of them. To act as if the reverse is true is the ultimate
foolishness.

We've read that the fear of the Lord is the beginning
of wisdom (Proverbs 9:10). Proverbs 3:7 implies that the
opposite of fearing the Lord is self-reliance. We absolutely
must understand the gap between us and God—and how
amazingly it was bridged—if we are to act wisely. We cannot
approach life without an overwhelming sense of the eternal
if we are to invest in what is truly valuable. Understanding
God will change how we spend our time, our money, and
our talents. It will change how we approach our circumstances, our relationships, our work, and our attitudes.

IN DEED   Have you noticed that those who make bad
decisions are usually acting out of extreme self-interest? A
focus on self leads to devastating shortsightedness and has
evil, destructive consequences. A focus on God—His character, His ways, His eternal nature—leads people to wisdom.

Try this exercise the next time you face a decision:
Instead of writing a list of pros and cons, write a list of
motives for each choice. Pros and cons are about outcomes;
but since we can't know the future, they are only guesses.
Motives are about perspective; they identify the center of
our lives. If we're centered on ourselves, we're fools; if on
God, we're wise.

The Road to Health

This will bring health to your body and nourishment to your bones. PROVERBS 3:8

IN WORD We don't try to drive our cars in the water and we don't try to speed our boats down the highway. Why? That's not what they were made for. So why do we use ourselves for purposes we were not made for? Why, when we were created to be entirely preoccupied with our Creator, do we become entirely preoccupied with ourselves? This does damage to our minds, and our minds affect our bodies. Our thoughts become distorted, our bodies become sick, and we end up a mess. A self-absorbed mess. We are misplaced vehicles on the wrong course.

Do you believe that? Do you understand that we were created to be fascinated by, overwhelmed with, and enraptured in our Maker? The fallen mind avoids this at all costs. We try to make a name for ourselves. We try to get in good with the right people. We read self-help books. We learn various philosophies and methods that will lead us to a better way of life. And it's all about us.

God points us away from ourselves and toward Him. He is to be our vision, our passion, our love. So far-reaching is this principle that it can bring health to our bodies. When we align ourselves with our created purpose, we are like the perfect part in a precision machine. We can function without undue wear and tear. Or we're like a beautiful piece of music played in the right key. We can perform without grating on everyone around us and depressing ourselves in the process.

IN DEED We place a high premium on good health. In a sick and fallen world, it is a valued commodity. We try to eat well, take our vitamins, select the right doctor, exercise often, and pray to avoid deadly diseases. But if we haven't immersed our minds in reality—that God is our all in all—we haven't taken the first step toward good health. Your mind has a profound effect on your physiology. Let it always be nourished by eternal truth.

MARCH 16
Proverbs 3:1-12

Our only business is to love and delight ourselves in God.

—Brother Lawrence

75

A Way to Give Honor

Honor the LORD with your wealth.
PROVERBS 3:9

Get all you can,
save all you
can, and give
all you can.

—John Wesley

IN WORD We're often not conscious of the statements we make, but they are more numerous than we think. We aren't aware of them because most are not verbal. They are revelations of the heart, spoken by our choices. As is often said, actions speak louder than words.

Consider, for example, what we are saying when we have no money for God's ministry but enough to pay the cable bill. Or when we see the starving and wish we could help—and then waste money on soft drinks with no nutritional value. Why does thirty dollars a month to save a child seem like so much, and thirty dollars for a steak dinner for two seem like such a bargain? What do our choices say of God? Not much. They say more about our values. They reveal what's in our heart.

God is no enemy of entertainment and taste buds. But He is an enemy of idols, and our choices reveal what they are. We deceive ourselves often—our enormous capacity for doing so came with the Fall. It's amazing how much we can't afford to do for God's Kingdom—the budget is always tight, right? Meanwhile, the vacations we really want to take are usually taken. The meals we really want to eat are usually eaten. The make and model we want to drive is usually in our driveway. We more comfortably delay God's gratification than our own.

IN DEED We need to snap out of our unconsciousness. Many of our idols have become automatic to us. We don't see them as intentional choices that reveal the treasures of our heart. But deep down we know: If we loved God with all of our being, if we treasured His Kingdom above all else, He would see more of our treasure given for His use.

Why is this so important? Does God have insufficient funds? Probably not. The Owner of all isn't short of cash when He really wants to accomplish something. He wants more than cash. He wants us to value faith, the currency of His Kingdom, over the currency of this world. More than that, He wants us. He wants our choices to reflect an intense, unbridled love. He wants them to honor Him.

The Means to More Means

Your barns will be filled to overflowing, and your vats will brim over with new wine.   PROVERBS 3:10

IN WORD   The purpose of all creation is to honor God. So it only makes sense that when He is honored—in this case, by our firstfruits—that He will grant increase and give His blessing. Honor begets more honor. Those who have dealt faithfully in small things will be given greater things. Those who have glorified Him with their wealth will be given more by which to glorify Him even more.

This is no guarantee that those who tithe will become rich. The Bible never says such a thing. It *is* a promise, however, that God will never be stingy with those who are generous toward Him. It is not in His nature to take and never give. Quite the opposite, in fact. He always gives more than He receives. He who did not withhold His own Son for us will not give grudgingly with any of His unlimited bounty.

This is what Kingdom living is all about: taking the stuff of this world and using it for eternity. The physical becomes spiritual. The corruption of money is redeemed as an investment in lives. We have an opportunity with our income to declare our agreement with our created purpose. Will we honor God, as He intended? Or do we only look for enough means to get by? The means to greater means is to abandon all to Him, for His glory. He will not take it and refuse to support you. He can't. That's not who He is.

IN DEED   Have you stated unequivocally that you are in line with God's purpose for creation—to give Him honor? It's more than a verbal statement, of course. It reaches into every area of our lives and is demonstrated by our actions more than our words. One way to honor Him is by dedicating all of our resources to His use, giving a generous portion to His work in this world. By this He is glorified. And by this we are proven trustworthy to handle more resources.

God calls us to be like Him. He has proven over and over again that He is by nature an extravagant giver. Are you?

MARCH 18
Proverbs 3:1-12

God is more anxious to bestow His blessings on us than we are to receive them.

—St. Augustine

The Struggle toward Godliness

Do not despise the LORD's discipline and do not resent his rebuke. PROVERBS 3:11

MARCH 19
Proverbs 3:1-12

Discipline and love are not antithetical; one is a function of the other.

—James Dobson

IN WORD Our natural reaction to rebuke—from anyone, even God—is to get offended. We don't want anyone telling us what to do, and we don't think anyone has a right to do so. We know God does, of course, but we think He's always on our side. When He works through others to correct us, we tell them our relationship with Him is personal and they have no business interfering. When He works through our circumstances, we cry out our whys without considering that He might be looking for a change in our hearts. We have a hard time accepting correction.

This is human nature, of course. We flee any kind of discomfort. We spend most of our lives trying to become a little more comfortable, to make things a little bit easier, to climb a little bit higher, avoiding pain and hardship at all costs. And when it's personal—like a rebuke—we treat it like a contagion. We'll even break friendships with people who remind us of our shortcomings, however gently they may do it. We are creatures looking for superficial peace and comfort.

We cannot afford that luxury as disciples. We begin as abject sinners and we want to end up as redeemed children of God. What did we expect? Do we think we can grow from one to the other without a painful shock to our system? We can't. We must endure a lot of correction along the way. Otherwise, we can never be remade into His image.

IN DEED Our problem is confusing God's rebuke with His disapproval. We must understand that His correction is never to condemn and always to edify. It's a painful edification, but it is well worth it. One day we'll stand in eternity and pour undying gratitude at His feet for the difficult things we went through and the discipline He imposed on us. It will have made us more gloriously radiant in the everlasting Kingdom. Temporal pain for eternal blessing is a bargain. Always cooperate with His discipline, and thank Him for its promise.

The Sign of a Son

*The LORD disciplines those he loves, as a father
the son he delights in.*   PROVERBS 3:12

IN WORD   We give no correction to strangers. Why? It's
not our place to do so; there's no relationship there. We can
take comfort, then, in the fact that God disciplines us. It
implies a relationship, and not just a casual one. It implies
that He loves us as children and is intent on our becoming
more like Him. He does not discipline those He has given
up on. He disciplines those He treasures.

Imagine a sculptor with a vision that consumes him as
he works night and day on his creation. Little by little he
chisels and shapes. Carefully he lets his vision take form. As
the sculpture nears completion, imagine this artist dropping
his tools and walking away. Ludicrous? Of course. So is the
idea of God dropping His tools before He's made us wise.

Or imagine a caring father spending years of intensive
attention on his child, only to walk away before the child
reaches maturity. Only a father with a drastic personality
change would do such a thing, and God does not have drastic personality changes. He loved us in the beginning, and
He loves us now. His correction will not cease until His work
is complete and we are mature. It's a sign of His delight.

IN DEED   Are you going through a hard thing today? It
may be discipline from the Lord to urge you to change something in your life. Or perhaps it is simply a divine stress
test, planned for your greater endurance and character.
Regardless of its specific cause, it is designed to shape you
into His image, and it is monitored with great care—even
delight—by the hand from which it comes. You would not be
going through it if He did not care. You would not be in the
painful process of conforming to His likeness if you were not
His child. Cooperate with His work, no matter how uncomfortable His tools are. He does not use them recklessly. He
uses them as lovingly as a father touches his child.

MARCH 20
Proverbs 3:1-12

Discipline is
a proof of our
sonship.

—Erwin Lutzer

One Mind

Your attitude should be the same as that of Christ Jesus. PHILIPPIANS 2:5

MARCH 21

Philippians 2:1-11

If you are looking for an example of humility, look at the Cross.

—Thomas Aquinas

IN WORD Euodia and Syntyche were at odds with one another. The two women, each a valuable member of the church, couldn't agree on some point (Philippians 4:2-3). We don't know what the issue was, only that it was somehow divisive. It interrupted the unity of that body of believers.

Paul could have stepped in and settled the disagreement. He claimed apostolic authority on other occasions; he could have acted as a judge in this one. If he had, however, one party could have resented the decision, and the other may have taken pride in it. And neither would have learned any lesson other than the fact that Paul was in charge. No, there was a better way. Paul gave them a deeper remedy.

What was the remedy? To have the mind of Christ. Paul had told the Corinthians that Jesus' mind was their inheritance (1 Corinthians 2:16). Now he tells the Philippians what having His mind implies: It means thinking like Him, having His attitude, and most of all, having His humility.

IN DEED When we think of having the mind of Christ, we usually think in terms of getting His direction and following His will. We're focused on action. But God has a higher purpose. He is focused on character. When He gives us the mind of Jesus, He is giving us the one gift that will fundamentally alter our sinful, conflict-prone nature. It is a gift that will shape us into the very image of God.

What is Jesus' mind like? Paul goes on to tell us of Jesus' humility—though He was God incarnate, He was a humble, obedient man. A servant. A dying servant, in fact. That's usually not our goal when we strive for godly thinking, but it's the first element of character that God will work in us. If we haven't learned the humility of Jesus, we'll never really understand His resurrection power. Our prayers will lack strength because they lack the nature of a servant. Our work will lack power because it doesn't conform to His character. And our fellowship will lack unity because, unlike Jesus, we aren't looking out for each other's interests.

A Lowly Mind

*[He] made himself nothing, taking the very
nature of a servant.* PHILIPPIANS 2:7

IN WORD Human beings rarely aspire to become nothing. Most of us want to be "somebody." We want to make a name for ourselves, or at least to succeed at our goals. We may not have set our sights very high, but we have set them somewhere. We want a good reputation, plenty of affirmation, and a satisfying life. We're trying to climb higher.

The mind of Jesus will take us in the opposite direction. Think of what He exchanged in order to serve us in our fallenness—all the things the devil tempted Him with, like kingdoms and immediate glory (see Matthew 4:1-11); a display of His own deity in the face of those who mocked and ridiculed Him; and, perhaps the thing we can most relate to, a pain-free existence. Jesus voluntarily accepted pain, humiliation, contempt, and disgrace. Why? Because it is in the very nature of God to serve and to love. And humanity, in our fallenness, needed such love.

Jesus' mind found satisfaction in deferring to others' needs. He didn't cling to deity because, in the long run, a demonstration of power would be less satisfying than a demonstration of character. The godly agenda aims for wholeness and unity over authority and comfort. The divine program for exaltation and glory is to go through humility and meekness to get there.

IN DEED If our minds are ever to be transformed into the likeness of Jesus, we have to learn to think that way. We must embrace deference, holding the welfare of others to be more valuable than our own. We must embrace service, working for the benefit of each other rather than trying to get ahead ourselves. And we must humble ourselves under the mighty hand of God in order for that hand to lift us up.

When we pray for Christlikeness and then aim for the aspirations of our fallen human nature, we are undermining our own prayers. We have not embraced the mind of Jesus. But if we readily accept servanthood and the value of others, we bear a striking resemblance to Him.

MARCH 22
Philippians 2:1-11

Our Lord lived His life . . . to give the normal standard for our lives.

—Oswald Chambers

A Surprising Mind

He humbled himself and became obedient to death.
PHILIPPIANS 2:8

MARCH 23
Philippians 2:1-11

Are you laying a feather bed for me? No, that shall not be. My Lord was stretched on a hard and painful tree.

—Brother Lawrence

IN WORD The mind of Christ is offered to us in Scripture, and it sounds so appealing. We think of the gentle Jesus of Galilee, the Shepherd who cares for us and who can cure any disease. We want that Shepherd as our guide; He will feed us when we're hungry and cleanse us of our filth. He will wash our feet and settle our disputes. *If we could only be like Him*, we think. And when Scripture offers us such a treasure—the blessedness of Christlikeness—we ask God to make Him real in our lives.

What a surprise, then, when we find that being like Jesus means more than healing and helping, preaching and teaching, feeding and clothing, and blessing at every turn. It also means obedience—hard, painful obedience. The kind of obedience that every bone in our bodies wants to resist. The kind that sweats drops of blood when confronted with God's plan for our lives. The kind that requires ultimate humility, compelling us to subdue every dream we once held dear. The mind of Jesus led Him not to glory first, but to death. Yes, that kind of mind is a surprise to us. It is radical and unexpected.

IN DEED Does that mean that we shouldn't pray to have His mind? Of course not. But it does mean that we should understand what our prayers will mean. God will not take us down easy paths to conform us to Jesus. He does not lead us on a walk in the park, but toward a struggle in the garden of Gethsemane, where strong wills are subdued, and the glory of God and the welfare of others compete with our own personal plans. And we know, when we get there, that He will lead us into death.

It's a painful death, but a glorious one. The other side of it is resurrection, which God has planned all along. Our ultimate, humble obedience will lead to high exaltation. Why? Because a lowly-then-exalted Jesus has called us. The very mind of the Resurrection has become our guide.

A Passionate God

I am my lover's and my lover is mine.
SONG OF SONGS 6:3

IN WORD There is quite a divergence on how Christians interpret the Song of Songs. Many interpret it entirely as an allegory of God's love for His people—or, more specifically, of Jesus' love for His bride, the church. Others interpret it purely as a divine sanction of erotic love within its appropriate boundaries. Others are able to accept it as both—God's love expressed in a human relationship as a reflection of a greater love from above.

It is right to see all love as coming from God. The world will take that argument and say that all expressions of love—as the world defines "love"—are from God, but that is a gross distortion of biblical truth. Nevertheless, all true love *is* from God, whether it is the love of friends, families, or couples. God created the range of emotions that we have, and it seems logical that He never created a kind of love that He Himself has not experienced. He would not establish a sort of love that is foreign to His own mind. The romantic love expressed in Song of Songs must also be somewhere in the heart of God. He must have first conceived romantic love before creating a romantic humanity. But if so, whom does He love so intimately?

We're afraid to utter the answer for seeming too presumptuous, but we know what the Bible says. It is us. We are the ones for whom God has created romantic love—not just to have between ourselves, but first to have with Him. Intimate love between humans is not the prototype; it is a reflection of the divine romance.

IN DEED We can easily say of another person that "I am my lover's and my lover is mine." Can we say it of God? Have we approached that level of intimacy? Don't be afraid. It does not profane the glory of God to approach Him this way. It honors Him. It values the love that flows from His heart and does not leave it tragically unanswered.

MARCH 24
Song of Songs 6:3

Romance is at the heart of the universe and is the key to all existence.

—Paul Billheimer

A Penetrating God

Surely you desire truth in the inner parts; you teach me wisdom in the inmost place.   PSALM 51:6

MARCH 25
Psalm 51:3-6

God is not deceived by externals.

—C. S. Lewis

IN WORD   David's confessional psalm contains an acknowledgment of one of God's greatest desires for us: integrity. The "man after God's own heart," the favored king of Israel responsible for much of the Bible's most beautiful praise, has found within him a gross inconsistency. On the one hand, he has sought God with all his heart and declared his heart upright on numerous occasions. On the other hand, he has sinned. Not just a little, but grievously. There is a vast gap between his stated beliefs and his inner condition. He has discovered within him what we must all discover: God wants His truth and wisdom to reach to our core, not just adorn our outward expressions.

God has made it clear, first through the Law and prophets, then through Jesus, that He has no tolerance for hypocrisy. None. It is one of the most abominable sins in Scripture. Those who speak pious words in public and then treasure their own corrupted nature privately are far from the heart of God.

David's sin does not nullify his devotion. Neither does ours. But it reflects the shallow depth to which God's Word has penetrated us. To the degree that His wisdom does not reach to our innermost parts—that His Spirit does not transform the very core of our being—then to that degree we have become like the scribes of Jesus' day: experts in the Word but devoid of its power. In other words, we are hypocritical. Our mouths speak godliness, but our hearts deny it.

IN DEED   None of us is perfect in our integrity. We all have inconsistencies. But those inconsistencies should be steadily disappearing if we are growing in the strength of God's Spirit. Test yourself often. Do the words of your mouth reflect the thoughts of your heart? Like David, we must know that God is zealous for our consistency. We must reflect Him from within, or we don't reflect Him at all.

A Persuasive God

The LORD gives wisdom, and from his mouth come knowledge and understanding. PROVERBS 2:6

IN WORD Human nature takes whatever wisdom and understanding we have and gives itself the credit. We pat ourselves on the back, feel a little more enlightened than our neighbors, and have a hard time understanding why others just don't have sense enough to receive the gospel like we did.

When we think this way—and most honest people will confess that they have, on occasion—we are forgetful of our own sinfulness and ignorant of the Word of God. Wisdom, knowledge, and understanding come from Him. We do not earn it, we do not discover it on our own, and we are not just naturally gifted in spiritual things. It comes straight from His mouth, and if He had not spoken it and opened our hearts to it, we would be like billions of others on this planet—living in total darkness. Pure grace gave us the truth.

Not only is this an effective warning against spiritual pride, it is a comfort to those of us who have loved ones who reject the gospel. The key to their understanding is not our convincing words or our clear explanations. No matter how impressive our spirituality is, it won't just rub off on those who need to know Jesus. That understanding comes from God. Our most effective approach, to be supplemented by proclaiming the message and demonstrating love, is to pray that He would open their eyes as He has opened ours—by His unsearchable, unfathomable grace.

IN DEED God is the consummate persuader. He is able to convince the mind of the scientist and to sway the heart of the poet. No corner of the human psyche is out of His reach. No mental or emotional wall can withstand His strongest overtures for long. The key to someone receiving His truth is prayer on behalf of the receiver. Does someone come to mind? Pray—diligently, persistently, repeatedly. Pray that God will open eyes and hearts to His wisdom.

MARCH 26
Proverbs 2:6

God shapes the world by prayer.

—E. M. Bounds

Fidelity

Do not lust in your heart after her beauty or let her captivate you with her eyes. PROVERBS 6:25

MARCH 27
Proverbs 6:20-29

God did not call us to be successful, but to be faithful.

—Mother Teresa

IN WORD We may read over this verse too quickly. After all, prostitution does not seem to be a rampant problem in the contemporary church. There are certainly indiscretions among its members, and adultery is tragically more common than in the past. But for those to whom soliciting a prostitute is not a viable temptation, this verse and others like it might often go unnoticed.

That is unfortunate. Why? Because there are deeper things at stake here than literal sexual immorality. Those who are wise know that the human heart is tempted by all sorts of adultery. Our opportunities for betraying the heart of our Lord are vast in their number and diversity. When Solomon warns us against lusting after the beauty of another, he knows—and the Spirit behind the Scripture speaks—of thousands of lusts by which we are drawn away from God. Did we think this passage was only about husbands and wives? It is also about the marriage between the Son and His bride, the church. We cannot be captivated by another. Fidelity to our Bridegroom is paramount.

IN DEED What are your temptations? They do not have to be of a sexual nature to carry the warnings of this passage. Any infidelity to our God is dangerous business. He is a jealous God; the devastation of a damaged relationship with our Creator is far worse than the devastation of a beloved husband or wife having an affair with another love.

Is your relationship with God like a lovers' union? If it isn't, it falls short of the divine romance for which we were created. If it is, then you know the importance of commitment and the dangerous power of other lusts. Flee from them. Your Lover wants all of you to Himself.

The Deeper Pursuit

*Keep my commands and you will live; guard my
teachings as the apple of your eye.*   PROVERBS 7:2

IN WORD   Why would we want to have the mind of
Christ? There are many appealing aspects of having the kind
of wisdom that comes from above: Our God has knowledge
of the future, He knows the foundations on which He laid
this universe, and He knows the fabric of our being. Access
to this kind of insight is attractive indeed. It would help us
make decisions, understand other people, and live in peace
and fulfillment. But there is a higher reason we should want
God's wisdom, a more noble appeal to His understanding.
We should first and foremost want to have His mind not
because it benefits us but because we love who He is.

We often take a utilitarian approach to God. We want to
be filled with His Spirit because it will lead to more fruitful
ministry, more fulfilling relationships, and more power in
our personal growth. In other words, we want God's Spirit
and His mind as a means to self-improvement or better
circumstances. But God is not primarily our self-help technique; He is the Lover of our souls. No love relationship ful-
fills its purpose when one party selfishly uses the other for
his or her own benefit. Love relationships are about love.

IN DEED   Is your relationship with God about love? Or
is it about getting more of Him for your own personal
improvement? His mind and Spirit are available to us, and
His presence in our lives will, in fact, change us dramatically.
But do you pursue God simply for the change He can bring
you? If so, take a step back and try another approach.

Come to God with a confession of your love for Him.
If you can say it honestly, tell Him you want a deeper experience of His presence because you love who He is—His
purity, His mercy, His love, His holiness, His power, His
wisdom. Do not move on to requests; bask in His character.
Have fellowship with Him. Your service and your place in
His Kingdom will grow out of this foundation of love.

MARCH 28
Proverbs 7:2

I would hate
my own soul
if I did not find
it loving God.

—St. Augustine

Living Martyrs

Whoever wants to save his life will lose it, but whoever loses his life for me will find it. MATTHEW 16:25

MARCH 29

Matthew 16:24-27

He who has no vision of eternity will never get a true hold of time.

—Thomas Carlyle

IN WORD Most people in this world have an approach to life that is all about them. It isn't necessarily selfish, it's just self-oriented. Those without very much in terms of material wealth live in survival mode, just trying to get by for now. Those a little better off live in prosperity mode, just trying to get ahead for a while. In each case, we tend to look for "the next thing." The next job, the next paycheck, the next big event, the next relationship, the next purchase—we are on an endless track toward improving our lives.

What's wrong with that? It isn't how Jesus defines discipleship. No, Jesus calls His followers to "lose" their lives. Those who are wise will not focus on "the next thing," they will focus on "the last thing"—God's Kingdom and the reign of His Son as Lord over all. Jesus isn't speaking to His disciples about martyrdom in this passage. He is speaking of lifestyle. Those who know about eternity will live for it. That has powerful implications.

We'd prefer to think that we can do both, living for now and eternity at the same time. But we can't. Many of our decisions will compel us to choose one or the other. Yes, we can have a fancy sports car or a dream vacation and still go to heaven. But we can't have those things and still invest the cost of them toward something eternal. Likewise, we can waste time recklessly and still go to heaven. But we can't waste time *and* invest that same time in an eternal work. We frequently make choices between the now and the eternal.

IN DEED Jesus never tells us to live spartan lives, as though we were ascetic monks isolated in a desert of self-denial. But He does tell us to be wise. We can enjoy His bounty, but we will be much happier if we realize what makes for a bountiful eternity. How do we do that? We stop trying to "save" our lives and we lose them. Take your focus off "the next thing" and invest in "the last thing"—the Kingdom of God.

Mysteries of Majesty

As you do not know the path of the wind, or how the body is
formed in a mother's womb, so you cannot understand the work
of God, the Maker of all things.   ECCLESIASTES 11:5

IN WORD   Human nature likes to boil things down into understandable parts. We like elegant theories that explain varied situations with one simple truth. We like to analyze books and movies, categorizing their parts and breaking out their themes. And we like theological truth; we like to fit everything into doctrines and creeds so that we can understand the nuts and bolts of God.

The problem is that God doesn't fit. Whatever systematic way of thinking man can come up with, it is too small to explain God. Whatever principles we can identify in His Word, they are too narrow to define how He relates to us. We simply can't get a handle on Him. He's too expansive. We're like earthbound ants trying to get a handle on the moon. We know God's there; we can describe what we see; and we can speculate about how He will behave. But we can't know.

That doesn't mean that doctrine and theology aren't important. They are—extremely so. They give us a framework to discuss the glory of our Creator, and they help us understand patterns He has used in His dealings with us. But they do not define Him, and they do not capture Him. They do not reduce Him to manageable formulas.

IN DEED   We can count on God's character. We know He is holy, righteous, omniscient, omnipotent, loving, merciful, and more. And we know that these attributes of His will not change. They, along with His Word, are forever reliable. But that doesn't mean that we have a handle on Him. No one has explained Him fully. No one has come up with His formulas, because He is not a formula God.

Is that unsettling? It is to many people. We like predictability and explanations. But a god we can explain isn't God. Remember that when your life seems out of control. It isn't. It is under the hand of the mysterious, mighty God.

MARCH 30
Ecclesiastes 11:5-6

A religion without mystery must be a religion without God.

—Jeremy Taylor

The Unseen Battle

What I have forgiven—if there was anything to forgive—I have forgiven in the sight of Christ for your sake, in order that Satan might not outwit us. For we are not unaware of his schemes. 2 CORINTHIANS 2:10-11

MARCH 31

2 Corinthians 2:5-11

If you don't believe in the devil's existence, just try resisting him for a while.

—Charles Finney

IN WORD Any wisdom we acquire that does not include a very real sense of the unseen world is severely deficient. The enemy has designs on us as the body of Christ—to destroy our unity—and on us as individuals—to keep us ignorant of our union with Jesus. He is no abstract force; he is a malignant personality with a malicious plan. We who believe are in his sights.

The enemy will draw near to you, but Jesus will draw even nearer. Never forget that. For the Christian, our proximity to Jesus is always greater than our proximity to the evil one. "The one who is in you is greater than the one who is in the world" (1 John 4:4). That perspective must always be maintained, or the battle is lost. The enemy can't steal your salvation, but he can steal all its pleasure—your joy and your peace.

IN DEED Spiritual warfare looks awfully physical sometimes. It takes wisdom to see the battle behind your battles and to respond appropriately. Know that the enemy loves your conflicts, not simply because they are conflicts, but because they distract you from God's business—and, if you aren't careful, from His character. Satan loves to obscure the glory of God's name, and when he can degrade your spiritual health in a conflict, the glory of God's name is certainly obscured. Satan retreats when you stand firm—when you keep your peace, maintain your joy, act in humility, and demonstrate love—even in the midst of conflict. *Especially* in the midst of conflict. He would rather not give you an occasion to show God's character in the fire, so if you're going to show God's character anyway, he'll eventually put out the fire. He'll be back with another strategy later, but he'll lose this one—if you stand firm.

Waiting in Faith

It is good to wait quietly for the salvation of the Lord.
LAMENTATIONS 3:26

IN WORD   Waiting quietly is not what most of us do best. We prefer to be activists, at least in the matters that pertain to us. Perhaps we like to maintain an illusion of control. Perhaps we just don't trust other people as much as we trust ourselves. Regardless, it's against our nature to wait patiently when we think we might be able to affect an outcome.

We make a statement when we act. We are answering all our questions about God: Does He care? Does He have a will in the situation? Does He intervene in our affairs? Does His Word have something to say about our situation? Every time we act, we are answering these questions one way or the other, at least for the matter at hand. Maybe we don't realize how loaded with meaning our behavior is, but it is profound. Almost everything we do indicates our beliefs about God.

God tells us how to approach life. We are to come to every situation with faith, an expectation of His goodness, and a desire to do His will. While we would like these heart attitudes to be instantaneous, they rarely are. They take time, and therefore we must approach each situation with time and thoughtfulness. Whenever we find ourselves in a difficulty, instead of barging our way out of it along the path of least resistance, as we are prone to do, we must first ask the Lord His will, wait for His answer, and let Him take the initiative by preparing the way before us. His is not an instant way.

IN DEED   Ask yourself why it is hard to wait sometimes. Is it impatience with the situation? A desire to be in control? A suspicion that God is not going to intervene? Let God search your motives, and then search His will. Wait quietly until He reveals it. Doors will open and victories will fall into your hands, rarely in your timing, but always in His. Waiting quietly demonstrates trust like nothing else. It is a way to honor Him.

APRIL 1
Lamentations 3:26

Simply wait upon Him. So doing, we shall be directed, supplied, protected, corrected, and rewarded.

—Vance Havner

Avoiding Wastelands

*Do not be deceived: God cannot be mocked. A man
reaps what he sows.* GALATIANS 6:7

APRIL 2
*Galatians 5:16-26;
6:7-8*

We share in the
divine nature
through our shar-
ing of the Spirit.

—Athanasius

IN WORD What would you say if someone offered to
sell you a piece of beach property at a seemingly affordable
price? Sounds good, doesn't it? But what if the property was
a wasteland—the site of toxic dumping, the end of a sew-
age line, or used for some other objectionable purpose? The
prospect of owning it would be unappealing, to say the least.
Why? Because there is no value in such an investment.

The image is an accurate picture of a choice we must all
make. We can either live in the Spirit or in the flesh. If we
sow seeds of the flesh, we are investing in worthless land. It
won't last. It can't be developed. It will leave us with nothing in the end; the sinful nature is destined for destruction.

When we think of sowing to please our sinful nature,
as Paul says (v. 8), we immediately think of overt, fleshly
sins: sexual immorality, substance abuse, greed, etc. But we
rarely consider the more subtle seeds of our sinful nature.
If we sow seeds of self-effort, we will reap its rewards: a
few accolades, perhaps, but nothing lasting. If we sow seeds
of self-righteousness, we end up with self-righteousness; it
cannot stand before God. If we sow seeds of self-sufficiency,
we reap only what we can provide for ourselves; and it is
never enough. Living in the power of the flesh is perpetual
futility. It accomplishes nothing eternal.

IN DEED One of the great mysteries of sin and self is why
we invest in them. Like the beachfront, the investment may
have natural appeal. But a self-directed life is deceitful. It
promises us success but delivers nothing that lasts. Even its
noblest works are corrupt. What a disastrous investment!
When we buy bad merchandise we get—well, bad merchandise. When we cultivate the flesh, we get the flesh.

Sow eternal seeds. Live by the power of the Spirit. Be
forever joined to the plan, the purposes, and the Person
of the incorruptible God. And enjoy reaping what you've
sown.

Flexible Obedience

At the LORD's command they encamped, and at the
LORD's command they set out. NUMBERS 9:23

IN WORD We serve an unpredictable God. He is not
unreasonable, and He is not inconsistent, but He *is* unpredictable. No human has ever fathomed His ways. As much
as we try to make the spiritual life of discipleship a formula—and check out the shelves of your local Christian
bookstore if you don't believe we have done that—God will
change directions on us. Why is that? Does He enjoy being
elusive? Does He like to taunt us by always staying out of
our reach?

APRIL 3
Numbers 9:15-23

The evidence of
knowing God is
obeying God.

—Eric Alexander

No, God does not tease. But anyone who follows Him
must quickly learn: He is not a formula. He does not repeat
the same methods over and over again. He does not let
us get into a habit of obedience-by-memory that does not
engage the spirit. There is great mercy in that. He is a God
of relationship, and He only allows us to relate to Him. We
cannot memorize Him, we cannot learn His principles apart
from His person, and we cannot substitute His Law in place
of His Spirit. He desires to be known, and while His past
deeds help us know who He is, His present direction can
only be found in a vital relationship with His person.

IN DEED God is looking for those who have the flexibility to pick up and go when He says to pick up and go, and
to sit down and stay when He says to sit down and stay.
Sometimes He will have us camp for several days, sometimes only for several minutes. Sometimes He will lead us
for miles, sometimes for a few feet. The disciple who says,
"The God who led me five miles yesterday will lead me five
miles every day," does not know the God he serves. He's
into religion, not faith. There's a huge difference.

In your discipleship, are you depending on principles,
or are you looking for God? You must be available to do
what He commands today, not what He commanded you
last time. Know the difference. Know your God.

Watch Your Diet

Whatever is true, whatever is noble, whatever is right, whatever is pure, whatever is lovely, whatever is admirable—if anything is excellent or praiseworthy—think about such things.
PHILIPPIANS 4:8

APRIL 4
Philippians 4:8-9

No one would allow garbage at his table, but many allow it served into their minds.

—Fulton John Sheen

IN WORD What would we expect of someone who feeds only on fast food and unhealthy snacks filled with sugar and fats? A healthy body? Long life? No, we would expect physical health to be largely the product of physical intake. Is it any different in the spirit?

Modern culture is saturated with unhealthy spiritual food—from the lusts of the flesh and the eyes, to the human pride of the self-life, to elaborate and deceptive worldviews and philosophies. Hundreds of television channels, dozens of newspapers and magazines, unlimited cyberspace images, and a number of other media compete for our attention. We let many of them actually win our attention. And much of what we feed on is unhealthy. In our pursuit of wisdom, our minds often hunger for genuine nutrition.

It is unreasonable to think that hours of digesting unhealthy material will result in healthy minds and spirits. "You are what you eat" applies not only in the physical world, but also in the spiritual. Consuming all the wrong things will have all the wrong results. It's a natural law. There's no way to take in junk without becoming junky.

IN DEED God calls us to watch our diets. It pleases Him when we care for His temple, our bodies. But it pleases Him much more when we care for our minds. Our thought life is where His Spirit most prefers to work, shaping uncluttered hearts and imparting wisdom to uncluttered minds. Even so, we do not make a smooth highway for Him into our souls. Through our entertainment, we let ourselves be bombarded by an incessant PR campaign for the ways of the world. Find a balance. Watch what goes into your mind. Without hindrance, let His thoughts nourish you.

A Pageantry of Need

Blessed are those you choose and bring near to live in your courts! We are filled with the good things of your house. PSALM 65:4

IN WORD Imagine a homeless man pushing his grocery cart on the sidewalk in front of an open-air buffet restaurant. Hungry for a meal—just one good meal—he stumbles back and forth. People sit at sidewalk tables, feasting on a lavish spread of the finest foods. Imagine a sign in front of the restaurant reading: "Free buffet. All you can eat. Everyone welcome." Still, the man wanders on the sidewalk. Everything he needs for the moment is offered, but he won't sit down. Perhaps he doesn't understand the sign, doesn't believe it applies to him, or feels like he's too dirty to fit in. Perhaps he just doesn't want to leave his empty bottles outside in his cart. Regardless of the reason, he hungers while others eat.

That's how many Christians approach God's promises. We loiter in front of His Word, but we don't understand it, don't believe it applies to us, or think we're too dirty to fit in. Often, we won't let go of the trash we're hoarding. Regardless of the reason, we hunger while others eat. The banquet of God waits for us, but we can't relate to it, so we don't even ask. We won't go sit down. We take some sort of perverse pride in our homelessness, mistaking our poverty for true spirituality. We think we're much less pretentious than those who are feasting. We just don't get it. The buffet is for us. God's promises are lavished upon us with His own Son as the guarantee.

IN DEED Blessed are those who accept God's promises like children, who are too innocent to ask questions or to be suspicious of His extravagance. While homeless people parade in front of His storehouse, clutching their carts, those who simply take Him at His Word avoid the absurdity of the picture. They understand: We have a God of enormous abundance, and we are a people of enormous need. It's a simple relationship. He invites us to display our poverties before Him so He can show the world His mercies. What prevents us from receiving His bounty with open arms?

APRIL 5
Psalm 65

You never pray with greater power than when you plead the promises of God.

—William J. C. White

95

An Enemy's Hunger

If your enemy is hungry, give him food to eat; if he is thirsty, give him water to drink. PROVERBS 25:21

APRIL 6
Proverbs 25:21-22

In Jesus and for Him, enemies and friends alike are to be loved.

—Thomas à Kempis

IN WORD If we ever needed any evidence that God's character is not instinctual for us, this is it. Giving our enemies food to eat and water to drink goes against every principle of justice we've cultivated from the early days of sibling rivalries and onward. The self-promoting impulses of fallen humanity do not allow us to look out for our enemies and bless them with favor. If we *wanted* to do that for them, they wouldn't be our enemies.

It takes a lot of faith to act in such a way. The Holy Spirit must radically renew our minds, and then our minds must trust that God will honor our behavior. It feels like going out on a limb, doesn't it? To treat an enemy well risks the possibility of his taking advantage of us, of his getting the upper hand, of our accounts being so out of balance that we're even more vulnerable than when we first felt offended. Treating an enemy with favor means that we have decided, in faith, that God is the keeper of our enemy's account as well as our own. We cannot do it unless we trust that He will work justice out in the end, and that we're actually improving our own welfare by improving the welfare of our rival. Human logic does not lead us to such conclusions. Only faith can do that.

IN DEED How do you treat your enemies? Perhaps you claim to have none; congratulations. But there are certainly people who rub you the wrong way. How do you deal with them? Do you hold grudges? Do you look for ways to avoid them? Do you secretly hope that God will humble them and vindicate you?

Perhaps He will. If you really believe in His goodness, you are free to let Him handle justice on your behalf. You are free to behave in extraordinarily unexpected and godly ways by blessing those who curse you, giving to those who have cheated you, or complimenting those who have insulted you. Trying to make their lives uncomfortable, though natural, tells God we don't believe in His justice. Treating an enemy well honors His merciful will.

Deepen Your Shine

Those who are wise will shine like the brightness of the heavens, and those who lead many to righteousness, like the stars for ever and ever.   DANIEL 12:3

IN WORD   People spend thousands of dollars to last longer. Exercise, cosmetics, plastic surgery, self-help advice, nutrition plans—in other words, the entire self-preservation industry—is huge business. We like life, and we want it to last, not just in some ethereal, nondescript expectation of a life hereafter, but in a real, fulfilling, purposeful eternity. We don't just want "forever." We want to know we will enjoy it.

Daniel is told what makes or breaks eternity in the resurrection: righteousness. Loving it, drinking it in, leading others to it, investing in it. Righteousness is the key. The quality of our righteousness on earth has everything to do with the quality of our eternity. And those who are wise know it.

Those who are wise also know that there's a problem. We are inherently unrighteous. An eternity based on earthly righteousness is a devastating predicament for people who are, in their very genetics, infected with corruption. Are there any who can really lead others to righteousness? Will any shine like the brightness of the heavens? Or is the promise empty?

We who know Jesus know the answer, of course. Righteousness is a gift from a holy heaven to an infected race. It comes from outside of ourselves, available only through faith in its Giver. Those who are wise will tell others about this gift. Those who want to shine will know the Source of light and will be completely preoccupied with Him.

IN DEED   You probably know of the Bible's imperatives about evangelism: We are commanded to spread the gospel of salvation throughout the world. Have you known also of this promise in Daniel? Evangelism is one way to make an investment that never, ever ceases to bring abundant returns. God promises that sharing the Light with others will forever deepen your own shine.

APRIL 7
Daniel 12:1-4

Eternity to the godly is a day that has no sunset.

—Thomas Watson

Eternal Returns

The faithless will be fully repaid for their ways, and the good man rewarded for his.   PROVERBS 14:14

APRIL 8

Proverbs 14:14

God has given us a short time here upon earth, and yet upon this short time eternity depends.

—Jeremy Taylor

IN WORD   Can you imagine being one of the first stockholders in the automobile industry, when the horseless carriage was seen as a foolishly impossible endeavor? How much would your stock be worth today, over a century later? Wise and early investments, given time, become amazingly profitable. In fact, almost every economic investment, given enough time, produces exponential returns far overshadowing its initial cost. A few dollars wisely invested hundreds of years ago could be worth millions of dollars now.

The principle of "investment plus time equals profit" not only applies in the world's economy, but also in God's. Faithfulness, given time, has profitable results. And in God's economy, the time is not measured in years but in eons. Our investments are eternal. Their profits *never* stop coming in.

The same principle also applies in the negative. Faithlessness bears a burdensome interest, and it never stops accruing without divine intervention and a repentant reversal. Or, as Paul says hundreds of years after Solomon: "A man reaps what he sows" (Galatians 6:7). It is foolish to expect otherwise, as so many do, thinking that recklessness will have no negative outcome. It is just as foolish to think that faithfulness may never be rewarded, even though it may be long in coming. God does not operate that way. Wisdom recognizes His character and knows that He is a rewarder of those who diligently seek Him.

IN DEED   Learn to see your actions today as eternal investments. They may not bear immediately visible profits or losses, but the profits and losses are given an eternity to work themselves out. Their scale can be massive. A wise word, a timely gift, or a simple act of service can compound daily for all eternity. God already knows their future value. When we've been there ten thousand years, how much will today's investments be worth? More than we can imagine.

How to Honor God

He who oppresses the poor shows contempt for their Maker, but whoever is kind to the needy honors God.   PROVERBS 14:31

IN WORD   For most of us, caring for the poor is an afterthought. We're not unconcerned; we're just not very intentional about our efforts. For God, caring for the poor is essential. It is an emphatic theme in His Word. It is written into His Law, it is expressed in His wisdom, it is measured by the prophets, it is characteristic of Jesus, and it is a substantial ministry in the New Testament church. From cover to cover, the Bible tells us of God's concern for the poor.

Modern Christianity maintains ministries for the poor, but they are often peripheral ministries. For most Christians, our efforts include donating things we no longer value and urging our denominations to help the needy. But God is a hands-on God, and we are to be hands-on people.

The message of Proverbs 14:31 is that our view of the needy reflects our view of God. Do we see in the destitute the image of God? Perhaps it is veiled, but it is there. Though the image is fallen, it is God's nonetheless. Don't let its obscurity fool you; all humanity was created in His image, and our attitude toward other people is symptomatic of our attitude toward God. Or, to put it another way, our love of God will determine how we treat other people—even the very least of them. If we can easily let His creation suffer, we probably don't think much of God.

IN DEED   Why is it so important to God that we be kind to the needy? Because if we aren't, we've forgotten who we are. We were needy. He was kind. Did we learn anything from His example? Do we consider His love valuable only because it was applied to us? Did mercy really sink in?

The poor remain because God wants to know: How much do you value His ways? Give Him a demonstration today. Show kindness to those who need it most.

APRIL 9
Proverbs 14:31

World poverty is a hundred million mothers weeping because they cannot feed their children.

—Ronald J. Sider

A Heart at Peace

A heart at peace gives life to the body.
PROVERBS 14:30

Peace rules the day when Christ rules the mind.

—Anonymous

IN WORD The relationship between the spirit and the body is deeper than we might think. Not all physical infirmity is a product of spiritual turmoil, but much of it is. When God is on the periphery of our lives, our bodies can't stand the void. Ask anyone who has heart trouble. Stress is often a big part of it. And stress is the result of a too-distant God.

Peace has prerequisites. One of them is a surrender of all the self's attempts to earn God's approval. Instead, we are to understand that God approves of Jesus and we are related to Jesus by faith. Another is an inspired ability to trust God, even when circumstances seem to dictate against trust. But there is one often assumed prerequisite to peace that is a decidedly misguided assumption. Peace is *not* dependent on circumstances. Not real peace, anyway. The real peace that comes from God is available in spite of circumstances. And it is often revealed *only* in the difficult times. We never know the truth of our relationship with God until it is burned in the fire. Does it remain? Then it is gold; it is true. Or does it collapse? Then it was combustible from the very beginning, worth nothing at all. Peace from God must be tested. If it isn't, we never know whether it's genuine.

IN DEED We human beings are a strange mixture of mind, body, and spirit. We like to think of these as separable entities, but they are not. They interrelate at levels we can scarcely understand. Sin has physical effects. Mental stress has physical effects. And a heart at peace gives life.

Whatever you are going through—and it is a safe assumption that we are always going through something—it is not to affect your peace. God is above your circumstances, and He is greater than your sin. Bring it all to Him—your sin, your trials, your everything. Bind yourself to the things that really matter and the One who can govern them. And rest. Be at peace and be well.

Envy Rots

A heart at peace gives life to the body, but envy
rots the bones.   PROVERBS 14:30

IN WORD   Envy is a subtle enemy. We think we're free from it, but it is often the silent root of our sins. We can make ungodly decisions because we want the quality of our lives to match that of our neighbors. We can make unwarranted judgments because we are compelled to mentally reduce other people in order to mentally enlarge ourselves. And we can avoid God's plan for our lives because we want too strongly to fit into our culture. Our constant tendency is to compare ourselves to others, and comparison leads to envy. It affects the way we spend our money, our time, and our talents. It affects the careers we choose and the relationships we cultivate. Deep within us all is a drive to "make it," to succeed well beyond the average person. We want success because we've seen others have it.

This envy-rooted drive for success-by-comparison carries many physical symptoms with it. It sucks us into a consuming "rat race," a treadmill that undermines good health. It keeps us spending more than we have to spend, impressing more than we need to impress, and controlling more than is ours to control. It tells us that we're never quite good enough and that there is always more to be done. It stresses us out.

IN DEED   How do we get beyond such a corrosive attitude? There can be no room for envy when we measure ourselves by how God sees us rather than by how others see us. If we are all abject sinners saved by extravagant mercy, who is there to envy? Only those who have taken hold of God's unfathomable grace, which is available in equal measure to all who will take hold of it.

If you are eaten away by the stress of the rat race, first recognize the envy that underlies it. Then try this: Perform one act per day that defies "success" as you once defined it. Choose not to impress someone; refuse to invest in an image; compliment someone you once judged. By all means, let your heart be at peace.

APRIL 11
Proverbs 14:30

Envy is a denial of providence.

—Stephen Charnock

Detestable Pride

The LORD detests all the proud of heart. Be sure of this:
They will not go unpunished. PROVERBS 16:5

APRIL 12

Proverbs 16:5;
1 Peter 5:5-6

Pride is utter
poverty of soul
disguised as riches.

—John Climacus

IN WORD Our world honors pride. We often give the most media attention to those who demand it. Athletes make arrogant claims and then are lauded for their competitiveness. Entertainers shamelessly promote their own image and then are praised for their confidence. Political and military leaders proudly wield their power over vulnerable people and are rewarded for their assertiveness. Making a name for oneself is an honorable business in the world's culture.

We might easily be drawn into that philosophy if we don't continually remind ourselves of God's hatred for pride. It is a consistent biblical theme: Pride is repulsive. It directs glory inward instead of upward. It seeks the honor of the gifted rather than the honor of the Giver. It is far too impressed with the ingenuity and resourcefulness of human abilities. In its very essence, it ignores God. If we want to avoid it, we must always honor Him. We also must honor His hatred of it.

That's hard to do. Pride is the foundation of self-will, which is the ultimate foundation behind every sin. It is deeply ingrained in us. We hate it in others, but we wallow in it when we're allowed to. Whenever a little glory comes our way, we drink it in as though it's the sweetest thirst-quencher. But like other sweets, it has little substance. Eventually, no amount of honor will cover the fact that we're needy on the inside. Something deep within us craves glory, but something deeper reminds us that we aren't worthy of it. The depth of our soul knows that God is the only worthy recipient of praise.

IN DEED Let every hint of pride be repulsive to you. Let God deal with those who seek their own glory; it is not our job to humble anyone. But the Bible repeatedly tells us to humble ourselves. Hate the pride that you are prone to love. Agree with God that it is a detestable thing. Send it away and seek His glory. His honor comes to those who do.

Blessed Fear

*Blessed are all who fear the LORD, who walk
in his ways.* PSALM 128:1

IN WORD Our logic tells us not to fear the God who defines Himself as "love" and who offers His grace freely to all who will accept it. Yet, as we've seen, fear is where wisdom begins. Those who fear Him will become wise, and those who do not are fools. The Scripture makes that clear.

The one who does not fear God takes a casual approach to life. The awesome beauty of creation is taken for granted. The preciousness of time and of life become less precious. Little by little, relationships become more trivial. And sin becomes a nonissue, something that doesn't really exist or that God will just overlook without much thought. The one who does not fear God does not understand himself.

Those who do fear God, however, begin to see all things as holy. Creation is a blessing, life a privilege. Relationships and resources turn into responsibilities for stewardship, and sin becomes a tragic defamation of the character of our Father. The one who fears God begins to see sin as ugly graffiti defacing the divine property and as high treason against the divine plan. And for God-fearers, that will unsettle their minds and gnaw at their sensibilities.

What is the blessing in that? How can such a painful discontent be called a "blessed" life? Because it gives us the right perspective and puts us on the right track. It unites us with the heart of God—not a God we're terrified of but a God who captivates us in reverence and awe. It sobers us up from our once-random, once-reckless existence. We see things as they are, and we can never take life casually again.

IN DEED What is the measure of your fear? Are you casual about the precious gifts of God? Do you take grace for granted and see your sin as tolerable? Are your relationships take-them-or-leave-them propositions? Are your time and resources carelessly managed? Let any symptoms of fearlessness alarm you. Laugh and enjoy life, but fear God. Love Him warmly, but respect Him deeply. You will know what it is to be blessed.

APRIL 13
Psalm 128:1-2

Fear the Lord, then, and you will do everything well.

—Hermas

The Wisdom of the World

Has not God made foolish the wisdom of the world?

1 CORINTHIANS 1:20

APRIL 14

1 Corinthians 1:18-31

We were deceived by the wisdom of the serpent, but we are freed by the foolishness of God.

—St. Augustine

IN WORD The wisdom of the world would never have chosen a cross for its salvation. The wisdom of the world always chooses the path of obvious victory. It knows nothing of the deeper battles and subtleties of faith. It acts on what it sees on the surface and grabs as much visible glory as it can. It will not wait; it seizes the day.

We are not born of that spirit. We are born of the Spirit of God, and the Spirit of God will lead us to the Cross. He points us toward eternal realities, not temporary glory. While earthly wisdom tells us to get what we can while we can get it, God's wisdom shows us the reality of eternity that lies beyond the visible nature of this corrupt world. It shows us the Resurrection beyond the Cross.

Those of us who seek true wisdom do not simply desire information from God. We want to know what He is like. We must come to see Him as the source of all truth, and we must take our cues from Him. We shouldn't be satisfied with Him just telling us what to believe. We need to see it in action. What is *His* wisdom like? What would *He* do if He were clothed in human flesh?

God has given us the answer, of course. We can examine the wisdom of Jesus, which led Him to death for a greater good. What He did in surrendering to the Cross was absolute foolishness in the eyes of the world. And it still is. But we can see beyond the Cross if we are wise, and based on what we see, we can walk toward it with confidence.

IN DEED The first lesson of wisdom from the Cross is this: *Never exchange eternal glory for temporary gain.* Jesus forsook the temporal because He knew the eternal. But the world will always urge us to seek a superficial victory today. Don't. It's a foolish world, and God has shamed it. See what God has done, learn the wisdom of the Cross, and embrace it.

The Wisdom of God

In the wisdom of God the world through its wisdom did not know him. 1 CORINTHIANS 1:21

IN WORD The world lived in darkness. Why would God ordain such ignorance? Why would He *not* want the world to recognize Him through its own wisdom? Doesn't He want to be known? Why isn't He more easily found?

Think about it this way: Who would receive glory if we found God on our own? He would be the hidden One, we would be the seekers, and the credit in this divine hide-and-seek would go to the intellect of the pursuers. God did not ordain it this way. He is the Pursuer, and He receives the glory. The world, in its "wisdom," refuses to play that game—to its own detriment. But those who *really* desire God are glad when He reveals Himself and are not reluctant to give Him the glory for finding the seekers before their own wisdom could find Him.

There is nothing in the human mind that can discern eternal realities without a revelation from above. It is all on His own initiative. If it were not, He would be the passive object of our activity. We would never be sure of His love; we would never know His ways; we would never see Him work. We would only find Him, and we would never be certain of what we found. But in His active pursuit of human rebels, His character is displayed. We see the intensity of His love, the wisdom of His ways, and the power of His works. His glory falls from above.

IN DEED The second lesson of wisdom from the Cross is this: *Never forget the divine initiative.* We think we pursued God, forgetting that He supplies all revelation, all strength, and all means of knowing Him. That's a stressful—and futile—pursuit. We must cooperate with Him, but we must also rest. Knowing Him requires our diligence, but it is a diligence of reception, not a diligence of acquisition. We receive only what He has already given. As a result, we cannot celebrate our wisdom or the world's—only His.

APRIL 15
1 Corinthians 1:18-31

His wisdom's vast, and knows no bounds, a deep where all our thoughts are drowned.

—Isaac Watts

The Wisdom of Jesus

You are in Christ Jesus, who has become for us wisdom from God—that is, our righteousness, holiness and redemption. 1 CORINTHIANS 1:30

APRIL 16

*1 Corinthians
1:18-31*

Nothing in my
hands I bring,
simply to thy
Cross I cling.

—Augustus Toplady

IN WORD The life of faith begins with a confession of bankruptcy. In order to accept our Savior, we must accept our need. We cannot have His righteousness without denying our own; we cannot have His holiness without confessing our sin; and we cannot receive His redemption without owning up to our bondage. We are bankrupt before Him, and fools if we do not know it.

The beauty of the Cross is its ugliness. God left us no aesthetic religion to idolize, no self-effort to perfect, no Law to fulfill. He completely undid us by doing it all Himself. The way to become godly now is not to become godly; it is to declare our ungodliness and cast its cost on Another. The way to become pure now is not to be pure; it is to declare our impurity and ask for the heart and mind of Another. The way to live is not to seek life; it is to die and let Another live in our place. We thought the wisdom of God would be to make us better people—through works, service, intellect, philosophies, religion, and more. But in His wisdom, Jesus did not come to make us better. He came to do away with the old entirely and to birth something new. We take hold of that by embracing the ugly, ignoble Cross. Only then can newness come.

IN DEED The third lesson of wisdom from the Cross is this: *Never despise the humble appearance of God's plan.* Make no mistake—the Cross was not at first gilded with gold to adorn our steeples and necklines. It was first a place of disgrace. It was the symbol of death. It was brutal and ugly, horrid and shameful. But it was God's way! From the foundation of the world, He ordained that His priceless treasure be dressed in very plain clothes.

If you're ever tempted to avoid the unattractive path God has planned, turn to Jesus on the Cross. See Him as a reminder that priceless treasures are in broken vessels.

The Wisdom of the Spirit

The Spirit searches all things, even the deep things of God. 1 CORINTHIANS 2:10

IN WORD Leave it to God to exercise His perfect wisdom. Somehow, we thought that a God who is Spirit might give us a salvation of the flesh. But the One who bears children must bear children in His likeness. It's the way of genetics—physical or spiritual.

Brought into a spiritual kingdom—though its spiritual nature encompasses body and mind, as well—we must learn of its culture. You cannot expect to prosper in another country without learning something of its customs and speaking its language. So it is with the Kingdom of God. We must be immersed in its culture and come into its character. The means for doing this is the Spirit of God.

Becoming wise in the ways of the Kingdom is like putting on a set of strange, new clothes. We look different and we feel different. This is no illusion; we *are* different. And we can take comfort in the fact that while a multitude of Christians—only God knows if they're genuine or not—are content with a superficial spirituality, God has called us to go deep. The Cross is our holy invitation. We are not saved for superficiality. We are beckoned into the wisdom that underlies the foundation of this universe, called to understand its purpose, its dynamics, its direction, and its needs. The invitation is more remarkable than we might think; it is a summons to participate in the works of God.

IN DEED The fourth lesson of wisdom from the Cross is this: *Never be afraid to go deep.* The privilege of the believer is to share in the deep things of God. The Cross was a secret mystery from before the beginning of time, but now it is revealed for our glory (2:7). We are colaborers with Him, sharing in His likeness! All creation must marvel at the sight.

Never be content with staying on the surface, and never assume you've learned enough. God is deeper than most people know. Dive into the depths of His wisdom.

APRIL 17
1 Corinthians 2:1-16

The Holy Spirit
of grace desires to
disturb your sleep.
Blessed are you
if you awaken.

—Lars Linderot

The Wisdom of the Believer

We have not received the spirit of the world but the
Spirit who is from God, that we may understand what
God has freely given us.   1 CORINTHIANS 2:12

APRIL 18

1 Corinthians 2:1-16

The Spirit breathes
upon the Word,
and brings the
truth to sight.

—William Cowper

IN WORD   This verse is the conclusion of the remarkable story of God's wisdom being made manifest in this world. We started with complete bankruptcy. We end with being let in on the deep mysteries of God. Paul makes an astounding claim: "We have the mind of Christ" (2:16).

Most Christians believe at some level that God is unknowable. It is true that we can never know everything there is to know about Him. We will explore His depths for eternity and still be near the surface. But the unknown God of speculative philosophies has made Himself known in the Cross. There He is Judge and Redeemer, wrath and love, holy and merciful, mighty and wise. The power of God was revealed one black day on a hill in the Middle East, and no one expected it to look like that. It seemed shameful, but it resulted in victory, life, and peace. Everything we will ever need was made available there.

Need salvation? It is given to us on the basis of Jesus' blood and the power of His resurrection. Need wisdom? It is freely given at the Cross, too. Need anything at all from God? He calls us to meet Him there—every time, for every purpose. The Cross and Resurrection were God's ultimate intervention in this world and the basis of all meetings between the holy and the profane. The mysteries of the sacrificial Lamb run deep, but they are available to us, always and forever.

IN DEED   The fifth lesson of wisdom from the Cross is this: *Never underestimate the availability of God.* God did not just scratch the surface at the Crucifixion. He reached into the depths and drew us out. He invites us into its victory and the resurrected life that follows—to know it, to savor it, and to tell it. Never cry out to God, "Where are You?" without looking first at the Cross. Understand what He has freely given and base your life on it. At the Cross, His wisdom is yours.

Where's Your Heaven?

Meanwhile we groan, longing to be clothed with our heavenly dwelling.   2 CORINTHIANS 5:2

IN WORD   There is an impulse deep in our hearts for the things of heaven. God placed it there. He shaped us for eternity, and somewhere deep within us, we know that. We may have distorted that impulse when our first parents ate the forbidden fruit or when we deliberately sinned against God, but we still have it. We want heaven, and we want it now.

Have you noticed all the ways we try to get it? We look for heaven in lots of places—the spring catalogs, the vacation brochures, the real estate guides, the novels and movies that engross us, the satisfying relationships we pursue, the American dream we're promised, and more. You name it, we've placed our hope in it. We welcome poor substitutes.

Perhaps we thought of our personal goals as an innocent search for satisfaction, but they went deeper than that. We were driven by our impulses for the eternal kingdom, trying to satisfy our hearts with things that don't measure up. That's why we always want more, no matter how much we have. Everything we think will satisfy us won't—not in the long run. Eternal impulses are not content with temporal treasures. Our hope is like an itch; it is cured with a divine balm, not an impatient scratch.

IN DEED   Where have you sought to secure your heaven? Even if you've placed your hope in the Kingdom of God, you still may be tempted to secure your kingdom by your own means. Have you insulated yourself in the most comfortable neighborhoods, padded your accounts with the most comfortable margins, gotten away from it all with the most comfortable respites, and escaped into the most comfortable fantasies? You may be entertaining false hopes. You may have cultivated your own parallel false kingdom next to the eternal Kingdom of God.

Resist that urge. God has called us into a relationship with Him. Let that be your treasure. Handle the things of this world loosely. Look for heaven where heaven really is.

APRIL 19
2 Corinthians 5:1-4

Heaven will be the perfection we have always longed for.

—Billy Graham

Fallen

There is not a righteous man on earth who does what
is right and never sins.   ECCLESIASTES 7:20

APRIL 20
Ecclesiastes 7:20;
Romans 3:10-18

We are not part
of a nice, neat
creation . . . ;
we are part of a
mutinous world
where rebellion
against God is the
order of the day.

—Samuel Shoemaker

IN WORD   Ecclesiastes is a depressing book. No one can accuse it of pious platitudes designed to put a positive spin on the world around us. It tells the truth, at least from the perspective of where a fallen humanity sits. If we depend on our eyes for truth, we will end up saying the same things as "the Teacher" who wrote it: "Everything is meaningless" (1:2).

The good thing about Ecclesiastes is that it sends us in search of a Savior. In its cold, hard assessment of who we are, it drives us toward the only One who can remedy our situation. But in order to know Him, we first need to embrace the harsh reality: "There is not a righteous man on earth who does what is right and never sins."

We accept this truth as basic, but we hardly live like we believe it. We put our hopes in politicians and policies. We admire entertainers and athletes as role models. We feed on the affections of friends and loved ones. We build up our own potential as the thing that, if we apply ourselves diligently enough, will make our lives meaningful. We invest such extreme emotions in fellow human beings—and ourselves—forgetting one critical foundation stone on which the gospel is laid: Every human being has the potential, even the probability, of letting us down.

IN DEED   It's only natural. We take our eyes off the invisible God and put them on visible mankind. We expect our dreams and desires to be fulfilled by others, or at least by ourselves. We develop a worldly focus and invest our energies into the plans, people, and places of this planet. Then, when we least expect it, our dreams are shattered. We should have expected that. No human being can live up to the expectations we have. No one is righteous enough.

There is one exception, of course. It's the exception Ecclesiastes points us to: the Savior sent by God. In a fallen world, we need to keep turning our eyes toward Him—for everything. He will never disappoint us.

Mercy's Victory

Mercy triumphs over judgment!
JAMES 2:13

IN WORD   When someone sins against us, we are driven by a sense of fairness. We want the sin acknowledged, repentance demonstrated, and restitution made. Within our minds are detail-sensitive measuring devices that scrutinize others' actions to make sure we are treated fairly.

When we sin against someone else, we have an entirely different approach. We are driven by a sense of mercy. We expect people to cut us a certain amount of slack since, after all, only bitter, judgmental people get uptight about the little things. We forget that we ourselves are often uptight about the little things.

Jesus said to take that mercy-driven mind we have when we offend and apply it to the times when we are offended. "Do to others as you would have them do to you," He said (Luke 6:31). The sense of fairness we have when we are wronged was assumed by God Himself and poured out on the crucified Jesus. We are no longer entitled to it. He declared once for all that justice is His, not ours. We are left only with mercy. And thank God for that. It's all we need.

IN DEED   God's judgment is the natural result of His righteousness. It is integral to His character. But His mercy exceeds His justice. Only God could have conceived of a plan to exercise judgment in such a merciful way. In condemning our sins, He laid them all on His own flesh and took the condemnation Himself. His judgment was undergirded by grace.

God tells us to be like Him. If we are to have His mind and be steeped in His wisdom, we must let our own mercy triumph over our indignation. God has given us sure footing for grace and none at all for judgment.

The next time you need someone to cut you some slack and forgive, make a note of the feeling. Savor it and cultivate it. Then remember it the next time you are outraged at another's fault. In doing so, you will apply mercy's victory to your own heart. And you will understand God's.

APRIL 21
James 2:8-13

The more godly any man is, the more merciful that man will be.

—Thomas Benton Brooks

Solidarity in Suffering

Remember those in prison as if you were their fellow prisoners, and those who are mistreated as if you yourselves were suffering. HEBREWS 13:3

APRIL 22

Hebrews 13:1-3

Tell me how much you know of the suffering of your fellow men, and I will tell you how much you have loved them.

—Helmut Thielicke

IN WORD At any given time, many of God's saints are in prison. The prison may be literal, or it may be a product of circumstances. It can be financial debt, a broken relationship, a physical ailment, or any other constraining situation.

A huge problem in the church is when Christians look at their imprisoned brothers and sisters and assume that God has not favored them. Paul probably had experienced such a phenomenon. We read his prison epistles and marvel at his suffering for the cause. But many of his contemporaries may not have marveled. They may have seen his trouble as a sign of God's disfavor and wondered why someone with so much potential had fallen to such depths.

God's prisons are full of His loved ones. He uses those experiences mightily, as He did with Paul, Joseph, John the Baptist, John the disciple, and numerous other biblical examples. In fact, most of those whom He has used in powerful ways have experienced an imprisonment, captivity, or loneliness ordained directly by Him.

IN DEED Are you in prison? You are probably not literally behind bars, but your circumstances may make you feel as if you are. Don't despair; it will not last. It is ordained by God and is designed either for your current witness or future usefulness. He is refining you and molding you into His image, the exact likeness of His crucified Son.

Do you know someone in prison? Do not condemn. God is highlighting the current witness of His saints and preparing them for future fruitfulness. It is never His intention for His church to turn on its visibly fallen. Solidarity is His prescription for believers. Pray for those who suffer and meet their needs however you can. Demonstrate your solidarity with a captive saint today.

Repentability

Then David said to Nathan, "I have sinned against the Lord." 2 SAMUEL 12:13

IN WORD Scripture is rich with the theme of humility. Jesus' first beatitude should not have been as shocking as it was: "Blessed are the poor in spirit, for theirs is the kingdom of heaven" (Matthew 5:3). Peter's mini-sermon on Proverbs 3:34 was nothing new: "God opposes the proud but gives grace to the humble" (1 Peter 5:5-6). Humility is good in God's sight. It always has been.

Nowhere does humility show itself more clearly than in our ability to repent of our sins. David was confronted with his sin by Nathan's incisive parable on sheep-stealing. Many of us would have responded with an indignant "How dare you?" or a "Who do you think you are?" But not David. David's response, when he saw his sin, was grief. He was humble enough to acknowledge his own depravity. He was firmly rooted in the reality of man's corruption. His level of "repentability" ran high.

IN DEED What do you do when confronted with your sins? Do you get defensive? Are you resistant? That may depend on the one pointing your sins out to you. A friend's rebuke is hard to take, a stranger's harder still. The Bible rebukes us frequently, but we find it easy to ignore the Word when we want to. There are lots of pages to turn to when we want a more uplifting, encouraging thought. Regardless of where the rebuke comes from, we don't usually want to be bothered with messages about our own corruption. We'd rather dwell on how far we've come than how far we have to go. We don't like reminders that no matter how long we've been disciples, we are in need of great mercy.

Test your level of "repentability." Evaluate your response when you are confronted with your sin, either by another person or by the Word of God. Take your cues from David. Let humility be your guide, and see the mercy of God.

APRIL 23
2 Samuel 12:1-13

No man ever enters heaven until he is first convinced that he deserves hell.

—John Everrett

Real Refuge

The LORD helps them and delivers them; he delivers them from the wicked and saves them, because they take refuge in him. PSALM 37:40

APRIL 24
Psalm 37:39-40

Dear Lord, although I am sure of my position, I am unable to sustain it without you. Help me or I am lost.

—Martin Luther

IN WORD What does it mean to take refuge in God? It means to have faith that what He says is true; He will deliver those who call on Him. It means to appeal to Him in times of trouble; prayer is a powerful resource. But most of all, it means that we decide not to take refuge in ourselves, in others, in worldly wisdom, or in human strategies. We take refuge in Him, *and Him alone.*

What do you do when you're in trouble? If you're like most believers, you figure out a strategy and ask God to bless it. In His mercy, He may. But He calls us to a better way. When God tells us He is our refuge, He asks us to forsake our former allegiance to other sources of protection. Are you sick? First acknowledge that no medical treatment will work unless God is the Healer behind it. Are you in conflict with someone else? First acknowledge that no words of yours will change another's heart unless God is the agent of change. Are you in financial distress? First acknowledge that no amount of income will help unless God is the source. And having acknowledged all of this, look to Him constantly. Follow His instructions for action, but know first that your action is God-directed and not a futile means of self-help.

God is a Deliverer for those who recognize how helpless and vulnerable they are. He is not a Deliverer for those who try to add Him to their own self-effort.

IN DEED "God helps those who help themselves" is a catchy saying, but it is not biblical. Rather, God helps those who know how helpless they are and who appeal to Him—on His terms—for deliverance. That's not quite as catchy, but it's true. Those who want God to be their stronghold in times of trouble must actually *depend* on God as their stronghold. The deliverance is His, and His alone.

The Faith in Thanks

He who sacrifices thank offerings honors me, and he prepares the
way so that I may show him the salvation of God.
PSALM 50:23

IN WORD To most of us, giving thanks comes in the aftermath of a gift. We receive, and we are grateful to the giver if, in fact, we welcome the gift. It would be odd among sinful human beings to give thanks before a gift is given. Generosity can never be presumed among us. We must see it before we acknowledge it.

Negative as we are, we often treat God like a sinful human being. We will give Him thanks when we see His blessing. If we don't see it, we withhold our gratitude. We base it on a false assumption about His character—that He might not be a Giver. Why? Because we haven't seen it with our own eyes. But God doesn't work that way. His character is constant. We can assume His generosity. He is a Giver by nature, and we can acknowledge Him as such right now, even before we think we've received His bounty. Not only is it appropriate to give Him thanks after a blessing, it is right to give Him thanks beforehand. And it is not only right, it is often a prerequisite. If we don't, we may not receive what He is prepared to give.

IN DEED It is a strange dynamic to human eyes: Those who have never seen or expected God's blessing will never receive it, while those who have will receive more. Does this seem unfair? It isn't. Pessimism about God is faithlessness, and God does not honor faithlessness. He honors faith. Faith sees God for who He is before He has proven it yet again. It sees past blessings in the life of the believer, in the history of His servants, and in the inviolable Word. It knows that when God says He will deliver, He will. When He says He will provide, He will. Faith does not wait to find out who God is and what He is like. It already knows. It takes Him at His Word, and it is thankful in advance.

APRIL 25
Psalm 50

He who can give thanks for little will always find he has enough.

—Anonymous

115

Anatomy of a Temptation

"Did God really say . . . ?"

GENESIS 3:1

Genesis 3:1-7;
Proverbs 16:25

Temptation has
its source not in
the outer lure but
in the inner lust.

—D. Edmund Hiebert

IN WORD We don't need the serpent to speak these words to us anymore. We speak them to ourselves. That's where all temptations begin: questions and confusion over what God really said. Sometimes it's a legitimate confusion, but frequently it's not. Somewhere deep inside us, we *want* a reason to go ahead and disobey. We want to "unintentionally" miss the will of God because we have our own will to appease, and it's far more appealing. So we question the clear wisdom of our Creator and muddy the waters, trying to arrive at a point where we can say, "I just didn't know. The right thing to do wasn't clear to me. It was a complex issue."

You know the routine. Every human being has practiced it. The gymnastics that the human heart will go through to justify our wants is impressive. It takes considerable training and remarkable flexibility. But it is a tragic exercise with tragic consequences.

Psychologists call our thought processes "rationalizing," but the biblical word for it—or at least what precedes it—is *temptation*. The cravings of our flesh, the lust of our eyes, the pride of the self—these are the drives that compete with the holiness offered by our God. The enemy has done a masterful job of coloring those impulses brightly and painting holiness blandly. He doesn't want the latter to have any appeal because it would result in a glory that he can't stand. It would honor God and it would fulfill the image of God in us. To him, that would be an ugly, ugly scene.

IN DEED Are you skilled in the art of rationalizing? If you are a human being, you must answer yes. The clever serpent got the ball rolling in the Garden, but it has rolled freely ever since. There are depths to this art form of talking ourselves into disobedience that we are often not aware of. Ask God to reveal them to you. He wants you to have discernment.

Can you pray that today? Ask God to give you clear insight into the mind games we play. Let His Word hold full sway over your thinking. Learn to recognize temptation.

Seduction of a Soul

There is a way that seems right to a man, but in the end it leads to death. PROVERBS 16:25

IN WORD It doesn't begin with a well-marked road map to our destruction. No, our departure from God's path is a series of shady grays and mixed desires. The nuances of our temptations have a way of making the wrong decisions look right—even appealing. The seduction of a soul is a sensitive and subtle business.

That's why a spiritual life without vigilance is incredibly irrational. If we are not watchful and well-guarded, we can be led step by tiny step into the snares of the enemy and the ways of the world. God never tells us simply to do what seems right at the time. What *seems* right and what *is* right are often two vastly different things.

The redeemed soul who has not yet learned the mind of God—been saturated with it, shaped into it, and trained to trust it—is in a dangerous place. Questions of the genuineness or security of our salvation are not the only issue; a child of God can be rendered practically fruitless if pulled by the allure of what seems right but isn't. God has a greater desire for His children than the fact of their eternal salvation. It is a salvation that is to be lived and enjoyed now. The deception of false moralities and misplaced values can thoroughly undermine the experience of that salvation, if not its essence.

IN DEED The Christian will face many forks in the road throughout his or her life and often will not notice them. The main road—the broad, well-traveled path—seems like the right one. Everyone is on it, and the exits are often hard to see unless you're looking for them.

So look for them. Don't be driven down the seemingly right path without asking hard questions about it. Understand the high call of the Kingdom—that God has us do more than what's right, more than what's expected. Ask Him for His mind and open your own to receive it. Let His Word cultivate a sharp discernment in your spirit. Never let yourself be seduced by anything but the good love of God.

APRIL 27
Genesis 3:1-7;
Proverbs 16:25

Every temptation leaves us better or worse; neutrality is impossible.

—Erwin Lutzer

Good Intentions

When the woman saw that the fruit of the tree was good for food and pleasing to the eye, and also desirable for gaining wisdom, she took some and ate it. GENESIS 3:6

APRIL 28

Genesis 3:1-7;
Proverbs 16:25

Right intention is to the actions of a man what the soul is to the body, or the root is to the tree.

—Jeremy Taylor

IN WORD It seemed to make sense at the time. Eve was probably convinced that this way, the way of eating what was forbidden, was right. She didn't remember (or believe) that it would lead to death. The serpent had convinced her— or politely helped her convince herself—that perhaps she had misunderstood God. Or maybe He was even holding out on them—although if God knew the *full* story, as she now did, He would probably allow this fruit fest. After all, it was *only* an attempt to enjoy His creation and learn more of it. What could be wrong with that? God wants us to enjoy His bounty and He wants us to become wise. Surely He would be okay with a little pleasure that honors His creation.

The mind games we play during our times of temptation do not seem as evil as they turn out to be. We often have good intentions, or at least we convince ourselves that we do. Forsaking the clarity of God's Word, we embrace the fuzziness of human reasoning. Things become relative rather than absolute. And while we maintain a sense that our motives are right, our decisions are wrong. We have determined to "do good" rather than to obey God.

IN DEED You know what they say about the road to hell. It is paved with the distorted, often-inactive motives of our hearts, those good intentions that aren't so good. We must always be suspicious of them. There is usually a deep dishonesty beneath them. We have told ourselves we want to do what's best, when in fact we really want to compromise God's clear instructions.

The result is a dangerous illusion. We *feel* righteous. We think a sincere heart makes us good, and that's a dangerous place to be. Intentions are worthless until God is the entire focus of them and we are diligent to carry them out. Determine to obey Him exclusively. Have no other desire.

Better Intentions

Faith by itself, if it is not accompanied by action, is dead. JAMES 2:17

IN WORD When God has convicted our minds, purified our hearts, and put His wisdom within us, our motives do, in fact, often become good. They aren't always self-deception simply because they proceed from within us. God has put Himself within us by faith. Sometimes our intentions are the product of sincerely seeking His will with an undivided heart.

Even so, there is nothing practically worthwhile about them until they are carried out. Perhaps they honor God in spirit, but who will see His honor if they are buried deep within? A good plan without proactive diligence is pointless. The vision that God has given His servants, the works He has called them to, the glory He wants them to reflect—all begin in the heart, but they do not end there. They end by moving us into action. We become His children by faith, but we become His servants by work.

Do not be mistaken: God weighs motives. They matter deeply to Him. William Borden left his wealth in America in 1913 to serve as a missionary in Egypt. He died soon after from cerebral meningitis, having accomplished virtually nothing in the way of visible fruit. Would God count his motives as fruitfulness? Our righteous Lord could do no less. But Borden did not falter in his plans simply because he never got around to them. He died in obedience. There's a difference.

IN DEED We may not fulfill all of our truly good intentions in this life. God has His purposes for us, and they may not include the outworking of every godly desire within us. But we must pursue those desires anyway. Good, godly intentions are meant to be lived, not dreamed of. They are planted in our hearts to move us, not to entertain us. The impulses of a Spirit-filled person are a call to action.

Is there anything you have always felt God might want you to do, but you have never gotten around to it? Is His agenda always a matter of "one day" to you? Put feet on your intentions. Live them well. Our wonder-working God is calling His people to action.

APRIL 29
James 2:14-17

When you are able to do good, defer it not.

—Polycarp

Meaningful Hope

Utterly meaningless! Everything is meaningless.
ECCLESIASTES 1:2

APRIL 30

Ecclesiastes 1:1-11

Other men see only a hopeless end, but the Christian rejoices in an endless hope.

—Gilbert Brenken

IN WORD Conquerors win countries, politicians win elections, competitors win championships, and corporations win takeovers. Sometimes such victories will have an effect for years, centuries, and occasionally even millennia. More often, their memory fades with the passing of a generation. Either way, they are never permanent. Like sandcastles on the beach, the works of an ingenious and ambitious race are susceptible to the incoming tide. We are created with eternal longings but have fallen into the bondage of time. Nothing we do lasts.

That was the view of an old king who had seen empires flourish and die, and who had come to know the fleeting nature of his own riches. He was right, of course—from a purely human perspective. He was facing the angst common to all who look back on their life's work with any depth of perspective.

But that perspective is limited by the boundaries of human wisdom. It is the conclusion at which we all arrive when we depend on our own reasoning. It is wisdom without revelation—all brain and no Spirit. We who depend on God's revelation in all its fullness know the foundation for hope: An eternal Kingdom is being built, and what we do today can bear eternal results.

IN DEED Statistics say one of the most common maladies of our generation is hopelessness. There is a pervasive sense among our peers that this visible life is all there is—and that's just not enough for most people.

We have two necessary responses: (1) We must not let the hopelessness of our age infect us. We are to fix our hope on eternity. And, (2) we must share that hope with an anxiety-ridden generation. They are convinced that our hope is groundless. We must convince them that it isn't. That is, we are told, one of the most meaningful, lasting things we can do.

Meaningful Desire

The eye never has enough of seeing, nor the ear
its fill of hearing.   ECCLESIASTES 1:8

IN WORD   Human nature is never satisfied. Whatever gifts God has given us, we want more. When we've gotten a taste of God's generosity, our appetites are whetted, not filled. We are always waiting for the next good thing.

The good thing about our constant quest for more is that, when rightly directed, we can have it. This may be surprising to those of us who have heard sermon after sermon on the virtues of contentment. It's true that desire for the things of this world, as Solomon describes, is never fully satisfied. But there is a godly craving that is rewarded with blessing upon blessing. If our dissatisfaction moves us toward God and His Kingdom rather than toward temporal fulfillments, it is a holy dissatisfaction. It will eventually be rewarded. God never denies those who want more of Him.

Solomon says: "The eye never has enough of seeing, nor the ear its fill of hearing." Is this bad, as he implies? Or can it be good? That depends. It's bad if our eternal cravings are misdirected toward temporal things. It's good if we're seeking first the Kingdom of God and His righteousness.

IN DEED   Are you dissatisfied with life? Ask yourself why. If you are filling your life with things that don't last, you will never be satisfied at all. How can you be? The things you seek are not inherently satisfying.

But God is. If you are filling your life with Him (and letting Him fill your life with Himself), He will satisfy, and when you grow discontent again, He will give more. You will find yourself fully content for a time, and then realize there is so much more of Him to discover. Your holy craving will drive you deeper into His presence. That's not a problem. He is inexhaustible in His riches. We can forever explore Him, and if we want more, there will be more to find.

MAY 1
Ecclesiastes 1:1-11

Let temporal things
serve your use,
but the eternal
be the object of
your desire.

—Thomas à Kempis

Meaningful Riches

I thought in my heart, "Come now, I will test you with pleasure to find out what is good." ECCLESIASTES 2:1

The real measure of our wealth is how much we'd be worth if we lost all our money.

—John Henry Jowett

IN WORD An exceedingly wealthy businessman who recently had bypass surgery was asked in an interview how the experience would change his life. He responded that he would spend more money and never, for one example, let any wine that cost less than one hundred dollars per bottle pass through his lips. His great insight in his time of crisis was that life is short and must be lived to its fullest. That's not a bad philosophy, if one knows how to define a "full" life. But his definition reflected a faulty foundation based on very short-lived values.

A mature Christian disciple can recognize the fallacy of temporal pleasure as a life goal. We live for something much more lasting than the cult of earthly empires and personal gain—real pleasure based on the realities of God's Kingdom and our fellowship with Him. This, at least, is our ideal. But if we examine ourselves carefully, we'll often find a conflict within us—a revulsion toward the businessman's philosophy but a lifestyle that reflects it. Human nature since the Fall is to build a heaven on earth, to reconstruct Eden. Though we are promised an eternal heaven, we want heaven here, too. Can't you see it in the comforts we crave and the prayers we raise? Eden is always just out of our reach, but we keep reaching.

IN DEED Solomon tells us in Ecclesiastes 2:1-11 what a life of investing in the temporal accomplishes: nothing. His resume of investments is impressive, but he is disappointed—even disillusioned—with the profit. It's all meaningless, he concludes. One day we will die, and unless we've invested in the eternal, nothing remains.

Contrast the futility of Ecclesiastes with the riches of the gospel of Jesus. There is an inheritance that comes from God. The rich businessman missed it, even when confronted with death. Multitudes do. But the eyes of faith can see the riches of the Kingdom of God. Learn to live for them, at all costs.

Our Highest Purpose

God created man in his own image, in the image of God he created him; male and female he created them. GENESIS 1:27

IN WORD No one can live wisely and with purpose without realizing where we came from, where we are going, and why it all came about in the first place. That is the foundation for everything. If we don't understand that, we don't understand the gospel and we don't have the context to make daily decisions that will align with God's plan. We must know: We are created from Him, for Him, and in His likeness.

It's a remarkable truth. We were meant to be the image of God, and though the image was shattered in the Fall, God's original intention lives on. He was not surprised by the Fall, and His plan included fashioning a people who would reflect His glory. He still means for us to bear His image. That's why He has put His Spirit in the heart of sinful but redeemed mankind—these earthen vessels that we are. Humanity *will* bear His image. He *will* be seen in this creation. Never mind that His image-bearers once forfeited that privilege. Even before we lost it, He had determined to recraft it in us. He bears His image in us Himself.

IN DEED We get caught up in jobs, mortgages, family business, relationships, and pastimes, trying to find some sense of fulfillment in all of them. It's easy to get distracted that way. But we have a higher calling lying underneath it all. *We are made to be like Him!* That's the point of it all. That was the purpose of our first parents, and that is the purpose of our redemption. Adam and Eve were modeled after Him; but we are even inhabited by Him. We are daily being conformed to the image of God in Christ (2 Corinthians 3:18).

Do you live with that awareness? Are your mundane, daily decisions made with that in mind? Meditate on this amazing truth daily and let it guide your life. Whatever your other desires, there is no higher calling than this. It's what we were made for.

MAY 3
Genesis 1:26-28

The rule of life for a perfect person is to be in the image and likeness of God.

—Clement of Alexandria

One Too Many Voices

"Let all who are simple come in here!" she says to those who lack judgment. PROVERBS 9:4, 16

MAY 4

Proverbs 9

Common sense suits itself to the ways of the world. Wisdom tries to conform to the ways of heaven.

—Joseph Joubert

IN WORD Wisdom and Folly both take on a human voice in Proverbs; they are principles personified. Repeatedly throughout the book, Wisdom calls. So does Folly. Wisdom promises everlasting blessing; Folly promises a moment of pleasure. Their voices are incessant.

So which one is quoted in the verses above? Both. Wisdom in verse 4; Folly in verse 16. They say exactly the same thing. They speak to those who are simple and lacking in judgment; the only difference between the two sayings is in the response of the hearer.

Perhaps we are unaware of the constant call. Perhaps we do not realize that every choice is a response to a voice—the voice of Wisdom or the voice of Folly. When you are tempted, both are speaking. When you are in search of security, both call out. When you are making your plans, both compete for your attention. When you are spending your money and your time, they beckon. Have you not heard them? They always say the same thing: "Come in here!"

Wisdom is like a spouse—a permanent partner who is always there supporting you for your own good. Folly is like a prostitute—the promise is enticing, but the result is brief and disappointing. When Proverbs speaks of wives and prostitutes, faithfulness and adultery, it speaks in literal terms. But it also speaks figuratively. We make choices daily. We are faced with a repeated choice between Wisdom and Folly, and their voices can sound so much alike.

IN DEED Whose voice do you hear? Wisdom isn't flashy, rarely impresses, and never demands. Folly is brash, showy, and frequently pushy. She says you were put here to have a blast. Wisdom disagrees: You were put here to have—and to be— a blessing. Can you tell the difference? When they both call, to which voice are your ears attuned? Train them well—a lot is riding on your ability to hear.

Sin and a Holy God

To fear the LORD is to hate evil; I hate pride and arrogance,
evil behavior and perverse speech.   PROVERBS 8:13

IN WORD   The progression is a very natural one, but it is exceedingly dangerous. We struggle with our sin; we find we can't overcome it, so we accept it as part of who we are; and then we begin to redefine our own nature. We did the best we could, after all, so our human nature must not have been that bad to begin with. We end up with an "I'm okay, you're okay" perspective. We aim to do better, but we're comfortable if we can't.

MAY 5
Proverbs 8

No sin is small.

—Jeremy Taylor

The problem with being comfortable with sin is that it is entirely contrary to the nature of God. God is not comfortable with sin. He never just lets it slide. He paid for it—in full and with great sacrifice. From Genesis 3 through Revelation 20, it was never a light matter.

The book of Proverbs has told us that the fear of God is the beginning of wisdom. How? If we have a fear of God, we got it by rightly understanding how awesome He is. We got a glimpse of His holiness that drove us to our faces. We understood our need to plead for a reconciliation with an offended Creator. We saw His goodness, and by comparison, everything else looked evil. And since God is the standard by which all things are measured, our own nature didn't just *look* evil to us; it *was* evil. We grew to hate it.

IN DEED   There is a false attitude in many segments of the contemporary church. It is the belief that sin, being universal to human nature, is not all that serious. That belief leads one to a god who is lenient, as opposed to a God who forgives. The first god is nonexistent; only the latter can save.

Do you hate sin? Is it detestable to you? Then you are in line with God's wisdom. You know the difference between a lenient deity and a forgiving One, and you know which one to bow to.

Sin and a Way Out

I love those who love me, and those who seek me find me. PROVERBS 8:17

MAY 6
Proverbs 8

A sight of His
crucifixion
crucifies sin.

—Charles Spurgeon

IN WORD Though the bad news is devastating—that we are, in our sinful nature, contrary to God's character and out of line with His foundation of wisdom—the good news is that we can change. Wisdom does not remain forever elusive, no matter how firmly we have rejected it in the past. Even if folly has hounded us for years, we can still turn in a single moment to the voice of wisdom calling from the streets. It is not too late to become unfit for a sinful world and fit for the Kingdom of God.

The wisdom of God will lead us to the cross of Jesus, of course. That is where all of our former futility is redeemed and our rebellion forgiven. A humble bow before the sacrificial Lamb will cleanse us of the muck of this world and put us on a path of discipleship. But once we have passed through that Cross, we must cultivate our love for the eternal. We must pursue wisdom with a passion. We must become enamored with the righteous ways of the world as it was meant to be. When we do, we will find it.

IN DEED If you are ever lacking in perspective, read the first two and the last two chapters of the Bible. Genesis 1–2 and Revelation 21–22 are pictures of perfection. From paradise to paradise, from the Garden of Eden to the city of God, from the dust of the earth to the bride of Christ, wisdom rules. Take away the huge parentheses on the sin problem—Genesis 3 through Revelation 20—and you'll clearly see the holiness of God and the beauty of His handiwork. It's often hard, in this parenthetical interim, to see such beauty, but it's there. It's our origin and our destiny, all rolled into one.

As you read those four chapters, the eternal bookends on either side of the temporal sin-problem, let your love grow deep for your Creator and Redeemer. As a plant stretches toward the sunlight, let your life grow toward His wisdom. Open up before Him, and let yourself love His ways.

Sin and Assurance

*I was appointed from eternity, from the beginning,
before the world began.*   PROVERBS 8:23

IN WORD   Our human pride often reverses the order of things. We think God came into our lives rather late. Our identity was firmly established, and then He invited Himself in, trying to woo us into a relationship with Him. Those who are reading this have likely accepted His overtures, but even that acceptance can carry a certain pride with it. We were in control of the heart that opened up to Him. Or so we thought.

MAY 7

Proverbs 8

Lord my God, You have formed and reformed me.

—St. Anselm

In spite of our sense of independence, God has a prior claim on us. He created the world that became our necessary environment. He began the genetic process that eventually resulted in our birth. He even fashioned us in the womb (Psalm 139:13, Jeremiah 1:5). He is no late-coming Redeemer. He and His wisdom have been there all along.

This is extremely important to know when it seems as if your life is falling apart. It isn't. The life *you* have constructed may be falling apart, but the life God has fashioned is not. His wisdom has known all things before the foundation of the world—including you. If God has let you be undone, He has allowed it for a reason. He is bringing you to the end of your sinful self and to the beginning of life in His secure arms. He is stripping away your falsely constructed identity in order for you to find your identity in Him and His ways. Wisdom was appointed from eternity past; you are the latecomer. God is bringing you home.

IN DEED   Do you realize how thoroughly rooted in eternity your life is? It was not an afterthought in the mind of a play-it-by-ear God. Did you think your sin was a surprise to Him? It wasn't. He has already made provision for it. Before the foundation of the world, He did at least two things: He brought forth His wisdom; and He thought of you (Ephesians 1:4). His wisdom and your existence went hand in hand. Does that boggle your mind? It should. Rest in the assurance of a forever-wise God.

Sin, the Intruder

I was the craftsman at his side.
PROVERBS 8:30

With the Fall, all
became abnormal.

—Francis Schaeffer

IN WORD "In the beginning God created the heavens and the earth," begins the Bible. We can scarcely imagine a creation *ex nihilo*—something out of nothing. From the fingertips of God came things that did not previously exist. Emptiness was filled with substance. Life was spoken into a lifeless, formless cosmos.

That thought is staggering to our finite minds, but we must also remember that this was not only a material creation. The character of God lay under it all. The things that the voice of the Almighty spoke into being were placed on a preexistent foundation—wisdom. She was "the craftsman at his side," as this verse tells us. There is order and purpose there. All that we see that doesn't make sense to us—the violence of a self-obsessed world, the mayhem and madness, the death and disease—came into this creation as a virulent intruder through sin. It was not invited by wisdom's voice. It has no legitimate foundation, no legal right to be here except through the human rebellion that introduced it. God's creation was founded on inviolable principles; our sin is a vicious criminal trespassing on the Creator's property.

We have grown comfortable with this alien element, this sin pathology, but it has no place in a world built on wisdom. The very wisdom that underlay the creation of the world now calls to us. We can build our lives on the same principle that formed the foundation when God spoke in the beginning. But we have to forsake the intrusion of sin.

IN DEED Do you understand how violent sin is? Do you see it as an invasive cancer, the antithesis of life and a violation of the created order? Or do you see it sympathetically, as a series of understandable human flaws? Those who come to understand sin as the ultimate contradiction of the Creator's voice suffer genuine pain, but they become wise—and cleansed—in the process. They align themselves with the first foundation. They finally fit in a world based on wisdom.

Sin and God's Favor

Whoever finds me finds life and receives favor from the LORD. PROVERBS 8:35

IN WORD The stage is set for God to call forth those whose heart is His. He created His world on a foundation of wisdom, and wisdom beckons. Though we became misfits in the eternal plan, we were resurrected and refitted by the work of Wisdom Incarnate—Jesus. We now have all eternity lying before us. What will we do with it?

We have not yet entered into our rest. If God has not yet called us home to heaven, we are still living the eternal life on earth for a reason. But countless Christians have taken the treasure of eternal life and squandered it on foolish living. The wisdom of all eternity, the foundation of this world, is offered to us, and we so easily fail to take hold of it. Why?

The choice should be obvious. On the one hand, we have been offered the reliable Word of God, the cleansing blood of the Cross, the resurrected life, the power of the Holy Spirit, the fellowship of the body of Christ, the inheritance of the Son, and the very favor of God. On the other hand, we see momentary pleasures to be had, things to own, places to visit, people to use, money to spend, time to waste, rights to be defended, and comforts to be enjoyed. Only a fool would choose the latter, but we live in a foolish world. We have partaken of its passions and imbibed its philosophies. Eternal wisdom is offered so generously, yet we handle it so carelessly.

IN DEED We are always pursuing something. It may be material, like wealth, possessions, or pleasure. It may be less tangible, like status and accomplishments. It may even be spiritual, like peace of mind and heartfelt joy. But unless it's from God's own mind, it's futile.

The Christian who lives by God's wisdom finds that sin is not so much something to be overcome as it is something that becomes irrelevant. He finds a greater pursuit, and its benefits outweigh all other pursuits. What sin can compete? The favor of God flows like a fountain on those who seek His mind.

MAY 9
Proverbs 8

Sin forsaken is one of the best evidences of sin forgiven.

—J. C. Ryle

129

Guard the Inside

Above all else, guard your heart, for it is the wellspring of life. PROVERBS 4:23

Proverbs 4:20-27

Let us learn to cast our hearts into God.

—Bernard of Clairvaux

IN WORD If you're typical, you think of guarding your heart in terms of keeping things out. Corruption, false ideas, temptations—all are to be held at arm's length, never to be allowed in the inner depths of your affections. But there's another side to this vigilance. We are to keep things in. In fact, if we can master that, the corruptions and temptations will often take care of themselves.

Think about it: The things that can assail a heart from the outside are innumerable, far too overwhelming to manage. But the things we are told to keep within—the spirit of Jesus, the humility and gentleness, the servanthood and sacrifice, the worship and thankfulness—these are one Spirit. While most religions tell us to avoid the bad, God tells us to embrace Him. We are better equipped to focus on His character than on the enemy's devices. In fact, we are commanded to do so. Paul emphasizes this radically new discipleship: "Live by the Spirit, and you will not gratify the desires of the sinful nature" (Galatians 5:16). Nowhere are we told to live against the sinful nature and hope that the Spirit will show up. We're told to live by the Spirit and expect the sinful nature to have no power. We get confused about that often.

IN DEED Too many Christians guard the way into their hearts to keep things out. That may be appropriate at times, but try a different approach. Guard the way out. Stand at the inside of the gate, and be careful about what may be leaving. Once in a while, we get a life-altering glimpse of true worship. By all means, keep it in! From time to time, we'll see a picture of true servanthood. Don't let that picture go! Occasionally, we are touched by a spirit of sacrifice, moved by a ministry, or convinced by a powerful word from the Lord. Hold on to these things! Treasuring the wellspring that God has birthed in your heart will leave little room for those corruptions you once obsessed over. And the wellspring is a much more pleasant preoccupation.

Dreamers and Doers

He who works his land will have abundant food, but he who chases fantasies lacks judgment. PROVERBS 12:11

IN WORD Dreams are wonderful. God gives us dreaming hearts because He wants us to accomplish things. In the heart that dreams, God can plant visions of widespread, effective ministries, of preaching the gospel and helping the poor, of finding innovative ways to build the Kingdom of Heaven. He can inspire millions and set the course of nations. Dreams are the beginning of all good accomplishments.

The problem with dreams is that they are just the beginning. In themselves, they don't accomplish anything. They may be the fuel that feeds the fire, but they aren't its substance. A life full of fantasies, no matter how worthy the fantasies, is futile if no action ever springs forth from its ambitions. Though God plants dreams in our hearts, He does not simply leave them there. He expects the keepers of the land to till the soil, water the seeds, and cultivate their growth. God wants our visions to have a plan of action.

Jesus told a parable that illustrated that principle. A man had two sons. One of them said he would work in the vineyard but never did. The other said he wouldn't but eventually did anyway. Which one did Jesus praise? The doer, not the dreamer (Matthew 21:28-32).

IN DEED Do you have big plans? Do you have a vision you're convinced God has given you? If so, what are your plans? God is expecting you to take the visions He has given you and move them forward. Write the steps down. Then take them. Don't let your dreams become faint memories of the night.

Are you unsure of your dreams? Still trying to determine whether they are self-ordained or God-given? Then ask God specifically to encourage the ones that are also His dreams for you. But once you know the difference, don't let them sit. Ask for His timing. Ask for His wisdom. And act on His promises.

MAY 11

Proverbs 12:11;
Matthew 21:28-32

Dreams grow holy put into action.

—Adelaide Proctor

Why Not?

MAY 12
Psalm 9:1-10

Trust involves
letting go and
knowing God
will catch you.

—James Dobson

IN WORD Something is holding us back. Perhaps it is a fear that maybe we are wrong about God. Maybe we feel presumptuous. It is possible, if we have been disappointed in the past, that our misunderstanding is haunting us. We hear a voice in the back of our minds that says, "What if God doesn't come through? What if He makes it more difficult than I can handle? What if all my hopes are illusions?" So we hesitate to trust God. We pray and we hope, but faith remains incomplete and doubts linger. We'll ask Him to help us, but we withhold judgment until we've seen His response.

The call of Scripture is contrary to our natural inclination. We are called to believe God with reckless abandon—not just believe that He is there and that He is involved with us somehow, though we're not sure exactly how; but that He is actively, personally seeking our good and answering our prayers. We are to give up our own strategies and ambitions, to relinquish all "Plan Bs," to recklessly, irrevocably cast ourselves completely into His arms. But we're reluctant, and the problem always comes back to us: In spite of His track record, we don't seem to completely trust Him. Why not?

IN DEED God called Abraham to leave Haran and go to a place to be revealed later. Jesus invited Peter to step out of the boat and walk on water. That kind of call is scary, though typical in God's Kingdom. But why is it scary? Where could He lead us that we'd regret? Would He ever lead us into danger but not out of it?

God calls us to "reckless" trust, the kind that prepares no safety net and reserves nothing for a spiritually rainy day. That kind of trust, if broken, leaves no room to save face. But it can't be broken. Try to find someone God has forsaken, observe His faithfulness, and ask yourself: "Why *wouldn't* I trust Him wholeheartedly?" Think about it. Why not?

All-Seeing Eyes

*The eyes of the LORD are everywhere, keeping watch
on the wicked and the good.*   PROVERBS 15:3

IN WORD   Our knowledge of God's omnipresence is
somewhere in the back of our minds, but are we really aware
of it? There are few thoughts as sobering as this: Whatever
we do, whatever deep motives prompt us to do it, wherever
we go, and the reasons we go there, God sees. He knows our
every impulse, whether good or bad. We cannot tell Him a
story He does not already know the truth behind. We cannot
paint a pretty picture of our ugly scenes. He has seen it all.

That is more than a little disarming. We know, deep
down, what we are like. We know the little white lies we
tell others in order to make ourselves look good. We know
the real body under the cosmetics and the clothes, both literally and figuratively. We even know, at some level, that we
deceive ourselves about many things. When we strip away
all of the false securities we've constructed and the image
we've presented, we shudder to think of what we might see.
But that's exactly what God already sees.

There is great comfort in knowing about this all-seeing
God, too. Why? Because once we realize that He sees us as
we truly are, and understand that He has offered us this
wonderful invitation to be saved and loved by Him *anyway*,
we can relax in utter security. He has seen our worst and
it has not sent Him running in the other direction. He still
pursues us. He still asks for our fellowship. He sees all, and
it's okay.

IN DEED   There is no fooling God. Our acting ability is not
that good. The best relationship with Him is an honest one.
He learns nothing new by our honesty, but we cannot learn
anything about Him without it. When we drop the pose, we
find our security in Him rather than in our image. We know
His love must be deep; He loves *us*!

Be sobered by God's all-seeing eyes, and let that acute
awareness guide your every step. But rest in that awareness.
You can't take a step He hasn't already known.

MAY 13
*Proverbs 15:3;
Psalm 139:1-17*

God is always
near you and
with you; leave
Him not alone.

—Brother Lawrence

A Refuge and a Ruin

The way of the LORD is a refuge for the righteous, but it is the ruin of those who do evil. PROVERBS 10:29

MAY 14

Proverbs 10:29

The center of God's will is our only safety.

—Betsie ten Boom

IN WORD Early explorers who dared to cross oceans quickly learned a valuable lesson: The currents of the sea could carry them to their destination, if followed correctly. Those currents could also divert them from their journey, if ignored. The very same currents can have either a positive effect or a negative effect on a sailing vessel; it all depends on the knowledge and the response of the crew.

God's wisdom is, in some ways, like the currents of the sea. It can carry us where we need to go. It is our refuge, the means to keep us safe and bring us to our desired destination. But only if we follow it. The benefit of His wisdom only applies to those who are willing to line up with it and set their course accordingly. Otherwise, those same beneficial currents will lead to ruin.

History is filled with millions who have tried to follow a path contrary to God's wisdom. It may be a false religion or philosophy, a personal ambition, a political agenda, an economic strategy, or any other thing that we humans, in our ignorance, may set our hearts on. Millions have sailed against the currents of God and failed. Their end is miserable. What looked so promising was found to be futile. Anything that contradicts the eternal wisdom of the living God always is.

IN DEED Do you have a personal agenda? Plans for your future? Strategies for living a comfortable or rewarding life? Examine them closely and ask yourself if they are thoroughly consistent with God's ways. If not, you could sail comfortably for thousands of miles, thinking you're headed toward the right destination, only to find out you're far, far away. Even slight variations in the beginning can lead you way off course in the end. If you find out when you finally hit shore, it's too late. Plan now. Learn the currents. Take refuge in the wisdom of God.

The Battle Within

Give me an undivided heart, that I may fear your name. PSALM 86:11

IN WORD Is there a Christian alive who has not struggled with a dual nature? Probably not. We who are gloriously born of the Holy Spirit of God are also genetically confirmed, card-carrying descendants of Adam. The Spirit enables us to live godly lives, but our tendency to do so is sporadic. While our spirit is often willing, the flesh remains weak. The Jekyll-and-Hyde syndrome may be common to all mankind, but it is especially common to the redeemed. Two natures in one body can make for an exhausting struggle. Are you exhausted yet? Don't think you are alone. You're not.

The burden of the divided heart is common in Scripture. It is the burden of which Paul wrote in Romans 7—"I have the desire to do what is good, but I cannot carry it out" (v. 18). It is the same contradiction Peter felt, claiming one evening that he could never forsake his Lord, then denying Him three times the same dark night. Every one of us has—at least occasionally—known the anguish of a divided soul.

A false solution to the problem has become epidemic. It is to resign oneself to the lower of the two natures, forfeiting the call to be holy as God is holy (1 Peter 1:15). Mistakenly calling true holiness "legalism," we can become far too accepting of our corruption. We sometimes even embrace it. We give up the battle and let the old nature win.

IN DEED There is a wiser way, and it is the work of God's Spirit, not of ourselves. We will never be completely delivered from the fight until we are in heaven, but victory is possible. Paul said so (Romans 7:24-25), and after Pentecost, Peter would agree. God answers the prayer of the psalmist; an undivided heart is possible. *Ask for it daily!* Be aware of all that would compete for the throne of God in your heart. Take your attention off of it, whatever it is, and put it on the breathtaking beauty of God. Be captivated by Him alone. If your heart is immersed in Him, sin will have no room to thrive.

MAY 15
Psalm 86

No one ever lost out by excessive devotion to Christ.

—H. A. Ironside

Resist Flight

I said, "Oh, that I had the wings of a dove! I would fly
away and be at rest—I would flee far away and stay
in the desert; I would hurry to my place of shelter, far
from the tempest and storm."   PSALM 55:6-8

MAY 16
Psalm 55:4-8, 16-18

Nothing great was
ever done without
much enduring.

—Catherine of Siena

IN WORD   David was a man after God's own heart and a great, anointed king. But in many ways, he was just like us. Psalm 55 is an example. When the pressure was on, David just wanted to run away.

All of us have had similar urges. When life gets intense and troubles seem to offer no way out, we just want to get out of the situation. Every Christian who has been prepared by God and stretched to his or her limits can relate: There are times when we would do anything if God would just remove us from our trial. We'll pray for ways of escape, but God often leaves us surrounded until His time is right.

God has no scorn for such feelings. He made us and He knows our frailties. He understands our impulse to flee from whatever difficulties we face. But He also insists on our endurance, because it has spiritual results that nothing else can accomplish. And there is no way to learn endurance other than simply to endure. We can't learn it in principle or in theory; only pain can teach it to us. We must be put in a position of having to lean on our God and to learn of His ways. Experience is the only way to know Him.

IN DEED   The good news for those who go through intense trials and suffering is that once the impulse to flee is broken, God delivers. When endurance is complete, God removes the tribulation we endure. Every fear of verses 4-8 is followed by every blessing of verses 16-18. Our God does not leave us in our troubles. He has put us there to discover His provision; He will not withhold it indefinitely. There *will* be a day of deliverance. It is God who is enthroned forever (v. 19), not suffering. We don't have to flee; we simply call on the One who dwells above our trials.

The Perfect Word

Every word of God is flawless; he is a shield to those who take refuge in him. PROVERBS 30:5

IN WORD   In a world of shifting loyalties, devious cons, and ever-evolving ideas, we need to know where to anchor our souls. We aren't diligent enough to analyze every counterfeit that comes our way, nor are we perceptive enough to expose every false philosophy. Human rationalism is not equipped to establish eternal truth. That's why we need help. Only God can point us in the right direction.

It's a comfort when we are searching for absolutes to actually find them. According to this proverb, such absolute truth will shield us. What from? Every subtle deceit, every malicious word, every doctrinal error, and every false messiah. Much to our dismay, the world is full of empty promises. If we are left to ourselves to figure them all out, we will spend our lives tossed around on tumultuous waves of competing "truths." By the time we obtain understanding by our own efforts, it's too late to settle on the foundation of God's wisdom. In short, we need to be anchored in revelation.

IN DEED   How do we do that? A daily time in God's Word is a good first step. It works truth into our minds on a regular basis. But is that really enough? Is a daily quiet time, often on the run, enough to protect us against error?

Here's a good pattern to follow: First, ask God every day to convince your heart of His truth and to give you discernment of lies. Second, find at least one verse a week to memorize. Chew on it, let it sink in, look at it from every angle, and come up with specific ways to apply it. Third, don't just study God's Word. Fall in love with it. Consume it as voraciously as your favorite meal. God has a way of working into our hearts the things that we love. If we love the flawless Word, the flawless Word will dwell within us.

The New Testament affirms the proverb. We are to let the Word of Christ richly dwell within us (Colossians 3:16). Perhaps that would be a good memory verse to start with. Let it richly dwell in you this week. In a world of lies, isn't it good to know you can embrace something flawless?

MAY 17
*Proverbs 30:5;
Colossians 3:16*

We must both affirm the inerrancy of Scripture and then live under it.

—Francis Schaeffer

Unshakeable

When calamity comes, the wicked are brought down, but even in death the righteous have a refuge. PROVERBS 14:32

MAY 18

Proverbs 14:32;
Psalm 71:1-3

As sure as God puts His children in the furnace, He will be in the furnace with them.

—Charles Spurgeon

IN WORD How do you react in a crisis? Or, to ask an even more revealing question, how do you react in the minor irritations of everyday life? The answer is not a matter of what you say you believe. It's a matter of your familiarity, even intimacy, with your Father. As much as we say that He is trustworthy and true, our tower of strength and our shield, those are only words until they are tested. And in this world, they are tested often.

Have you ever known Christians who believe the right things about God but who panic at every difficulty? It's hard to believe that someone's belief in the sovereignty and faithfulness of God are more than skin deep when his panic sets in. The truth of our relationship with God comes out when the heat is on. We discover whether we really trust Him or not when we're put in a position of having to trust Him. A belief in God's providence means little until one lacks essentials, and a belief in God's strength means little until one is completely helpless. Then the truth comes out.

Those who have not put their trust in the Refuge, who ignore Him and go their own way, are wicked, according to the Bible. That may seem harsh, but that's the true assessment of the human rebellion. And those who do not really trust Him will be brought down by every calamity. Those who do trust Him can't be brought down by anything—even death.

IN DEED So where do you stand? Do you have a shallow belief in God's faithfulness, applying His promises to others' situations but not to your own? We are called to live in a different dimension than we once lived in. We must *know* who our Fortress is. We are not to become strong; we are to find our strength in Him. We must let His peace speak louder to us than our trials do. God stands firm when everything else moves. Can you?

Taming a Destroyer

The tongue also is a fire, a world of evil among the parts of the body. It corrupts the whole person. JAMES 3:6

IN WORD Every summer, the news story is repeated. Someone in the western United States fails to completely put out a campfire, and from a single ember, a forest blazes. Firefighters battle the consuming enemy from ground and air, and governments spare no expense to extinguish it, but it is relentless. There is virtually no stopping a raging forest fire until the rains come. Before they do, millions of acres are destroyed. And it all starts with one spark.

Such is the power of the tongue, says James. Words burn. Once they've ignited, there is no undoing them. The only way to prevent massive damage is to prevent the sparks that start it all. Once spoken, words cannot be unspoken. Combined with the gossip-prone nature of the human community, words spread rapidly. It is virtually impossible to put them out.

The tongue must be tamed. Its destructive capabilities call for the utmost carefulness. Its corruption spreads outward and it also works inward. Words not only distort the perceptions of others, they train our own minds to follow. A careless comment becomes a deeply held conviction all too quickly. There is no such thing as idle chatter. Words matter.

IN DEED How careful are you with your tongue? Biblical wisdom has much to teach us about the power of speech. "The things that come out of the mouth come from the heart, and these make a man 'unclean,'" Jesus said (Matthew 15:18). Words reveal our inner impurities, and those impurities may offend others. The childhood saying about sticks and stones simply isn't true. Words can hurt.

Guard your tongues. They can set the whole course of your life, according to James. Anything with that kind of power must be tamed.

MAY 19
James 3:1-12

Cold words freeze people, hot words scorch them, and bitter words make them bitter.

—Blaise Pascal

139

Releasing a Blesser

With the tongue we praise our Lord and Father, and with it we
curse men, who have been made in God's likeness.   JAMES 3:9

Kind words also
produce their
image on men's
souls; and a beau-
tiful image it is.

—Blaise Pascal

IN WORD   Positive words seem less volatile than negative words, but their power can be surprising. A good word
can edify. It can confirm the talents, skills—even the life
direction—of someone who only needed a little encouragement to keep going. It can change the course of someone's
day, which in turn can change the course of that person's
week, month, or year. The snowball effect of a comment can
run in an edifying direction just as easily as a destructive
one. Why would anyone neglect such a powerful tool?

Not only can our mouths bless others, they can also
draw attention to the glory of God. They can tell of His great
works, witness to His unfathomable mercy, and marvel at
His remarkable ways. They can be heard in the darkest corners of this world, in the assemblies of the saints, and in the
halls of heaven. They can enter His gates with thanksgiving
and tell of His marvelous greatness. They can shout with a
voice of triumph and proclaim His mercies to all nations. In
fact, our mouths were created entirely for such purposes.

It is a violation of the tongue's created design to degrade,
denigrate, demean, or destroy. It is even a violation to exces-
sively express its discontentment and criticism. The tongue
was formed exclusively—or at least primarily—to bless. It
was given to bless others and to bless God. In so doing, it
will bless our own selves.

IN DEED   Do you have this remarkable tool stashed away
somewhere? Have you failed to use this potent source of
blessing? If negative words come out of your mouth, reverse
the trend. Use your mouth to bless at all times. You will find
the current of your life to flow in a corresponding direction.
When blessing comes out of your heart, God makes sure
that blessing comes into it. Release your tongue to do what
it was meant to do.

Accept No Substitutes

If I have put my trust in gold or said to pure gold,
"You are my security," . . . I would have been
unfaithful to God on high.   JOB 31:24, 28

IN WORD   Moses once gave a very long discourse on the blessings of obeying God and the curses of disobedience. God had entered a covenant with His people, one on which He would never default. Would His people? Moses explained what would happen if they did. Their enemies would lay siege to their cities "until the high fortified walls in which [they] trust fall down" (Deuteronomy 28:52).

That is one of the dreadful results of sin: We begin to trust our best efforts rather than the ever-dependable God. Our faith in God crumbles, and we must come up with substitutes, however flawed they may be. In Moses' speech, it was the high walls of cities—protection, just in case God happened to fail! In Job's lament, it's gold—provision, just in case God happened to lack! There is no shortage of securities that we set up to ensure our safety, health, comfort, or pleasure. We can depend upon them heavily. When we do, we take a huge risk: We may gradually learn to place more trust in them than in God. By God's standards, that's unfaithfulness.

IN DEED   Where do you look for your sense of peace? An account? An education? The national defense? Airport security stations? Standard airbags? The list could go on for pages. Not that there's anything wrong with earthly insurance in the various forms it takes. But our trust in wealth or walls can be a veiled statement of mistrust in God. He must let our false securities fail before our trust turns back to Him.

Don't you remember? His eye is on the sparrow and the hairs on your head are numbered. The *only* thing that can undo you is your deliberate disobedience, and even then it's under His supervision. Let yourself trust the One who is unfailingly trustworthy. Accept no substitutes. Rest in His sovereign arms.

MAY 21
Job 31:24-28

It is not our trust that keeps us, but the God in whom we trust who keeps us.

—Oswald Chambers

141

Responding to Pain

No harm befalls the righteous, but the wicked have their fill of trouble. PROVERBS 12:21

MAY 22

Proverbs 12:21

Trials enable people to rise above religion to God.

—Brother Andrew

IN WORD Several years ago, a rabbi wrote a popular book asking why bad things happen to good people. It's a legitimate question; we see godly folks go through some very difficult things. So doesn't our experience contradict this proverb? Must we generalize this verse and water it down to get anything out of it? Not necessarily. We need to approach this proverb with some clear definitions. We need to define "harm," and we need to define "righteous."

Who is righteous? Surely not those who have it all together. None of us do. The proverb would be unrealistic if it meant that, and the Bible isn't unrealistic. Those who are righteous know who God is and hang on to that knowledge regardless of the situation. They desire God enough to trust Him. Their past may not be righteous, but their direction is.

What is "harm"? Surely not difficult circumstances or pain. Otherwise, the proverb would be a shallow assumption based on fantasy, and the Bible's not a shallow fantasy. No, trials and pain are not ultimately harmful unless they diminish our relationship with God. But the righteous will not let them do that. They let their trials draw them closer to God. They see His grace more clearly in the aftermath of pain; they trust Him more truly when obstacles hinder trust; they serve Him more sacrificially when it costs something. Through pain, we see Him better, and He becomes more real to us. There is no harm in that.

IN DEED This proverb is less about the trials that befall us than our reaction to them. Nothing that the righteous go through is truly harmful if faith is maintained. But troubles are troublesome indeed to those whose faith is conditional. Their love of God depends only on what He does to make them feel good.

Trials come to all, and our reaction defines us. Are we righteous or wicked? The test of pain will make it clear.

Shedding the Past

Forgetting what is behind and straining toward what is ahead,
I press on toward the goal. PHILIPPIANS 3:13-14

IN WORD It's easy to live with regrets. Some people are able never to look back, but most of us can point to a few decisions that keep us wondering what life would have been like if we'd done things differently. Those kinds of thoughts can cripple us. They haunt us and keep us preoccupied with the past.

Two truths will keep the past from stealing our joy in the present: our identification with Jesus and our faith in God's sovereignty. The enemy will seize the opportunity to remind us of our failures and accuse us of disobedience. He may be right, of course, but we aren't living on the basis of what we have or haven't done. We live fully identified with Jesus. We stand before God on the basis of what *He* has done.

A firm conviction that God is sovereign will also protect us from our regrets. Even when we've made missteps, we can trust that God knew about them before the foundation of the world and planned to compensate accordingly. Nothing we've done has surprised Him. He has known all along how to bring us in line with His will—even when we've walked far away from it.

IN DEED God never asked us to check the rearview mirror in order to lament about our shortcomings. We confessed when we came to Jesus that we were sinful failures, and He saved us. It's time to move forward.

Do memories of the past hound you? Take an active stance against them. Point the enemy to Jesus as the basis of your righteousness—his accusations are irrelevant once you've found your identity in the perfect Son of God. And remember the sovereignty of God. Find heroes of the faith in Scripture who failed—it's a pretty easy task—and see how God sovereignly worked out His purposes in spite of their failures. Rest in the present and look forward with hope. Nothing in your past can thwart God's plan.

MAY 23
Philippians 3:12-14

God is not defeated by human failure.

—William J. C. White

An Illusion Undone

When your judgments come upon the earth, the people of the world learn righteousness. ISAIAH 26:9

MAY 24
Isaiah 26:7-11

The gem cannot be polished without friction, nor man perfected without trials.

—Anonymous

IN WORD The strange tendency of human nature is to thrive under distress and to stray under prosperity. We usually don't see it that way because we define thriving in terms of our circumstances. But God defines it in terms of our attitude and growth in Him. And we grow best when we're in trouble.

Why is that? Pain has been the catalyst for spiritual growth ever since the early pages of Scripture. We see it most dramatically in the book of Judges: Every time the people prospered, they strayed from God. Every time they cried out, He delivered them. Then the cycle would be repeated all over again. It's a cycle we know well in our individual lives, and the principle is almost mathematical in its precision. Ease equals apostasy and pain equals a heart hungry for God. Why?

Because we are motivated by need. When all seems well in our circumstances, we don't think we have needs. It's a dangerous illusion because it masks the spiritual poverty we all share. Somehow, a set of circumstances that highlights our need—one that corresponds directly with our spiritual poverty—gets us to see the lack of self-sufficiency we should have known all along. It turns our eyes toward God in the physical, which in turn can turn our eyes toward Him in the spiritual. It's His mercy that puts us in a crisis. Crises drive our once-passive hearts to Him.

IN DEED Do you consider this principle when you're in the midst of a trial? It may not be the only reason for your trouble, but it is certainly one possibility. Your crisis may be the perfect occasion for you to "learn righteousness"—to direct your attention to God and to wait for His Word. He draws us close through such occasions. We are always given a chance to grow deeper into Him when our outward situation matches our inner condition. We learn to seek the One who matters. If you're in trouble, seek Him zealously.

Holy Satisfaction

Death and Destruction are never satisfied, and neither are the eyes of man. PROVERBS 27:20

IN WORD Nearly every child has sworn an oath to his parents: "Just buy me this one thing, and I'll never ask for anything else again." It's a hollow promise from the beginning; every parent knows it isn't true.

Nearly every Christian has offered a similar prayer to God: "Just answer this one thing, and I promise I'll be satisfied." It's a hollow promise. God knows better. Deep down, so do we.

What is it about human nature that is always craving but is never content? We've all approached milestones in our lives with the thought that once the milestone is accomplished, we'll be happy with our lives. But we never are. As soon as the next job is realized, the next house is bought, the next car is driven, the next relationship results in marriage, or whatever we're looking forward to is accomplished, we set our sights on something new.

Whatever the reason, we can know at least one thing about our cravings: They indicate that we're missing something deep within us. We have a gnawing hunger for more meaning, more purpose, more results. We can thank God that He made us that way; it's His design for our fruit-bearing and our growing relationship with Him. But we also have to be aware of how sin has distorted that design. We turn it toward possessions, people, places, and personal agendas. Instead of letting a holy discontentment drive us toward God and His Kingdom, we let a twisted discontentment drive us toward fulfilling our needs in unholy ways. We're looking for life in all the wrong places.

IN DEED The proverb is true; the eyes of man are never satisfied. But a maturing relationship with God will shine light on our dissatisfaction. It will also turn it toward the things that really fulfill us. We will find that it is, in fact, possible to be content with the things of the world and still be driven by a desire for God. He is the only One who satisfies.

MAY 25
*Proverbs 27:20;
Ecclesiastes 6:7*

It is so important not to waste what is precious by spending all one's time . . . complaining over what one does not have.

—Edith Schaeffer

Fleeting Emotions

We live by faith, not by sight.
2 CORINTHIANS 5:7

MAY 26

2 Corinthians 5:1-7

Faith is the bird that sings while it is yet dark.

—Max Lucado

IN WORD We fallen humans generally make decisions by sight, and sight usually takes one of three forms: (1) We let our emotions be the guide. In other words, we do what we want to do, and pride and feelings rule; (2) we take a commonsense approach, evaluating the pros and cons and the risks involved in each course of action; and (3) we seek supernatural guidance, often in pagan ways—by stars and horoscopes, mediums and spiritists, and even best-selling self-help gurus.

There are profound problems with each approach. Consider the first one today. It traps many believers. God created our emotions and He intends for them to be fulfilled, but He does not intend for them to rule us. If they did, our lives would be roller-coaster rides, up and down with every whim and trend. There can be no consistency in such an approach to life, and there can be no worship of God. God transcends our feelings, and when we elevate them above His wisdom, we are placing ourselves on the throne of our own heart—where only He belongs. Emotional guidance is a disastrous way to live. It sets the course of our lives based on the mood of the moment. We end up living with immeasurable regrets. Sooner or later, we find out: He who does whatever he wants at any given moment is like an animal—and a fool.

IN DEED God's prescription for our wisdom is to find His. His is constant; His is eternal; His is deeply rooted in reality—the way things *really* are. It is not trendy, and it is not superficial. In short, His wisdom is everything our emotions are not.

A believer who forsakes his or her own feelings for the much more reliable guidance of the eternal God has become wise. That believer must realize that feelings are not forever shunned; God created us for emotional fulfillment. But we are much more fulfilled when He fills us, not when we try to fill ourselves with our own shortsighted cravings. Sight is limited; faith is not. We must walk by faith, not sight.

Fallible Logic

We live by faith, not by sight.
2 CORINTHIANS 5:7

IN WORD   Consider the second approach of human wisdom—common sense. It is higher and more noble than the selfish life of those who are subject to their emotions and desires. It is based on the best logic we can muster. We make lists of pros and cons; we evaluate the risks involved in each course of action; and we determine the clearest, safest, most profitable direction. It is the best, most reliable path that human reasoning can offer. But it is still profoundly human. And it is still sight, not faith.

In essence, the commonsense approach is an intellectual way of "playing the odds" in life. It is not much different than a gambler at the track who has thoroughly studied the horses and calculated the best candidates to win, place, and show. We can approach life with the same mind. We aim for the best education, locate in the safest, most comfortable area, plan for the most satisfying career, and save for the future. Nothing is wrong with any of those activities if they are built on a foundation of eternal wisdom and under the guidance of God. But we often skip the foundation and miss the guidance. We trust in our own devices and place our bets on the best life we can. In short, we exalt our limited logic over the voice of the Eternal. Even if we succeed in the eyes of men, we fail in the eyes of heaven.

IN DEED   As we have learned, God's prescription for our wisdom is to find His. His is thoroughly sensible, but it only appears so with the eyes of faith. Eyes that see beyond the ambitions of this world to the true values of the eternal Kingdom will have different criteria for making decisions. Faith often forsakes the things of this world for the lasting treasures of the Kingdom. Faith looks not for the longest physical life possible but for the most fruitful life possible. Faith understands that God's wisdom often appears absolutely senseless to those with worldly sense. His Word is full of examples: Conservative sight does no miracles; "risky" faith does nothing else.

MAY 27
2 Corinthians 5:1-7

Everything Jesus Christ taught was contrary to common sense.

—Oswald Chambers

Fallen Faith

We live by faith, not by sight.
2 CORINTHIANS 5:7

MAY 28
2 Corinthians 5:1-7

The essence of faith is being satisfied with all God is for us in Jesus.

—John Piper

IN WORD Of the three approaches to decision making we usually take, the third—supernatural guidance—can be the most rewarding. It can also be the most disastrous. It all depends on where we place our faith. Just as it is possible to walk by faulty sight, it is possible to walk by faith and still be wrong. Living by faith rather than sight is no guarantee; faith can be misplaced.

Consider all of the supernatural offerings our world lays before us: seances, mediums, horoscopes, channelers, spirit guides, psychics, and more. The more overt of these are laughable to the ordinary believer. But they can also take highly subtle forms. Don't believe it? Go to a bookstore and read excerpts from the self-help section. Some of it is human or even biblical wisdom dressed up as something new. But much of it has cultic connotations. Our age is not lacking in mystics proclaiming the way to happiness, the way to fulfillment, the way to self-actualization. The problem is that unless it comes from God's revelation of what's *really* real, it's always the wrong way.

All supernatural sources of guidance apart from God are forbidden in Scripture—even when dressed up as "advice" and marketed to a general audience. The Christian who seeks them is an idolater. It is a slap in God's face to seek advice from horoscopes, unbiblical gurus, and anyone else falsely claiming wisdom from above. It suggests that there might be a higher—or at least more accessible—source than God. But He is the ultimate authority and He is available. Why go anywhere else?

IN DEED Seeking supernatural guidance is a biblical mandate. But we must take this mandate with care and discernment. It cannot be just any supernatural guidance; it must be God's revelation. Do not trust your emotions, your common sense, or the spiritual seductions of this age. Depend on God alone. Dare to live by genuine, exclusive faith.

Fearful First Steps

We live by faith, not by sight.
2 CORINTHIANS 5:7

IN WORD The problem most of us encounter in this life of faith is that we must base our decisions, our futures, our families, our jobs—our everything, in fact—on realities we cannot see. Not only can we not see them clearly—though God will open our eyes to them more clearly if we ask—those around us cannot see them, either. That's where the misunderstandings, the rejection, and even the ridicule come in. When we live by faith, we are at first uncertain of where we're going. We can't see very far in front of us. And our family members and friends are watching. While we're barely understanding our next steps, they can't understand them at all.

The principles of this world are all based on sight. Our human culture likes tangible evidence. It has learned to thrive on the limitations we've been given. But start bucking those limitations and see how quickly your peers back off. When you refuse to live by sight, you refuse to play the games of this world. You reject its most foundational beliefs. Religion is only speculative, we've been told. Our world doesn't mind us believing whatever we want, as long as we don't base our lives on the unseen. But when the eyes of faith are opened to the greater reality of God's Kingdom, the label of "unstable" or even "crazy" comes quickly.

Just ask Abraham, whose mission it was to move to a place he would be told of later, and who was promised a most improbable son. Or Moses, who was called to demand from a hostile ruler the release of a million profitable slaves. Or Elisha, who was surrounded by a vicious army, but more greatly encompassed by heavenly hosts. Or Mary, who bore the Son of God by quite unconventional—and socially unacceptable—means.

IN DEED Are you afraid to live by faith? Welcome to the club. But the Faith Hall of Fame in Hebrews 11 was made of such a club. Be bold and forsake nearsightedness. Faith sees more than sight ever can.

MAY 29
2 Corinthians 5:1-7

The ultimate ground of faith and knowledge is confidence in God.

—Charles Hodge

149

Fertile Lives

We live by faith, not by sight.
2 CORINTHIANS 5:7

MAY 30

2 Corinthians 5:1-7

You honor Jesus
when you act in
faith on His Word.

—Ed Cole

IN WORD Most of us try to get through life on human
wisdom. Some of us succeed. Others of us make so many
mistakes that we die with innumerable regrets. If only we
could get guidance from above, we would get this "life"
stuff right. If only we could hear the voice of the One who
knows. If only.

The truth is that we can. The Voice has spoken. His
words are available to us. But there's a catch. We have to be
willing to obey it. Otherwise, we won't have what Jesus calls
"ears to hear." Those who obey what they already know of
God have their ears opened to more; and those who have
their ears open are readily obedient. It's a precious cycle,
conceived in the mind of God: Obedience begets hearing,
which begets obedience, which begets hearing, which . . .
you get the picture.

The life of faith is a life of obedience, and a life of obedience is a life of faith. The root of the problem is that most of
us have trouble, however minor it may be, with obedience.
We lose our "ears to hear," and as a result, we fall back on
human wisdom. Our lives never match those of the biblical heroes. Why? Human wisdom would not have pushed
Abraham up a hill to sacrifice his son; it would not have led
God's people to the edge of the Red Sea with an army in
pursuit; it would not have marched around Jericho seven
times and blasted a trumpet for the wall to fall; it would not
have matched David with Goliath in the valley; and, most
strikingly, human wisdom would not have vilified the Son
of God on a cross in order to save a wretched race.

IN DEED Really, when it comes down to it, would you
prefer to live by the human logic that results from losing
your ears to hear? Or would you prefer the cutting-edge,
risky-but-real life of a true, radical believer? The answer isn't
clear for everyone. But we've seen who lasts. Your Bible is
full of their stories. They lived by faith, not by sight.

Humble Reminders

Those who walk in pride he is able to humble.
DANIEL 4:37

IN WORD Somewhere deep inside, we know the truth about ourselves: Everything we have was given to us. None of us asked to be born or specified the conditions under which we came into this world. We did not choose our talents or our physical features. We did not select our place of birth or our native language. We may have been industrious and careful in choosing our paths, but our drive and our wisdom was given to us by our Creator. We did not make our own circumstances, build our own brains, or control our own relationships. Everything we have is a gift.

Even so, we take an awful lot of credit for the good things God has given. We take pride in our work, display our accomplishments, advertise our abilities, and use our relationships for our own esteem. For people who were created, we act an awful lot like creators.

Nebuchadnezzar, king of Babylon during the time of Daniel, made that mistake. Having seen ample evidence of God in Daniel's dream interpretations and in the survival of three guys in a furnace, Nebuchadnezzar nonetheless gave himself glory frequently. He had built a golden representation of himself to be worshiped, and he credited himself with the power and glory of Babylon.

God gave the king a clear reminder that all gifts, all power, all wisdom, and all authority come from above. He humbled Nebuchadnezzar with insanity. He demonstrated the lowliness of human achievement. He undid the king's pride.

IN DEED God will undo our pride too. Perhaps we aren't as arrogant and bold as Nebuchadnezzar was, but we often need reminders of our neediness. We can't relate to God properly unless we understand that all we have and all we are is by grace. When we take credit, we deny God's generosity. That is not a minor offense. His love will correct us.

Wake up each morning with a self-reminder that your life is all about grace. It will keep you humble and it will open God's arms to you. It will ground you in the truth.

MAY 31
Daniel 4:28-37

He that is down need fear no fall, he that is low no pride.

—John Bunyan

Kingdom Currency

You are all sons of God through faith in Christ Jesus, for all of you who were baptized into Christ have clothed yourselves with Christ. GALATIANS 3:26-27

JUNE 1
Galatians 3:22-29

Ultimately, faith is the only key to the universe.

—Thomas Merton

IN WORD How do you relate to God? Most people, after being saved by grace through faith, then quickly embark on a hybrid life of faith and legalism. It isn't that we don't believe in God, or even that we don't trust Jesus for salvation; the problem is that our belief is often based on the quality of our works. When we serve God well, we assume He looks on us favorably. When we stumble, we assume He turns His back on us until we repent.

There's an element of truth in that; we know that God looks with favor on the righteous, and that He disciplines His children who tolerate sin and rebellion in their lives. But in accepting these truths, we often take it a step further: We begin to relate to God on the basis of what we have and haven't done. We pray with more confidence when we've been good, and we serve with more enthusiasm when we've been obedient. We forget how dependent we are as children of grace. We begin to base our faith on how well we've done rather than how good He is. We begin to think of obedience as a means to stay in His good graces and not as a response to the fact that He has already made us righteous.

We stand holy before God. No, we aren't righteous in ourselves, but we've been clothed in the righteousness of Jesus. We've been given a sacred right to speak to the Eternal about the problems of today. And while we speak, we dare not assume that the quality of our works procured that right. God only accepts one currency in His Kingdom, and there is no exchange rate. Our business with Him must be done only with the currency of faith.

IN DEED What currency do you try to pass off in the Kingdom of God? Is it ever anything other than faith in the righteousness of Jesus Himself? If so, remind yourself daily: Only Jesus is acceptable to God—for prayer, for ministry, for anything. And we are only "in Jesus" by faith.

Radical Transformation

Just as he who called you is holy, so be holy in all you do; for it is written: "Be holy, because I am holy."   1 PETER 1:15-16

IN WORD   Our familiarity with the gospel often dulls us to history's most spectacular truth: Human beings can have a relationship with the unimaginably awesome God. Perhaps having heard this so many times has led us to take it for granted, but it's Scripture's most startling claim and a truly overwhelming thought for anyone who will let it sink in.

JUNE 2
1 Peter 1:13-16

To love Jesus is to love holiness.

—David Smithers

What makes this possible? The cleansing sacrifice of Jesus removes our impurity and makes us pure. But this is the legal side of the issue. What makes an ongoing, intimate relationship with the Almighty a practical reality? Holiness. The process of becoming like Him. Those among us who need impressive theological terms to validate a doctrine call it "sanctification." If the substitutionary sacrifice of Jesus is the basis for our relationship with God, our sanctification is its practical application. We cannot know Him well without it.

That's what makes this truth of a relationship with God so startling. When we first learn who He is, we come face-to-face with an overwhelming obstacle: A thoroughly sinful man cannot get along with a perfectly holy God without one of them having a radical change of character, and we know God isn't going to be the one to change. He can't. It must be us.

IN DEED   Far too many Christians are content with the legal basis of their salvation without taking much thought to apply it to their daily lives. But we cannot know Him— *really* know Him, as in a relationship—unless we become like Him. That will hurt. It does painful damage to our sinful nature to become holy. We are slow to let it go.

Have you assumed that God would never ask you to forsake some of your natural tendencies? Don't. He certainly will. That sin you tolerate? Let it go. However painful it is, let Him rework you. Abandon all that isn't just like His pure, perfect character. Be holy.

Radical Abandon

Just as he who called you is holy, so be holy in all you do; for it is written: "Be holy, because I am holy." 1 PETER 1:15-16

1 Peter 1:13-16

The serene beauty of a holy life is the most powerful influence in the world next to the power of God.

—Blaise Pascal

IN WORD Our personal holiness is not a picky prerequisite handed down by a morally demanding God. It is the means to a fountainhead of blessing. Perhaps we thought it was a necessary inconvenience, something God required in theory, but which we could never fully attain. Perhaps we thought it was all for His benefit and not really for ours. That's likely a problem for every Christian who straddles the fence between the call to holiness and an indulgence of misdirected desires. When it comes down to it, we don't really believe that our becoming like Jesus—our sanctification—will really benefit us where we live today.

But we are dreadfully wrong. There is immeasurable blessing for those who will single-mindedly pursue the righteousness of God that is found in Christ. "Seek first his kingdom and his righteousness, and all these things will be given to you as well" (Matthew 6:33). "The eyes of the LORD range throughout the earth to strengthen those whose hearts are fully committed to him" (2 Chronicles 16:9). We are offered all sorts of riches in unthinkable abundance, yet we hang on to our withered, sinful natures as if our only security is found there. That's often the posture of the human flesh when it is threatened by a holy calling, and it's pitiful.

IN DEED Does a deep suspicion of holiness lie beneath your struggle to forsake sinfulness? In faith, do all you can to abandon it. Read of Joseph, who reaped amazing long-term benefits from his commitment to remain pure. Read of Job, who was doubly blessed because of his commitment to maintain his belief in God's faithfulness. Read of any biblical figure—Old Testament or New—and try to find someone who was all-out faithful to God and yet was not blessed. Yes, that's a challenge. Accept it, and be encouraged by what you discover.

A Place of Rest

*Do not be anxious about anything, but in everything, by prayer
and petition, with thanksgiving, present your requests to God. And
the peace of God, which transcends all understanding, will guard
your hearts and your minds in Christ Jesus.* PHILIPPIANS 4:6-7

IN WORD We are easily caught up in anxious thoughts. Anxiety can keep us thinking obsessively about a certain problem, occupying all of our time and energy. We pray about the situation, asking God to intervene. But still we are consumed with it. Shedding our anxiety does not come easily.

Paul gives us wise advice. It is, in fact, a command: "Do not be anxious about anything." How can we follow this? We can go through the motions of prayer, but how can this kind of peace sink into our hearts in the midst of a difficult problem? By praying with thanksgiving and full trust that the problem is God's. In this kind of prayer, we transfer ownership of our situation to God. We do not need to be wrapped up in it; it is His.

There is no way to come to this place of rest unless we are able to relinquish our agenda in the situation. We must become willing for God to work it out any way He chooses, whatever the result to us. It seems scary to relinquish control, but we were never really in control anyway. And what outcome might God work out that would not be entirely good? He is completely trustworthy with our problems.

IN DEED Are you going through a difficult trial? Relinquish your goals in it. In your heart, transfer ownership of the situation to God. Our anxiety comes from a false sense of control—a sense that we perhaps are responsible to manipulate the crisis to work out for good. That's God's job. Let go of your will, and let your heart and your mind be at peace.

JUNE 4
Philippians 4:4-7

Pray, and let God worry.

—Martin Luther

Humble Deeds

Who is wise and understanding among you? Let him show it by his good life, by deeds done in the humility that comes from wisdom. JAMES 3:13

JUNE 5
James 3:13-18

He who knows himself best esteems himself least.

—Henry G. Brown

IN WORD If Proverbs is the wisdom book of the Old Testament, James is the wisdom book of the New. There, the profound theology of the early church is applied. Real faith is demonstrated and good works are the result. The truth of the gospel comes to life for the poor, the widows, the tongues of the saints, the suffering church, and the faithful who pray. And, according to James, it is all characterized by humility.

Why is humility a natural by-product of wisdom? Because wisdom knows who God is and it knows who we are. It sees the remarkable contrast between the two and accepts that God has saved us anyway. It acknowledges the utter depravity of the human condition, but affirms the glory of redemption. Where can pride fit into such an understanding? It can't. Wisdom rules it out. Humility grows in those who see things as they really are.

When we find pride in the church, we can be sure there are believers there who don't really understand the gospel. Pride can never exist where the gospel is clearly understood. The fact that we all struggle with pride doesn't alter that truth at all; we all struggle with the depth and the majesty of the gospel as well. It takes a lifetime to really sink in.

IN DEED Ask yourself a probing question. Do your good works result in pride or in humility? If in pride, then you are doing them to earn favor from God. That is not the gospel, it is legalism. If in humility, then you are doing them because of the amazing grace you've experienced.

Be extremely wary of pride, but do not mistake it for satisfaction. The wise and understanding life of which James speaks is deeply satisfying, but it is not proud. How can it be? The good news of the mercy of God precludes it. Grace removes all sense of worthiness. We do our deeds in humility because we have no other reason to do them.

God's Good Favor

A good man obtains favor from the LORD, but the LORD condemns a crafty man.   PROVERBS 12:2

IN WORD   We might think that the opposite of a good man is a bad man. Not so, according to this verse. A good man is contrasted here with a crafty man. God bestows no favor on those who—like the serpent in the Garden—are devious.

Our world praises shrewdness. But shrewdness has a devious side; craftiness manipulates people for one's own ends. Why is it so tolerable to the world and so odious to God? Because the desire to serve self is common to all humanity. Those who do it best are often admired. But craftiness says volumes about a person's belief in God. Those who are cunning do not expect God to help them; they must help themselves. They do not expect God to honor goodness; they must seek their own good. They do not believe God is watching; they are in this world for themselves. In short, a crafty person denies who God is.

All of us have a tendency to manipulate circumstances. We want to stack the odds in our favor, to set the best course before us, to get everyone else on our side. But the more focused we become on our position in this world—whether at work, at home, at church, or in any other social situation—the less focused we become on God. We cannot have our eyes on our own agenda and God's simultaneously unless ours is perfectly in line with His—and it rarely, if ever, is.

IN DEED   Being "good" in the eyes of God and in the definition of Scripture involves a hands-off approach to the things that belong to God. He is the Master of our circumstances; there is no need for our guile. The opportunities He wants us to have will be opened before us. The people He wants us to know will come into our path. No manipulation is necessary—or even welcome. All that He requires from us is our willing obedience to His plan. That, above all else, obtains His favor.

JUNE 6
Proverbs 12:2;
Psalm 5:12

When you get your own way, you nurse a hideous idol called self. But when you give up your way, you get God.

—Janet Erskin Stewart

157

The Power of Pleasantness

*Pleasant words are a honeycomb, sweet to the soul
and healing to the bones.* PROVERBS 16:24

JUNE 7

*Proverbs 16:24;
Colossians 4:6*

Kind words can
be short and easy
to speak, but
their echoes are
truly endless.

—Mother Teresa

IN WORD There are few things in this world as contagious as words. Rumors spread like wildfire, lies inflame
deadly passions, and bitterness hardens the heart of both its
speakers and its hearers. On the other hand, encouragement
cultivates the will, praise establishes the praiseworthy, and
truth always begets wisdom. Words can do great things.

Speech is an awesome responsibility. It's hard to imagine that our casual comments can have eternal implications,
but they can. God anoints them for blessing, and Satan uses
them for cursing. Both blessings and curses have a dramatic
impact on the heart and soul of human beings. They often
dictate the direction we go—forever.

That's why pleasant words are sweet and soothing.
They have deep spiritual impact. They are not neutral claims
of neutral people; they are vehicles for both the power of
God and for the corruption of this world. They can be
inspired by the Holy One or hijacked by the evil one. They
matter—a lot.

IN DEED Have you ever considered the implications of
your words? They can be powerful, whether you realize it
or not. Through your speech, you can pour out wrath and
condemnation, and you can pour out blessing and encouragement. You can set the mood of a room and cultivate the
direction of a life. You can stop people dead in their tracks
or put them on a course of fruitfulness. One way or another,
what comes out of your mouth is rapidly contagious. It will
either build up or tear down. It all depends on what you say
and how you say it.

Try this mental exercise: Learn to consider each of your
words as a powerful spark, a small investment in a vast
future. See the implications beyond the moment. Discipline
your mouth to be silent until you are sure your words are
(1) consistent with Scripture and (2) flavored with grace.
That doesn't mean you'll never say anything harsh—some
situations beg for rebuke. But let your speech be redemptive.
Most of all, let it point to God.

The Source of Conversation

*Let your conversation be always full of grace,
seasoned with salt, so that you may know how to
answer everyone.* COLOSSIANS 4:6

IN WORD If words are as powerful as a raging fire, able to both warm the heart well and to burn it to a crisp, it might be important to consider their source. Words are not random utterances from absent minds; they are the fruit of the soul. They indicate what's growing within us, whether the Spirit of God or the spirit of corruption. They are a true measure of the spiritual life. They tell us what's inside.

Jesus said all the evils of sin "come from inside and make a man 'unclean' " (Mark 7:23). His assessment of human corruption is startling, but experience and wisdom bear Him out. The human heart comes up with all sorts of mischief, and though we often keep it secret, it inevitably flavors our speech. We cannot disguise the condition of a sinful soul. Corrupt words are the fruit of that rotting tree.

But when we have been raised to life by the Spirit of God, our words become the fruit of a living, thriving tree planted by streams of water. Our conversation can be full of grace because *we* are full of grace. We can speak with the flavor of salt because *we* have been seasoned with salt. We can bear eternal fruit because we *are* eternal fruit. The Word of Life fills a faithful heart with words of life. He makes fertile what once was barren.

IN DEED Analyze your speech. Are you frequently making negative comments? Do you seethe with anger and bitterness? Do you spread discouragement and criticism when you open your mouth? If so, it's a reflection of what's inside. It indicates a lack of fellowship with the Spirit of life and hope and grace.

Do not make the mistake of thinking your speech and your spiritual condition are distinct. One reflects the other. If the reflection is negative, don't just clean up your mouth. Bask in the fellowship of the Spirit. God doesn't want to change your tongue, He wants to change your heart. When He does, your words become His.

JUNE 8
*Proverbs 16:24;
Colossians 4:6*

Take my lips, and let them be filled with messages from Thee.

—Frances Ridley Havergal

Do the Word

Do not merely listen to the word, and so deceive
yourselves. Do what it says. JAMES 1:22

Faith without works
cannot please, nor
can good works
without faith.

—The Venerable Bede

IN WORD Who sees the behavior of Christians? First of all, God. God is interested in the motivations that guide our decisions and the thoughts that fill our minds. But He is interested in more than a people who will think right. His desire, expressed repeatedly throughout Scripture, is for a people who will do something about what they know.

Who else sees? Other Christians. We do not encourage one another primarily by our words but rather by our actions. A brother or sister in need may need to hear a kind reminder of the love of God, but he or she may need a visible illustration of it more desperately. Faith that says only "God bless you, I wish you well," grieves the heart of God, as James implies later on (see 2:16). It accomplishes nothing that God can use. It must result in action, in prayer, in *something*. Otherwise, it is wasted faith.

And an unbelieving world watches too. It does not care about the intricacies of our theology, and apart from college philosophy majors, no one will really ask the questions we want to answer. Unbelievers want to see what faith looks like, and the only way to speak on those terms is to act. When Jesus told His disciples that the world would know them by their love for one another, it was not a sentiment hidden deep within. He called for acts of love. Faith, love, hope, and every other spiritual virtue remain invisible to a lost world—until we act according to our beliefs.

IN DEED Listening to the Word is immensely profitable, but it can be dangerously deceptive as well. When we hear the Word, mull it over, and let it become a part of our thinking, we often make the mistake of believing it has become a part of our lives. That's an illusion. The Word is only ours when we have acted on it. It is only effective when we've allowed God to move it from our minds into our hearts, and then outward into our actions. Anything else will lull us into a false sense of security. Do not be deceived. "Do what it says."

An Hour of Need

The jar of flour will not be used up and the jug of oil will not run dry until the day the Lord gives rain on the land. 1 KINGS 17:14

IN WORD A drought had made food scarce in Israel. Elijah the prophet had been fed by ravens, but God had a new command: *Go to a widow in Zarephath.* She would supply the need. Elijah did, and though the woman was preparing to die of hunger, God miraculously provided enough for her, her son, and the prophet.

Have you ever wondered why God told the prophet to go to a woman who had nothing? She was no source of great wealth, no prominent benefactor. She was about to make her last meal so that she and her son could then die. But God's providence comes in barren places, and the woman learned a valuable principle: Obey God first, even when He asks for your last meal. Then your supply is up to Him.

Can you imagine giving your last dollar to a ministry while your stomach gnaws at you for attention? This is exactly what God ordered. The deep principles of providence kick in only after we've demonstrated a greater desire to invest in obedience than to invest in ourselves. No one ever received the blessing of God by desperately hanging on to his last dime. The greatest inflow of providence comes when we determine that nothing will hinder our outflow. God is looking for those who will do what He says before fulfilling their own desperate plans—just as the widow of Zarephath gave Elijah what she thought might be her last meal.

IN DEED At what point do you have so little that you stop giving to God? That is the point where God will demonstrate the futility of your plans—not because He enjoys frustrating us, but because He has greater plans for His people than their self-preserving instincts will allow. The miraculous flow of His providence is only miraculous to us when it seems unlikely. Our hour of greatest need is His hour greatest supply. A Phoenician widow survived a famine on that principle. So can you.

JUNE 10
1 Kings 17:7-16

You will never need more than God can supply.

—J. I. Packer

Regarding the Weak

Blessed is he who has regard for the weak; the LORD delivers him in times of trouble. PSALM 41:1

JUNE 11
Psalm 41:1-3

He who demands mercy and shows none ruins the bridge over which he himself is to pass.

—Thomas Adams

IN WORD Imagine having a child who doesn't seem to care much for other people. He or she is completely absorbed in self-centered activities, always planning for personal gain and never making any real sacrifices for anyone else. Even when confronted with desperate need, this child seems not to be moved.

How will you feel about this child when he is in trouble? As a parent, your sympathies will naturally lead you to take care of your child. But with what enthusiasm? If the child has demonstrated no feeling for others, you will likely have a strong desire for him to learn compassion.

On the other hand, how would you feel about a child who has always gone out of his way to help everyone else? Your compassions are stirred for someone who is by nature compassionate. When a sympathetic person is in deep trouble, he has the sympathy of others to draw on.

So it is with God. He loves every one of us, even those who are coldhearted. But He delights in rescuing a compassionate person. If we rarely focus on others, God will often let us sit in our difficulties for a while until we learn how others have felt in their need.

IN DEED Those who have regard for the weak always have God's sympathetic ear. The problem is that we get so completely wrapped up in our own agendas at times that we hardly notice the needs around us. It isn't that we don't care about other people; we just don't care enough to feel their pain or even to notice their hardships. We're too occupied with our own business.

In His mercy, God cares for our needs regardless of our level of compassion. But He cares for them more readily, more powerfully, and more demonstrably if we have demonstrated His nature toward others. Do we withhold grace? Then grace will be hard to find. Or are we examples of mercy? If so, we will have mercy in abundance.

God of Justice

Many seek an audience with a ruler, but it is from the
LORD that man gets justice.   PROVERBS 29:26

IN WORD   God loves justice, and we who have been created in His image love to see things work out in a way that
is fair for everyone. We hate inequity, especially when we're
on the short end of the imbalance. No matter how many
times someone tells us that life isn't fair, we still want it to
be. We're afraid we might not get our piece of the pie.

Our sense of fairness is really rankled when God's timing does not equal our own. We're hardly content with the
thought that things will be made right at the judgment seat
of Christ. That's too far off in the future. And what if the
offender repents! Then there's *never* any payback, just a free
ride. Never mind that we received the same free ride the day
we accepted Jesus' sacrifice. When we're offended, we're all
for justice.

Such indignation has led us throughout the centuries
to establish all sorts of courts and punishments. And God
would have it so; He is never in favor of chaos in this world.
To the degree that our justice systems reflect His standards,
they are pleasing to Him. But they are never perfect, and
they don't handle our every grievance. We are left, at least
with some offenses, either to steam and stew about them or
to let them go and forgive, trusting God to handle them well.
We often choose the anger over the trust. God seems much
less urgent about our complaints than we are. We want restitution now.

IN DEED   How do you make things right when you've
been wronged? Revenge is not a biblical option; God insists
that vengeance is His, not ours. And perfect fairness is not
a biblical option either; we who have received a clean slate
from our Savior can have no complaints against our God
of justice. Justice once directed at us was poured out on
Another. We can hardly insist that others must receive it.

Does that bother you? Relax. God *will* make all things
right, in His time and in His way. He is patiently waiting for
all who will repent; a verdict now would be premature. Seek
justice now, when appropriate, but don't place your hope in
it. God's is worth waiting for.

JUNE 12
Proverbs 29:26;
Isaiah 30:18

God's justice
guarantees that
ultimately all
that is unfair will
be dealt with.

—Joseph Stowell

An Obligated God?

Who has a claim against me that I must pay? Everything under heaven belongs to me. JOB 41:11

Job 41:1-11

Between here and heaven, every minute that the Christian lives will be a minute of grace.

—Charles Spurgeon

IN WORD Imagine a father giving his daughter an extravagant Christmas gift every year: an expensive piece of jewelry. At first, she might squeal with delight and hug her father's neck as tightly as she could. After a few years, her reaction to the annual gift might calm to a respectful "thank you." Eventually, she might begin to expect the extravagance as her right. Suppose that one year the father didn't have enough money for expensive jewelry and bought her something much more humble. How would she react?

We know human nature well enough to know that once we're accustomed to generous grace, we expect it not as a gift but as a right. Perhaps we've noticed this dynamic in our spiritual lives as well: God gave us salvation, to which we rejoiced as undeserving recipients should; then we began to take His mercies for granted; now, we often expect them as our rightful inheritance. We might even complain when He doesn't answer our prayers the way we want Him to, or when He doesn't make life as easy for us as we think it should be. What happened to us? We made a dreadful mistake. We misunderstood the consistency of God's mercy. Somewhere along the way, we decided that His extravagant promises entitled us not only to trust in them, but to demand them. Perhaps we've been spoiled.

Job's many blessings may have led him to expect that God would always bless him in exactly the same ways. God didn't. Job couldn't understand that, and he even hinted that God might have dealt unfairly with him. Like us, he forgot that we were fallen, corrupt, and spiritually dead. We deserved nothing. Grace gave us everything.

IN DEED Be careful how you address God. Don't be a spoiled child; be a grateful one. Remember that everything you have—even life itself—is a gift that springs from His fabulous, unfathomable mercy.

Unburdened

An anxious heart weighs a man down, but a kind word cheers him up. PROVERBS 12:25

IN WORD One of the most persistent problems for Christians is anxiety. One of the most consistent exhortations in Scripture is for us to not be anxious. It's a curious contradiction, isn't it? Or perhaps it makes perfect sense. God's command for us not to be afraid, not to be anxious, not to fear, and to be strong and courageous is so complete and frequent for a reason: He knows that fear will be one of our worst problems.

Why is God so concerned with our level of anxiety? Because, as this proverb says, an anxious heart weighs a person down. It is a heavy burden. It is the antithesis of the abundant life that Jesus has come to give us. It will cripple us from doing God's will and enjoying His presence. When we are absorbed in the threat of difficult circumstances or difficult people, we are not absorbed in God. When we fear the things that seem to steal our lives away, we are placing them on a higher pedestal than the One who gives us life.

God emphatically does *not* want us to be weighed down. He may give us many responsibilities, but He does not *burden* us with them. His burden is light, because Jesus is the Burden Bearer. And as long as we are anxiously stressing over our burdens, we are not letting Jesus bear them. We simply cannot experience His strength while bearing the weight of life in our own strength. We must choose one or the other. We must choose the burden-bearing God.

IN DEED What is the solution to our anxiety? There are several, prayer ranking first among them. But the proverb gives us another: kind words. Let your life be full of them. Tell them to yourself. God's truth is kind to you, after all; rehearse it often. Tell them to others. God's primary vehicle for expressing Himself in this world is through people. Verbally demonstrate His kindness to others. And when others offer kind words to you, accept them. God has sent them to you. Accept them, and do not be anxious.

JUNE 14
Proverbs 12:25;
Philippians 4:6

Beware of anxiety. Next to sin, there is nothing that so troubles the mind, strains the heart, distresses the soul, and confuses the judgment.

—William Ullathorne

Fruit and the Spirit

The fruit of the Spirit is love, joy, peace, patience, kindness, goodness, faithfulness, gentleness and self-control. GALATIANS 5:22-23

JUNE 15
Galatians 5:16-26

Work designed for eternity can only be done by the eternal Spirit.

—A. W. Tozer

IN WORD All those who desire to live godly lives have prayed for these fruits. We want more love, so we pray for God to increase our love. We want more patience, so we pray for patience. We all know the routine. We've all sought the gifts of the Spirit with a shopping-list mentality.

But there is a better way. Instead of seeking more of the fruits, we must seek more of the Spirit. When we think we need more love, we really need more of Jesus in us. Or, perhaps more accurately, we need Jesus to have more of us. The same goes for our joy, our peace, our patience, and so on. These are not nine individual characteristics that we can isolate and work on individually. They are integral parts of the mind of Christ. The more we abide in His Spirit, the more we will have them. When we lack certain fruits, we lack fellowship with the Spirit who gives them. The means to be more fruitful is to ask for closer fellowship with the Source. When we have that, the love, joy, peace, etc., will come.

This is God's design for His people. His plan is not simply to improve us and make us better people. His plan is to inhabit us. The fruit of the Spirit is not about us and our deficiencies. It is about God and His presence in this world. If you find yourself lacking, the problem is not an isolated characteristic; it is fellowship with the personal, living God. He aims to live His life in you.

IN DEED Believe it or not, you—along with other believers—are the means to display God's character in this world. If we don't display Him, He won't be seen. That's an awesome responsibility. It's also an awesome privilege. Do you lack His fruitfulness? Then you lack Him—not necessarily His salvation, but His Lordship and His fellowship. Don't just ask for love, joy, or anything else. Ask for Him.

Love

His banner over me is love.
SONG OF SONGS 2:4

IN WORD The Song of Songs is an amorous book because our God is an amorous God. Does it seem irreverent to say so? It can't be, not when we realize the most passionate kind of love could not have originated anywhere but in the passionate heart of God. It is certainly not Satan's invention, nor that of a depraved human condition. It is experienced by emotional beings made in the image of an emotional God. Our love reflects His.

Like the bridegroom in the Song of Songs, our Bridegroom, Jesus, has set His love over us as His declaration of victory. It is our identity. We know that He loves us, and because of that, we love Him (1 John 4:19). Not only do we love Him, we love each other. It is the identifying feature of a Spirit-filled Christian. Where love is absent, so is the Spirit. Where the Spirit is absent, so is love.

So important is this characteristic that Jesus spent the major part of His last words to His disciples on the subject. In John 13–16, He first demonstrates love and then preaches on it: love and obedience, love and the Spirit, love and prayer, love and His friendship, love and joy. Then in His parting prayer, He asks this of the Father: "May they be brought to complete unity to let the world know that you sent me and have loved them even as you have loved me" (John 17:23). It is an intimate love—"I in them and you in me"—between a loving God, the beloved Son, and a love-hungry people. If there is any single mark of belief, it is love.

IN DEED Does your life bear the banner of love? Are you aware of God's great love for you? Do you have great love for Him and for others? Do not be deceived: No matter how spiritually mature a believer is, it is a false spirituality if he or she is not thoroughly saturated in love. "God is love. Whoever lives in love lives in God, and God in him" (1 John 4:16). There is no way around it. The Christian life is a loving life. An unloving life is not Christian. Let love, above all else, define you.

JUNE 16
Song of Songs 2:1-4

Love of man necessarily arises out of love of God.

—John Hooper

Joy

The joy of the LORD is your strength.
NEHEMIAH 8:10

JUNE 17
Nehemiah 8:1-12

Joy is the experience of knowing that you are unconditionally loved.

—Henri Nouwen

IN WORD It was a day of grief and repentance, that day the scribe Ezra read "the Book of the Law of God" in the hearing of the assembly. A generation of Israelites suddenly realized what many previous generations had forsaken—a covenant of love with the great and mighty God. And, according to Nehemiah, they wept.

Have you ever wept over your failures? It's a humbling experience, pouring out your heart over grievous sins that can't be undone. The human heart never feels weaker than when it is faced with its undeniable shortcomings. Our humanity is shot through with sin, and there's nothing we can do about it. We're weak and helpless.

Believe it or not, that's a great place to be. God meets us in our weakness and He exalts the humble. "Blessed are those who mourn, for they will be comforted" (Matthew 5:4). It is a blessed frailty to have no claim before God, no words with which to justify ourselves, no bargaining power whatsoever. When we can accept that, we can accept His provision; and there is no greater joy than His provision. It is all we need. It takes us from weakness to strength because God's power—His very presence—is greatest when we are most visibly vulnerable. We can lay down our stressful, painful attempts at self-sufficiency, and we can accept His sufficiency instead. What greater joy is there than to realize it all falls on His shoulders and not on ours?

IN DEED Do you know God's joy? Have you ever heard Him speak into your grief and say, with Nehemiah, "This day is sacred to our Lord. Do not grieve, for the joy of the LORD is your strength"? The joyless Christian is bearing burdens no human is capable of bearing. The joyful Christian has come to grips with his weakness and accepted God's strength by casting all burdens on Him. Learn the art of casting those burdens; be joyful and be strong.

Peace

Let the peace of Christ rule in your hearts.
COLOSSIANS 3:15

IN WORD Peace is elusive. Not only is it elusive to governments in the world's hot spots of conflict, it is elusive in public and private institutions. Unfortunately, it is also elusive in churches and families. And, most unsettling to us, it is elusive in our own hearts.

Ever since the Garden of Eden, the human heart is by nature unsettled. We are restless creatures because we have separated ourselves from our created purpose. The natural dependence our first parents felt for God has been lost on us. Insecurity reigns within; and where insecurity reigns, peace doesn't.

The reason we live in a world that is in conflict is because we have hearts in conflict. We want to institute the rule of Christ in our hearts, but He must replace the reign of self—with all its fears, ambitions, passions, and false hopes—and that takes time. Human beings in such turmoil find it difficult to live in peace with others, whether it is on the job, in the church, or at home. Those who do not get along with others are invariably uncomfortable with themselves. Those who are at peace within are almost always at peace with others. Even when others rage against them—as they did with Jesus on the cross, Stephen before the Sanhedrin, and Paul from city to city—they do nothing to fuel the conflict. They have no need. They are at peace with themselves and at peace with God.

IN DEED Paul says we are to let the peace of Christ rule in our hearts. He doesn't say peace is simply to exist in our hearts. He doesn't say it is to influence our hearts periodically. It is to rule.

Take this diagnostic test: Are you in conflict with others? It is likely a reflection of the condition of your heart. Ask God to still your turbulent waters. Let Jesus rule in the deepest corners of your being. Know the depths of His peace.

JUNE 18
Colossians 3:15-17

You have made us for Yourself, and our hearts are restless till they find their rest in You.

—St. Augustine

Patience

A man's wisdom gives him patience; it is to his glory to overlook an offense. PROVERBS 19:11

JUNE 19
Proverbs 19:11;
Ecclesiastes 7:8-9

Be as patient with others as God has been with you.

—Anonymous

IN WORD It is profoundly ironic that those who are most aggressive in asserting their rights and establishing themselves are least likely to earn a respectable reputation. There is something disturbing about those who are rash and overly assertive. They must have what they want *now*. They are ruled by their whims. They carry the defining marks of this world, and they are unimpressive to everyone but themselves.

By contrast, those who are patient—slow to anger, deliberate in their steps, reluctant to speak or to judge hastily—are those held in highest regard by others. They do not assert their reputation, they simply earn it. They lose the argument but win respect. The world takes notice because they are noticeably unlike this world. They carry the marks of wisdom. In fact, whether they intend it or not, they are like Jesus.

Jesus could have won the kingdoms of this world at the Temptation, but He waited. He could have established His kingdom when He rode into Jerusalem, but He waited. He could have condemned those who crucified Him, but He waited. He could have called legions of angels to defend Him, but He waited. He could have returned yesterday, but He waited.

Why is He so excruciatingly patient? Because the greater the investment in His people—in both time and spiritual maturity—the greater the benefit in the eternal scheme.

IN DEED Have you learned that principle for yourself? Sometimes the best answer is a slow one—or none at all. Sometimes there is no pressing need to defend yourself when you know your position will be established in the end. Sometimes the person who offends you will eventually come around—if you give him time. If you are patient in all things, you are like Jesus. Your wisdom will be to your own glory, and also to His.

Kindness

A kind man benefits himself, but a cruel man brings trouble on himself. PROVERBS 11:17

IN WORD Kindness is defined as an attitude or action that benefits others. It is directed toward others, enjoyed by others, and edifying for others. Cruelty, too, is defined as something directed toward others. But this proverb doesn't focus on the effect of kindness (or lack thereof) on others. It skips the basic definitions and goes straight to the side effects. It focuses on the results on oneself.

Just as patience ironically promotes those who are most reluctant to promote themselves, so kindness builds up those who are most interested in building up others. Cruel people try to give themselves a boost by harming others, but the strategy backfires. Harming others will eventually cause trouble for the cruel person. Likewise, kindness will eventually be returned to the kind. People who help others also help themselves, and so does God.

But we must be careful how we define kindness. True kindness will prompt a person to speak the truth in love (Ephesians 4:15). No one would question Jesus' kindness, but it could be a very confrontational kindness toward those who distorted truth and righteousness. A wise person will accept that: "Let a righteous man strike me—it is a kindness; let him rebuke me—it is oil on my head," wrote David (Psalm 141:5). Kindness is an intentional effort to pursue what is good for another person.

IN DEED Have people been unkind to you? There's a chance that the reason lies within yourself—not that you are unworthy of the kindness of others, but perhaps you have not made an effort to be kind. A person reaps what he sows, and if one has sown kindness, he will reap it as well.

Perhaps others take your kindness for granted. God will not. An unbiblical saying asserts that God helps those who help themselves. Biblical truth says that God helps those who help others. Do you qualify? Then they, and you, will benefit.

JUNE 20
Proverbs 11:17;
Colossians 3:12

Kind words can be short and easy to speak, but their echoes are truly endless.

—Mother Teresa

Goodness

Surely goodness and love will follow me all the days of my life.
PSALM 23:6

Goodness is something so simple: always live for others, never to seek one's own advantage.

—Dag Hammarskjöld

IN WORD   For something to be worthwhile in our age, it must be amazing, outstanding, remarkable, or awesome. We are so overwhelmed with superlatives that we must keep coming up with more attention-grabbing adjectives with each new season of advertising. But God often advertises Himself in refreshing simplicity. He is good. Through and through, pure and simple, He is good. His attitude toward us is good, His will toward us is good, and His works on our behalf are good. We are unaccustomed to pure forms in our world—everything is tainted with corruption—but with God, no superlative is necessary. From any angle we look at Him, we see goodness.

There's a remarkable transformation for us in His goodness. God blesses so that His people will become blessers. He gives so that we will give. He loves so we will love. He forgives so we will forgive. His demeanor toward us is to be reflected in our demeanor toward others. It isn't just a responsibility to fulfill; it's a natural reaction. When we've been treated so well, it's natural to treat others well. His goodness takes root in us; we become good, like Him.

IN DEED   Most of us are busy trying to impress others with a remarkable personality, amazing skills, or our outstanding achievements. God's Spirit in us, however, will not make us flashy. He will make us good.

If others do not see in us a simple, uncorrupted goodness, they do not see the Spirit of God. We forget that behind every miracle, behind every teaching, behind every revelation and prophecy, there is the goodwill of God. Goodness underlies everything He does. He is a beneficent Creator, and a beneficent Creator births beneficent children. Do you bear His goodness? Demonstrate it to someone today. Show your world what God is like.

Faithfulness

O Lord God Almighty, who is like you? You are mighty,
O Lord, and your faithfulness surrounds you.   PSALM 89:8

IN WORD   If you were to do a biblical word study on "faithfulness," you would find something mildly surprising: The vast majority of biblical references to faithfulness are about God, not about us. God's faithfulness is an established fact in Scripture; man's is not. We are encouraged to be faithful, but we are always found wanting. God, however, is constant. His faithfulness reaches to the skies (see Psalm 36:5; 57:10; 108:4), and His love and faithfulness are semantically paired so often that they are clearly intertwined. His love is unchanging; there is nothing fickle about it—not even from generation to generation (Psalm 100:5). True faithfulness endures forever (Psalm 117:2). It can do no other.

This is why faithfulness *must* be a fruit of the Spirit. It cannot be of the flesh. Humanity measures faithfulness in terms of months and years; God measures it in terms of eternity. We cannot maintain such commitment unless the power to do so is given from above. It simply is not within us to be covenant-keepers for long. Nearly every biblical covenant originates in heaven and is maintained unilaterally by the covenant-keeping God. *His* faithfulness alone is everlasting.

IN DEED   If you needed any sense of security about your salvation, there it is. God keeps you because He is faithful. He knows the fickleness of those He pursues, and He pursues us nonetheless. He knew how unstable we were before He committed to keep us.

But we cannot remain unstable, not if we're filled with His Spirit. The flesh is weak, but we no longer live according to the flesh. Never use the excuse, "I'm only human." You're a human with the Spirit of the living God dwelling within. Faithfulness is possible for us when we are wholly dependent on Him. His faithfulness surrounds His throne. Enthrone Him in your heart, and it will surround you, too.

JUNE 22
Psalm 89:1-8

The faithful person lives constantly with God.

—Clement of Alexandria

Gentleness

Let your gentleness be evident to all. The Lord is near.
PHILIPPIANS 4:5

JUNE 23
Philippians 4:4-5

Nothing is so strong as gentleness, nothing so gentle as real strength.

—St. Francis de Sales

IN WORD David was gentle toward his rebellious son (2 Samuel 18:5). Jesus came into this world with a spirit of gentleness (Matthew 11:29; 21:5). Paul had a tender attitude toward the churches he had founded (2 Corinthians 10:1; 1 Thessalonians 2:7). Throughout Scripture, we are instructed to put on gentleness as though it's a required garment. Why? Because God has been gentle with us. It's who He is, and we are to be like Him.

We may not envision God as being gentle. We read of His anger toward humanity before the ark was built; of His command for Israel to ruthlessly conquer the Canaanites; of His judgments on Israel in the prophets; and of His harsh condemnation of our sin when He laid our iniquity on a bloodied, beaten Jesus. But all of this points to His absolute, uncompromising, holy purity. His heart is thoroughly gentle. When our confession and humility allow for His gentleness, He *always* chooses it over His judgment.

Have you felt His gentle touch? When you received mercy rather than condemnation, it was there. Every day when He feeds you, clothes you, and surrounds you with air to breathe, you feel His tender provision. If there is anyone out there who loves you as you are, you have seen a reflection of His gentle nature. In Jesus, we know a gentle God.

IN DEED If the fruits of the Spirit are God's display of His character through the church to a searching world, then gentleness is one of the most needed elements of that display. The world does not know of this gentle God—it portrays Him as either viciously judgmental or blandly irrelevant. It has not seen enough examples of righteous, patient, redemptive gentleness. Be one of those examples. Find a hurting person and demonstrate God's gentle touch.

Self-Control

Like a city whose walls are broken down is a man
who lacks self-control. PROVERBS 25:28

IN WORD   The contemporary church is plagued with problems of self-discipline. Sinful behaviors have infiltrated our congregations possibly at unprecedented levels. One reason self-control is such a problem for so many Christians is that it feels like a work of the flesh. We are told to live Spirit-filled lives, so we become passive. We have incorrectly assumed that any effort on our part is "works," a product of the flesh and a symptom of legalism. We end up with a faith without works, and as we find out, that kind of faith is dead.

Self-control is perhaps the most confusing of all the fruits of the Spirit. How can it involve the self and the Spirit at the same time? If it's self-control, how can it be Spirit-control? It can't. But, contrary to popular teaching, the Bible never tells us to be controlled by the Spirit, at least not in the sense that we lose our personality and will. We are to be born of the Spirit, filled with the Spirit, led by the Spirit, inspired by the Spirit, and sealed by the Spirit. But we are not controlled by the Spirit. The Spirit enables us to have self-control.

A lack of self-control will cause us to neglect necessary disciplines like prayer, Bible study, contemplation, evangelism, and more. It will also cause us to indulge even godly desires in inappropriate ways. A lack of discipline distorts work, sexuality, entertainment, nutrition, and stewardship of time and money. If our lives were compared to an ancient city, self-indulgence would be the weakness in our walls. Erosion will eventually cause our protection to collapse and allow our enemies to raid.

IN DEED   A life of godly discipline is useful to God. He can accomplish much with it, because it can steward His vast resources appropriately. The uncontrolled life squanders God's treasures—spiritual and material—and invites attack. At all costs, let the Spirit empower you to learn self-control. It is the key to managing all other fruitfulness.

JUNE 24
Proverbs 25:28;
2 Timothy 1:7

If you would learn self-mastery, begin by yielding yourself to the One Great Master.

—Johann Friedrich Lobstein

Too Many Identities

Those God foreknew he also predestined to be conformed to the likeness of his Son. ROMANS 8:29

We cannot help conforming ourselves to what we love.

—St. Francis de Sales

IN WORD Many young people find their identity in a pro athlete or team, while others idolize and emulate a rock star. Adults are more subtle, but we, too, will identify ourselves by our careers, our family roles, our hobbies, or trends set by our favorite celebrities. It is human nature to pick an appealing image—any image—and then try to live up to it. We enthusiastically become like the people or ideals on which we set our affections. When we want to, we conform easily. Our desired image becomes a part of us.

When we became Christians, we may have found that we continually struggle to become Christlike. Why? If our affections are set on Him as they once were on the trends and icons of our culture, wouldn't a godly transformation be a natural process for us? Perhaps that is just the problem. Perhaps our affections are not entirely Christ-ward. We easily let our love grow stale, losing the excitement that newness and discovery naturally brought us at first. Other images—cultural trends and newfound interests—become the object of our infatuation, while Jesus subtly and imperceptibly passes from our adoration to our obligation.

When this happens, we find godliness more of a struggle. It is hard to let ourselves become conformed to the image of Jesus when we hold another image in higher esteem. Other passions pull us in other directions, often making conflicting—or at least superfluous—demands on our character. Godly character cannot thrive in such a context. Our spirits will not fit into two molds simultaneously.

IN DEED Is your growth toward godliness a difficult struggle? Examine your desires. How do you envision yourself? How would you like others to perceive you? What image do you aim for? If you find any image other than Jesus shaping your soul, abandon it. It will hinder your growth. Find your identity entirely in Him.

Spiritual Diversity

There are different kinds of working, but the same God
works all of them in all men.   1 CORINTHIANS 12:6

IN WORD   The gifts of the Spirit are a glorious treasure. They are evidence that God has grafted us into His plan and made us His coworkers. Think of that! Partners with the eternal God! No achievement or recognition in our labor can compete with that. There is no higher honor for the work of our hands.

Such an amazing reality only comes to life in those who have the mind of Christ—those who are spiritually minded and filled with the Spirit of God. It is all the more amazing, then, when human nature distorts this blessing and makes it a fleshly point of contention. But how often this happens! The gifts of the Spirit become our occasion to judge the work of grace in others. If God has given us the gift of mercy, we have contempt for those who demonstrate a lack of it. If God has given someone a burden for a specific social problem, how easy it is for that person to assume all others should have the same burden. How common it is for us to think of our own gifts as spiritual and those who lack them as unspiritual. Our giftedness and convictions are a true measure of spiritual maturity only in our own minds—never in Scripture.

IN DEED   Church unity is often disrupted by the assumption that all causes are to be equally defended by all believers. Or that all ministries are to be equally served by all members of the body of Christ. We forget that our God loves variety. We forget that He has not distributed His gifts with absolute equity. Does that seem unfair? No, He will judge in fairness. Everyone is accountable for the resources he or she has been entrusted with. No more, no less. The distribution is determined by the wisdom of God.

Spiritual maturity is not found in having all gifts or defending all causes. It is found in accepting the diversity of God's people and working within it.

JUNE 26
1 Corinthians
12:1-20

Spiritual gifts are no proof of spirituality.

—Samuel Chadwick

Wisdom in Community

The way of a fool seems right to him, but a wise man listens to advice. PROVERBS 12:15

JUNE 27

Proverbs 12:15; 15:22

Seek the advice of your betters in preference to following your own inclinations.

—Thomas à Kempis

IN WORD How do the wise know their decisions are sound? How do fools know theirs are not? Neither question can be answered by looking within. The human heart is not reliable in matters of wisdom. We hope our perspectives are based on reality, but there are always distortions, always perceptual filters through which we receive our information. The way that seems right to us may—or may not—be right.

The history of Israel is filled with two contrasting approaches to life. In Deuteronomy, God and Moses repeatedly urge the people to do what is right in the eyes of the Lord. In Judges, everyone did what was right in his or her own eyes. Thereafter, Scripture clearly points out that godly kings did right in God's eyes. Ungodly kings did right in their own eyes. But nearly all thought they were doing right.

Our period of history is one in which most people do right in their own eyes. Ethics are considered by most to be relative. People live as ships with no anchor. Each has his own god. We are urged by popular spiritual leaders to look within for the answers, for deep in the human heart we will find our true calling and follow our course. Nothing could be more unbiblical. Fools aren't aware of their foolishness. How can we know what is right? By feeling? By following momentary or self-derived desires? Is there any objective standard by which wisdom is measured?

IN DEED There is, of course. The Bible gives us solid wisdom on which to base our lives. But while it is absolute, its interpretation can vary widely. That's where advice comes in. Never underestimate the body of Christ. He has crafted us to live in community. Wisdom usually comes not to godly individuals but to godly fellowships.

Are you seeking direction? Know your heart, but do not trust it entirely. Measure it by biblical wisdom and the counsel of those who follow it well.

Wisdom in Waiting

*They soon forgot what he had done and did not
wait for his counsel.* PSALM 106:13

IN WORD You've asked God for direction. It has not yet
come. You feel as if you must act. Surely God must want you
to go with your best instincts. If He did not, He surely would
have answered by now. His silence can mean nothing other
than to go ahead and do what you think is best, right?

Psalm 106 recounts the history of Israel's rebellion. One
aspect of their disobedience was following the urge to act
when God had not yet given counsel. They forgot His goodness. Had they remembered, they would have waited; but
human nature finds waiting to be difficult. When clear memories of God's benefits are absent, we feel we must seek our
own benefit. The people of Israel forgot that God was their
defender, provider, protector, deliverer, and all-purpose
miracle-worker. So which direction did they pursue? "They
gave in to their craving" (v. 14).

The impulse to act quickly always leads us to our own
human devices. On what else can we base our decisions
when we have not waited for God's direction? We have
no other recourse. We choose to do what we think is best,
and we are left then with the limitations of our thinking.
God rarely works in a rush. Forming Jesus within us—the
renewal of our minds—takes time.

IN DEED There is virtually no way to discern God's will
without waiting quietly. Self-generated desires must be
quelled. God must be asked. We must listen. The Word must
take root in our hearts. The counsel of others in the body of
Christ must be sought. The options must be weighed. In
time, one course of action will stand clear. The voice of God
will whisper in your ear: "This is the way. Walk in it."

How much do you trust the wisdom of God? Enough
to wait until after it's "too late"? God won't heed our deadlines, but He is never too late. His direction will come, His
way will be clear, and His timing will be perfect.

JUNE 28
Psalm 106:1-23

He never comes
to those who
do not wait.

—Frederick William
Faber

Necessary Prayers

Far be it from me that I should sin against the LORD by failing to pray for you. 1 SAMUEL 12:23

JUNE 29

1 Samuel 12:19-25

Pray as if everything depended upon your prayer.

—William Booth

IN WORD You have wondered if your prayers are effective. You have felt, at times, as though you were trying to persuade a reluctant God to intervene in a situation that He'd prefer to leave alone. Deep in your heart, it sometimes seems as though your prayers and your God are moving in opposite directions. You've let your feelings result in inactivity.

It is safe to assume that you've followed this pattern, at least occasionally, because virtually all Christians have. No genuine believer is convinced that he or she is adequate in prayer. We have a nagging feeling that we could and should pray more. Part of the reason that we don't is that we're not entirely convinced that our prayers are necessary.

The picture in Samuel is of a God who has made prayer an integral part of His activity in this world. We are not commanded to convince a reluctant God to do what He is loath to do; we are commanded to be a catalyst for His intervention. Not only is it acceptable to make our appeals to Him, it is required. God gives us the impression that His activity in the affairs of men is somehow contingent on the prayers of intercessors. If we don't pray, He doesn't act. In His divine arrangement with this planet, our prayers are essential. It is His plan for us to ask; when we don't, we violate His plan.

IN DEED Has the Holy Spirit prompted you to pray for someone? You *must* follow through on it! His prompting was not superfluous; He is efficient with His directions, and He would not have led you unless your prayers were an essential aspect of His intervention. We must continue in our prayer assignments until God's work is done. When His Spirit assures us that our prayers are complete, we may move on to others—but not before. His plan may hinge on your pleadings. Plead however—and whenever—He leads.

One Extreme to Another

The brother in humble circumstances ought to take pride in his high position. But the one who is rich should take pride in his low position. JAMES 1:9-10

IN WORD Believers have a tendency to fall into one of two extremes: wallowing in the fact of our depravity, or boasting in the benefits of the faith. Each extreme can be further cultivated by our position in this world. For some reason, we draw conclusions about our poverty or wealth, that they are possible signs of God's favor. But they aren't. And James tells us how to retrain our minds on the matter.

Those who are of low position in this world may need to be reminded frequently that they are beloved children of the Most High God. Those who are rich and successful may need to be reminded frequently that they are thoroughly corrupt sinners and called to be servants. But at one time or another, we all need to know both. Only a balanced knowledge of truth will preserve a right perspective: We are unbelievably, insufferably depraved and naturally divorced from the living God; *and* we are unimaginably, gloriously redeemed and blessed with eternal treasures, including knowing Him. Both extremes are unalterably true. Nothing can change the fact that we came from such a lowly place, and nothing can take away the thrilling promise of where we are headed. From the decay of this rebellious planet to the family of the King—what a story!

IN DEED Do you tend to dwell on your sinful condition? Humble circumstances might lead you to such an imbalance. Meditate on the riches of the Kingdom. Do you tend to feel superior to others? Worldly success might lead you to such an imbalance. Remember our corrupt origins and our call to sacrificial service.

But regardless of your circumstances—material or spiritual—know that both extremes are true for every believer. The Bible is clear. The story of grace is altogether amazing. We've been lifted from one extreme to another.

JUNE 30
James 1:9-11

The one sole thing in myself in which I glory, is that I see in myself nothing in which I can glory.

—Catherine of Genoa

181

The Word of Life

I meditate on your precepts and consider your ways. I delight in your decrees; I will not neglect your word. PSALM 119:15-16

JULY 1
Psalm 119:9-16

Some read the Bible to learn, and some read the Bible to hear from heaven.

—Andrew Murray

IN WORD Is the Bible an obligation, something that we know we should read whether we have enthusiasm for it or not—like finishing our vegetables before we head on to dessert? If so, we have perhaps not accurately understood the weight of this Word that God has given us. It is more than literature, more than history, more than theology. It is life.

Many a reader has gotten bogged down in the "begats" and "thou shalts" of the Bible, missing the relevance of those sections in establishing our faith as historical and human. But think about our condition: We are lost in this world, not knowing which way is up. Every midlife crisis or pang of existential angst will force us to admit it, whether we want to or not. Meanwhile, the Bible smolders on the shelf, burning to answer our ultimate questions on meanings and mysteries. It is the revelation of the divine. It has all the wisdom we need.

IN DEED Your culture and whichever elements of it you dwell in—whether it's your work environment, your entertainment choices, your conversations with friends, etc.—will constantly try to pull you into its value system and its own sense of morality. God's Word, if we will let it, will pry us back out of it. Only the Word can resist the currents of this world and shape us according to God's design.

Does this mean we should avoid our culture? No, we cannot escape. In fact, we *should* involve ourselves in our world in order to influence it for God's kingdom. But we cannot be swayed by it. Let the Word be a stronger influence in your life than any other philosophy or value system. Not only *should* we give it proper attention; we should *delight* in it, crave it, and savor it. When we do, it will accomplish in us all that God means for it to accomplish. It will make us everything we are meant to be.

The Word of Delight

Oh, how I love your law! I meditate on it
all day long.   PSALM 119:97

IN WORD   Even when we are convinced of the necessity of reading our Bible daily and applying its truths, we can get bogged down in the obligation of doing so. Somehow, perhaps not coincidentally, when we determine to learn Scripture with an open heart, the rest of life seems to close in around it. Schedules get more complicated, demands get more intense, pressing needs seem to preclude our time of meditation. Our enemy makes sure of it, and God allows him to—it's a test of our devotion to the Word of life.

But even when we stick with it, there are times of delight and times of passive indifference. It's human nature. What thrills us one day can often bore us the next, even when the subject is something as substantial as God's Word.

What are we to do? How can we maintain our delight in the Bible? Perhaps it is a matter of perspective. We can easily come to view the Scriptures as irrelevant relics of a different age—one that has little consistency with an era of global multiculturalism and technological marvels. We need to remember that the human heart and its relationships are essentially the same as they were thousands of years ago—steeped in self and sin and prone to conflict and dissatisfaction.

IN DEED   If you see the Bible as a collection of ancient writings, it might impress you, but it will not change your life very much. If, however, you see it as the vessel that holds the deep mysteries of God, the key that opens life's secret ways, it will have amazing transforming power. The Word of God could do no less—it breathes life into dead souls and causes all that was stale and stagnant within us to flourish.

When the Bible becomes boring to you, perhaps it's because you have reached a spiritual plateau on your journey into God's heart. Ask Him to take you deeper. It is hard to imagine any good father who would reject such a request from his child—least of all ours.

JULY 2
Psalm 119:97-104

The Bible is a window in this prison-world, through which we may look into eternity.

—Timothy Dwight

The Word of Power

I lift up my hands to your commands, which I love,
and I meditate on your decrees.   PSALM 119:48

JULY 3
Psalm 119:41-48

Meditation is holding the Word of God in the mind until it has affected every area of one's life and character.

—Andrew Murray

IN WORD   Modern hearers of the Word often hear so much truth with so little change in our lives. We hear a sermon at church or on the radio or TV, or we read a Christian book, and even though the message may be powerful and true, we've often forgotten it within a matter of days or even hours. Why? One reason is that we don't take time to meditate on what we hear.

Most of us have busy lives. Church is followed by other Sunday activities. Personal Bible study is followed by work or family responsibilities. Our days are packed with clutter, and we have little time to sit and think. But sitting and thinking are essential. When we don't take time to think, we jump from truth to truth, with the illusion that hearing is the same as learning. Truth needs time to seep from the intellect to the depths of our soul.

When we hear or read the truth, our mental agreement is only the first step. For many, it's also the last step. God has so much more work for His Word to do in our hearts. Meditation takes it deeper until it becomes a part of our lives. Only then does it affect us. Our minds are not changed until our hearts are transformed. Only in the hours of meditation are the deep truths of the gospel stirred into our whole being, changing us from within. Without such stirring, we are as those who agree with the gospel without really *believing* the gospel. True belief comes out of the core of our hearts.

IN DEED   Does the Word lack power in your life? If so, perhaps you lack time in the Word. And no mere addition of minutes or hours will help. The time spent in the Word must be time spent chewing on the Word, figuring out its ramifications, allowing it to sink deep, and letting it refresh your life in the Spirit. We must ask questions of God's Word and allow Him to answer. Only then does it become a powerful tool for change. Our lives can then be transformed.

One Birth

Lowborn men are but a breath, the highborn are
but a lie; if weighed on a balance, they are nothing;
together they are only a breath.   PSALM 62:9

IN WORD   We human beings have all sorts of ways of dividing ourselves. In some cultures there is an overt, recognized caste system. In others, it is much more subtle. The Western world, for example, tends to classify people in terms of economic status, race, or skill level. We'll do nearly anything to define ourselves in tight, distinguishable groups.

There's nothing wrong with identifying with a group of like-minded or similar-background people. The problem comes when we attribute relative worth to our different groups. We get hung up on ideology and education, pedigree and ancestry, or spending power and net worth. There's a reason Wall Street barons and welfare mothers don't usually hang out together, and it's not just because they have little in common. Our sociology is not just an accident. We like our class distinctions and we want to keep them.

We are naturally divisive, but the Kingdom of God makes no such distinctions. We will all commune together at the throne. When members of every tribe and nation meet together to praise Him, there will be no borders between them. When rich and poor are gathered in His name, there will be no first-class seating. The Kingdom of God knows only one species of human beings: His children.

IN DEED   If the Kingdom of God in heaven looks like a united fellowship of saints, shouldn't the Kingdom of God on earth look pretty similar? The psalmist is right: In God's eyes, there is no difference between the lowborn and the highborn. Centuries later, Jesus' teaching would make only one distinction—between the born again and the lost. Only one kind of birth matters in His Kingdom, and it has nothing to do with pedigree. It's all about grace, right now, here in this world. So are we.

JULY 4
Psalm 62:5-10

The union of men with God is the union of men with one another.

—Thomas Aquinas

Constant Change

There is a time for everything, and a season for every activity under heaven. ECCLESIASTES 3:1

JULY 5

Ecclesiastes 3:1-8

After winter comes the summer. After night comes the dawn. And after every storm, there come clear, open skies.

—Samuel Rutherford

IN WORD The human experience is filled with anticipation of the good things and dread of the bad. We have dreams, goals, hidden desires, and needful impulses. When we most expect fruit and fulfillment, we find none. Often when we expect barrenness, God gives fruit. The seasons of life frustrate us.

The writer of Ecclesiastes—Solomon, most likely—is aged and philosophical, and while he does not embody the hope that Christians have been given, he knows a thing or two about finite life in this physical world. He has seen emptiness and futility. And, apart from God, he has seen meaninglessness. If there is no God, if no afterlife, if no hidden hope that we cannot see, then there's no point to any of this life that we're living. And still, blind to a discernible purpose, Solomon is able to say: "There is a time for everything."

Solomon has seen seasons come and go. He knows the cyclical pattern of living is not just a matter for meteorologists, it's also a matter for relationships, labor, and the myriad emotions we have. In our lives, there *will* be unfruitful seasons. There *will* be times of discouragement and even despair. There *will* be pointless tasks and intractable conflict. Interspersed with all the joys of the human experience, there will be latent seasons, periods of fallow ground and backward regress. It won't be all good, all the time.

IN DEED That's important for us to know. We'll drive ourselves crazy if we don't understand that there are seasons in our lives. If you're particularly fruitless now—or even fruitful—know that it's only for a time. If a relationship is difficult—or even perfect—it, too, is only for a time. We have to get used to constant change.

Many Christians kick themselves or question God when life isn't running smoothly. Don't. It's only for a season. Do not expect your entire year to be warm and sunny. Part of it will be cold and rainy. And if you're in winter now, know that spring is on the way. Its time always comes.

A Time for Good

A time to be born . . . to plant . . . to heal . . . to build.
ECCLESIASTES 3:2-3

IN WORD We have no trouble seeing God as the source of life, health, and happiness. But those who are alienated from God, both within the body of believers and without, may consider themselves excluded from such blessings. For people whose lives have been marked with pain and strife, the blessing of God seems far, far away. Perhaps they've even lost sight of the benevolent, loving God. Perhaps they've grown hopeless.

Dark seasons in a person's life will do that. They will obscure the goodness of God and make us think that we're all alone in this world. They turn faith into skepticism, hope into cynicism. In the dark night of uncertainty, people who once held on to God will either hold Him tighter or let go altogether. When the temptation to let go comes, it's important to remember: There's a time to be born, to plant, to heal, to build. There's a time for life and blessing. There's a season for the goodness of God in the life of one who believes, and it's certain to come.

A popular interpretation of this passage—perhaps aided by the melodies of past generations—implies that a season for everything means we can take just about any approach to life we choose. "A time for everything" can mean, if misinterpreted, that anything goes. But the heart of this passage is all about discernment. It keeps us from becoming proud and reckless during times of prosperity and from becoming dark and dreadful during times of scarcity. It keeps our perspectives in balance so that we don't get too high during high times or too low during low times. And it reminds us to discern the difference, knowing that our actions depend on the big picture of changing seasons, not on the weather today.

IN DEED If you are a believer going through a low time, know that it will end. God has His seasons, and many of them are good. He never deprives His children of all good seasons. The light will come, the cold will thaw, and God will bless your life—in its time.

JULY 6
Ecclesiastes 3:1-8

See that you are not suddenly saddened by the adversities of this world, for you do not know the good they bring.

—John of the Cross

Fruits of Sin

A time to die . . . to kill . . . to tear down . . . to weep . . . to give up . . . to throw away . . . to hate . . . for war. ECCLESIASTES 3:2-8

JULY 7
Ecclesiastes 3:1-8

The world rings changes; it is never constant but in its disappointments.

—Thomas Watson

IN WORD Far from giving us license to kill—or to hate, destroy, or any other such negative activity—the Scriptures give us perspective on the fruits of fallenness. We live in a broken world, and we are broken people.

If everyone got along, living according to God's righteousness, there would never be a time to kill or to go to war. But such is not the case. There is evil in this world, and there are times to oppose it, even violently. If sin had not introduced death into this world, there would never be a time to uproot, to tear down, or to throw away. But again, such is not the case; there is decay in this world, both physically and with our projects, ideas, and dreams. Seasons cultivate productivity, but they also imply an end to it. The cycle of life includes both origins and expirations, celebration and sacrifice. Such is the stark reality of trying to build permanence in a transient world. It can't be done. Nature and God dictate against it.

IN DEED Think of Ecclesiastes as a description of life in a fallen world, and contrast it with the promises of God's Kingdom. Are all of these times inherent in both? No, the Kingdom of God will not be a place of war and weeping, death and destruction, or any other such evidences of corruption and decay. The Kingdom of God will flourish with life, love, and a Lord who does not change with the seasons. It will take our former futility and turn it into future fruit.

But for now, understand the broken world we live in. Don't try to dress it up as your heaven. Don't hope for the times of love and faithfulness while ignoring the times of grief and despair. God has not redeemed a nation of escapists; He is cultivating a people of perspective. We understand the nature of our world, and we look forward with hope toward the nature of His Kingdom. Even now, we have begun to get seasonal glimpses of it—all in His time.

God of All Seasons

A time to tear and a time to mend, a time to be silent and a time to speak.   ECCLESIASTES 3:7

IN WORD   If we really want to understand how this passage is to play out in our lives, we need only to look to Jesus. We could make a case that every time under heaven was fulfilled appropriately by Him. A time to be born? Yes, in the fullness of time, in fact. A time to die? Yes, at God's appointed moment. A time to kill or to tear down? Yes, an evil climate of false beliefs had to be assaulted. A time to heal or to build? Yes, and He is still healing and building today. Moreover, He scattered and gathered, embraced and refrained, tore and mended, was both silent and outspoken. He loved people and hated sin—He still does both. He declared war on the kingdoms of this world and proclaimed eternal peace, the "shalom" of God. Jesus did not make His seasons either/or propositions. He understood God's timing better than any other.

We need to be similarly discerning about God's timing. We need to know the circumstances that call for war against evil and those that call for peace instead of conflict. We need to understand when to violently plow unbroken soil and when to gently plant seeds. We need to remember how God confronted us with our own sinfulness and yet patiently led us to repentance. We need to consider the God who has a time for everything from bold opposition to humble encouragement. Most of all, we need to dispense with the idea that Jesus came to affirm everyone and take hold of the idea that He came to radically reorient people, cultures, and kingdoms. And we must remember: The new creation will not coexist with the old one forever.

IN DEED   By observing God's own activity, we can know that there is, in fact, a time for everything. The God who stepped into His once-perfect, now-rebel world has a plan for uprooting and planting, killing and birthing, warring and making peace. Blessed are those who understand what He is doing and get in on it.

JULY 8
Ecclesiastes 3:1-8

The only significance of life consists in helping to establish the kingdom of God.

—Leo Tolstoy

Beautiful Timing

He has made everything beautiful in its time.
ECCLESIASTES 3:11

JULY 9

Ecclesiastes 3:11;
Romans 8:18

God's fingers
can touch noth-
ing but to mold
it into loveliness.

—George MacDonald

IN WORD Some flowers will bloom within days of their planting. Others will not bloom for years, and then only for a short time. What is the difference? Only the God who has ordained the beauty of His creation to be made manifest in different ways and at different times.

You probably know people who bloomed as soon as they were planted. Perhaps you are one of them. Many of us, however, find the early bloomers frustrating. They remind us of what we would like God to accomplish in our lives. We grow impatient with the seasons of God, wondering if He will ever bring us into our own personal promised land, as we once hoped He would. We forget the valuable lesson of this planet's diverse flora. Growth, maturation, and fruition vary widely among species. And in God's mind, every Christian is a distinct species. We are all different.

We are all one in Christ, of course. But nowhere in Scripture do we find a God who deals uniformly with His people. There are people who never seem to suffer, and people who seem to suffer incessantly. There are people who bear fruit nearly their whole lives, and those who bear fruit only for a moment. There are people who live for decades and people who live for brief minutes. And God has His hand on all of them.

IN DEED Are you a people watcher, frustrated with how bountifully God has dealt with other Christians and wondering if He will ever do the same with you? There are many possible reasons for the delay, ranging from sin in your life to the special nature of the gifts He has given you. But consider the God who makes all things beautiful. He is crafting a global testimony to His glory (Habakkuk 2:14). Why would He leave you out?

Consider the promise of Romans 8:18: Current sufferings do not compare to future glory. Then set your heart on the future glory. Know that in His time, God will make all things—even your life—extremely beautiful.

190

Escape to Reality

Set your minds on things above, not on earthly things.
COLOSSIANS 3:2

IN WORD   The core of wisdom, the heart of this transformation that we call sanctification and Paul calls the renewal of the mind, is summed up in this verse. We set our minds on different things than we once set them on. In our thinking, we exchange the temporal for the eternal, the worthless for the valuable, the profane for the holy, and the self for Christ. We no longer pursue darkness, only light. We no longer pursue money, only treasure. We no longer pursue our reputation, only His. We stand in a radically different place.

That place is where Christ is. Did you know that we are with Him? That's the basis of Paul's declaration: We have been raised with Him. We are seated where He is seated, and He lives in the depths of our hearts, where we once thought we reigned. It only makes sense, then, that we would be thoroughly absorbed in our new dwelling and our new life. Not to be preoccupied with eternal realities would be ridiculously out of touch with the fact of our new nature. We would be escapists, fantasizing about worthless things and neglecting unimaginable riches. We would be like pigs transformed into princes, but who still prefer slop. We'd have no sense.

Yet this is where many Christians live. We have a hard time thinking about the reality we can't see, though it is very, very real. We're well trained in the ways of this world, immersed in false philosophies. We harbor old thoughts. So Paul must instruct the Colossian believers who, like us, are hounded by false perspectives. Set your minds where Christ is and where, in fact, you are too.

IN DEED   This is a discipline. We've perhaps been taught that disciplining the mind to think in a certain way is similar to brainwashing, an artificial escape from reality. But for us, setting our minds on the things above is an escape *into* reality. It puts us practically where we are positionally. It renews our minds and it makes us truly wise.

JULY 10
Colossians 3:1-10

May the mind of Christ my Savior live in me from day to day.

—Kate B. Wilkinson

Your Mind, God's Thoughts

Put on the new self, which is being renewed in knowledge in the image of its Creator.   COLOSSIANS 3:10

JULY 11

Colossians 3:1-10

Think through me, thoughts of God.

—Amy Carmichael

IN WORD   When we are born again, we are spiritually renewed. The Bible makes that clear. We are a new creation—the old has passed away and the new has come (2 Corinthians 5:17). What does that mean for our bodies? Though they will die, they will be resurrected. What does that mean for our hearts? Though they were hard and resistant to God, they are now soft and inclined toward Him. What does that mean for our minds? Paul tells us here. We are given a new knowledge.

This new knowledge isn't just a change of opinion. It's an invasion of truth into our once-deceived souls. Now we have a radically new perspective, a vital understanding of who God is and how His Son has saved us, and a new means of making decisions. We also have a kindred wisdom with our Creator, an ability to think His thoughts and live His life. We are in a holy process of becoming like Him.

Isn't that amazing? While many cults and false philosophies make us gods unto ourselves, Jesus makes us humans with God's mind. It's a foundational principle of Christianity: We who were fallen and dead are now inhabited by One who is risen and alive.

Does that mean that our thinking will never err? That we will never disagree? That our logic will be infallible? Obviously not. But it does mean that, to the degree we submit our thinking to Christ, we can have His mind. We can be led and guided, renewed and transformed, crafted ever increasingly into the divine image.

IN DEED   Are you aware of God's goal for your thought life? It is perhaps the most challenging battleground for a Christian. We all too easily give in to depression, negativity, deception, misconceptions, and all sorts of false perspectives. God changes that, if we will let Him. You do not have to convince Him to do so—He loves to. He wants us to think like Him. Shed the old and embrace the new. Be conformed to His image daily in your mind.

Constant Need

Elijah was afraid and ran for his life.
1 KINGS 19:3

IN WORD   James was right when he wrote that "Elijah was a man just like us" (James 5:17). Though most of us don't have a ministry the magnitude of Elijah's, we have a fear reflex equal to his. Elijah had spent the last few days proving the power of God over the empty religion of Baal. He had been viewing eternal truth with his very human eyes. Suddenly, when Jezebel sought his life, he viewed his circumstances through those same lenses, but with unexpected fear. This time, those eyes didn't see the glory of God, only the wrath of Jezebel. He was afraid—just like us.

What is it about us that can see eternal majesties at inspired moments and then can cower at ungodly threats at other moments? Does the Holy Spirit come and go that freely from our hearts? Perhaps it's just that we are so thoroughly infused with human frailty that we can only get glimpses of divine power. Perhaps we are simply inconsistent in our devotion. Perhaps faith is a muscle that is sometimes, for some reason, reluctant to work. Though faith is, in a sense, our resting in God, we can still get tired. We pass seamlessly from anxiety to divine glory to anxiety again, hardly ever realizing what empowers us one day and not another.

A heart of wisdom will come to grips with such human inconsistencies. We must settle in our own minds the fact that we are never self-sufficient and always dependent. Great successes do not eliminate deep needs; it's a fact of the human condition. We have to get used to it.

IN DEED   We must battle constantly against two relentless urges: the urge to think great victories should be followed by self-sufficiency; and the urge to let visible circumstances rule our thinking. Elijah, the great prophet of Israel, gave in to both. So do we. Frequently.

Never let the visible rule. Your victory yesterday does not decide your status today. Neither do your enemies. You need God desperately every day equally, regardless of how threatening—or how successful—things look.

JULY 12
1 Kings 19:1-18

O God, never suffer us to think that we can stand by ourselves, and not need Thee.

—John Donne

The Prowler

The LORD said to Satan, "Where have you come from?"
Satan answered the LORD, "From roaming through the
earth and going back and forth in it." JOB 1:7

JULY 13
Job 1:6-12

No matter how
many pleasures
Satan offers you,
his ultimate pur-
pose is to ruin you.
Your destruction is
his highest priority.

—Erwin Lutzer

IN WORD The wise believer understands the nature of the enemy. We won't know all of his schemes, and we won't ever get to the point where we can outsmart him. We live in a world that he has shrouded in darkness and confusion, and we are incapable of piercing that darkness—on our own, at least. No, our task in this reconnaissance mission is to understand that (1) the enemy exists; (2) he has an agenda that aims at every one of God's people; (3) he is *not* omniscient or omnipresent; but (4) he gets around.

When God encounters him in verse 7, Satan is before the heavenly throne. God knows, of course, where he has been, but He makes Satan admit his unholy agenda. He had been roaming throughout the earth in order to find and expose evidence of "unglory"—impurity and evil that might ruin God's reputation. Peter also mentions the activity: "Your enemy the devil prowls around like a roaring lion looking for someone to devour" (1 Peter 5:8). This is no medieval superstition; this is war.

The wisdom of the believer comes in knowing of this enemy. We do not have to study his ways or obsess about his capabilities; we need only to look to Jesus. But we need to be aware that there is an evil, personal entity prowling around our doorsteps, looking for moments of opportunity. We cannot casually give them to him.

IN DEED Several places in Scripture urge the saints to be "sober-minded." The activity of the enemy is the major reason for such instructions. It doesn't mean we can't enjoy life and the gifts of God; it does mean, however, that we can never let down our guard.

Look to Jesus in all things, but especially for protection. He has won the victory against Satan and holds all power over him. In a world of prowlers, that's extremely important to remember.

Assaulted for Glory

Then the L<small>ORD</small> said to Satan, "Have you considered my servant Job?" JOB 1:8

IN WORD We'd like to think that in our resistance against the enemy, God is our refuge. He is, but not in the way we think. Far from being Job's hiding place, God became his PR firm. He makes no attempt to shield Job's reputation from the enemy. He specifically points to His servant as a target.

Why would God do such a thing? Job has served Him well. Is this really the reward he gets? Does all of his righteous behavior really warrant the transaction made in the heavens, when Satan approaches Job's Refuge and the Refuge points to Job? Why would God set His faithful servant up for temptation, even disaster?

Because there is an overarching purpose in this universe, and it is not the comfort of man. We like to think that God exists for our benefit, that He's a heavenly wish-granter and need-fulfiller. And while He has committed to grant us our heart's desires—assuming those hearts are godly—and to fulfill all of our needs—assuming we look to Him in faith—His actions are not guided primarily by the welfare of man. His actions are guided first by the glory of His name. And in this case, the glory of His name called for a demonstration.

IN DEED We often get caught up in human-centered thinking. We assume that God's salvation is first and foremost about our well-being, and we even try to define "well-being" for Him as comfort, prosperity, success, and health. God is interested in all those things; after all, He cares for us passionately. But there's a higher purpose: His glory. This is a God-centered universe, not a man-centered one.

When you are under attack from the adversary, ask God to protect you and deliver you. But more than that, ask Him to preserve His reputation in you. Ask for His glory to be made manifest in the conflict. Ask for victory for His sake first, and for your sake second. Understand that this conflict revolves around issues much higher than you. It revolves around the glory of God.

The glory of God . . . is the real business of life.

—C. S. Lewis

Grief and Worship

At this, Job got up and tore his robe and shaved his head.
Then he fell to the ground in worship. JOB 1:20

JULY 15
Job 1:13-22

His love in times
past forbids me
to think, He'll
leave me at last
in trouble to sink.

—John Newton

IN WORD What is your response when your trials are most severe? If you're like most, worship is not your first reaction. In fact, we often criticize God, question His goodness, and ask pointed questions about why this had to happen to us—a whole ritual of self-pity—long before we come to a place of true worship.

Worship was Job's first reaction. His livelihood (i.e., his oxen and donkeys) had been stolen. His transportation (i.e., his camels) had been stolen. And his children (i.e., his legacy) had been killed. All of this in one day! And Job's first reaction, after his initial shock and grief, was not anger, not questions, and not apostasy. It was worship. He violated every psychologist's formula for the stages of grief.

How could Job do such a thing? Did he know he was under a divine microscope? No, the questions he and his friends wrestle with in the ensuing chapters indicate that he had no idea what was going on. Did he assume that his sins had finally caught up with him? No, he maintained his righteousness throughout the book. So how could he worship? He knew, deep down in his heart, two essential facts that most of us question from time to time: (1) God is sovereign, and (2) God is good. Those were givens. Job could worship because whatever was happening, it was under the sovereign hand of a really good God. He didn't know why bad things were happening, but he knew who watched over him. And despite circumstances, he knew that the One who watched over him was worthy.

IN DEED It goes against our human nature, doesn't it? When our lives fall apart, we're inclined to accuse God of not living up to His end of the bargain. Job remembered that he was not in a bargaining position—never had been. All he had received from God was from His mercy. He knew that the fact that it was now gone had nothing to do with God's character. When our trials weigh heavily upon us—even when crisis strikes—we must remember the unchanging, merciful nature of God.

Our Deepest Love

The LORD gave and the LORD has taken away; may the name of the LORD be praised.   JOB 1:21

IN WORD   No, Job wasn't thrilled with this turn of events. He made no effort to mask his grief. He was not just being stoic, and he was certainly not a Pollyanna. He was devastated, and he couldn't hide it. But in his devastation, he remembered the character of God. He remembered that all things he had ever been given were gifts from a merciful hand. He had never really gotten attached.

That's the problem in many of our trials. The things or people that are threatened are deeper attachments to us than the Lord Himself is. With many of our loves—whether they be possessions, people, places, or positions—we would almost rather lose God than lose them. We live with a sense of permanence in this world, and when that permanence is shaken, our security is shattered.

God has a better plan for us. He wants us to love the people He has placed in our lives and to appreciate His gifts, but He does not want us to lose sight of Him. In a crisis, when our world is shattered, He wants to be the foundation that never moves. If we've built on that foundation, we can say along with Job: "Naked I came from my mother's womb, and naked I will depart" (v. 21). We will remember that we will be what He wants us to be—nothing more, nothing less. We will live as though our lives are not ours, but His. And He can do whatever He wants with them—even if it's tragic.

IN DEED   It's hard to maintain such an attitude. We have our agendas. We are filled with dreams and goals, attachments and loves. We have constructed our lives with all of the things we think we need most and many of the things that will comfort us. And when God lets His archenemy take one or all of those things away, we think our lives have been shattered.

The wise heart does not get overly attached to the things of God, but only to God. Measure your attachments with honesty. When you are enduring a trial, consider the value of your losses compared with the glory of God's name. And let His name be praised.

JULY 16
Job 1:13-22

Our heavenly Father never takes anything from His children unless He means to give them something better.

—George Müller

Measured Words

Do not be quick with your mouth, do not be hasty in your heart to utter anything before God. ECCLESIASTES 5:2

JULY 17

Ecclesiastes 5:1-3

When you pray, rather let your heart be without words than your words be without heart.

—John Bunyan

IN WORD If you had an appointment to confer with the president in the Oval Office, would you prepare? Would you plan what you were going to say before you saw him, or would you just play it by ear? All but the most reckless and careless of us would consider our words wisely. We'd realize we're meeting with someone who has the power to change things. We'd think about what we want changed.

But we rarely approach God that way. Perhaps it's our awareness that our time with Him is unlimited. Perhaps we've heard so many pastors and teachers tell us that even our smallest concerns are His concerns. Perhaps we've interpreted His generous time and detailed care as reasons that prayer can be casual. If so, we've misunderstood. God does give us unlimited time, and He does care about the details. But prayer is anything but casual.

Jesus rebuked both religious hypocrites and pagans for their many words. Maybe He was zeroing in on their annoying repetitions, but He also pointed out their false idea that many words get God's ear (Matthew 6:7). He also warned that we will be accountable for every careless word we've spoken (Matthew 12:36). And we can assume that His standards for prayer are probably not lower than His standards for conversation.

IN DEED God encourages us to come to His throne with boldness and confidence (Hebrews 4:16). But He does not encourage us to come to His throne with carelessness. Our words in prayer carry incredible weight. They should be well considered.

Perhaps a good approach to prayer would be to take Solomon's advice. After all, God surely has more important information to share with us than we have to share with Him. Yes, He wants to hear our desires. He also wants us to listen to His. Both are extremely important.

Called to Be Comforters

I saw the tears of the oppressed—and they have no comforter. ECCLESIASTES 4:1

IN WORD Solomon's wisdom in Ecclesiastes is a biting, bitter assessment of life as it is "under the sun" (1:3). It does not take into account the intervention of a redeeming God that gives purpose to all things. No, this is what life with a distant God looks like; in this picture, "everything is meaningless" (1:2). So when this teacher looks at the oppressed— the widows, orphans, and captives found in every society in every era—he sees no comforter. There is no one on their side.

God sees the same situation. We are told that He is "a father to the fatherless, a defender of widows" (Psalm 68:5). But more than that, He is constantly calling His people to take care of those who are needy. The people of God are never to be the oppressors, but are always to side with the oppressed. We are to work for their justice, sacrifice for their welfare, and provide for their needs. We may have various political, social, or spiritual philosophies on how that is to be done, and we may argue over which institution is best equipped to meet the needs. But there is one scriptural principle that we cannot argue with if we believe God's Word: It is our job to show God's compassion for those who need it.

Think of the commands. In the Law of Moses, God always made provision for widows, orphans, and others in need. Proverbs tells us that whoever oppresses the poor shows contempt for God (14:31) and that God will not answer the prayers of those who neglect the poor (21:13). And unless we think God's concern for the needy is an Old Testament phenomenon, consider James: Real faith always involves looking after widows and orphans (1:27).

IN DEED How do you treat the poor and oppressed? Your answer is essentially a barometer of your relationship with God. You can measure the degree to which your heart beats with His by your visible, active concern for the needy. Solomon's observation that the poor have no comforter begs a response. God calls His people to be that response.

JULY 18
Ecclesiastes 4:1-3

When we turn our backs on the poor, we turn them on Jesus Christ.

—Mother Teresa

Guilty Fear

The wicked man flees though no one pursues, but the
righteous are as bold as a lion. PROVERBS 28:1

JULY 19

Proverbs 28:1;
Leviticus 26:14-17

A guilty mind can
be eased by noth-
ing but repentance.

—Benjamin
Whichcote

IN WORD Saul was relentless in his hatred for David. David demonstrated on numerous occasions that he meant no harm to Saul and would wait patiently for God's plan, whatever it might be. But Saul was disturbed by an ungodly, jealous fear. He thought David's popularity was his greatest threat. He wanted to maintain his throne, whether it was God's will or not. And he would use any treacherous means to do it.

Those who have an evil disposition toward others are often imprisoned by their paranoia. It hounds them relentlessly wherever they go. They make the mistake of thinking that others are as manipulative and ill-willed as they are, and that assumption keeps them in constant fear of everyone. There is no rest for them, only flight. A guilty conscience has no peace.

Those who are pure in heart, however, have nothing to fear. They assume the goodwill of others because they have it in themselves. They trust the power of God to protect and establish them because they have seen His power at work within their own hearts. They are not worried about the judgment of God because they know His righteousness, and they are not worried about the judgments of men because they know God's love. A clear conscience is always at peace, and it feels the power of the Almighty.

IN DEED Much of the anxiety we feel is the product of a restless guilt deep within. We don't trust God because we're convinced we have failed Him. Our conscience will not let us rest. And we cannot trust anyone else, either. We are jumpy and paranoid, ready to flee. We are sure our sins, however large or small, will find us out.

What is the remedy? The cleansing that comes from the One we flee. He pursues us, but not for vengeance. It's for redemption. He wants to replace our guilty conscience with a heart at peace. Trust Him. Let Him make you bold before Him. His righteousness is freely offered to you.

Supernatural Delight

Blessed is the man who fears the LORD, who finds great delight in his commands. PSALM 112:1

IN WORD The greatest turning point in a person's life is when salvation comes by grace through faith. Even so, many people struggle endlessly with the remnants of the sinful nature. Failure upon failure casts many of us into a sort of spiritual despair. We know we're saved, but we can't seem to live like it. We're a living contradiction.

The greatest turning point in a believer's life—after salvation, that is—is when pursuing God's righteousness changes from an obligation to a delight. Trying to be holy always results in failure after failure. Falling in love with a righteous God results in progress. Failures still happen, but there's a noticeably different approach to them. Instead of obsessing about shortcomings, we begin to obsess about God's goodness. We can put sin behind us as the exception when we press on into our love for a holy God. Our focus is taken off of our works and placed appropriately on our Savior. Law no longer consumes us; grace does.

That doesn't mean that the rules for living a godly life become less relevant. It means only that our method of growth changes. Instead of trying to eliminate all unrighteousness with legalistic rules, we focus our faith instead on the Righteous One. A fascination with His goodness has remarkable power to change us. A dread of the Law has none.

IN DEED There's no question that God calls us to live a holy life, and there's no question that God's righteous standards are to be our standards as well. The only issue is how to attain our growth. Is it by hypervigilance toward an unattainable Law or by a delightful fascination with the One who is holy? The standards of the two are not incompatible; but the power each one wields definitely is. No one has been made righteous by strict legalities (Galatians 3:11). The Law cannot impart life (Galatians 3:21).

How do we acquire this delight? Through faith, through prayer, and through the Holy Spirit of the delightful One. You *can* do the humanly impossible: Enjoy His commands.

JULY 20
Psalm 112

The righteousness of Jesus is the righteousness of a Godward relationship of trust, dependence, receptivity.

—Michael Ramsey

201

Blessings Forever

Surely he will never be shaken; a righteous man will be remembered forever. PSALM 112:6

JULY 21
Psalm 112

All earthly delights are but "streams"; but God is the ocean.

—Jonathan Edwards

IN WORD The promises for those who delight in God's commands are astounding. Anyone making us such promises today would be greeted with our deepest suspicions. But we know the Source of this promise. He is no slick salesman. This promise is the Word of the living God, our absolute anchor in a world of inconsistencies.

What does God promise those who have found that unlikely combination of fear and delight (v. 1)? Blessed descendants (v. 2); lasting prosperity (v. 3); light even in the worst times (v. 4); goodness (v. 5); freedom from fear (v. 7); security and victory (v. 8); and honor (v. 9). The extravagance of the promise overwhelms us. We're ready to sign on the dotted line.

What's the catch? The catch is a heart that fears God without dreading Him; a heart that *wants* His holiness rather than fleeing from it. The fallen nature finds God's Word restricting and confining, a difficult limit imposed on freedom-loving impulses. The godly nature, on the other hand, *loves* God's Word—even its hardest stumbling blocks. It may not find His Word easy or comfortable, but it finds the prospect of Christlikeness compelling and ultimately worthwhile. It pursues holiness with a passion. Like the blessed fourth Beatitude, it is driven by a craving for righteousness (Matthew 5:6). The hunger and thirst of the one who is fascinated and delighted with God will be filled.

IN DEED Who would not want such promises to be theirs? Only the highly cynical, who doubt that God can accomplish a radical change of the heart's desires within them. In their final analysis of the offer, the condition of righteousness is too prohibitive. They know themselves too well, and God not well enough. They give it up as hopeless.

We cannot afford to pass up such treasures. Blessings upon us and our descendants? Security and freedom from anxiety? We *must* ask God to put His delight in our hearts. It's the only way to His ultimate blessing.

Satisfied Longings

The longings of the wicked will come to nothing.
PSALM 112:10

IN WORD Most of us don't consider ourselves wicked. Neither do we consider ourselves righteous. No, as we perceive ourselves, we fall somewhere in between. We read of magnificent promises for the full Godward life and think of ourselves as below them. And we read of the ominous warnings to the wicked and think of ourselves as above them. Yet the Bible doesn't give us much information about a mediocre spirituality. It is always classifying people as either godly or ungodly, good or evil, holy or profane, saved or lost. In the Word, there is no middle ground.

Maybe that's comforting for those who are sure they aren't wicked or alarming for those who are sure they aren't righteous. For those of us who know our own tendency to default to the sinful nature when we're not specifically inspired otherwise, this verse drives us toward God's righteousness. We don't want this promise fulfilled in our lives. We want our longings to be good ones, validated by God Himself.

How can we be sure that our longings are godly? We can examine their source. What needs do they spring from? What purpose will they fulfill? If they exist to satisfy our own insecurities and plans, we need to reconsider them. They should spring from a love of God and His Word. When they do, they *will* be fulfilled. God has promised.

IN DEED Everyone has longings. Most of them are morally neutral. The real question we should have about them is where they come from.

God has assured us in His Word that desires coming out of a self-centered, amoral heart will be utterly frustrated. They will never be fulfilled in any lasting sense, because there is a fundamental principle in this universe: God's heart rules.

Is your heart in line with God's? Do you love Him? Do you love His Word, His will, and His ways? Then it's certain: Your longings will be satisfied.

JULY 22
Psalm 112

O Lord our God, grant us grace to desire Thee with our whole heart.

—St. Anselm

What If

Faith is being sure of what we hope for and certain of what we do not see.   HEBREWS 11:1

JULY 23
Hebrews 11:1, 6

Faith is the sight of the inward eye.

—Alexander Maclaren

IN WORD   You've prayed and tried to muster up faith. You've been through difficulties and tried to cultivate hope. You've read headlines and tried to maintain confidence. All the while, you've struggled with doubts. You've wondered if God will really come through, if trials really will be resolved, if circumstances really will work together for good. You've questioned God.

The human mind is filled with "what ifs." "What if I'm interpreting God's promises wrong?" "What if the Bible is mistaken?" "What if my prayers aren't answered?" "What if I'm not really saved?" Honest doubts nag at us, and they are relentless. Many of our "what ifs" are strategically suggested by the enemy of God; many of them are the natural thinking of a fallen flesh. Either way, we are restless within until we are able to rest in God.

That's part of the reason for prayer—extended, persistent, worshipful prayer. It brings us from a place of doubt to a place of faith. Once we're there, God can answer according to His Word. The time we spend crying out to God is not so much to convince Him as to convince us that He can and He will meet us in our needs. Our worship reminds us of who He is. And knowing who He is will nurture faith like nothing else.

IN DEED   When you are faced with "what ifs," how do you respond? Do you cultivate them, thinking of variable upon variable until everything that could possibly go wrong fills your mind? That is not the way of faith. God calls us into the kind of worship that will soak our minds in His unfailing power and love. Wisdom begins with a knowledge of who God is, and wisdom is often a prerequisite to faith. We cannot approach God in belief unless we have first determined that His will toward us is good. Only then can we be certain of what we do not see. Only then can we take hold of His promises. Only then will He reward those who earnestly seek Him.

The Raging River

When the people broke camp to cross the Jordan, the priests
carrying the ark of the covenant went ahead of them. Now the
Jordan is at flood stage all during harvest. JOSHUA 3:14-15

IN WORD Have you ever wondered why God chose a
harvest time for the Israelites to cross the Jordan into the
Promised Land? The Jordan is a less-than-formidable bar-
rier for much of the year, and forty years of wandering
would have provided ample opportunity for them to cross
at a more convenient time. But no, Moses' death and the
Israelites' arrival on the eastern bank of the river took them
to their boundary at exactly its highest moment. Why?

God wants us to follow His wisdom—His guidance,
His timing, His purposes. But we often let our circumstances
dictate the path we take. The circumstances are formidable?
Then we go another direction. The situation is an easy one?
Then we follow the path of least resistance. Those whose
lives are guided by this dynamic are following the ways of
the world. The ways of God will lead us to the Jordan at its
highest level. He will promise us deliverance in our darkest
moments. He will provide for our needs most abundantly in
a barren land. He will be for us a God of the impossible.

IN DEED Do not let the currents of your circumstances
dictate the direction you'll take. That's God's domain. His
voice is to speak more loudly to us than the boundaries that
box us in. We must learn to see Him as the unconstrained
God, the God who is not limited by the gaping need of our
situation or the restrictiveness of our circumstances.

Why does God work this way? Maybe simply because it
brings Him greater glory. When we take only humanly possible steps, we give our humanity the credit. God alone can
be praised for overcoming an impossibility. Miracles point
to Him. Expect them. Ask for them. Never let the raging
river drown out His voice.

JULY 24
Joshua 3:9-17

Faith sees the
invisible, believes
the unbelievable,
and receives the
impossible.

—Corrie ten Boom

A Matter of the Heart

Man looks at the outward appearance, but the
LORD looks at the heart. 1 SAMUEL 16:7

JULY 25
1 Samuel 16:1-13

The first and great
work of a Christian
is about his heart.

—Jonathan Edwards

IN WORD David had seven brothers. He was the youngest, and all the others looked stronger and abler than he did. Samuel the priest was a godly man, but he looked at the eight sons of Jesse as everyone else did—with human eyes. He anticipated the anointing of God with earthly measurements, a mistake no one can afford to make but that everyone does. Samuel learned a divine principle on that day of selecting the new king: He learned that God's anointing doesn't follow human standards. It is held secret in His unfathomable wisdom until He is ready to reveal it.

Think of what that means in our churches. We define the anointing of God on a preacher by how well he relates to people and preaches a sermon. We define the anointing of God on a ministry by how impressive it has made its reputation. We define the anointing of God on each other by how we dress, how we part our hair, how socially smooth we are, or how talented and knowledgeable we appear to be. And all the while, the wisdom of God is peering into each person's heart, looking beyond talent, appearance, gifts, intellect, resources, and everything else. Character is the key. Obedience and submission are the cornerstones of His anointing. He will bless people we least expect Him to bless and shelve people we least expect Him to shelve, all because He's looking in places we can barely see.

IN DEED That doesn't mean that gifts, talents, intellect, resources, and even appearance are irrelevant. It simply means that not one of those things can fulfill the will of God in a person if the heart is not right.

That should say two profound things to us: (1) We can't judge people by the standards we normally use, and (2) we can't be disciples based on the gifts we think He has given us. In both cases, popular opinion is irrelevant. The piercing eye of God is not fooled. The quality of anyone's discipleship, at all times, depends on the condition of the heart.

Deeper by the Day

I know, my God, that you test the heart and are pleased with integrity.   1 CHRONICLES 29:17

IN WORD   So many people think biblical faith is about changing our behavior. Many of the Pharisees and experts of the Law in Jesus' day were convinced that religion was an outward expression only. Our culture often makes the same mistake. Rules and regulations are substituted for a genuine change of heart. All the while, God points us back into His Word. There is nothing in it—nothing at all—to encourage a righteousness that is skin-deep.

Isn't it easy for us to get caught in that trap? We know the truth, that the gospel is about getting a new heart. But we look for the outward evidence of our new heart—as we should—and allow that evidence to become the substance of our faith—which we shouldn't. The outward works of righteousness are only the by-product of the inward work of faith. They must be a very intentional by-product, as we train ourselves to put feet on our faith. But they are by-products nonetheless. There is no requirement of God for our behavior that is not to begin down in the depths of our spirit.

God desires truth in our inmost parts. Do we? God wants to plant His wisdom deep within. Do we? Perhaps we have failed to realize the radical nature of the gospel. Perhaps we have sought guidance for our behavior without first seeking a change in our character. Perhaps we have wanted easy words to follow rather than a traumatic Word that changes us.

IN DEED   God will not let us be content with that. His Spirit will continue to hound us as lovingly as He can hound; He will not stop His work in us until it has penetrated our core. He will not settle for appearances.

Do you settle for appearances? Are you content with superficial acts of faith while a sinful heart fights and wins the battle deep within? Adopt God's desires. Never cease your prayers for change until the change runs deep. Always let God take you deeper than the day before.

JULY 26
1 Chronicles 29:14-19

Spiritual growth consists most in the growth of the root, which is out of sight.

—Matthew Henry

When God Tarries

I thought, "Now the Philistines will come down against me. . . ." So I felt compelled to offer the burnt offering. 1 SAMUEL 13:12

JULY 27

1 Samuel 13:5-15

Patience is the companion of wisdom.

—St. Augustine

IN WORD Saul was vastly outmanned and outarmed, surrounded by vengeful Philistines. He waited for Samuel to come and make the offerings that would secure the Lord's favor. But Samuel tarried. We don't know why; we just know that the longer he delayed, the more desperate Saul became. The moment Samuel was officially late, Saul acted. He made the offering himself. He wasn't a priest and had no authority; but someone had to do it. Israel was at stake.

Have you ever prayed desperately for God's help, only to see the deadline pass with no reply? God frequently tests us this way. Providence is slow in coming and we take matters into our own hands. We don't mean to be disobedient; we just assume God hasn't answered our prayers and wants us to help ourselves. He doesn't. He's waiting to see what's more important to us: our obedience or our survival.

Would God really give us that difficult a test? Just ask Abraham, Esther, or Peter. And remember Saul. Our obedience will be tested, usually in smaller degrees. But it always comes down to this: When things are really desperate, when our whole lives seem to depend on the next step, what will we do? Take it upon ourselves to intervene or continue to trust God?

IN DEED Life is filled with these little acts of impatience. We pray, but we don't wait long enough for the answer. Like Samuel, God tarries too long. Our deadlines pass—not God's, just ours. We think He has left us out to dry, that perhaps our prayers were not on target enough. But it's our timetable that is not on target. The Bible is abundant and emphatic in its commands for us to "wait on God."

Saul's impatience cost him his reign. Like him, we don't live in a waiting society. But God's Kingdom is exactly that. He will try us to see how long we wait for Him. Hang on to faith; the answer will come, and it's never too late.

Weak Strength

If you falter in times of trouble, how small is your strength!
PROVERBS 24:10

IN WORD   Paul struggled with a thorn in his flesh. Three times he asked God to remove it, but the now-familiar answer was clear: "My grace is sufficient for you, for my power is made perfect in weakness" (2 Corinthians 12:9). Paul heard straight from God's mouth how to persevere in a trial. It is God's strength that carries us through.

Jesus assured us that we would have trouble in this world (John 16:33). How negligent would our Father be if He knew this and did not prepare us for the tough times! We are not designed to cruise through this life with ease. We are built for endurance by the God who has planned an eternity for us. He knows trouble will come. He simply *must* prepare us to handle it in grace and His strength.

Newly manufactured products are often given a stress test. An extreme amount of pressure is applied to them— more than they will experience in regular use—so that their strength can be verified. God does the same for us, as painful as it is. But there's a difference. He's not testing us for our strength. He is testing us for our inclination to depend on His strength. His power is the only power that can carry us through.

We would agree with the proverb above. We *do* falter in times of trouble, and our strength *is* small. But we have learned a secret. Small strength allows room for God's power. It sends us in search of a Sustainer and a Deliverer, and there is no more worthwhile search. We will find Him if we are under no illusions about our own self-sufficiency.

IN DEED   Are you going through a trial? It is more than a lesson in tolerance. It is for your endurance and it is a lesson in dependence. Know your weakness. Know your potential for faltering. Then know the power of your God. Blessed is the person who can say, "How small is my strength!" with the knowledge that there is a greater strength available. And blessed is the Giver of sufficient grace. Where we are weak, He is strong.

JULY 28
Proverbs 24:10;
2 Corinthians
12:9-10

When a man has no strength, if he leans on God, he becomes powerful.

—D. L. Moody

In Your Trials

In all this, Job did not sin by charging God with wrongdoing.
JOB 1:22

JULY 29
Job 1

It is trial that proves one thing weak and another strong.

—Henry Ward Beecher

IN WORD When adversity strikes, our true spiritual maturity comes to the surface. Many of us can play the game of godliness, appearing to be mature while undisciplined attitudes rage within. But when adversity hits, all is exposed. Our true feelings about God come out in the questions we ask and the actions we take.

Job was a genuine saint. His faith surpassed that of all others of his time. Crisis came, and Job guarded his thoughts and his words. He did not sin by accusing God of doing him wrong.

Can we say the same? Often, when we're in a crisis, we ask God, "Why are You doing this to me?" Sometimes it's an honest question, but often it has undertones of accusation in it. We're just sure we don't deserve the trials that have come upon us, unaware that often trials have nothing to do with what we do or do not deserve. Our trials can be, as they were in Job's case, an opportunity to demonstrate the validity of our worship. They can develop our character and help us grow closer to God. When we assume that our trial is an unfair judgment or repayment from God, we expose our true feelings about ourselves. It means we were in a *quid pro quo* relationship with Him based on rights rather than grace.

IN DEED Adversity tells us a lot about what we really believe. Perhaps that's why God allows it to strike us from time to time. It answers the questions we need to have answered. It displays the accurate measure of our growth and the true nature of our relationship with God.

How do you react when you're in a crisis? Is your first impulse to charge God with unfairness? Go back to the Cross and remember that His righteous judgment against us would have been fair. God gave us grace instead. The crisis means something else. Worship God in the midst of it, and let Him use your trials to draw you closer to Him.

Implicit Trust

Though he slay me, yet will I hope in him.

JOB 13:15

IN WORD   When faith can look death in the face and say that God is good, it is true faith. It was not contingent on miracles and blessings, and it was not uprooted by trials. When Satan's savagery intimidates and wounds, the truly faithful heart can say that God is faithful. It does not let superficial evidence impugn the steadfast character of the loving God.

This does not mean, however, that those with faith cannot ask questions. We cannot ask accusing questions—that would be sin—but we can ask God to show us His ways. We can ask if our pain is the result of our own sin or of some other divine purpose. We can ask God to show up in our trial and use it to reveal Himself in a deeper way.

Job certainly did. His great statement of faith—"though he slay me, yet will I hope in him"—was a preface to another declaration: "I will surely defend my ways to his face." In other words, Job committed to hang on to faith regardless, but in the meantime he was going to ask some questions. Faith does not imply ignorance. It allows us to discover God.

A story is told of a doctor in the jungle who was forced to do surgery on his young son without anesthesia. Would the son look at his father's scalpel with horror or with trust? That would depend on the relationship. In this story, though the pain was excruciating, the son lay still in compliant trust. He knew who his father was, and he knew his father's love.

IN DEED   Do you? Can you look at the Father's scalpel with an implicit trust that He knows what He's doing? Are you certain of the love that is behind your trial? Even if He appears to slay you, will you still trust in Him? Genuine faith will always come to that point. It may ask a lot of "whys" in the meantime, but it knows that the answers, whatever they are, are not going to destroy the faith. That is certain. Regardless of our crisis, God is trustworthy.

JULY 30

Job 13:13-19

Hope can see heaven through the thickest clouds.

—Thomas Benton Brooks

Punishment or Love?

He brings the clouds to punish men, or to water his earth and show his love. JOB 37:13

God tries our faith so that we may try His faithfulness.

—Anonymous

IN WORD Elihu's observation in Job 37:13 is perceptive. The clouds God brings into our lives could be judgment. They could also be mercy. Either way our focus during trials needs to be less about God's intent than our response.

Often, God's actions have diverse effects on people. His presence can be soothing for one and extremely uncomfortable for another, depending on the prior relationship. His blessings can prompt the gratitude of one or cultivate the corruption of another. Again, it all depends on the prior relationship we have with our Creator. So it is with our trials. In some people, trials illustrate that their worship is genuine and draw them deeper into God. In others, trials drive them away. They will have nothing to do with a God who lets them suffer.

In adversity, that middle ground of indifference is taken away. When World War II ended, some people walked away from concentration camps with deeper faith, and some walked away with none. What was the difference? Their prior relationship with God probably had something to do with it. The adversity only highlighted the difference between the genuine and the false. It removed the illusion of lukewarm faith, driving people either to hot or cold extremes.

IN DEED God will bring clouds into your life. Perhaps they are hovering now. Will they be your punishment? Or will they refresh you and show you His love? The answer may be less a matter of His intent than of your response. It all depends on how you choose to see them.

Let the clouds of adversity drive you into God's presence. Let them stir a passion in your heart to know Him more deeply and to worship Him more authentically. Do not flee from them. Let them linger long enough to see His mercy fall from heaven in the end.

Master of the Morning

Have you ever given orders to the morning, or shown the dawn its place? JOB 38:12

IN WORD This is God's question to the human ego. He has a way of reminding us of our limitations whenever we get too comfortable with our understanding. When things just don't make sense to us, God reminds us that they don't have to. We're not in charge. Our understanding isn't key to the operation of this creation. We can participate in it without being in control or knowing everything there is to know. In fact, we must. Control and omniscience are not options for us.

Why does God so frequently put us in our place? Because He has to. We repeatedly grow out of our dependence on Him and try to manage things on our own. We sometimes ask questions that implicitly accuse Him of being inept or unknowledgeable. We seek to control our world and master our resources. God has to remind us that we can't. That's His job. Our role is dependence and trust.

That shouldn't make us feel too bad. Righteous Job had to be reminded as well. He got caught up in thinking his trials were all about him—what he had or had not done, or what he could do to get out of them. He didn't realize that his trials were all about God and the true worth of worship. Job's questions were presumptuous. Sometimes, so are ours.

IN DEED Do you have a tendency to want to control your environment? Do you feel out of control when your situation gets out of hand? That isn't a problem. You were never in control anyway, no matter how much you thought you were. God is our Master. He commands the dawn and holds the vastness of His creation in His hand. He has put everything in its place. When our circumstances feel out of place, we are to go to Him. The answer is always there, and we cannot be impatient for it. The wisdom of God is entirely trustworthy. Wait for it. Believe in it. Rest in the knowledge that He will help you in His perfect timing. He will break into your trial like the dawning of the day.

AUGUST 1
Job 38:1-21

Immortal, invisible, God only wise, in light inaccessible, hid from our eyes.

—Walter Chalmers Smith

The Sovereign God

I know that you can do all things; no plan of yours can be thwarted. JOB 42:2

AUGUST 2

Job 42:1-6

It has often been my delight to approach God, and adore Him as a sovereign God.

—Jonathan Edwards

IN WORD At the end of his trials, Job affirms God's sovereignty. This is a knowledge at which we do not arrive easily. Faith and experience may bring us to it, but before we arrive at such a statement, we are plagued with numerous questions of doubt. Will this turn out for good? Will God show up or just leave me hanging? Has my sin caused me to miss out on God's plan?

We know the right answers to these questions, but our trials invariably cause us to doubt the right answers. Circumstances can be awfully persuasive. We see negative things, and though we know the Word of God is more trustworthy than the vision of our eyes, we tend to put more faith in the latter. When God calls us to walk by faith and not by sight, He wants us to believe in the invisible more than the visible. He wants us to trust His Word. He wants the questions to be answered for us.

God's will is not undone by our trials. It is not even undone by our sin. We may lose out on participating in it and enjoying it if we are persistently disobedient, but His purposes *will* be accomplished. No plan of His can be thwarted. We may take the long and painful way to fit into it, but God has accounted even for that. He has seen all things from the beginning. He knew ahead of time what your crisis would be and how you would respond to it. He has had a plan all along to bring you into a deep, deep faith.

IN DEED We may ask our questions of God, but we must know in the end: He can do all things and no plan of His can be thwarted. Job's repentant confessions in chapter 42 were the most accurate he had yet uttered. God is God, and He knows what He is doing. He has a handle on our future. He calls us to participate in it willingly, but it is already well planned. Take heart in that, and know that God is sovereign.

A Cry in Our Crisis

Turn your steps toward these everlasting ruins,
all this destruction the enemy has brought
on the sanctuary.   PSALM 74:3

IN WORD   The scene is one of devastation. God's temple has been destroyed by the enemies of His people. There seems to be no deliverance, no way around the catastrophe. It's an utter disaster.

Such was the scene behind Psalm 74. But this psalm wasn't only relevant those many centuries before Jesus; it is relevant to us. It offers us a picture of a soul desperate for God. No, the ruins are not physical, and the temple is not made of stone. The picture is relevant for us because we now know that the dwelling place of God in the Old Testament pointed to the hearts of His people in the New. And all of us, at some point or another in our lives, have probably felt the need to ask of God: "Turn your steps toward these everlasting ruins, all this destruction the enemy has brought on the sanctuary." We want Him to visit the devastation that is us. We need Him to step into the ruins of our lives.

It is God's mercy that brings us to that point, though it doesn't feel like mercy at all. It feels cruel. God lets us run the way of our rebellion, and He lets our apathetic hearts lead us to pathetic consequences—conviction, despair, brokenness, and deep need. But it is all of grace. We cannot know Him unless we cry out for Him to visit our devastation. For that, we have to be brought to the point of crying out.

IN DEED   Has your life ever looked like the scene of a disaster? If not your own, have you ever had to counsel a brother or sister whose life lay in ruins? We can know that the cry of Psalm 74 is a legitimate cry. It is a necessary point for us to get to, that painful point when the raw nerves of the soul are exposed and God's comfort seems far away. Learn to see it as a necessary step of coming closer to Him. Do not let it discourage you. God will meet you there. He would not have let you fall if He'd had no plans to catch you.

AUGUST 3
Psalm 74

Our extremities
are the Lord's
opportunities.

—Charles Spurgeon

A King in Our Crisis

You, O God, are my king from of old; you bring salvation upon the earth.   PSALM 74:12

As Christ is the root by which a saint grows, so is He the rule by which a saint walks.

—Anonymous

IN WORD   That's what our crisis needs: a King. It needs Someone who will restore order, Someone who will tell us how to get back in sync with the Kingdom program, Someone who will know what went wrong and how to fix it. Every human life needs His touch.

There are two profound implications when we call God our King: (1) We acknowledge His ability to reign over our circumstances, making Him the object of our praise and the heart of our worship; and (2) we acknowledge His right to reign over us, submitting ourselves to His authority and removing ourselves from control of the situation. Both are necessary responses in crisis; the King will inhabit the ruins of a person who knows both His power and His authority.

An easy trap for us fallen creatures to get caught in is the tendency to ask God for His control of every aspect of our situation except us. We want Him to control the people who are making us miserable, the circumstances that are causing us stress, and the threats to our well-being. But we are much more hesitant to offer Him complete authority over our lives. We want Him to fix things. We don't want Him to fix us.

God will usually not work that way. In fact, He often allows our crises specifically to bring us to a point of willingness, where we cry out for Him and are willing to sacrifice anything—even our own self-will—for Him to intervene. He must break our self-direction if He is to direct us. For Him to take control, we must relinquish it. There is no other way.

IN DEED   God brings salvation upon the earth—on His terms, not ours. We want to be saved from our situation, but God is much more loving than that. He must save us from ourselves—our plans, our false hopes, our determination to be self-fulfilled and hang on to our means to accomplish it. We are often not willing until crisis comes; then we'll do anything to see God. It was grace that brought us there; it is grace that will now bring His salvation into our ruins.

A Cause in Our Crisis

Rise up, O God, and defend your cause.
PSALM 74:22

IN WORD When crisis first hits, it's all about us. We wonder how we will be affected, how we can get out of it, how we will survive. But if we're living God-centered lives, our prayers should turn quickly to a greater cause than the immediate impact on ourselves. Our prayers should be all about God and His purposes.

Many people assume that God's and their own interests necessarily coincide. We cannot afford to make such assumptions. Often, the purpose of our crisis is to break us of such thoughtlessness. After our typically human reaction of obsessing about ourselves, we must realize God's greater purposes—and we must get in line with them.

The writer of Psalm 74 knows the appropriate prayer agenda. By the time he gets to the end, his problem is not his; it is God's. He is not bending God to comply with his own agenda; he has realized that he is part of God's agenda to reveal Himself to this world. His crisis is not about the devastation in his life; it's about the harm being done to God's fame. He is no longer asking God to answer his prayers for personal reasons; he is asking Him to answer for Kingdom reasons. There's a world of difference.

IN DEED When you pray for God's help, what is your motivation? If you're average and normal, you pray for your own needs. There's nothing biblically wrong with that. But there is a maturity that needs to develop. Biblical prayers must eventually fall in line with the biblical agenda: displaying the glory of God. There is no better way to gain victory in crisis than to shift our focus from our purposes to God's. Our prayers must move from "Lord, defend my cause" to "Lord, defend Your cause." The cries for help that begin with our own desperation must end with a deep concern for the work of God and the reputation of His name. Our cause must give way to His. Our will must be shaped like His. Our ruins must be rebuilt for the glory of His name.

AUGUST 5
Psalm 74

To pray effectively, we must want what God wants.

—A. W. Tozer

Humility and Pride

When pride comes, then comes disgrace, but with humility comes wisdom. PROVERBS 11:2

AUGUST 6
Proverbs 11:2;
1 Peter 5:5

It is our self-importance, not our misery, that gets in His way.

—Daniel Considine

IN WORD God hates pride. He opposes it at every turn. Scripture hints that pride is what led to Satan's fall from heaven, and it leads to our fall as well. This proverb and its familiar companion verse in 16:18—"Pride goes before destruction, a haughty spirit before a fall"—are only two of the many biblical references to God's hatred of this root of sin. First Peter 5:5 is explicit: "God opposes the proud."

For every seeker who has wanted to know how to get on God's good side, here's a clue: God embraces the humble. True humility and an understanding of sin will lead us to Jesus, and that's God's only path for us. But that path can *only* be traveled by the humble. Human pride is its biggest roadblock. No one who puts too much stock in himself can enter the Kingdom of God.

When we became Christians, we humbled ourselves. It was a prerequisite. No one can accept the sacrifice of Jesus without realizing that he or she needs it, and that acceptance does violence to the ego. But after our salvation, we have an all-too-human tendency to let pride creep back in. We strive in our own strength to do the work of the Spirit. We start thinking that our righteousness is actually ours and not Christ's. We think our loyalty to God is praiseworthy rather than the product of pure grace. In other words, our God-centered lives can become self-centered quickly and subtly. Our pride must then be uprooted.

IN DEED Has God let you fall? If so, it was because of His grace. He undermines our pride because He loves us. He *wants* us to have the key to His heart. He divulges the secret to His pleasure. It is humility. Humility allows for confession and repentance, it allows for service and fellowship, and it allows for worship. It also allows for His blessing. Pride obstructs all of the above. At all costs, forsake it.

Malleable Hearts

Whoever gives heed to instruction prospers, and blessed is he who trusts in the LORD. PROVERBS 16:20

IN WORD The human race from its earthly abode looks up to heaven and assumes that God requires our righteousness. It's a natural impulse, one that was placed within us in the Garden of Eden. But it has become a futile quest, this righteousness that we seek. We can only find it in Another. It has to be provided for us, and we have to accept it by faith as an act of amazing grace.

We must let go of the impulse to please God with our goodness and embrace what He is really looking for: hearts that can be molded. Our master Artisan is seeking gold that He can hammer into whatever shape He pleases. He desires material that can be melted, formed, pounded, and purified. The righteousness is up to Him. The willingness to conform is up to us.

Whoever gives heed to instruction is a submissive servant of the Creator. He or she has learned that our discipleship is not achievement-focused but form-focused. We are being shaped into the image of the Son, who Himself is the exact image of the invisible God. The blueprint of our creation—drawn up to fit the image of God Himself, according to Genesis 1:26-27—is now being fulfilled. We thought we'd squandered that priceless calling, but it has been restored. The Image now lives within us. He is conforming us even now.

The hard part of heeding instruction—being a malleable enough material for God to shape—is that it requires a tremendous amount of trust. We don't like to relinquish that much control. We have our own agenda for what we should look like. But we must give it up. Only he who listens to instruction prospers. He who hardens his soul to God's work will miss out on the blessing of being shaped like Jesus.

IN DEED Do you subject yourself to the mallet of God? Submission to the Artist's hand is to be our constant pose. The pure image that results is too valuable to miss. Give heed to His instruction. The prosperity that follows is an unearthly treasure.

AUGUST 7
Proverbs 16:20;
2 Corinthians 3:18

O Lord, forgive what I have been, sanctify what I am, and order what I shall be.

—Thomas Wilson

219

The Highest Standard

It is the Father, living in me, who is doing his work.
JOHN 14:10

AUGUST 8
John 14:8-14

No man can do the work of God until he has the Holy Spirit and is endued with power.

—George Campbell Morgan

IN WORD Christians commonly take one of two approaches to a verse like this. The first approach is assuming that because Jesus was God incarnate, His relationship to the Father was unique and exclusive to Him. A logical conclusion, following that assumption, is that Jesus is the only One who can ever say these words about the Father doing His work in Him. With this understanding, we may marvel at Jesus' identity, but we can never participate in it.

The second approach assumes that the relationship Jesus had with the Father—while unique in the sense that He is the only begotten Son of God—is nevertheless an example for us to follow. If so, He demonstrates the full potential of a human being completely surrendered to God and immersed in His will. With that understanding, we not only marvel at Jesus' identity, we can participate in it.

Which of these approaches should we take? Is Jesus one of a kind in His relationship with the Father? Or does He offer that relationship to us? The rest of the New Testament makes it clear. If we are obedient and request this amazing relationship, we can quote these words of Jesus for ourselves: "It is the Father, living in me, who is doing his work."

Is it presumptuous to say such a thing? Paul did. See Galatians 2:20 and all the other verses in which he refers to Christ living in him. The Scriptures scream this truth at us, from Jesus' declaration a few verses later about doing His work (John 14:12), to Pentecost, to Revelation. It is implied everywhere. Jesus is not just our Savior; He is our life.

IN DEED Do you see Jesus' life and works as an impossibly high standard? They are, if we rely on our human capabilities. But Jesus offers His Spirit to live within us. Accept Him. Rely on Him. Ask for a greater display of His life within you. Do not settle for less. Our knowledge of His presence and strength within us makes all the difference.

Unlimited Compassion

Who is my neighbor?
LUKE 10:29

IN WORD The question was asked by an expert in the Law wanting to justify himself. It seems like a legitimate question on the surface, but behind it is a suspicious agenda. The lawyer wanted to narrow his responsibility in the eyes of the Lord. If only a few are really neighbors, then only a little is required when God says to love our neighbor. He was looking for a reduction in the requirement, an easier way out.

As much as we would like to hold the lawyer in contempt, we cannot. We ask exactly the same questions. God's grace and love are huge, unlimited, able to cover every sin and every soul. His compassion has no bounds. If we are urged by Scripture to be like Him and to be conformed to His image, we know that such boundless love and grace are also required of us. We don't quite know how to handle that. We want boundaries. We want God to define it for us: "Who is my neighbor?"

Think of all our attempts to minimize the expanse of God's ways. "When it says to forgive others, that only means when they come and ask us to forgive, right?" "When it says to love our enemies, that only means to stay out of their way, right?" "When Jesus tells us to go into all the world, that's only for a select few, right?" The questions could go on. We want qualifications. We want God to define for us the limits of our love and compassion and mercy.

IN DEED God will not define limits for our love because His love has no limits. He does choose to judge people, of course, but, unlike ours, His judgments are righteous and untainted by sin. Only He knows the right time for them. The vastness of His compassion, however, is enough to cover every person on the planet, and He calls us to be like Him. That means loving in the extreme, forgiving in the extreme, and sacrificing in the extreme. Can we do that? No. But He can do that in us and through us. Let Him live in you without limits. Let Him open your eyes to a world of neighbors.

AUGUST 9
Luke 10:25-37

He who is filled with love is filled with God Himself.

—St. Augustine

221

Trustworthy Mouths

When words are many, sin is not absent, but he who holds his tongue is wise. PROVERBS 10:19

AUGUST 10
Proverbs 10:19;
Matthew 12:36

Converse as those would who know that God hears.

—Tertullian

IN WORD The human tongue is hard to tame. James likens it to a wildfire and calls it a world of evil (James 3:6). That's not a very complimentary assessment, but it's reality. The more we talk, the more we expose the thoughts within us. Sooner or later, the sinful ones will come out.

Jesus said we would be accountable for that. Every careless word will need to be justified before God. That's a frightening thought, especially for those who talk a lot. Slanders, untruths, gossip, faithless thoughts, and any other corruption that proceeds from our mouth will need an accounting. It's terrifying to think that something we give so little thought will carry so much weight. But all things carry weight with God—especially things as powerful as words.

God frequently encourages us to measure our maturity by our ability to restrain our tongues. He who can hold it is wise, the proverb says. God assures us that the spoken word is far more potent than we think. Words can cripple emotions, ruin reputations, incite wars, spark jealousies, and create bitter rivalries. Discretion is the better part of conversation.

IN DEED That won't be true in heaven. We can speak freely there, because sin will not gush from our hearts. We will utter praises in worship of our God, and all we say to others will be edifying. That's the nature of a heaven from which all sin has been cast out. But that's not the nature of this world. Here, professionals are paid to gossip while millions tune in, debaters are required to argue, and talk shows encourage comments so offensive that they result in riotous violence. Sin gushes, and the mouth is usually where it comes out.

But followers of Jesus are a separate people. We have been called to a discipline of discretion. Our silence is often more golden than we think. The well-being of others is often in our hands. God risked a lot by giving us mouths with which to praise Him and fellowship with others. We are called to be utterly trustworthy with them.

Numbered Days

Teach us to number our days aright, that we may
gain a heart of wisdom. PSALM 90:12

AUGUST 11
Psalm 90

Time is given us
to use in view
of eternity.

—Anonymous

IN WORD   Against all evidence to the contrary, we grow up thinking we are invincible. There is something deep in the human soul—something placed there by the God who created us for eternity—that tells us life is endless. It is, but there is a substantial difference between the life we live now and the life we live in eternity. They overlap, but in only one can we bear fruit for the other. What we do today can have everlasting consequences. We can invest in the treasures of the Kingdom of God.

So many lives end in regret over this revelation. Many of us let our days pass by in survival mode or in entertainment mode, never balancing such concerns with the eternal fruits that matter more. We are to plant so that our God may reap and reward. And in order to sow effectively, we must sow with a clear awareness that the time to plant is extremely short. The window of opportunity for fruit bearing is narrow indeed.

James tells us our life is a vapor. David agrees: "Each man's life is but a breath" (Psalm 39:5). In the grand, eternal scheme of things, we are a small point on the timeline. By the time we learn what we need to know and are equipped to serve, we have but a moment left. But God has given us an awesome privilege. We can accomplish in that moment works of such significance that they will last forever. God can change people's lives through us. He can shape our children and our spouses and our friends through us. He can feed the hungry, encourage the outcast, redeem the lost, heal the sick, cultivate worshipers, and build His Kingdom through us. But only if we're wise and have numbered our days.

IN DEED   Paul tells us to redeem the time because the days are evil (Ephesians 5:16, KJV). They are fleeting days, slipping by us before we've hardly noticed. We must number them. We must live with an eye on the limitations of time and the certainty of death. Wisdom fills the hearts of those who can live with such perspective.

The Substance of Our Lives

I am the way and the truth and the life. No one comes to the Father except through me. JOHN 14:6

AUGUST 12
John 14:1-6

It is not your hold of Christ that saves you—it is Christ.

—Charles Spurgeon

IN WORD Have you ever noticed how often Jesus says, "I am"? Is He hinting at the divine name of Yahweh—the I AM WHO I AM—that God revealed to Moses (Exodus 3:14)? He is especially emphatic in John: "I am the bread of life" (6:35, 48); "I am the light of the world" (8:12; 9:5); "I am the gate for the sheep" (10:7); "I am the good shepherd" (10:11, 14); "I am the resurrection and the life" (11:25); "I am the true vine" (15:1); and here in John 14:6—the way, the truth, the life. He is all the things we need to get by in this world.

Jesus did not come to us and promise to show us the way, to feed us the bread, to shine the light on us, to tell us the truth, or any other such direct assistance. No, He is much closer to us than that. He does not just offer us these things; He *is* these things. In a very real and literal way, Jesus *is* our life now. We do not ask Him for His help in living our lives; we ask for Him to live His life more profoundly, more transparently each day. That is why it is never appropriate simply to see Him as our Teacher, Guide, Counselor, Healer, Deliverer, and the like, insofar as we think these roles belong to a person outside of ourselves. He is genuinely in the depths of our heart, asking us to get the junk out of the way for Him to shine through us. We are crucified; He is alive (Galatians 2:20).

IN DEED Do you see Jesus only as someone who has come along to assist you? Or do you rely on His dwelling in your heart? He is not just your example or your copilot. He is the substance of your life. You cannot know the Father, and you cannot get to heaven, with Him only showing you how to get there. He must *take* you there. Having been born of His Spirit, we must let His Spirit actually live in us.

This is a profound, life-altering truth. Meditate on it. Realize every morning that Jesus is present within you by reason of your faith and that He intends to conform you thoroughly to His likeness.

The Poor in Spirit

*The sacrifices of God are a broken spirit; a broken and contrite
heart, O God, you will not despise.*   PSALM 51:17

IN WORD   In Matthew 5, Jesus opens His mouth to begin His great sermon. The first eight proclamations are blessings. We call them the Beatitudes. Perhaps they sounded strange to their first hearers; blessings were imparted to unexpected subjects. But the blessings should not have sounded so strange. They are scriptural themes throughout the Word. The sacred mouth that spoke to them on the mount was the sacred mind that had inspired them centuries before.

Consider the first Beatitude: "Blessed are the poor in spirit, for theirs is the kingdom of heaven" (Matthew 5:3). Consider also the emphasis on humility throughout God's Word: "He crowns the humble with salvation" (Psalm 149:4), as well as the verse for today. Jesus told people that understanding their bankruptcy would prepare them for the riches of the Kingdom. Was that really a surprise? For a nation that had modeled itself after Pharisaical spirituality, it was. But the Bible had made it clear from the beginning: Self-sufficient pride is the wrong model.

IN DEED   Self-sufficiency continues to be the wrong model. As it was in the Garden and will always be, pride kills. We were not made for independence. There is nothing self-sufficient about us other than the ability to get by for a few decades, and even then we depend on God's resources. No, we were made for absolute dependence. We have a poverty of spirit that only God can enrich. There is a hole in the human heart that no self-effort can fill, though we try desperately.

That's our way out—to quit trying to fill it and just be desperate. That's where life with God begins. Do not let desperation drive you to frantic self-effort; let it drive you to utter dependence on God. There can be no pride in such a pose, only blessing. God always responds to those who seek Him.

AUGUST 13
Psalm 51

Humility is nothing else but a true knowledge and awareness of oneself as one really is.

—The Cloud of Unknowing

Those Who Mourn

I am bowed down and brought very low; all day long I go about mourning.   PSALM 38:6

AUGUST 14
Psalm 38

In every pang that rends the heart, the Man of Sorrows has a part.

—Michael Bruce

IN WORD   We would not normally consider those whose eyes are rubbed raw with grief to be blessed. But there is a despair that is honored by God. It is despair over the human condition, despair over our sin, despair over the ravages that this planet has seen since the Fall. God gives us a word of hope: There will be comfort in the end.

David grieved over his sin with Bathsheba (Psalm 51). But that is not the only psalm that begins with despair; many of them do, and they almost always end in joy. Those who cry to God in their distress will eventually find their crying utterly worthwhile. It's a promise: He turns our mourning into dancing (Psalm 30:11). Those who sow in tears will reap with joy (Psalm 126:5). It's a repeated story throughout Scripture: Dread, despair, hopelessness, tears, and pain will end in victory, promise, hope, comfort, and peace when God is involved. He always brings life.

IN DEED   What do you do with your pain? Do you allow it to discourage you and destroy your faith? Do you lose hope in the midst of a trial? Don't. God does not mean for you to become so preoccupied with trouble that you lose sight of Him. He especially does not want us to become so preoccupied with our sin that we lose sight of His forgiveness. There is no comfort in that. And God is a God of comfort.

The sorrowful soul is blessed indeed if the sorrow is one of repentance and truth. Our lament over the ways of this world and the ways of our own heart is entirely appropriate, and God wants all of us to spend some time there. But He does not want us to stay there. In the midst of our pain, God speaks promises. In the depths of our sin, He speaks redemption. In the far reaches of our grief, He reaches even farther. He promises comfort to those who know the grief of this world. He offers Himself in comfort.

The Meek

The meek will inherit the land and enjoy great peace.
PSALM 37:11

IN WORD When a wild horse is trained for service, he is ridden until his will is broken. It may take great patience, but if the rider can persevere longer than the horse can buck, the victory is won. The will is broken and the horse is compliant, ready for useful service.

When Jesus told the meek they were blessed, He implied a gentleness, a humility, a submission that an untamed will does not know. He also invoked Psalm 37. It was a promise that those whose will is ruled by God—in other words, those who have been broken—will come into His inheritance. It applies to Israel's kingdom and the ever-elusive Promised Land, as this verse may have originally intended. It also applies to anyone who knows good things come from God. We are His children and He will bless us with a lavish inheritance. We are suitable for it if we are meek.

Why is meekness so valued by God? Because it defers to Him. It does not take matters into one's own hands, but acknowledges the ability of the One on whom we depend. God is honored by such deference. It allows Him to work in our lives without onlookers confusing His work with our self-efforts. It does not accomplish its own agenda to the negligence of Kingdom concerns. It's the appropriate way for a flawed and finite human being to relate to a holy and infinite God. It lets Him accomplish His will.

IN DEED Where are you on the meekness scale? No, God is not asking you to be timid and weak. He is, however, asking you to be gentle and unassuming, compliant and broken. He does not honor an untamed will. He honors those who rely on Him to accomplish His purposes in their obedient lives. Eternal fruit can grow from such a life. And eternal fruit is a greater inheritance than we can imagine.

AUGUST 15
Psalm 37:1-11

Meekness is the mark of a man who has been mastered by God.

—Geoffrey B. Wilson

Those Who Hunger and Thirst

As the deer pants for streams of water, so my soul pants for you, O God. My soul thirsts for God, for the living God. When can I go and meet with God? PSALM 42:1-2

AUGUST 16
Psalm 42

It is a sure mark of grace to desire more.

—Robert Murray M'Cheyne

IN WORD When Jesus told His disciples that those who hunger and thirst for righteousness are blessed and will be filled (Matthew 5:6), was He reminding them of this psalm? Perhaps. Or maybe He was reminding them of Isaiah's prophecy: "Come, all you who are thirsty, come to the waters; and you who have no money, come, buy and eat!" (Isaiah 55:1). Those who are poor in spirit, those who mourn, and those who are meek will find in themselves a holy hunger gnawing at their souls.

Jesus was no stranger to Old Testament imagery. His Spirit had inspired it, and His humanity had been educated in it. When He announced the Beatitudes, He had recently reminded the enemy that "man does not live on bread alone but on every word that comes from the mouth of the LORD" (Deuteronomy 8:3; Matthew 4:4). Later He would announce Himself as the bread of life and the source of living water. It was true that all who hungered and thirsted would be filled, and it still is; we can be filled with Him.

IN DEED We tend to think of discontentment as an ungodly character trait, but there is a godly side of it. The discontent soul knows that something is wrong deep down inside. It knows that hole that Augustine, Pascal, and many others have referred to: the God-shaped vacuum in every human heart. And no matter how much it tries to fill that hole with pleasure, work, people, or things, the vacuum remains. It was carved out for God, and only God can make it whole.

Do you hunger and thirst? Do not make the mistake of trying to satisfy your cravings with worthless things. Only God can effectively occupy your heart. Commune with Him there. Ask Jesus to bless you with His presence today.

The Merciful

I knew that you are a gracious and compassionate
God, slow to anger and abounding in love, a God who
relents from sending calamity.   JONAH 4:2

IN WORD   One of the more colorful examples of the need for mercy in the Old Testament is a negative example: Jonah. He knew that God was a compassionate God, and he did not want God to show compassion to the Ninevites. So he disobeyed. When he was compelled to obey, he complained. Somehow, the compassion of God did not translate into the compassion of Jonah.

Do we find ourselves in such a predicament? Having been abundantly blessed with God's mercy—the unmerited grace and forgiveness we've received for our rebellion against the Most High—do we then stand in judgment of others? The idea is ludicrous, but nearly all of us are guilty. Jesus has a Beatitude He'd like us to hear: "Blessed are the merciful, for they will be shown mercy" (Matthew 5:7). The implication is sobering: Those who are not merciful will not be shown mercy. That has to hurt. We know it has applied, at least in some degree, to each of us.

Those who have not shown mercy have never understood God's. They just don't get it. They don't understand the depths from which we've been saved and the relative pettiness with which we judge others. They still think an attainable righteousness is the key, and they compel others to strive for it.

IN DEED   Have you ever found yourself passing judgment on someone else and then remembering the guilt that we have all shared before God? That is the prompting of the Holy Spirit, reminding us that we, too, are worthy of judgment and unworthy of mercy. Let the reminder sink in. God overflows with compassion for those who are lost and sinful, and if we are to be like Him at all, we must share that compassion. We must understand mercy.

AUGUST 17
Jonah 3:1–4:11

Do you wish to receive mercy? Show mercy to your neighbor.

—John Chrysostom

The Pure in Heart

Create in me a pure heart, O God, and renew a
steadfast spirit within me.   PSALM 51:10

AUGUST 18
Psalm 51

If there is joy in
the world, surely
the man of pure
heart possesses it.

—Thomas à Kempis

IN WORD   Jesus calls the pure in heart "blessed." It is an elusive purity for us. We have a hard time maintaining inoffensive thoughts for long periods of time. We are tainted with misplaced motives and petty agendas. If we're really honest with ourselves and our God, we know the truth: Our corruption runs deep.

Jesus knows the impossibility of a pure heart, and He offers to fill us with His purity. We have the Holy Spirit dwelling in us, with an emphasis on the *holy*. Even so, our purity fluctuates as widely as does the vibrancy of our relationship with Him. What can we tell ourselves to avoid discouragement?

We must remember the essence of biblical purity. It is single-minded devotion to God. It does not imply that we will always have perfectly sinless thoughts. It means that the direction of our lives will be solidly, irrevocably invested in Him. When arguments between self and sacrifice resound in our hearts, the godly impulse will eventually win the argument. Perhaps we may fail many times. Regardless, our desire for godliness must remain steadfast. The "steadfast spirit" must constantly be renewed.

IN DEED   God knows the frailties of our character. The human heart is a fickle thing; it caves in to the voices of this world and the compulsions of our flesh. But it is redeemable, utterly redeemable. "He is able to save *completely* those who come to God through him, because he always lives to intercede for them" (Hebrews 7:25, italics added).

Have we forgotten the call of the holy God? He understands our imperfections, but He calls us above them. The pure in heart—the steadfast, passionate, faithful lovers of the Savior—are a work in progress. But it is a relentless work. Our direction never changes. God will always show more of Himself to those blessed enough to crave purity.

The Peacemakers

*Consider the blameless, observe the upright; there is
a future for the man of peace.* PSALM 37:37

IN WORD How do you feel when someone offends you?
It's usually a burning reaction, a sense that your reputation
has been assaulted and the offense must be addressed. We
react to insults and pushy people with outrage, at least internally if not externally as well. It is nearly impossible for us
to resist the urge to get the last word in, to settle the verbal
score, and to put people in their place when our dignity has
been slighted. We want to fix their misconceptions.

Many people are confrontational by nature. Others
avoid confrontation on the outside, but steam about offenses
on the inside. Neither approach makes for peace. Human
relationships can be volatile, and our handling of them
determines whether we live at peace in this world and at
peace in our hearts. A person in conflict does not generally
rest well at night. We know, deep down, that we were made
for fellowship.

Jesus blessed the peacemakers. He gave profound
promises to those who would pursue relationships of integrity and support. When we do, we find a common theme:
The greatest threat to peace is the pride of the human heart.
It isn't content to let others be wrong about something. It
feels compelled to set things straight. The result is an escalating competition to determine whose opinion will win.

IN DEED It requires a deep maturity to respond to criticism and complaint with affirmation and encouragement.
The pride within us does not want to just let offenses go
unanswered. The person who can respond to an insult with
a compliment is a person who has mastered pride. In doing
so, he has become a peacemaker—an ambassador whose
interest in his King's reputation is deeper than his interest
in his own.

Jesus told us to respond to evil people with good intentions. That's an honorable, peaceful response. It doesn't
deny legitimate conflict, but it defuses it. Have you mastered
pride enough to do that?

AUGUST 19
Psalm 37:30-40

Peace is such a
precious jewel that
I would give any-
thing for it but truth.

—Matthew Henry

The Persecuted

O Lord, see how my enemies persecute me! Have mercy and lift me up from the gates of death, that I may declare your praises in the gates of the Daughter of Zion and there rejoice in your salvation. PSALM 9:13-14

AUGUST 20

Psalm 9

Prosperity has often been fatal to Christians, but persecution never.

—Amish Bishop

IN WORD The book of Hebrews tells of Old Testament heroes who were persecuted—stoned, sawn in two, put to death by the sword, destitute, and mistreated. They suffered such things because they were looking ahead to a resurrection, a new Kingdom, a city built by God. They knew where their true lives were invested, and they refused to hang on to the pleasures of this world. Why? Because the pleasures of this world are superficial and short-lived. The Kingdom is deep and eternal.

You can always tell the difference between a believer who has planted his feet in this world and one who has planted them in the Kingdom. Though all Christians live in both worlds at once, we choose daily which one we will invest in. Those who invest in the things of this world are shaken when this world is shaken. Those who invest in Kingdom endeavors can persevere through anything. They lose nothing when stock markets fall, when wars threaten lives, when terrorists rampage, or when treasures prove transient. Their lives are not based on shifting sands but on eternal streets. They know where they're headed.

IN DEED Persecution, perhaps more than any other event, reveals how eternally focused a believer is. We never seek it, of course, but when it comes our faith is purified. We find out where we stand and what our hearts treasure. We discover whether we have been living an eternal vision or tolerating a temporary lie.

Do you know where you would fix your gaze if you were persecuted? Would suffering shatter your dreams or cause you to embrace them more deeply? Your answer will indicate where you've staked your life. Answer with an eye on forever.

Prayer and Purity

*The Lord is far from the wicked but he hears the
prayer of the righteous.*   PROVERBS 15:29

IN WORD   As much as we'd like to think that there is
no correlation between our sin and the depth of our prayer
life, the biblical witness is clear: The sin in the heart affects
the prayers of the mouth. There is a cleansing that must
happen before we enter the throne room of God. There is
an emptying that must take place before God occupies the
throne of our heart. The interference must be dealt with so
the communication will be clear.

God takes sin seriously, far more seriously than we do.
A heart that tolerates it is in no condition to commune with
the Holy One. If prayer is fellowship—and it is—there can
be none of it when a corrupt soul tries to get intimate with
a spotlessly pure God. Like oil and water, there is no inter-
mingling between the Holy and the profane. Sin and prayer
do not mix.

The principle raises a serious concern for us. We know
deep down that we are sinful. How then can we ever pray?
By the purifying that comes through Jesus. He has made
us clean. He has opened the curtain at the entrance to the
Holy of Holies. We may enter in and fellowship with the
righteous God.

But we take this for granted. Perhaps we thought that it
was a once-for-all event, that salvation implied a permanent
cleansing. It does, of course—we are forever seen as righteous in God's eyes. But that righteousness must be lived
if faith is to be vibrant. A disobedient soul will find little
in common with the Lord of all creation. Some know their
position in Christ but will not live it. Prayer cannot thrive
in such a context.

IN DEED   Have you ever felt that your relationship with
God, while genuinely secure, functions awkwardly? Do
your prayers seem out of sync with His will? By His mercy,
God is calling you closer. You must drop your sin to draw
near to Him, but it is an infinitely worthwhile exchange. Sin
hinders prayer and fellowship. Confess it, repent of it, right
your wrongs, and get closer to the heart of God.

AUGUST 21
*Proverbs 15:29;
James 5:16*

As long as we
meddle with any
kind of sin we
shall never clearly
see the blessed
face of our Lord.

—Julian of Norwich

Prayer and Poverty

If a man shuts his ears to the cry of the poor, he too will cry out and not be answered. PROVERBS 21:13

AUGUST 22

Proverbs 21:13;
Psalm 82:3-4

He who wants anything from God must approach Him with empty hands.

—Robert C. Cunningham

IN WORD When most of us cite hindrances to prayer, we mention the obvious: sin, misplaced desires, doubt, enmity with others, and the like. Few of us recall verses like this one that make God's response toward us contingent on our response toward others. But the Scripture is clear, and the book of Proverbs and other Old Testament passages are quite emphatic about it: God is intensely compassionate toward the poor, and His followers must be also.

There's logic behind that. Those who really understand what God has done will reflect His grace in their attitude toward the oppressed. In a very real sense, we were all broken and destitute. We needed compassion and restoration, and God gave it to us. He is the One who gives to the poor. He urges us to recognize our poverty so we will be blessed by His grace (Matthew 5:3; Luke 6:20). Anyone who understands that and accepts it must go and do likewise. Otherwise, we are guilty of an extreme hypocrisy. We receive mercy without extending it. We take but do not give.

We may be content to help the poor whenever we encounter them, but God is more intentional than that. He seeks them out, just as He sought us. He is the Provider who meets the needs of those who cry out to Him, and often He meets their needs through us. We must be available.

IN DEED So how does our reaction to poverty enhance our prayers? Those who understand God's compassion for the needy—those who have experienced it and then represent it to others—are best able to understand God's will and pray with passion for His purposes. The heart of compassion that beats in God's Spirit is the heart of compassion that beats in us. That puts us in deep fellowship with Him. And deep fellowship is what prayer is all about.

Are your prayers going nowhere? Check your concern for the poor. Does it reflect God's? If not, seek a change. Those who meet others' needs will see God meet their own.

The Spiritual Side of Money

If you have not been trustworthy in handling worldly wealth,
who will trust you with true riches?   LUKE 16:11

IN WORD   There is an unexpected subject of which the Bible speaks in more than 2,300 verses. It is referred to more often than heaven, hell, salvation, or many of the other key doctrines of our faith. To have been given such attention in the Word, it must be of great interest to God. But the topic is often considered unspiritual. The topic is money.

Mammon. That unrighteous stuff that implies that we must account for every ounce of productivity, every moment of work, and every act of service because we do not trust each other. Think about that: We only have money because we need to keep track of the things we've done and the products we've traded. We can't rely on others to be fair, so we've established a system of fairness. We've placed value on various currencies and used them to keep track of what is due to us. We compete with others for the limited resources at hand. We have money because we fell.

Heaven won't be like that. If we were to speak of heaven in human terms, we could trust everyone to freely provide their products and services because we would freely offer our products or services. The store would give us its goods because its workers would trust us to give ours. There need be no accounting in heaven, because all things are abundantly available and everyone is completely reliable.

The fatal flaw of communism was that it sought a heavenly economy in an ungodly society, and that just won't work. But we're under no such illusion. Money is inherently corrupt because of the context in which we live. Our use of it, however, is intensely spiritual.

IN DEED   Have you considered the emphasis your Father places on your use of money? Or have you wrongly seen it as peripheral to the spiritual life rather than a central means of grace? Use it often, but use it well. It is a deeper spiritual issue than you might have thought.

AUGUST 23
Luke 16:10-15

One fifth of all Jesus had to say was about money.

—Billy Graham

Exposed Motives

All a man's ways seem innocent to him, but motives are weighed by the LORD.   PROVERBS 16:2

AUGUST 24
Proverbs 16:2;
Psalm 139:23-24

It is not what a man does that determines whether his work is sacred or secular, it is why he does it.

—A. W. Tozer

IN WORD   In our constant quest for self-improvement, we focus on the things we do. As we grow spiritually, we measure ourselves by our actions. We're preoccupied with outcomes, and as long as those are improving, we think we are improving.

But God has a different agenda. He looks at our motives. In fact, Jesus was particularly harsh with a group of legal experts whose deeds were right but whose motives were wrong. The outward behavior, while important, could be ruined by misplaced intent. God wants internal integrity. If that is there, deeds will follow. But it is entirely possible for us to appear right on the outside and be hollow on the inside. Jesus referred to that phenomenon as "whitewashed tombs"—a beautiful exterior masking the death within.

The problem with our perception of ourselves is that we are rarely discerning enough. All of our ways seem innocent to us; we think our intentions are good. But God calls for a closer examination. Are we acting out of self-interest or a passion for God and His Kingdom? Are we focused on our reputation or on His? Are we disciples for the long haul or because we want something soon from God? The answers aren't as easy as we might think. We cannot arrive at them ourselves. We must be illumined by the Holy Spirit. He must shine heavy doses of reality into the hidden purposes of our hearts.

IN DEED   David asked God to search him and know his heart (Psalm 139:23-24). He knew that his intentions mattered to God. He knew well enough that he needed a more objective assessment than his own. There is always more to our designs than we see.

Do you want God to expose your intentions? Ask Him to. He who is motivated by holiness and compassion wants you to share His desires. He wants His motives to become yours. He wants you to share in a purity deeper than you can even imagine.

Praying an Agenda

Balak's anger burned against Balaam. . . . "I summoned
you to curse my enemies, but you have blessed
them these three times." NUMBERS 24:10

IN WORD In the strange story of Balaam and Balak
(Numbers 22–24), we read of a king convinced that it must
be the divine will to save his people. He summoned Balaam
to pronounce a curse against Israel's coming horde. We marvel at Balak's inability to understand. Poor simpleton; he just
doesn't get it. Blessing and cursing is not about his personal
agenda; it's about God's. Balaam even tells him the rules up
front, but Balak simply can't get it out of his head that if he
pays enough, pleads enough, and promises enough honor,
the sorcerer will be able to establish the divine will all by
himself. Obviously, he can't. Balaam can only do what God
tells him to do.

Balak is an easy target for our contempt. What a fool!
But aren't we often similar? Isn't this how we approach
prayer? We try to persuade God to bless our own agenda.
We come up with a plan in all confidence that it's surely
God's will. We miss a crucial step in the process. The first
item of business in any prayer request is not to ask God
to defend our position, establish our plans, or fulfill any
other aspect of our agenda; it's to ask Him what His agenda
is. Balak's bullheadedness led to utter frustration. Are you
utterly frustrated, too?

IN DEED How often do you pray for your agenda without consulting God for His? Are you absolutely sure that
what you're asking for is part of His plan? We don't have
to know every aspect of God's will before praying, but we
must pray with an understanding that His will, believe it
or not, may contradict ours. We simply must forsake our
assumptions and be open to that. Never be a Balak in disguise, using prayer as a sanitized form of sorcery. Use it
to get yourself in line with the divine program. Then pray
your heart out.

AUGUST 25
Numbers 24:10-14

You cannot alter the
will of God, but the
man of prayer can
discover God's will.

—Sadhu Sundar Singh

237

Beyond Pettiness

Starting a quarrel is like breaching a dam; so drop the matter before a dispute breaks out. PROVERBS 17:14

AUGUST 26
*Proverbs 17:14;
2 Timothy 2:23-24*

I have never yet known the Spirit of God to work where the Lord's people were divided.

—D. L. Moody

IN WORD What is it in the human psyche that compels us to pursue a matter straight into the heart of a conflict? Do we just enjoy a good fight? For some reason, we frequently feel we must establish truth—as we see it—in even the most petty of disagreements. We often value our opinions more than we value our relationships.

Why is that? What so captures our indignation that we will sacrifice friendships and feelings over something that just isn't worth it? Blessed are those who do not have a contentious spirit within them, but most people at some time or another have struggled with one. It is human nature. We feel offended when people disagree with us, and we are bent on establishing who is right and wrong. Even when there is no right and wrong.

Does this mean there's no place for conflict? Obviously not. We are called to stand up for what is morally and spiritually right—to a point. Even Jesus was no stranger to conflict, and He is our model. But we must develop the discernment to know what is worth fighting for and what is not. Most of us find ourselves frequently confused on the issue.

IN DEED When you sense a conflict escalating, what is your response? Do you take it as a challenge to win? Or can you step back and assess whether it is really worth fighting for? Broken relationships are no pleasure to God. He even inspires the writer to call a quarrel "sin" a few verses later (Proverbs 17:19). Petty squabbles once begun are hard to stop. They do not suit a child of God.

Learn to practice a discipline of restraint. Do not run from an important issue, but do not pursue a pointless one. Let relationships become more important to you than petty proofs and problems. God has done so with us. We must do so with others.

Secret Sins

Stolen water is sweet; food eaten in secret is delicious!
PROVERBS 9:17

IN WORD The truest measure of our spiritual maturity is always found in private moments. When no one is looking, how pure are our eyes? When we are alone, how honest are our prayers? When there is no threat of being contradicted, how accurate are our words? The secret life is the true life. It is who we are before God. He sees all.

Fallen human nature has a universal tendency: We are more concerned with our reputation among others than we are with our standing before God. We do not want friends or strangers to know our deepest secrets, but we have no embarrassment about them with God. Is it because we know He sees and understands? Perhaps so. But when sin is involved, His holy eyes are more grieved than those of any stranger. Yet we fear the stranger more.

That is why Jesus spent a lot of time encouraging His disciples to guard the integrity of their secret life. Their spirituality was to be most honestly lived behind closed doors—the prayer closet, the fasting schedule, the hand that gives tithes and offerings. These are the signs that maturity is real and not just for show. But this is the secrecy we save for our sins.

It is natural for us to keep our sins in darkness and to show off our spirituality. But God doesn't ask for what comes naturally; He calls for the opposite. We are to expose our sins—confess them to Him and others—and to be humble in our disciplines of the Spirit. Faith will show itself in works, but it will never show off. Sin, on the other hand, will hide itself from others, but it can never hide from God.

IN DEED If you are like most, your reputation is sacred to you. You guard it well. But which matters more—your reputation in the world or your reputation with God? The opinion that counts the most is His, and God's assessment of our secret sins is graver than we thought. Live transparently before Him. Confess them all in naked, heartfelt honesty. Let Him shine in your dark corners.

AUGUST 27
Proverbs 9:17;
Psalm 90:8

It may be a secret sin on earth, but it is an open scandal in heaven.

—Lewis Sperry Chafer

Spiritual Anxiety

He did it to demonstrate his justice at the present time, so as to be just and the one who justifies those who have faith in Jesus. ROMANS 3:26

AUGUST 28
Romans 3:21-31

Justification takes place in the mind of God and not in the nervous system of the believer.

—C. I. Schofield

IN WORD The gospel takes a lifetime to really understand. Perhaps we will always be exploring its depths and never finding its boundaries. Though we try to rest in the salvation God has offered to us, it still hasn't completely sunk in. We try to earn it, if not by legalism then by proving the earnestness of our faith.

How do we compromise the purity of the gospel? Every time we look at ourselves to see if our salvation is genuine, we have compromised it. When we ask whether we've done enough good works, we've made salvation something to achieve. When we ask whether we believe strongly or purely enough, we've made salvation a matter of our own resolve. Either approach will give a deep sense of anxiety; they both base salvation on the fickle heart of a human being.

There is a spiritual angst deep in the heart of many Christians. It is an unsettled feeling that perhaps we have not done enough, believed enough, struggled or sacrificed enough. Paul offers us the cure: God is both the just and the justifier. Salvation begins and ends in Him. Everything about it, other than our simple acceptance, is a gift.

IN DEED What does it mean that God is both just and the One who justifies? It means that the same One who demands holiness accomplishes it for us. The same One who orders a sacrifice of blood provides the sacrifice of blood. He requires of us perfection; in Jesus, He offers His own perfection in our stead.

The remedy for our salvation-anxiety, whenever it creeps back in, is to fix our eyes on Jesus. Don't look within at the quality of your faith, and don't look at the abundance of your works. Look at Jesus. Count on what He has done. Rest in His work. Know that He has satisfied God fully—for you.

Irresistible Guidance

In his heart a man plans his course, but the LORD
determines his steps. PROVERBS 16:9

IN WORD Balaam wanted to accept Balak's payment for cursing the Israelites, so he went when called. But an angel stood in the way of his donkey and would not let him pass. Jonah wanted to get as far from Nineveh as he could when God called him there, but a storm and a fish dictated otherwise. He became a very reluctant but very effective evangelist. Paul wanted to travel through Asia Minor preaching the gospel, but the Holy Spirit would not let him. There was a better plan. A vision directed his party to Europe, and a new frontier for the church was born.

Those examples vary in their godliness, but not in the means to their direction. Each had plans that didn't fit with God's greater agenda. God got them where He wanted them to go, either with or against their will. His agenda prevailed.

So it is with our plans. We determine the direction we want to take, and God intervenes. Sometimes it is even a godly direction, as in Paul's attempts to evangelize Asia Minor. But if God really wants to accomplish something, and our plans do not fit His purposes, His purposes win. He will intervene. Human will cannot thwart His overarching plan.

IN DEED We can never take that principle as an excuse to pursue our selfish interests. God wants us always seeking His will and obediently following it. But as much as we try to perfect that process, there is usually an element of insecurity in it. We are rarely absolutely sure of His directions. Even so, He determines our steps. We are not puppets, but His will cannot be usurped. The only question is whether we will be flexible and seek to fulfill it or stubborn and seek to defy it. Either way, whether in rebellion or compliance, God will accomplish His purposes in this world when He sets His mind to it.

Trust God's guidance, even when you're unsure of it. He *will* fulfill His plan. Open your heart to go wherever He takes you, and let Him lead.

AUGUST 29
Proverbs 16:9;
James 4:13-17

If a sheep strays from his fellows, the shepherd sets his dog after it . . . to bring it in again; even so our heavenly Shepherd.

—Daniel Cawdray

241

Inevitable Guidance

In his heart a man plans his course, but the LORD determines his steps. PROVERBS 16:9

Proverbs 16:9;
Genesis 50:20

Thy ways are past understanding, but Thou knowest the way for me.

—Dietrich Bonhoeffer

IN WORD Joseph's brothers had sold him into slavery. It was an unexpected turn, especially in light of the dreams he had recently had. Those dreams foretold his family bowing down to him. Becoming the property of wandering traders didn't seem to fit the plan. Neither did his years in an Egyptian prison. Had God abandoned him? Were his dreams really just the product of a self-righteous imagination? How could he be so far off track?

Joseph wasn't off track. The plans of his brothers for harm fit with the plans of God for good. Though everyone involved was quite unaware of God's hand, their steps were ordained by Him. He had seen the whole tragedy ahead of time and had woven His plan into it. Or He had seen the plan and woven the tragedy into it. We're not sure exactly how His sovereignty operates in the self-will of humanity, but we know that it does. Even when life throws the unexpected at us, it is never unexpected for God. He always has a plan.

That's hard for us to grasp. Sometimes life seems far off course. We think we're too far astray, or that circumstances are reeling out of control. But we forget: We are children of the God who sees ahead and who has already interwoven His good, sovereign plan with the strange, presumptuous will of human beings. We are not as off track as we think.

IN DEED If God's sovereignty applies to the actions of Joseph's jealous brothers, it certainly applies to our decision-making processes. We stress and strain over finding God's will, and it's important to seek His direction in all things. But if we've made that honest attempt and go forward in faith, there is no sense in turning back and wondering if somehow we missed His perfect plan. He has ordered our steps, even when we weren't sure of them. Long ago, He took our will even when we were willful and used it for His purposes. How much more will He keep us near His plan when we aim at faithfulness? Seek God's will and determine to pursue it, but don't stress about your steps. He always puts them in order.

Wealth, the Illusion

Why should I fear when evil days come, when wicked deceivers surround me—those who trust in their wealth and boast of their great riches?   PSALM 49:5-6

IN WORD   Psalm 49 is a wisdom psalm. It instructs us in the ways of God and warns us of the ways of men. It offers us a picture of the futility of human resourcefulness. It reminds us that those who hold power in this world— generally the wealthy—hold no power over the children of God.

Why would the psalmist fear when evil days come? Because we live under an illusion that our lives are at the mercy of others—the people we are indebted to, those who govern us, the bureaucracies and massive institutions, and more. You can't fight city hall, and you can't buck the status quo. When powerful people tell us what to do, we must either do it or come up with the funds to go to court. Since that isn't an option for most of us, we're left to swim downstream with the rest of the world. We feel bound by its ways.

The good news of Psalm 49 is that we really are not bound. We are not obliged to fit ourselves into the value systems of money and power. The cliques and clubs of a world gone wrong simply do not matter. They are false categories, figments of the world's imagination. Status—especially status based on possessions—is an ugly illusion. It will be shattered in the end.

IN DEED   Why is this a comfort? Because we easily feel discouraged when we view ourselves in the context of a distorted and deceptive world system. It swells with pride in its accomplishments, and we feel left out. But our status is not based on social, economic, or any other system imposed on us. It is based on who we are in Christ. Our value is based on what God has done for us. Our usefulness is based on the Spirit who dwells within us. Our significance is not defined by anything that we can't take with us when we go. Those who trust in such things will be brokenhearted. Those of us who do not can never be shaken.

AUGUST 31
Psalm 49

Theirs is an endless road, a hopeless maze, who seek for goods before they seek for God.

—Bernard of Clairvaux

243

Death, the Equalizer

All can see that wise men die; the foolish and the senseless alike perish and leave their wealth to others.   PSALM 49:10

The use of riches is better than their possession.

—Fernando de Rojas

IN WORD   It is one of life's deepest mysteries. We who were created for eternity and given the capacity for eternal affections often place those affections on transient things. We are all capable of the Sinai treason: While God was speaking eternal truth to Moses on the mountain, the Israelites were in the valley worshiping a golden calf. A piece of metal. No breath, no life, no power—just an earthly material that shines. God still speaks eternal truth by His Spirit and the Word, and we still worship gold. The mysteries of life rarely change.

Perhaps "worship" seems a little harsh. We all know that having wealth isn't the same as wealth having us. We can own it and use it without being controlled by it. But our sense of mastery over our possessions is often an illusion and always a dangerous temptation. Far too easily, our things begin to own us. We do not bow down and sing their praises, but we would bow down in grief if they were taken from us. We're far more attached than we think.

This wisdom psalm by the sons of Korah is right: Death is the great equalizer. Those who have wealth and those who do not will all have exactly the same amount when they breathe their last breath. We leave this world as we came into it—naked and destitute. We may have been well taken care of in our stay here, but none of our comforts last. Wealth for its own sake is only as meaningful as the dirt we're buried in.

IN DEED   What is our way out of this trap? Most of us do not resolve to go through this life as ascetic monks and nuns or as poor beggars. We have money and we use it often. What is the spirituality in that? We can leverage temporal wealth for eternal purposes. God has made that possible. The money that decays tomorrow can be invested in the lives that last forever. Riches and godliness can be a powerful combination. Wisdom ensures that they are.

God, the Redeemer

But God will redeem my life from the grave; he will surely take me to himself.   PSALM 49:15

IN WORD   This verse is what it's all about, for us and for others. This must be the first preoccupation of all our plans and purposes. It is not our productive work habits, inheritances, or any other windfall during our lives that divides the successful from the impoverished. The grave does that. Only then are true riches counted.

Is it not amazing how much time people spend securing their lifestyles, their careers, their education, and their living conditions compared to the little amount of time spent on the things of eternity? It is a sure sign of depravity when men and women cannot—or do not care to—see beyond the grave. One day in eternity, many will look back with astonishment. They will see how much effort went into things that do not last and how little went into things that do not die. And there will be gnashing of teeth.

"But God will redeem my life from the grave; he will surely take me to himself." That is the claim and the hope of everyone who has seen through the world's illusions of fame and fortune. Everyone who was snubbed by worldly elites will not care when he or she is redeemed from the grave. None of the games people play will matter then. No social, economic, or political rivalry will matter then. There will be two kinds of people—redeemed and not.

IN DEED   It is enormously important for us to keep life in perspective. It is dangerously easy to get sucked into the world's value systems. But a depraved culture is not a reliable source for what—or who—is truly valuable. God's Word is. Any other focus is a misplaced trust.

Do you get discouraged easily by your status in life? Then ask yourself: Who defined that status? God or the world? God only has two classes, and He always welcomes you into the better one. The world has many classes, and they're all false. Who would you rather believe?

SEPTEMBER 2
Psalm 49

God is the judge of all social systems.

—Oscar Romero

A Safe Refuge

Keep me safe, O God, for in you I take refuge.
PSALM 16:1

SEPTEMBER 3
Psalm 16

This is a wise, sane Christian faith: that a man commit himself to God; . . . that therefore that man ought not to be afraid of anything.

—George MacDonald

IN WORD   If we are to receive the wisdom of God, we must know who He is. Though knowing who He is begins with reading about Him in the Word, it does not end there. God is to be experienced. And, much to our anxiety, He is to be experienced in the crucible of life, where fires burn and hearts melt. It is in the trials that we learn the most about God. It is in having to trust Him that we become wise.

David often referred to God as his refuge. He would know. The would-be king had spent long seasons hiding in caves and fleeing the irrational wrath of Saul. But the caves were not his refuge. David knew that there was a surer, safer source of protection. When all of life seemed to be against him, David could hide in the safety of God.

Dictionaries define *refuge* as a place of safe retreat. No refuge conquers the threats and the dangers we face—it protects us from them. It will not promise us an absence of conflict or pain. But it will provide a haven of rest when the conflict or pain is intense. And we can take deep comfort in the refuge we are promised. It is not a cave or a bunker or a bank account or a good plan. It is God.

IN DEED   Do you know Him as your refuge? You can never know this side of God until a crisis strikes. But when it does, He is there to be found. He may seem absent at first, but He does not ignore your pleas. Though you pray for deliverance—and deliverance will come, in one way or another—He first wants you to know Him as the place of safety and rest. The Father's desire for His children is that we know, in the most treacherous trials of life, that His presence will welcome us home. When we just want to hide, we can hide in Him.

Storms rage, but the good Father never leaves His children out in the elements. He takes them in. They will have to wait out the storm, but they can wait it out within the solid walls of His presence, where a warm fire glows and His hand comforts. The wise will always go there first.

A Certain Providence

LORD, *you have assigned me my portion and my cup;*
you have made my lot secure. PSALM 16:5

IN WORD Many foolish decisions have been made out of the emptiness of discontentment. That's a frightening place from which to guide a life, but we do it often. We want something more, something better, because we're not quite happy with our lot in life. We forget one unwavering scriptural principle: God is the Author of our lot.

There's nothing wrong with a holy ambition. The key for us is to make sure it's actually holy. God has placed within us a desire to work and to accomplish things, especially for His glory. But we can deceive ourselves easily, thinking that we're working for God when in fact we're working to escape the place He's put us. Contentment is the fruit of godly wisdom and a wonderful attitude to hold, and it begins with the certain knowledge of this verse: "Lord, you have assigned me my portion."

We do not live in a content culture. Our society is moved primarily by restlessness. Deep down we know that things aren't right, and the knee-jerk reaction of a secular world is to try to fix the situation. We who are in Christ know better: He is the Fixer, and only our trust in Him will deliver us from our restlessness. That trust, if cultivated rightly, will give us the contentment that David expresses in this psalm. It will define for us our security.

IN DEED Did David write of his peace while he was sitting on a throne or hiding in a cave? Was he dancing in praise or grieving his son Absalom? It doesn't matter. The key to contentment is to refuse to define your life by your present circumstances. It is to know that you are where you are because God is sovereign. Even when the situation is desperate, we can say that "the boundary lines have fallen for me in pleasant places" (v. 6). Why? Because we've been given a glimpse of the end of the story and the One who guides it. Whatever we're going through, it will end well if we trust Him. Faith believes that truth, clings to it, and thrives on it. The result is the wisdom of contentment.

SEPTEMBER 4
Psalm 16

If we do not have quiet in our minds, outward comfort will do no more for us than a golden slipper on a gouty foot.

—John Bunyan

A Wise Counsel

I will praise the LORD, who counsels me; even at
night my heart instructs me.   PSALM 16:7

SEPTEMBER 5

Psalm 16

Let us learn to
cast our hearts
into God.

—Bernard of
Clairvaux

IN WORD   What a strange verse. David praises the Lord who counsels him; and in the parallel statement following, he attributes instruction to his own heart. That's the human heart, which Jeremiah called "deceitful above all things" (Jeremiah 17:9). How could David possibly trust it in the dark of night?

David's heart had been crafted on the right foundation. Consider all that he has said in this psalm: He takes refuge in God, he delights in God's people, he will not run after other gods, he is content with God's sovereign plan, and he enjoys what God has done in his life. A heart so saturated with God has been instructed by God. It has been changed and molded to conform with its Creator. It has fed on the will of God and trusted in His goodness. It is ready to give counsel.

Does that mean a godly person is infallible in his or her advice? Certainly not. But a person steeped in the ways of God will usually be able to discern the ways of God. A heart that desires His plan more than its own is likely to give good advice even in the darkness of the night. A spirit born of the living Word is apt to counsel according to the living Word.

IN DEED   Oh, for the wisdom of the living God! All other advice pales in comparison. Yet perhaps because we think the counsel of God is out of reach, we often strive for lesser recommendations. Or perhaps because we have such a hard time discerning between our own agenda and God's, we do not trust those inner impulses. Are they from God? Or are they from self? We often do not know.

God does not leave us there. Be encouraged; He is our Counselor and He will direct us. And when the dividing line between His will and your heart begins to blur, consider that the two might be falling in line with one another. Have you laid the foundation for that? Is God your refuge, His people your delight, His plan your joy? Then God has shaped your heart. Do not trust it naively, but trust the work that He has done in it. He has shaped it to beat with His.

A Joyful Life

You have made known to me the path of life; you will
fill me with joy in your presence.   PSALM 16:11

IN WORD   It is no coincidence that this psalm of trust is also a messianic prophecy. Peter quoted its last four verses in the Spirit-filled church's first sermon (see Acts 2:25-28). All of David's need for refuge, all of his need for providence, all of his need for counsel are summed up in Jesus. The Holy One's life, undecayed and eternal, are where we fix our hope. The people who have saturated their lives in God and let their hearts be crafted by His wisdom will see it. Jesus *is* the wisdom of God. He *is* the provision of our sovereign Lord. He is our refuge from this world of sin and death. All God-given roads lead to Him.

David, writing prophetically, says he has set the Lord always before him (v. 8), just as Jesus single-mindedly followed the will of God. That, according to all of Scripture, is the way of life. That is our path: a single-minded pursuit of the character and will of God, a wholehearted devotion to the pleasure of His company and the beauty of His glory. There is no real, lasting joy in this world other than the joy of His presence. The eternal pleasures are all found at His right hand.

Have you found it? Too many Christians have not. There are joyless souls filling our churches, souls who have not fully placed the Lord before their eyes. They believe He is up there, but they have not found Him relevant because they have not sought Him intimately. What is missing from that picture? Joy.

IN DEED   The promise of this messianic psalm is joy, eternal pleasures, safety and rest, a delightful inheritance—in short, everything the human heart craves. No wonder Peter quoted it. The wind and flame that blew and burned on Pentecost filled him with the knowledge of the Holy One. Everything the human heart craves can be found in the risen Jesus.

Do you know that joy? If not, here's how to get it: Ask. Tell God you want no more of stale belief, but only His heart, His Spirit, His love. Ask Him to stir His passion into you. Do not let the gift of His joy be wasted.

SEPTEMBER 6
Psalm 16

Joy is the most infallible sign of the presence of God.

—Léon Bloy

Living in an Out-of-Control World

As Paul discoursed on righteousness, self-control and the judgment to come, Felix was afraid and said, "That's enough for now! You may leave." ACTS 24:25

SEPTEMBER 7
Acts 24:24-26

There has never been, and cannot be, a good life without self-control.

—John Milton

IN WORD Paul went all over the Roman Empire preaching the grace of God and the salvation that comes only through faith in Jesus. He was quite emphatic about God's mercy, both in his arguments and his letters: We are saved *by grace alone*. So why, when defending himself to Felix, did he speak of "righteousness, self-control and the judgment to come"? Why didn't he speak of grace?

Perhaps Paul meant to portray himself as a lawful citizen, not a troublemaker who would stir up Felix's territory. Perhaps he was trying to tap into whatever moral sentiment had attracted Felix to his Jewish wife. But a likelier reason—one particularly relevant to our times—is that Felix was a Roman, largely unacquainted with the Law and satisfied with the options of the Roman pantheon. The empire's religion had numerous patron gods to pick and choose from, most with their own easy morality. In such a context, grace means nothing. Conviction must come first. Righteousness, self- control, and judgment must be taught.

IN DEED What does grace mean in our society? In the minds of those who are convinced of their sinfulness, it is a refreshing oasis of relief from a dry spiritual desert. But for those who have embraced a fuzzy, relative morality—the "whatever you like" ethics of our age—grace means nothing. Why would a generation that has defined its own easy standards need a merciful God? What is there to forgive?

That's why we must live in a way that conveys God's purity—not holier-than-thou judgment, but a radical, sacred change of lifestyle. Instead of fearing that our friends will respond as Felix did, we should rather fear a generation that has lost any concept of sin. Self-control is a foreign idea in our society. Exemplify it. Your life will stand apart, and your world just might see its need for God.

Tried by Fire

*We must go through many hardships to enter
the kingdom of God.*   ACTS 14:22

IN WORD   Paul and Barnabas had begun their mission work with a tour of duty through Cyprus and Asia Minor. People had responded with amazement. But almost immediately, leaders of the status quo began suppressing the new movement. The good news of Jesus was too threatening, so they threatened back.

So Paul and Barnabas declared that those who enter the Kingdom of God will enter through many hardships. Was this a new discovery for them? A developing theological principle? A major shift in Paul's perspective? Acts doesn't elaborate. Regardless, it is the early church's affirmation of something Jesus had told His disciples: "In this world you will have trouble" (John 16:33). Peter and John had already experienced it. Now Paul would discover the same dynamic. The Good News isn't considered "good" by everyone.

Many people in the world are now living this principle, but the Western church has lost the concept of the trauma of discipleship. We're caught up in our zeal for life, liberty, and the pursuit of happiness. We consider trials and persecution an aberration. We've forgotten that the gentle Kingdom of God and the vicious kingdom of darkness are competing for the same territory. We've forgotten that God makes disciples and displays His purposes by pressing His people into shape and refining them in the fire. It can be a violent process.

IN DEED   It is human nature to avoid trials. It is godly nature to persevere through them. They have an indispensable purpose in molding us into the image of Christ, who, as we recall, suffered quite a bit. Establishing the Kingdom of God in His name was a traumatic event for Him. Entering the Kingdom of God in His name is traumatic for us as well.

Don't pursue trials, but don't flee from them in a panic, either. God is doing something profound in them, either to shape you or to demonstrate His Kingdom. Patiently let Him.

SEPTEMBER 8
Acts 14:19-22

One sees great things from the valley; only small things from the peak.

—G. K. Chesterton

251

Rest in Danger

He who dwells in the shelter of the Most High will rest in the shadow of the Almighty.   PSALM 91:1

IN WORD   What do you do when the world seems dangerous? Hide? Obsess about self-preservation? Pray your heart out? All are instinctive, but God asks us to do something that is contrary to our instincts. He calls us to rest.

How can we rest when disasters threaten? How can we live safely in an unsafe world? It all depends on where we choose to dwell. There is a kind of trust that is more preoccupied with the rock-solid character of our Sovereign God than with the circumstantial evidence of danger around us. When the psalmist tells us to dwell in the shelter of the Most High, the Spirit is directing us to look at the God who is certain rather than the world that is not. He calls us to count on His utter dependability rather than the ominous headlines of impending doom. And He urges us to hang on to the truths we believe rather than the lies we see. The ability to so absorb ourselves in the character of the Almighty qualifies us as God-dwellers—those who know the strength of the walls of His house. In other words, those who rest.

The restless soul looks at the troubled world and is troubled. It hears the newscasts and panics. It cannot rest secure because it does not know the source of security. It does not understand that whatever happens in this painful world, there is an eternal reality behind it. In that reality is a peaceful kingdom where sins cannot follow and tears cannot stain. The God who reigns there urges us to find our citizenship with His people. The restless soul can find rest.

IN DEED   Where do you dwell? The dreadful things that cross our minds will attempt to toss us around like a rowboat in a hurricane. God tells us to anchor ourselves in Him. That means to place our hopes, our fears, our dreams, our sins, our faith, our weaknesses under His shelter. His shelter is our refuge, because there is nothing that can penetrate it—no terrorist, no war, no disease, no financial collapse, no broken relationship—nothing. The place of safety is available to us. Dwell there and rest.

Safety in God

If you make the Most High your dwelling—even the
LORD, who is my refuge—then no harm will befall you, no
disaster will come near your tent.   PSALM 91:9-10

IN WORD   How can any rational person accept such a claim? Didn't good Christian people die in the World Trade Center disaster? Didn't faith-filled soldiers die in Normandy, Vietnam, Afghanistan, Iraq, and all kinds of other brutal places in this world? Haven't floods, earthquakes, famine, and crime been rather indiscriminate, ravaging the faithful and the lost in the same places on the same days? Surely the psalmist didn't think this one through. Surely the Spirit of God was not the inspiration behind this shallow hope.

But we know such questions do not get to the heart of the issue. The Bible *is* true—it has proven itself to us on many occasions. So what does this promise mean? How can God assure us of seeming immunity to the world's brutal abuses? Because He insists on one vital truth: We are not of this world.

Yes, we were born into the world as children of flesh and heirs of sin. We have certainly not proven ourselves above reproach as we've walked through this life. But the Word contains glorious promises for God's people. We are born from above. No matter what spiritual slum we sprang from, we now dwell in our Father's house. And it is a place of ultimate safety.

IN DEED   The Bible and tradition are honest about the martyrs. Stephen was stoned, Peter was crucified, Paul was likely beheaded, and John was exiled. And they all knew this verse inside and out. They believed it with all their heart. The Spirit within them had inspired it centuries before. It is truth.

But those martyrs were miraculously preserved often; none died before his time. Moreover, they knew the real meaning of disaster and harm, and that they were ultimately protected. And they knew the true geography of their tent; they dwelled in an eternal kingdom not subject to threats. So can we. For that kingdom's citizens, there is nothing to fear—ever.

SEPTEMBER 10
Psalm 91

I'm standing on the promises of God.

—R. Kelso Carter

Know Your Roots

The righteous will flourish like a palm tree . . . ;
planted in the house of the LORD, they will flourish
in the courts of our God.   PSALM 92:12-13

SEPTEMBER 11
Psalm 92:12-15

On Christ the solid Rock I stand; all other ground is sinking sand.

—Edward Mote

IN WORD   The shifting sands of this world are fertile ground for nothing but fear. We see uncertainty all around us, in stock markets, in the comings and goings of military forces, in rapidly spreading pathogens, in red alerts and brown skies. We can easily panic under the illusion this world presents to us: that we are in a very fragile place where nothing is sure.

But that's not the place God provides for His people. Yes, this age, with all its chaos, can be frightening at first glance. That's why we cannot settle for first glance. We must look deeper, to the One who gives us promises of refuge and strength. He is our tower, our fortress, and our help, as so many of the psalms tell us. And in Psalm 92, He gives us a promise: "The righteous will flourish."

That's great news except for one unsettling fact: Deep down inside, we question our righteousness. We know we've earned nothing before God. So how can this passage encourage us? We know the Righteous One. *He* will flourish, and we are in Him. The Bible is very emphatic about that, and we can take it literally. In Jesus, we exist. His death was ours, His resurrection is ours, and His life at the right hand of the Father is ours (Ephesians 2:6; Colossians 3:1). He lives in us, and we live in Him. It's an unalterable, blessed fact.

IN DEED   What does that mean for our fear? It means that when the towers of this world collapse, we stand firm. It means that when the bombs of this world explode, we keep it together. It all depends on where we're rooted.

Do you feel rooted in shifting sand, vulnerable to the scarecrow tactics of a panicked society? Reconsider your position in Christ. Those rooted in the world will shake when the world shakes. Those rooted in Jesus will never shake when the world shakes, because when the world shakes, Jesus stands unmoved. Cling to Him. Trust Him. Remember that you live where He lives.

The World vs. God

*Do not love the world or anything in the world. If anyone loves
the world, the love of the Father is not in him.*   1 JOHN 2:15

IN WORD   "God so loved the world . . ." So begins one of
the most familiar verses of the Bible, John 3:16. But if God
loved the world, and we are to be like God in our affections, why does John tell us not to love the world? Because
"the world" of which Jesus speaks is the beautiful creation
of God, including the souls of men and women. But "the
world" of which John speaks is the corrupt systems we
encounter every day—economic systems, political systems,
cultural systems, and more. Anyone who falls in love with
these—who wants to hang on to them rather than to pursue
the Kingdom of God—has chosen the wrong kingdom. He
has forsaken the treasures of God for the trinkets of a sinful
humanity.

    This is one of the Christian's most chronic problems. We
want friendship with the world *and* friendship with God.
We want to love both. But our desires are like those of a
husband who wants to love two wives or a wife who wants
to love two husbands. A one-to-one relationship is corrupted
by multiple loves. And God always insists on a one-to-one
relationship with us. Though He has the capacity to love
billions—He is God, after all—we do not. If He is not our
highest affection, we are idolaters and He is jealous. He will
not be one of our many treasures. He wants all or nothing.

IN DEED   Our pursuit of wisdom will compel us to choose
between God and our other loves. As much as we'd like to,
our hearts cannot balance both God and anything else. And
our pursuit of wisdom will dictate which one is the rational choice. It should be obvious that the One who designed
us for Himself would leave us unfulfilled with our other
suitors. Only He can satisfy, because we were created only
for Him.

    Do you struggle with dissatisfaction? Perhaps you have
invested your affections in something that is ultimately
unsatisfying. Forsake it and turn your heart toward God.
He alone can fill our hearts.

SEPTEMBER 12
1 John 2:15-17

The things of
earth will grow
strangely dim in
the light of His
glory and grace.

—Helen H. Lemmel

God vs. the World

*Don't you know that friendship with the world
is hatred toward God?* JAMES 4:4

SEPTEMBER 13

James 4:4-6

The world has
advanced to the
very door of the
church, and is
seeking to draw
even the saints of
God into its grasp.

—Watchman Nee

IN WORD What does God have against the world He created? Only this: that there are many aspects of this world that He did not directly create. The result is a world that worships self and sin, the created rather than the Creator, the profane rather than the holy. We strive for comfort, prestige, power, security, and love, and then if we have the desire, we may strive for a god of our own imaginations. God hates that. He is the Jealous God (Exodus 34:14, among many other references).

God has often characterized His people in Scripture as faithless harlots. He is not nearly as indifferent about our affections as we are. When we place anything, any person, any ideal or belief above our Creator, we are like a wife who sleeps around. "They made me jealous by what is no god and angered me with their worthless idols," God says of His own people (Deuteronomy 32:21). He despises the unfaithfulness of His lovers. And yet we gravitate toward such unfaithfulness regularly. Our God is often a Lover scorned, and we can be quite callous about it.

A sign of our ignorance in our relationship with God is our frequent prayers for Him to bless our other loves. We ask Him to fulfill our desire for our idols of comfort and conquest. He will not answer such prayers any more than a husband would send his wife off to another man's bed. Friendship with this world—the corrupt world of power, lust, status, and greed—is a "Dear John" letter to God. It is our attempt to seduce and gratify His meanest rival—the spirit of the human rebellion.

IN DEED Friendship with the world is perhaps the church's most subtle yet dangerous enemy. It results in lukewarm hearts and fickle souls. It sends us in hot pursuit of compromise, and it's nauseating to God (Revelation 3:16).

What can we do? Pray for faithfulness, pursue intimacy, determine to be fulfilled *only* in the tender love of our Lover. Not to do so is to hate Him. But to be found in that love is pure delight.

God vs. the Evil One

The whole world is under the control of the evil one.
1 JOHN 5:19

IN WORD Perhaps we thought that our friendship with the world was a neutral relationship. Perhaps we thought that as long as we defer to God in most things, we are essentially free to pursue anything else our heart desires. Perhaps we thought only the really rebellious sins were sinful. But we are unwise lovers if that's what we thought.

When we drink in the philosophies of our world—the strategies of its false systems, the spirit of its idolatries, the pursuit of life, liberty, and happiness first before God—we have drunk poison. It's the enemy's lie that convinces us that all is neutral and that God doesn't care where our affections drive us. The whole world—all of its values, all of its humanistic endeavors, all of its ideologies—is permeated by the spirit of the evil one. He has his hand in *everything* on this planet. Even the church can be his playground—if we entertain him there.

The Christian life is a separated life. Why? Because there is a malevolent personality in this world designing his plans to undermine the true worship of God. We can recognize this malicious schemer if we're wise and discerning, but it requires the utmost diligence to do so. We must look with insight into our activities, and we must dive into the depths of our own hearts. We must ask the Spirit to reveal our self-deceptions. Otherwise, we end up aiding and abetting the enemy of the Most High God.

IN DEED This earth is a battleground between the Eternal One and His foe. This enemy respects no rules of engagement and abides by no morals or obligations. And we strike up a friendship with him casually and often. We don't mean to—we're only doing what seems acceptable to our culture and our conscience. But culture and conscience are unreliable, and God calls us to find ourselves entirely in Him. We must drink the cup of His holiness, eat the bread of His Word, and spend all of our time with His Spirit. He is our only refuge behind enemy lines.

SEPTEMBER 14
1 John 5:18-20

It is so stupid of modern civilization to have given up belief in the devil when he is the only explanation of it.

—Ronald Knox

Victory in Jesus

Now the prince of this world will be driven out.
JOHN 12:31

SEPTEMBER 15
John 12:31; 14:30

Faith is the victory!
Faith is the victory!
Oh, glorious
victory that over-
comes the world.

—John H. Yates

IN WORD We know that Jesus won the victory over the evil one. But we also know that the evil one is active to this day. We struggle with the implications of the victory of the Cross, because we don't always see them. Though we are inhabited by the Spirit of God, the spirit of this world often grips our hearts. And what a grip! No living human has yet fully been released.

Why not? Is the power of Jesus insufficient? No, He is able to save us completely. We are beyond the enemy's control. But he still attacks. If he can get us completely absorbed in the battle, then we cannot be completely absorbed with our God. We cannot focus on the war and maintain our focus on the Victor—unless we've learned to let the Victor fight our battles.

Jesus claimed all authority over the enemy—in heaven and on earth (Matthew 28:18). That has profound implications for us. When we are attacked, we know our source of victory. When we are tempted, we know our source of resistance. When we are discouraged, we know our source of hope. Everything the enemy threatens to do with us on the battleground of this world is countered in the arsenal of Jesus. But there's a catch. In order to realize this victory in the here and now, we must employ faith in the Beginning and the End. The Alpha and Omega, our Savior and Lord, gives us the key to every weapon. But we must take it and use it.

IN DEED Are you battle-weary? Be encouraged. This world is not an everlasting domain. Its ruler has been legally stripped of power, and his apparent resistance is deceptive. He holds no real power over the person of faith. The world and all that is in it is passing away (1 John 2:17). It's a dying and desperate regime. When we understand this—really get a grasp of it—the temptations we face and the trials we endure become much more easy to handle. Why? Because our faith is not in our ability to overcome, it's in the Overcomer. Jesus is the only One to truly transcend this world, and He brings us with Him into glory. Trust in Him. Know the victory that is His. The exiled prince has nothing on you.

Adversaries Remain

He did this only to teach warfare to the descendants of the Israelites who had not had previous battle experience. JUDGES 3:2

IN WORD When we're going through adversity, we have a lot of questions: "Why are difficult people allowed to cause so much disturbance in my life?" "Lord, why don't You remove these impossible circumstances?" "Why are my prayers taking so long to answer?" And the big one: "Lord, why is the devil still allowed to run rampant?"

Life's issues are complex. There is no single answer to these questions. But there is one answer we rarely consider: God has let adversity remain in our lives in order to teach us to wage holy battles. For some reason, now obscured by the mysteries of the eternal plan, we need to learn to fight. And not only do we need to learn to fight, we need to do so in the power of God's own strength and according to His own character. We need to understand His weapons, His ways, His goals, and His strategies. And we can never learn such things in a peaceful existence. There has to be war.

We don't like that. We don't understand it, either. God has promised us His peace—His "shalom"—and we fully expect to realize it one day. So why do we need to learn warfare, we ask? Why do our hands need to be trained for battle?

We don't know. Perhaps there are future battles to be fought before shalom comes—battles that only the hands and hearts of experience can wage. Perhaps we are to be critical instruments in God's violent opposition to evil. Regardless, for whatever reason, God wants us to have experience.

IN DEED Be encouraged. Your adversity is not meant to destroy you, or even to get you down—not by God, anyway. No, He has greater plans for it. He is teaching you to be a useful instrument in an other-worldly conflict. And the opposition of this world is your means to learn.

Do you have difficulties? conflict? enemies? pain? You are being trained. Learn your lessons well; fight the fight. God has left adversaries in your life for a reason.

SEPTEMBER 16
Judges 3:1-4

Smooth seas do not make skillful sailors.

—African Proverb

God's Unexpected Wisdom

You have too many men for me to deliver
Midian into their hands. JUDGES 7:2

SEPTEMBER 17
Judges 7

It will do us good
to be very empty,
very weak, very
distrustful of self,
and so to go about
our Master's work.

—Charles Spurgeon

IN WORD Gideon was only doing what God had called him to do: He was leading a revolt against the oppressive Midianites. And in the moment of decision, God pulled the rug out from under the deliverer. He told Gideon that he had too many soldiers. Victory itself wasn't the goal; *God's* victory was.

We can be entirely on God's side and still be in conflict with Him. Have you noticed the irony of our efforts? All throughout the Bible, faithful human beings who have given themselves to God are striving to be strong for Him. Meanwhile, God offers us weakness, desiring to be strong in us. We both want strength. We want ours to glorify Him; He wants His to glorify Himself. We who live for His glory better get used to a strange dynamic: It's our insufficiency that brings Him praise.

Our efforts on His behalf seem so godly. They have pure motives, an element of faith, His agenda in mind, and an abundance of human wisdom behind them. There's nothing wrong with the pure motives, the faith, or the agenda. It's the human wisdom that trips us up. God wants us to be used for His purposes even more than we do, but His means are radically different. For His glory to be demonstrated, human glory has to be minimized. We can't earn honor and then give it to God. We can only submit to Him and let Him display His honor. In this vision-impaired world, we have to be visibly low for God to be visibly high.

IN DEED The counterintuitive wisdom of God is only learned through many years and painful experiences. We don't like our weakness, and we want God to make us strong. But, as Paul reminds us centuries after Gideon, we are to be strong "in *his* mighty power" (Ephesians 6:10, italics added).

If God does not take the lead in our lives and win our victories on His own terms, there's a muddled picture of glory. Is it His or ours? Understand His purposes. Let your vulnerability be the occasion for His power.

Pure Devotion

That which is devoted is among you, O Israel. You cannot stand against your enemies until you remove it. JOSHUA 7:13

IN WORD God had given the Israelites clear instructions: After the fall of Jericho, they were to destroy all the treasures of the city. None of those items once dedicated to idolatry were acceptable in the holy camp. If not destroyed, Israel's disobedience would lead to its downfall. The people of God cannot thrive on false spiritual props.

Only one man violated the ban. Achan coveted, so he took just a few pieces of the spoils of war. Perhaps he didn't see the sense in destroying useful wealth. Maybe he was just a guy wanting to make a little profit on the side. Or maybe he really didn't trust in the provision of God, so he provided for himself. Whatever the case, God wouldn't let it slide. The fortunes of a nation—the *chosen* nation—hung in the balance. God let His great name suffer insult because of just one man's disobedience. A little bit of disobedience corrupted the whole godly effort. The holy purpose had an unholy element.

The parallels to our own lives are clear. We have entered the promised land in the power of God and are marching toward complete victory. He has assured it, if we remain faithful. But the eyes of Achan lust within us for a few small mementos of our sinful past. We want to leave most of our sin behind while taking a few of our highly treasured attachments with us. We want to obey *and* harbor a little impurity. We want to embrace God without letting everything else go.

IN DEED We can't. According to divine Law, it's a spiritual impossibility. The principle is inviolable: God will give us victory if we're wholly dedicated to Him; He will let us suffer defeat if we're not. Victory *and* divided hearts cannot coexist. God will not allow it.

Who or what are your enemies? Sin? Debt? Broken relationships? Difficult circumstances? God may have His purposes in all, but one thing's for sure: Your enemies will stand until your idols fall.

SEPTEMBER 18
Joshua 7:1-26

Quit all, strip yourself of all, and you will have all in God.

—Gerson

261

Wisdom Waits

The LORD rewards every man for his righteousness and faithfulness. 1 SAMUEL 26:23

SEPTEMBER 19

1 Samuel 26

God aims to exalt Himself by working for those who wait for Him.

—John Piper

IN WORD David had the opportunity that every oppressed, abused person dreams of: a chance to rid himself of his archenemy. As Saul lay sleeping in his camp, David sneaked through the ranks and put himself in position to thrust a spear into his rival. Surely he hadn't risked so much entering this camp just to prove a point. But, in fact, he had. As in a similar golden opportunity weeks before, he had no intention of laying a hand on "the Lord's anointed" (v. 9). David remembered what most of us forget: Our times are in God's hands.

Most of us would have thought as David's companion did. Abishai interpreted the event as God's provision, an ordained moment to throw off the yoke of an oppressive, mad king. Surely God had put David in this strategic position for a reason! And He had; but Abishai thought the reason was Saul's demise. David knew the reason was to make a statement about his intentions, his innocence, and God's sovereignty. He had not forgotten that God had placed Saul in his kingship. He dared not violate God's anointing—even when it had been abused.

Such sensitivity to the wisdom of God would serve us well. David knew Saul would die in God's timing; but he wasn't convinced that he himself was an instrument of God's timing. So he restrained himself. When it comes to God's will, assertiveness is only appropriate when the path is certain. This path wasn't certain. Restraint was the better part of faith.

IN DEED How do you approach God's will? When God's direction seems probable to you, do you forge ahead? Don't. God never asks us to move ahead on the basis of probabilities. He commands us to move ahead on the basis of His certain promises. But our actions should never be more definite than His timing. If His plan isn't clear, it is not time to move forward. God does *not* help those who help themselves. He helps those who trust His sovereignty. He honors faithfulness. When God's plan is unclear, wisdom waits.

Single-Minded Obedience

"I too am a prophet, as you are. And an angel said to me by the word of the Lord: 'Bring him back with you to your house so that he may eat bread and drink water.'"
(But he was lying to him.) 1 KINGS 13:18

IN WORD God had sent a prophet from Judah to Bethel to speak to the king, but with orders not to eat or drink until his task was done and he had returned. The king offered food and drink, but the prophet resisted the temptation. But on the way home, another prophet likewise tempted him, claiming God's permission. "An angel said to me . . . ," he asserted, and the man of God believed him. He ate and drank, contrary to God's command.

What was the prophet's downfall? What caused his disobedience? He chose unquestioned acceptance of another man's prophecy over his own instructions from God. He doubted what he had previously known to be God's voice. He did not keep his eyes fixed on the Word of God.

We run the same risk. Often God will speak to us straight from His Word. We hear the leading of the Spirit and the call of His voice, but we easily let others talk us out of our convictions. "They know more than I do," we might argue. "I must be missing something," we might confess. All the while, we are undermining the clear will of God.

IN DEED It is a biblically mandated task to check our interpretation of Scriptures with the body of Christ as a whole. We are never given permission to go off on personal tangents of doctrine or practice. We are, however, required to follow God's voice more closely than the voice of tempters. Just because someone says, "God told me . . . ," doesn't mean that God did. Discernment is paramount.

Do you hear the voice of God? Do His words jump off the pages of Scripture and into your heart? When they do, do not reject the Spirit who calls you. Fix your gaze entirely on His Word, and be single-minded in your obedience. Let *nothing* pull you off course.

SEPTEMBER 20
1 Kings 13:7-26

We must not trust every word of others or feeling within ourselves, but cautiously and patiently try the matter, whether it be of God.

—Thomas à Kempis

History Lessons

They forgot what he had done, the wonders he had shown them.
PSALM 78:11

When remembrance of God lives in the heart . . . then all goes well.

—Theophan the Recluse

IN WORD   God has done great things. Many of them are recorded in the written Word by generations who wanted their descendants to know of His faithfulness. Many of them are the subjects of biographies and church traditions. But many of them are relics of history, forgotten by a forgetful humanity. They are often buried in the minds of those who have passed on. Sometimes they are faint hints in our subconscious that God has done something good for us, but we can't remember what. The wonders were marvelous at the time, but they are wasted in the present. Far too often, we don't let the lingering goodness of God linger long enough.

Why not? What is it about us that can remember who insulted us decades ago but cannot remember the deliverance God gave us last year? We can hold a grudge for a lifetime, but when asked how God has answered our prayers in the past, we struggle for a response. It's not that He hasn't answered our prayers, even dramatically sometimes. No, the problem is that we are always focused on the next hurdle, the next problem, the next goal. God is only relevant in our minds when He is relevant to today's needs.

He would actually seem more relevant to today's needs if we could rehearse and remember His past victories. It's much easier to pray to the God who delivered us from an impossible situation when we remember the deliverance. We pray with faith when His miraculous strength stands out in our minds. We pray with ambiguity and doubt when it doesn't.

IN DEED   Make sure His strength stands out in your mind. If you are not in the practice of keeping a prayer log, begin the practice now. It doesn't need to be elaborate. Just make a list of what you ask God for, and then when He answers, check it off. Then in a day of distress, review all the checks—and watch your faith grow. The spiritual markers you put up in your life will largely determine the depth of your faith today.

Unholy Discontent

*They willfully put God to the test by demanding
the food they craved.* PSALM 78:18

IN WORD God had led the Israelites out of Egypt and
across the Red Sea. They were confidently on the way to the
Promised Land. After all, it had been promised.

A funny thing happened on the way to Canaan's bounty.
They had to go through a desert. The wilderness was wild
beyond their tastes. Yes, they had seen God do marvelous
things, but the sight of this desert seemed so much clearer
than the goodness of God. Was the problem a short memory? An evil nature with a propensity to sin? A bad habit of
complaining? Maybe all of these and more. Regardless, the
chosen people spoke against the One who chose them. They
had just been given the rule of God's Law, but their cravings
ruled them more. With transient, demanding desires, they
put God to the test.

We can relate. Human beings are complainers by nature.
We instinctively know that things aren't right in our lives.
We live in a fallen world that we somehow expect to give us
a better deal—for no reason in particular. When our desires
aren't satisfied, we cry out to God. He has already dealt
bountifully with us, but we have short memories. He has
provided manna, but we have a taste for something else. He
has created us for His purposes, but we have purposes of
our own. So we sit as judges while our God goes on trial.

IN DEED It's an absurd situation, really. Wandering
human beings—miraculously delivered from oppressive
slavery, fed with food from above, visibly encountered by
the Word of the living Lord, and promised an abundant land
of victory—don't like our lot. Every time we utter a prayer
asking, "Lord, why are You picking on me?" or express frustration that our plans are not exactly working out, we are
hugely underestimating the goodness of God. Whenever
we feel that the Deliverer, Savior, Redeemer, Victor, Guide,
Protector, and Provider has somehow let us down, perhaps
we should ask ourselves: Who is more likely to misunder-
stand this situation—me or Him?

SEPTEMBER 22
Psalm 78:17-31

The secret of con-
tentment is the
realization that life
is a gift, not a right.

—Anonymous

265

Amazing Mercy

He remembered that they were but flesh, a passing breeze that does not return. PSALM 78:39

The grace of God is infinite and eternal. As it had no beginning, so it can have no end.

—A. W. Tozer

IN WORD God's mercy is amazing. Repeatedly, the Israelites sinned against Him. If we're honest, so do we. The ravages of the fallen nature are not isolated setbacks. They are frequent failures springing from a chronic condition. Even after we are born of His Spirit, we feed other spirits and our own flesh with alarming ease. And still, after all the sin and rebellion, after all the complaints and rationalization for our complaints, God remembers that we are but flesh. He hesitates to stir up His wrath.

People have taken God's grace for granted for centuries. He offers forgiveness, and we interpret His mercy as license to do as we please. After all, if only a confession and some semblance of repentance are required, we can get away with practically anything. We abuse the character of God, *and He lets us*! If not forever, at least for a very long time. His patience is enduring, His faithfulness great. He much prefers to demonstrate mercy over justice. And in Jesus, He has demonstrated both.

We could spend our lives analyzing the fallen condition of mankind, with our lying tongues, flattering mouths, traitorous hearts, and futile ways (vv. 32-37). But our nature points to a greater object. Though our history certainly highlights our fickleness and frailty, it is more than a study of depravity. It is a study of God's mercy. The patience of God, the grace He has given, the compassion of the Holy toward the profane—all of His attributes are amazing. All creation must marvel that, literally and metaphorically, treasonous flesh has abusively, willfully slandered Him in the desert, and He still came to redeem.

IN DEED Do you ever think you've sinned past the limits of God's grace? Don't flatter yourself. If the wanderers in the wilderness did not provoke His destruction of this planet, neither have we exhausted His mercy. In all of our futility, in all of our struggles, we can hold on to the knowledge of the all-wise God: He remembers that we are but flesh.

Splendor Subverted

*He sent the ark of his might into captivity, his splendor
into the hands of the enemy.* PSALM 78:61

IN WORD We know from multiple Scripture passages
that God is intensely concerned for the glory of His name.
The Exodus event is filled with words from God to Pharaoh
through Moses that His works will establish His reputation
(Exodus 8:10 and 9:16, for example). Moses, David, Daniel,
and many others let the impetus for their prayers be the
glory of God's name rather than the success of their plans—
and God honored them for it. Even the heavens declare His
glory (Psalm 19:1). The whole earth will be filled with the
knowledge of His glory (Habakkuk 2:14). Clearly, a driving
theme of God's Word is the renown of His name.

God attached His name to a group of tribes in the
ancient Middle East. Surely He knew what that might do to
His reputation. God's glory displayed in humans? It seems
so absurd. And they proved it. After years of rebellion and
grievous sin, God pronounced judgment. It wasn't an unredeemable judgment, but it was harsh nonetheless. And the
God who loves the glory of His name, it seems, hates sin
with an even greater passion. He sacrificed glory, even if
only momentarily, in order to purge His people. He let His
splendor fall into the hands of the enemy.

IN DEED Do you take your sin casually? God doesn't. His
passion and zeal throughout Scripture to make His name
known among the peoples of the earth was subverted by
His own hand. Why? He hates sin. It cannot stand. It would
have been a greater offense to God for Him to defend a rebellious people for His name's sake than to let the symbol of
His name fall into the hand of pagan enemies. So He did the
latter. The glory of God was held captive for our sin.

Fast forward a few hundred years. Want to know what
God thinks of sin? Look at the brutality of the Cross. That's
the most accurate picture. On the Cross, the glory of God
was once again held captive for our sin. His Son became a
curse. His splendor became ugly. Only when we begin to
understand that—the hideous nature of sin—can we begin
to understand the depths of His mercy.

SEPTEMBER 24
Psalm 78:56-64

Sin is the dare of
God's justice, the
rape of His mercy,
the jeer of His
patience, the slight
of His power,
and the contempt
of His love.

—John Bunyan

267

A Shepherd Sent

David shepherded them with integrity of heart; with
skillful hands he led them. PSALM 78:72

SEPTEMBER 25

Psalm 78:65-72

I remember two
things: that I am
a great sinner,
and that Christ
is a great Savior.

—John Newton

IN WORD David is an Old Testament picture of the Savior. Messianic prophecies say the Son of David will establish the kingdom of David—an everlasting kingdom. Psalms about David are often quoted in the New Testament and applied to Jesus. There's a correlation between the human image and the divine fulfillment that we can scarcely grasp.

Even so, though we understand it dimly, we get the clear impression that the psalmist Asaph is not speaking only of David the king, but also of the Davidic King. Just as God's own hand provided a unilateral salvation after centuries of treasonous Israelite history, God's own hand has provided a unilateral salvation after millennia of treasonous world history. The God who stepped into Israel's affairs, despite its well-attested rebellion, is the same God who steps into our affairs, despite our own rebellion. Paul said it succinctly: "While we were still sinners, Christ died for us" (Romans 5:8). We have a Shepherd who will take our confused, distorted lives and lead us with integrity of heart and skillful hands.

IN DEED David is an apt image for the good Shepherd. The shepherd of Israel wrote the most familiar psalm about the shepherding nature of God, and it parallels the history of His people. Because the Lord was his Shepherd—and ours—both he and we shall not want. Despite our whining in the desert, we will be led to pleasant waters and green pastures. Despite our wilderness wanderings, He will lead us in paths of righteousness—for the sake of His name. Despite the fact that the wage of our sin is death, He will walk with us through death's valley. Despite God's rod of judgment, His staff will comfort us. Despite the vicious enemies in both the wilderness and the Promised Land, He will prepare our table in their presence—just to prove a point. What's the point? His goodness and mercy last a whole lot longer than our centuries—and years—of sin. Even after all that has happened, we will dwell in His house forever.

Enduring Plans

Everything God does will endure forever; nothing can
be added to it and nothing taken from it. God does it so
that men will revere him.   ECCLESIASTES 3:14

IN WORD   We live in an age of disposables. We have disposable containers, disposable diapers, disposable cameras, even disposable income. Whenever people lament that "they don't make things like they used to," they are invariably critiquing the quality of a product. Though the things craftsmen used to make didn't last forever, the things factories make now last even less time. We are a plastic generation with a plastic lifestyle. Everything we don't use immediately goes in the trash.

That may make for efficient consumerism (although one might argue just the opposite), but it doesn't make for meaningful spirituality. Even the work of God's hands, our world, is on a timetable. But God's real work, the salvation of eternal souls, is permanent. His character is eternal and constant, His plan is eternal and constant, and His people are, through Jesus, eternal and constant. There is nothing disposable about the Christian life. When God called us, He had planned it from before the foundation of the world and called us with "forever" promises. Nothing can take away from that, and nothing can add to it. God's work is complete in every sense.

Why does God craft such immutable works? "So that men will revere him." The shifting sands of time and culture have made us suspicious of everything. We are not impressed with temporary products. The infinite, on the other hand, blows us away.

IN DEED   This verse applies to all of God's works, but today, consider its application to your life. Do you wonder if God will change His mind about you? That perhaps you've overstepped His mercy? That maybe He won't complete what He's started in your life? Trust Him. The work that He does—including you—will endure forever. He promised it so you would revere Him.

SEPTEMBER 26
Ecclesiastes 3:14;
Philippians 1:6

Change and decay
in all around I
see; O Thou, who
changest not,
abide with me.

—Henry Francis Lyte

Satisfying Work

That everyone may eat and drink, and find satisfaction in all his toil—this is the gift of God. ECCLESIASTES 3:13

SEPTEMBER 27
Ecclesiastes 3:12-13

God's greatest gifts come through travail.

—F. B. Meyer

IN WORD Recent surveys indicate unprecedented dissatisfaction with work. As many as 80 percent of employees at any given time are looking for a new job. Why? Maybe they need more money, or perhaps they don't like the location, their coworkers, or their bosses. For most, however, the discontent isn't a matter of location or benefits. It is a matter of meaning. If we don't find meaning in our jobs, we find motivation difficult. Lack of motivation gets us behind in our work, which leads to stress, which leads to less motivation. It's a vicious cycle.

God created work. Somehow, we got the impression that it's a result of Adam and Eve's sin, but God had the couple tending the Garden of Eden long before they were tempted and cast out. Work became more difficult, but work had already been ordained. God means for His people to be productive and to enjoy the fruits of their labor. He wants us to be content in what we do, whether it's at home with children, in an office with coworkers, or elsewhere.

IN DEED Even when we know God's plan, we often miss out on His ultimate purposes. The surveys that indicate massive job dissatisfaction invariably have Christians among their respondents. Believers can be as dissatisfied as the secular world.

How can we be more content in our work? There are two simple steps to meaningful labor. (1) Ephesians tells us to work "as if you were serving the Lord, not men" (6:7). If we who love Jesus have it firmly fixed in our minds that our labor somehow honors Him, we will be more interested in our labor. (2) We can pray. It's acceptable to pray for a new job or role, but it's even better to ask God to build meaning into your current work until His timing for something new is right. He can show you how your work relationships honor Him, or how your godly service reflects His character. That sort of satisfaction is a gift God longs to give.

Meaningless Competition

I saw that all labor and all achievement spring from man's envy of his neighbor.   ECCLESIASTES 4:4

IN WORD   We like to think that our motives, at least on occasion, are pure. When we work hard and strive for success, we'd like to think we are doing so for the sake of our families and our God. But are we? Solomon's observation is all too relevant. Even on our best days, we compare ourselves with others. And much of our motivation for achievement comes from one self-centered impetus: rivalry.

When are our ambitions most powerfully fueled? When are our accomplishments the sweetest? When are we most driven to achieve? When a rival is in the picture. We do want to bear fruit for God and to have an abundant life in His name. But there are subtle competitions that propel us further and deeper into our work. There is more than His glory at stake; there is ours. We work not only for the sake of His name but for the sake of our name.

Don't believe it? Consider how often you compare your kids with those of others. Consider how you feel about your own house or neighborhood relative to others'. Consider your income and your position. Do we not strive for the best-sounding title on our resumes and business cards? When someone asks us what we do for a living, do we not cast it in the most impressive terms possible? Who are we trying to impress? It can't be God; He knows what we do and how we do it. He already knows the level of responsibility we have and the income it brings. Is it possible that we try to impress others with our station in life? Solomon says yes. Our strongest motivations often spring from envy.

IN DEED   Seek to consider only God's favor, no one else's. Force yourself to refrain from trying to impress people with what you've done, what you make, or how well you run your home. Consider yourself first and foremost a child of God, a position for which there is no rivalry. Make a conscious decision that prestige is like the wind, and you will no longer chase after it.

SEPTEMBER 28
Ecclesiastes 4:4;
Philippians 2:3

Envy of another man's calling can work havoc in our own.

—Watchman Nee

End-Time Priorities

It will be good for that servant whose master finds him doing so when he returns. MATTHEW 24:46

The fact that Jesus Christ is to come again is not a reason for star-gazing, but for working in the power of the Holy Ghost.

—Charles Spurgeon

IN WORD There is much speculation these days about whether we are nearing the end. Many people have an opinion, even a strong one. And while the Bible has given us many clues and tells us to live with a sense of expectation, let's face it: We don't know the day or the hour. Jesus assured us of that. In fact, when it comes down to it, we really don't know the century or even the millennium. We are to be watchful and wise, not cocksure and dogmatic. We have to confess a certain ignorance on the issue. Even Jesus did.

One thing we can know for certain, however, is that Jesus expected His followers to be ready. And as much as we look for His coming, many of us are clearly guilty of spending too much time trying to decipher biblical codes and headlines, and then gazing into the clouds for signs of His return. A little gazing is okay; Jesus urged our awareness of the signs. But He used stronger imperatives to urge something more: *We are to be about His business!*

Are you aware that as we stare upward, many millions of people—even billions—remain shrouded in darkness these two thousand years after the Cross, never having heard the gospel of grace, remaining under sin, and headed unforgiven into eternity? Are you aware that as we hold costly prophecy seminars, many emaciated children are waiting for someone to hand them a cup of cold water in His name? Wouldn't we be a little embarrassed if Jesus returned right now?

IN DEED Jesus told us to expect His return, but expectation is folly if it does not lead to a dramatic sense of urgency and readiness. *There is work to be done!* Jesus knows you love Him, but don't show your love by standing in the doorway passively awaiting His arrival. His house must be put in order. The other servants must be fed. Your Master isn't just dropping in to say hello. He's coming for an accounting. Are you ready?

Strength in Community

A cord of three strands is not quickly broken.
ECCLESIASTES 4:12

IN WORD   God doesn't produce loners. He makes some people more sociable than others, but He has not called anyone to a lifetime of isolation. Why? Because the body of Christ is made up of many parts. They cannot operate independently any more than fingers can operate without hands or muscles can operate without nerves. An isolated soul is, in a very real sense, separated from the fellowship of Christ. He can experience the Spirit of God in some ways, but not in others. An essential means of God's Spirit working in our lives comes only in community.

That should be obvious, but those of us who have grown up in an individualistic society have been trained to think of human beings as coexisting, not interrelating. We choose our relationships with a sense of independence, never realizing that we depend on the whole church in order to be complete in ourselves. Jesus may dwell in each believer for prayer and faith, but He does not dwell fully in any one believer for His works and ministry. That requires a body with numerous, diverse gifts. If we want to bear fruit in His name, we must bear fruit together. It's the only way.

IN DEED   The Christian church is horribly fragmented. Somehow we got the idea that separation was a casual matter. We change churches with relative ease. We move in and out of spiritual relationships with apparent apathy toward them. True believers develop overly exclusive theologies and divisive personalities and cliques. All the while, we forget a foundational biblical principle: In the body of Christ, as in many other venues, unity equals strength.

God gives us this principle of the three-strand cord because He wants us to be wrapped and bound together. He wants us to gather in His name. He wants a unified body of Christ, not many bodies of Christ. He wants individuals to find strength in tight, durable communities.

SEPTEMBER 30
Ecclesiastes 4:9-12

As we draw nearer to Christ, we shall be drawn nearer to His people.

—G. T. Manley

Confidence in God

Though war break out against me, even then will I be confident.
PSALM 27:3

Confidence in the
natural world is
self-reliance; in the
spiritual world it
is God-reliance.

—Oswald Chambers

IN WORD Feeling besieged? Don't be surprised. It's a
natural human condition. Few people go through life with
a sense of invulnerability. We question our strength, and,
when trouble strikes, we doubt our ability to stand. We don't
feel invincible, so we fear trials. When war or even minor
conflicts break out against us, confidence often disappears.

David was no stranger to conflict. He was also no
stranger to fear. His understanding of God's strength and
sovereignty did not come by birthright, it came by experience. When he tells us in verse 1 that the Lord is his light
and salvation, the stronghold of his life, he can make such
claims only because there were times when he was forced
either to lean on God or to wither away and die. The truth of
God's strength is only learned during times of vulnerability.
Strong, confident people learn to rely on themselves. Weak,
helpless people learn to rely on God.

David's introductory question in this psalm—"whom
shall I fear?"—is purely rhetorical. He knows the answer:
no one. If we can honestly claim with David that the Lord
is our light, salvation, and stronghold, we can ask the same
question without any fear of a valid answer coming up. We
can be afraid of no one.

IN DEED If you're trying to work yourself into a state of
confidence, be careful of where that confidence is placed.
The model of overassertive strength that the world urges
us to follow overestimates the power of man. Christians are
not called to follow it; we are called to place every hope in
the almighty God. If we need a source of strength, our inner
self will not encourage us very much. God will.

Learn to speak the words of David. Say them out loud
to yourself, if necessary. You are not playing psychological
games, you are rehearsing the truth. Though war break out
against us, we have every indication that our confidence
in God is well-founded. Our heart does not need to fear,
because we are children of the fearless One.

In His Dwelling

In the day of trouble he will keep me safe in his dwelling.
PSALM 27:5

IN WORD We tell ourselves frequently that God will keep us safe, and there are numerous scriptural promises that will back that up. But there's an often-neglected element of those promises that we need to emphasize. God will keep us safe *in his dwelling*.

What does that mean? David surely thought of the tabernacle and the planned temple when he wrote. Are we to view our church buildings—or even the now nonexistent temple of Jerusalem—as the locale of God's safekeeping? We know better, of course. But what does it mean, specifically, to be in God's dwelling? When can we know He's keeping us safe?

Dwelling in the house of the Lord is a state of mind and a condition of the heart. Or perhaps it would be better to consider it a state of faith. Our physical location isn't the key; the overflow of David's heart in verse 4 is. We are to dwell where God is, and, in New Testament terminology, let Him dwell in us. It is to be an everyday attitude. And we are to have a continual mind-set of awe and inspiration. If we are seeking God with all of our hearts; if our desire is to dwell wherever He is, regardless of what it takes to get there; and if we'd just love to gaze upon His beauty; then we are in the safety of His strength. We've got nothing—absolutely nothing—to fear.

IN DEED That doesn't mean, of course, that God only keeps us safe when we're perfect. It doesn't even mean that He never keeps us safe when we're recklessly out of His will. In His mercy, He often does. But we can't be confident in our rebellion. If our hearts are turned away from Him, either in hardness or lukewarmness, we lose our confidence in His shelter.

But the heart that is inclined toward Him, though it may go through hardship and pain, will never go through catastrophe. He will not allow it. Suffering is a part of this world, and He does not eliminate it for us yet. But the presence of the Lord is a safe place. Nothing touches us there without His specific permission. There's no better place to be.

OCTOBER 2
Psalm 27

I know not the way God leads me, but well do I know my Guide.

—Martin Luther

Timing

Be strong and take heart and wait for the LORD.
PSALM 27:14

OCTOBER 3
Psalm 27

On every level
of life . . . hurry
and impatience
are sure marks
of an amateur.

—Evelyn Underhill

IN WORD   Why does the Bible so insist on our waiting? We are given instruction after instruction to "wait on God." There is story after story about someone who wanted to rush Him—Abraham, Saul, Peter, and many, many more. Why are we always being told—not so subtly, either—to slow down?

Because our timing is almost invariably faster than God's. His agenda for a situation includes deep workings and intricate details. We just aim for superficial symptoms. He intends to grind His grain very, very fine—an excruciating work on our character that will not let coarseness remain. Or, to use another metaphor, He heats His ore long and hot, removing not just the impurities that can be seen with the naked eye, but all that exist. We usually don't care about such thoroughness. We want to get out of our difficult situation quickly or to achieve our successes suddenly. For us, time is of the essence. For God, time is essential.

A direct correlation to the wisdom we learn from God is the patience our hearts can tolerate. Foolishness is impatient. Wisdom knows the God who redeems us and can look patiently with hope toward His deliverance and His victory. We don't have to know how things will turn out; we know the God who is sovereign over the things.

IN DEED   What does that mean at a practical level? It means that answers to prayers often seem delayed in our own minds but are decisive in God's. It means that deliverance often seems slow to us, but to God it is already accomplished. It means that when we act on our impulses, we're violating His patient plans. It means that when our blood pressure is rising and our palms are sweating, God's voice is always saying, "Be still. Settle down. I am on My throne."

Can you hear Him? If you're in a rush, probably not. But how many times was Jesus in a rush? How often does the Word describe God as panicked? How many people who have invested their lives in Him have been let down in the end? Relax. Wait. Be strong and take heart.

The Voice of a Prophet

He who ignores discipline despises himself, but whoever heeds correction gains understanding. PROVERBS 15:32

IN WORD The bulk of the Bible between Genesis 3 and Revelation 19 is largely corrective. In many different ways, it addresses an utterly fallen human condition, through remedy and through judgment. It points out—repeatedly—that we are in need of a change.

That's not a very popular position in this world. We don't like to be confronted with our sin. Many have emphatically rejected Christianity because there are commands and judgments in its Scriptures. We often ignore the God who loves His creation enough to divert us from our own destructive ways. But whenever we're out of line, He must point it out. Through His Word, given through His prophets, God speaks. And whether we like it or not, His voice often calls us to be dramatically different.

The voice of a true prophet is always a voice crying in the wilderness. It is a lonely voice of redirection, showing all of us wanderers how to get to the city of God. It is often not welcome. If it were, it would not have been necessary to begin with. This world doesn't like correction, and it's often not interested in getting to God's city. We simply can't afford to absorb its independent ways.

IN DEED When the prophets speak—whether they are the prophets of Scripture or the prophets of our age—we must listen. The loving Father will always correct His children, and we must be open to His correction. Not to have ears that hear Him is suicide. It is like walking off a cliff because we've ignored the true path we were pointed to. It just doesn't make sense.

Do not stress about the affront to your ego that the Word of God will spark. It is a loving affront. Can you hear it? It is the voice of your Father, and it will lead to life. Be sure to heed the voice of discipline. It will bear the marks of love, and it will always point you home.

OCTOBER 4
Proverbs 15:32;
2 Chronicles
36:15-16

The voice of God is a friendly voice. No one need fear to listen to it unless he has already made up his mind to resist it.

—A. W. Tozer

Suspicion of God

I am the LORD your God, who teaches you what is best for you,
who directs you in the way you should go.   ISAIAH 48:17

OCTOBER 5
Isaiah 48:17-19

There are no disappointments to those whose wills are buried in the will of God.

—Frederick William Faber

IN WORD   A rich young man came to Jesus one day and asked Him some spiritually sensitive questions. He wanted to be right with God. Jesus gave him an answer, but in the end it wasn't what he wanted to hear. He would have had to let go of his idols—his wealth, his agenda, his will (Matthew 19:16-22). Underlying his refusal to accept the call of Jesus was a suspicion that perhaps God didn't have his best in mind. He would have to look after himself.

This verse in Isaiah only becomes relevant when there's a conflict between our desires and God's. When we and God want the same thing, we have no trouble walking His way. But when obedience contradicts the leaning of our heart, we have a heart problem. We find it difficult to conform to the will of God. Underlying that difficulty is the same suspicion the wealthy seeker had—the thought that perhaps God's way will not actually work out to our advantage in the end.

We must sacrifice a lot of good theology to believe that. We must reject the love of God or the wisdom of His will if we are to place our own agenda above His. But how easily we do that! It is imperceptible to us when we are making our decisions, but it is a prominent eyesore in the spiritual realm. Disobedience implies that we're more concerned about our well-being than God is. Such thin ice is a dangerous place to be.

IN DEED   God doesn't want us to consider His will as an option. He wants us to pursue it as an imperative. But He doesn't want us to pursue it with suspicion in our hearts. He'd rather we understand: Even when His will is hard, it really will lead to the best possible outcome for us.

How the heart of God grieves when His people will not follow His wise direction! It is like a father watching his son harm himself. It isn't rational, but sin never is. We must replace our irrational behavior with a deep belief in the goodness of God. His teaching is always the right one.

Peace Like a River

If only you had paid attention to my commands, your peace would have been like a river, your righteousness like the waves of the sea.   ISAIAH 48:18

IN WORD If only. Those two words are small in their grammatical placement but enormous in their tragic implications. They mean that things could have been different. Much different. They mean that if the response of God's people had been other than it was, much heartache could have been avoided. Blessing would have flowed, but it didn't. If only.

Like Isaiah, we've spoken them, too. Everyone has regrets. That's part of living in a fallen world. We know if we had been more diligent and faithful, our lives today could be radically different than they turned out. Even if we're happy right now, we wonder what could have been and what would have been. Why? Because sooner or later we come to a melancholy realization: Life can always be better.

We seek the God of comfort to tell us why bad things have happened—why we're in debt, why we lost that job, why our family isn't a happy one, why our dreams aren't fulfilled. But deep down we know. It isn't because God let us down; it's because we let Him down. We didn't live up to His instructions. That dreaded rebellious streak that we all seem to have has led us in futile directions contrary to the explicit teaching of our Maker. We don't know what we were thinking when we went away from Him, but we want to come back. His plan is better; we know that now. We want to be restored to a place of peace like a river and righteousness like the sea.

IN DEED That's the beauty of the gospel of grace. It never puts us in an unredeemable position. Whenever we say, "If only," God says, "Now you can." Maybe there are lost years, but they are past. God can redeem them for a bountiful future. The important thing is that we've learned that His voice is not demanding for His own ego but insistent for our own good. We can follow Him with trust that His way leads to peace and righteousness. We *must* follow Him with that trust. If we can, we'll be blessed. If only.

OCTOBER 6
Isaiah 48:17-19

Stayed upon Jehovah, hearts are fully blessed, finding as He promised, perfect peace and rest.

—Frances Ridley Havergal

279

Hope in Power

Was my arm too short to ransom you? Do I lack the strength to rescue you?   ISAIAH 50:2

OCTOBER 7

Isaiah 50:1-3

What is impossible to God? Not that which is difficult to His power, but that which is contrary to His nature.

—St. Ambrose

IN WORD   What keeps us from obeying God fully? What stands in the way of our turning that last vestige of personal autonomy over to His authority? It can't be that His will is questionable—we saw that in Isaiah 48:17. It can't be that His willingness to forgive and restore is lacking—we saw that in 48:18. Could it be that His power is insufficient to meet our needs? Do we question His ability to intervene in our deepest troubles and our darkest hours?

We would never overtly question in our minds the power of God: We know better. We believe that He created this world and that He holds it in His hand. But how relevant is that power to us? Sometimes we wonder. When a situation is somewhat difficult, we feel that prayer may still have a chance. But if a situation is *really* bleak, we give up our faith that an answer will come. The degree of difficulty influences our perception of God's ability to work.

Why? Why would the level of difficulty have *anything* to do with whether we believe God will answer or not? He has been clear throughout Scripture: There's nothing too difficult for Him. We believe in the God who parts the seas, who slays Goliaths, who heals the blind and the lame, who cleanses lepers, who turns water into wine, and who cannot be held in a tomb. What is it about our situation that causes us to give up our hope?

IN DEED   If you've ever maintained hope when problems are solvable and then given up hope when they are not, you have forgotten the God of the impossible. Your situation does not scare Him. He is not desperately trying to figure it out. He takes great pleasure in bursting into an impossible situation with an answer no one had thought of. His greatest reluctance is the lack of faith engaging Him from the middle of that situation. He looks for faith so that when He bursts in, He will be recognized. It must be genuine faith, persistent faith, and bold faith. Its absence, as in Isaiah 50, causes Him great grief. Remember that He stands ready to save.

Strength in Fellowship

He wakens me morning by morning, wakens my ear to listen like one being taught. ISAIAH 50:4

IN WORD Isaiah spoke words of judgment and words of mercy to a crowd that was skeptical of both. His calling flew in the face of other "prophets" who were representing God falsely. The judgments on other nations God told through him were welcome news; the judgments he foretold of God's chosen people were not. In short, he followed a calling that often went against his culture and challenged his courage. He represented a holy God to an unrighteous people.

So do we. Our calling is strikingly similar to Isaiah's. We may not be assigned the task of foretelling judgment with the specifics Isaiah saw. But we are assigned to live purely, speak truthfully, and witness to both the holiness and the mercy of our God. Sometimes the message is popular. More often, it is not. Our calling, like Isaiah's, often goes against our culture and challenges our courage. It sets us up for total dependence on our Creator.

Isaiah could fulfill his calling because he could hear the voice of God. When we think we might have heard something that sounded like it could have been the voice of God, we go out into our world with fear, trembling, and very little conviction. When, on the other hand, God wakens us in the morning and tunes our ear to His voice, we can walk in the strength of faith. Our teachable nature becomes the key to our confidence.

IN DEED Those who are not teachable are trying to talk themselves into security and confidence. They appear sure of themselves, but deep down they aren't. Those who are teachable, however, hear from God. There is no greater boost to one's faith than to know that however strange or countercultural the voice we've heard, it is the voice of the Almighty—the invincible warrior God, the Sovereign who sways human affections, the Beginning and the End. There's a calm assurance in the one who knows he or she is in fellowship with the Creator. A heart sensitive to Him will go forth in intensely certain faith. It has met with God.

OCTOBER 8

Isaiah 50:4-9

God desires and is pleased to communicate with us through the avenues of our minds, our wills, and our emotions.

—A. W. Tozer

The Beat of God's Drum

Do not fear the reproach of men or be terrified by their insults.
ISAIAH 51:7

Never forget that only dead fish swim with the stream.

—Malcolm Muggeridge

IN WORD Have you ever wondered what your life would be like if you had no concern for others' opinions? Would your choices be different? We'd like to think not; few of us consider how swayed we are by our desire for a good reputation. But think about it. How many things do we do (or not do) simply because of how it will look to our family, our friends, our coworkers, or even strangers? We're affected from the clothes we wear, to the parties we attend, to the jobs we take, to the neighborhoods we move to—and, unfortunately, to the words we say and the morals we live by. We are far more influenced by cultural norms than we want to be.

Consider all of those who really stand out in Scripture as obedient servants of God—Abraham, Noah, Moses, David, Elijah, Isaiah, Jeremiah, Ezekiel, Daniel, and so on. What do they have in common? They cared more about what God thought of them than what others thought of them. Their reputation in the eyes of God was of greater value than their reputation in the eyes of men. Even in the case of Jeremiah, who grieved over his adversaries' harsh words, obedience to God was more treasured than acceptance among peers. Those who make a difference in God's Kingdom are those who refuse to conform to the kingdom of this world.

IN DEED God calls us to a holy stubbornness. It's not a stubbornness that turns a petty disagreement into a major war or that will not be teachable under any circumstances. It's the kind of resolve that does not go with the flow of the culture. We cannot speak only what is politically correct— that's a terribly unprophetic thing to do. We cannot sacrifice biblical standards for modern moral expectations. We cannot bow to the pressures of our peers or blend with the contexts of elitism, corporatism, politicalism, classism, or any other -ism out there. We must march to the beat of the ultimately different Drummer—God Himself. We must seek only His voice and follow only His commands. We must strip ourselves of all hindrances to discipleship, and we must not be swayed.

His Prescription
for Obedience

Who are you that you fear mortal men, the sons
of men, who are but grass, that you forget the
LORD your Maker?   ISAIAH 51:12-13

IN WORD   Our actions are often guided by other people
more than they are guided by God's Holy Spirit. What a
travesty of the divine plan! The One who created us, who
has bought us back, who sustains us daily, is the One we
push to the back burner in order to please the fickle opinions of transient minds. How can we break out of this fear
of man?

We can escape only by an intentional, emphatic focus
on who our God is. We must rehearse His Word and His past
mercies in our minds. We must train our hearts to care first
and foremost for Him. We must understand the relative lack
of power of people compared to the almighty Lord of hosts.
We must remember that He holds heaven and earth, time
and eternity, welfare and calamity, and the keys to every
human heart in His hand. There is no one else we try to
impress who wields such power. Not even close.

God's prescription for our obedience is to let Him fill
our minds. But we so often fail at this. We're worried about
others laughing at us, criticizing us, looking down on us, and
shutting us out of their circles. Instead, we should be preoccupied with the awesome prestige of our God: He alone can
comfort us (v. 12), He made us (v. 13), He stretched out the
vast expanse of the heavens and laid the firm foundations of
earth (v. 13), He runs the currents of the oceans (v. 15), and
He established a people for Himself (v. 16). Who else would
guide our paths?

IN DEED   It is a delusion of fallen sinners that causes us
to place more value on human opinion than on God. And
we're hypocrites about it: We stress our independence and
freedom, yet enslave ourselves to public opinion and the
shifting sands of culture.

God calls His servants to be released from captivity. The
spirit that is full of Him will not be so deluded. His opinion
alone matters, and it is liberating. Stand firm on His truth,
never be moved, and let fear be far from your heart.

OCTOBER 10
Isaiah 51:12-16

It is only the fear
of God that can
deliver us from
the fear of man.

—John Witherspoon

283

Your Vindication

No weapon forged against you will prevail, and you will refute every tongue that accuses you. This is the heritage of the servants of the LORD, and this is their vindication from me, declares the LORD.   ISAIAH 54:17

OCTOBER 11
Isaiah 54:15-17

Patience is our martyrdom.

—Gregory the Great

IN WORD   A cold, hard truth in this fallen world is that those who side with God will share His enemies. They are numerous, and they can be vicious. They often have little regard for truth and a great capacity for scheming. David found it to be so with Saul, the prophets discovered it with their prophetic rivals, Jesus experienced it with Roman and Jewish leaders, and Paul heard it from other preachers and churches. Whenever God does a great work, either in your heart or in your world, it will be greatly opposed. Those who are His servants will face the opposition firsthand.

The key to victory in such a situation is not in retaliation or rebuttal. It is in calm faith and patience. None of the above examples went on the attack. We who claim God as our defender must not take up our own defense. We must stand firm, and that means we must sometimes speak out. But we can never challenge ungodly attacks with like responses. And those who trust God have no need to do so, anyway. He gives us His promise: He will protect us. No weapon will prevail, no accusation will stick—at least not in the long run. God has a way of vindicating His servants that is beautiful in the end. The aggressors fade into oblivion; the righteous remain in His glory.

IN DEED   Have you been under attack? It may be the overt work of aggressive people, or it may be the subtle work of devious spirits. Either way, your response is to be godly. God has allowed the attack, perhaps to strengthen you, to teach you godly warfare, or to instill faithful patience. So be faithful and be patient. The deeper your trouble, the more satisfying your vindication in the end. But the vindication can only come from God. When we try to work it out ourselves, it loses its savor. Let your accusers murmur. The promise of God will be forever fulfilled in its time.

Your Soul's Delight

Why spend money on what is not bread, and your
labor on what does not satisfy? ISAIAH 55:2

IN WORD We like to think we have a lot of resources at our disposal: a plan for the future, a diverse portfolio, a wealth of friends and family, a strategy for personal security, frequent entertainment, and more. Subtly and imperceptibly, our faith begins to shift from the God who gave us these things to our ownership of these things. Before long, we are imbibing secular wisdom and humanistic strategies for success, health, and welfare. We seek all our comforts without reference to God, except for our prayer that He will support our agenda. This path from God-reliance to self-reliance is surprisingly short in its distance, but very, very tragic in its implications.

God's penetrating question through Isaiah calls us to a better way. Why, when we have the God of all resources in our intimate fellowship, would we place our faith in the resources themselves? Perhaps that's the problem—we aren't in intimate fellowship with Him. It's easier to pursue self-sufficiency, we think, than to pursue the invisible God. But human ingenuity falls woefully short. We will find that out before long, if we haven't already.

IN DEED Why do we seek wisdom from any source other than God? Why do we trust in provision from the work of our own hands? Why do we find our security more in our human relationships than in our holy Father? The answers are part of the mystery of fallenness. Just as their sin drove the Israelites away from their covenant with God, so does ours. Supernatural faith becomes naturally corrupt all too quickly. Finite minds and fickle hearts are always in need of redirection.

God gives us His direction. He implores us to embrace it. It is the only way to life. It alone will delight our soul. It takes hold of His everlasting faithfulness. Is that so hard to remember? Our discipleship must always involve turning to what is truly bread and laboring for what really satisfies—daily, hourly, and moment by fulfilling moment.

OCTOBER 12
Isaiah 55:1-7

God's gifts put man's best dreams to shame.

—Elizabeth Barrett Browning

285

Deception's Promise

"Peace, peace," they say, when there is no peace.
JEREMIAH 6:14

OCTOBER 13

Jeremiah 6:13-15

We like to be deceived.

—Blaise Pascal

IN WORD Jeremiah was given a difficult assignment. He was called to preach destruction to a people who would never believe him. He knew up front that his message would fail. Other prophets would succeed with their false message. But God told Jeremiah to preach the truth anyway.

We live in an age of acceptance. Anything goes. Morality, we're told, is relative; truth is too complicated to pin down, commitment is defined by the mood of the moment, and there are many different paths to "God." *Tolerance* is a code word meaning, "Don't preach to me. I've got no intention of changing." The false prophets of our age have a clear, persistent message: "Peace, peace." But there is no peace.

How we wish peace would come. We pray to the Prince of Peace and ask Him to rule our lives. He does, and He will. But He will fulfill the message He preached long ago in Galilee and Judea: God will judge the human revolt, and Jesus is the only way to escape the judgment.

That's not a popular message in an age of acceptance. Nothing will bring out intolerance in the "tolerant" ones like a message of exclusive redemption. But like Jeremiah, Christendom is faced with a choice: Preach the truth, even where it goes unheeded, or lie about the condition our race is in and the judgment that awaits it—all for the sake of "peace."

IN DEED Deceptions abound in our world. Most of the effective ones sound pleasant to our ears; otherwise, they would not deceive us. God's Word sounds pleasant, too, but only to repentant ears. To the pride of self-sufficiency—the drug of choice for the human ego—His Word is anathema. It is as thoroughly rejected as Jeremiah was. But it is true.

Our generation has brought significant challenges to our faith. Our beliefs are not for the faint of heart. But as Isaiah promised, God's truth is the only water that quenches thirst and the only bread that is filling (Isaiah 55:1-3). Cling to it. Drink and eat of it with gusto. Stand firm in a truth-impaired generation. And never fall for the false promises of secular prophets.

Deception's Defeat

The heart is deceitful above all things and beyond cure.
Who can understand it?   JEREMIAH 17:9

IN WORD   Not only can we be deceived by the false prophets of our age, we can also be deceived by our own hearts. We often embrace lies if they are emotionally satisfying, never discerning the final result of believing them. God's wisdom takes a backseat to our affections when our affections have not been rooted in Him. The fact of the heart's treachery is a huge affront to our ego. It's a tragic affront to our Father.

Such is the nature of human wisdom. It is dark and deceptive, shifty and shallow, misdirected and myopic. It rejects the present reality of eternity for the future hope of personal glory. It builds on shifting sand. And, according to God's Word in Jeremiah, *it is beyond cure!*

How tragic. How scary. How can the God of hope give us such a hopeless word? How can the promise of salvation be so unpromising? How can we continue to read the Bible after we've come across this desperate declaration? How can we be redeemed?

The answer is glorious. God promises later in Jeremiah to give His people a new heart (24:7). So what if our hearts are beyond cure? They are not beyond resurrection. Our dead hearts are not reformed or healed; they are raised to new life. They are replaced with ones that are real. God says it even more precisely in Ezekiel: "I will give you a new heart and put a new spirit in you; I will remove from you your heart of stone and give you a heart of flesh" (36:26).

IN DEED   Only God can understand our hearts, and His assessment is utterly depressing if we do not know the rest of His plan. But He who discerns our deepest thoughts and most obscure deceptions (v. 10) offers us His pure and truthful Spirit to replace the corruption of our flesh.

These dreaded prophecies do not end with dread, and the wisdom of God does not end with death. Those who embrace it find life—answers now, direction today, and character always. *Daily* open your heart to His life.

OCTOBER 14
Jeremiah 17:5-13

O for a heart to praise my God, a heart from sin set free; a heart that always feels Thy blood so freely shed for me.

—Charles Wesley

Rock of Wisdom

Everyone who hears these words of mine and puts them into practice is like a wise man who built his house on the rock.   MATTHEW 7:24

OCTOBER 15
Matthew 7:24-27

When we speak about wisdom, we are speaking about Christ.

—St. Ambrose

IN WORD Perhaps we have come to assume too much about the character of Jesus. We ask, "What would Jesus do?" envisioning the pre-modern Man of peace who walked around Galilee so many years ago, just as the movies portray. We wonder how much relevance He has for a world of corporate takeovers and global communications. We wonder how much of His voice is our own psychology and how much of it is really His.

That's a flaw of human nature: We have difficulty distinguishing between our God-given but distorted consciences and the pure, convicting voice of our Lord. The Spirit of God dwells within us, but so do all sorts of misconceptions, anxieties, phobias, hang-ups, and habits. When we think we hear His voice, is it a matter of revelation or psychosis? In our discernment, there is a fine line between the two. In the reality of His kingdom, there is an unbridgeable division between them. We must learn how to tell the difference.

That is why a strict adherence to God's Word is paramount. We are not to make His words our occasion for petty divisions, but we are to hear His voice clearly. And Jesus offers it clearly. He has instructed us thoroughly. He has shed His light on the Old Testament—it is all summed up in Him—and He has shined His light into the New—things will always be summed up in Him.

IN DEED As our minds go through this renewal process—the transformation from old, worldly ways of thinking to grasping and embodying the deep mysteries of the now-revealed Kingdom of God—we must saturate them in His words. His teaching must become the first set of criteria used in our decision making. His wisdom must become the fire that melts us and the mold that shapes us. We must define truth by Him and define all that is outside of Him as untruth. We must build all our houses on the solid, unshakeable foundation of His Kingdom.

A World of Hate

Do not be surprised, my brothers, if the world hates you.
1 JOHN 3:13

IN WORD It has been the way of the world from the beginning. Cain was jealous of Abel, his jealousy turned to hatred, and his hatred turned violent. The tradition has been carried on by Joseph's brothers, Pharaoh's soldiers, Jews and Romans who hated the incarnate God and His followers, and on and on. People are killed simply for claiming Jesus. And we should not be surprised at all.

Why this enmity? Go back to the Garden of Eden. The serpent and the seed of God's children have been at odds since day one. There is a cosmic warfare raging, and we're in the middle of it. Now that the Messiah has defeated death and raised us to unspeakable heights, the enemy's sense of vengeance runs deeper than ever. We were born into that bad environment (Ephesians 2:1-3), but we've been delivered. And there is no halfway house. We chose sides. That didn't go unnoticed in the shadows of this world.

But it is a strange phenomenon that the world doesn't believe it is at enmity with God. Scripture is emphatic about its hatred (James 4:4, for example), but our culture thinks that tolerance for the possibility of a Creator is the same as friendship with Him. The truth of its hatred only comes out when His Lordship is asserted, never before. We think God's people are at peace with an unbelieving society until righteousness is preached. Then things get ugly, and we're surprised.

IN DEED Don't be. Abandon the illusion that we can be friends with the world and friends with God simultaneously. That's a fantasy that is never supported in Scripture. We can have a decent reputation, we can serve humbly and admirably in our society, and we can earn the respect of many. But it is a superficial respect. Don't be taken in by it; take it with a grain of salt. A mere mention of Jesus could forfeit all the acceptance you think you've earned. Never give the world's esteem much effort, and cling to the surpassing worth of the Lord you've chosen. Ultimately, only His opinion matters.

OCTOBER 16
1 John 3:11-16

Hold everything earthly with a loose hand.

—Charles Spurgeon

A Community of Grace

Let the word of Christ dwell in you richly as you teach and admonish one another with all wisdom, and as you sing psalms, hymns and spiritual songs with gratitude in your hearts to God. COLOSSIANS 3:16

OCTOBER 17
Colossians 3:16

Grace is love that cares and stoops and rescues.

—John Stott

IN WORD Wisdom is always lived in community. The popular image of the guru hidden in a mountain monastery or of the sage out in the wilderness is intriguing, but it is not the biblical pattern. God has gifted His people with interdependent gifts. They can only be exercised in the body of believers.

What does this body look like? It's the body of Christ, His physical presence in this world, so it should look like Him. The picture Paul paints is ideal: A fellowship that is rich in the Word, sharpening each other's understanding, singing with joy and gratitude—not just when the leader directs, but out of the overflow of the heart—is the kind of fellowship that reflects the peace and perfection of Jesus. But is it real? Don't we question the validity of such a spectacle and accuse it of superficiality? Don't we just know there are deeper issues that the community is suppressing?

That's the beauty of the body of Christ. If it's real, there is no suppression. It is a more realistic danger for Christians to suppress the joy of faith in order to fit better with this world than to suppress the ways of the world in order to express joy. And gratitude, singing, and mutual admonition do not imply that there are no problems in life. In fact, they depend on the problems. God has entered the context of this broken planet to show mercy, love, and peace. The fellowship that really believes is one that lets Him show those things within it.

IN DEED Cultivate this kind of community. It simply must begin with individuals, and we might as well be those individuals. Has God been gracious? Be gracious. Has God forgiven? Forgive. Has God healed? Then heal. The church is to mirror the Savior—the Bible calls it a reflection of His glory. The result is a community of grace. It lives grace, breathes grace, speaks grace. And it begins when someone decides, as Paul says, to "let it."

New Clothes

Clothe yourselves with humility toward one another.

1 PETER 5:5

IN WORD   At the heart of the temptation in the Garden of Eden, at the heart of the human rebellion and its slithering instigator, is a foundation of pride. Many have said that pride is behind every sin. It is pride that tells us to ignore God's will and follow our own. It is pride that tells us to enthrone our pleasures and pursuits within our hearts. And it is pride that places us in a heated competition with every other person on the planet—for status, for goods, and for glory.

God is emphatic throughout Scripture: He "opposes the proud but gives grace to the humble." Proud kings and priests in the Bible found themselves humiliated by God Himself. Humble supplicants were lifted up into His presence. And so the principle continues today. God becomes the archenemy of any who diminish Him by magnifying themselves.

That's why Peter tells us to put on new clothes. We are to strip ourselves of that fantasy that we are self-made souls and adorn ourselves with God's grace. We are to cast out our old clothes like they were last decade's fashions and stock up on the plain elegance of reality. Our new wardrobe is far more beautiful in its simplicity than was our old wardrobe in its attention-grabbing styles. Gaudiness does not fit in the Kingdom of God, and it does not unite us with others. Humility blends in perfectly.

IN DEED   Your attitude toward others will largely determine, in a practical way, how united you are with the body of Christ. Are you often at the center of discord? Is it because of a lack of humility? Dress yourself in new clothes.

Humility takes the first step, even when it is confronted with the pride of others. When it does, it disarms the proud like nothing else. Prideful people feed off of each other and stir up more pride. A step of humility undermines the whole process. It defuses the root of our sin and opens the way for the glory of God. It gives us an entirely new look.

OCTOBER 18
1 Peter 5:5-7

Nothing sets a person so much out of the devil's reach as humility.

—Jonathan Edwards

Choices

The way of the sluggard is blocked with thorns, but the
path of the upright is a highway.   PROVERBS 15:19

OCTOBER 19

Proverbs 15:19;
Deuteronomy 30:19

Every day the
choice between
good and evil is
presented to us
in simple ways.

—William Sangster

IN WORD   Every single moment of our lives, we face a choice. We choose when to speak and when to keep silent, when to sit and when to stand, when to breathe and when to hold our breath. We could get incredibly detailed about all of our many momentary options if we wanted to. But that's an excruciating exercise, sort of like listening to every beat of our heart. It requires too much attention and stress. We prefer to let things happen naturally and automatically.

But Proverbs urges us to step back and look at our choices from time to time—not just the major ones, but also the little ones that determine the subtle directions of our lives each day. And its message is consistent: Righteous choices, while sometimes harder in the short term, are always easier in the long run. They lead to life. Laziness and evil put us on hard roads. The path of least resistance is often the path of greatest grief.

That doesn't mean that righteous choices will always make things easy for us. Anytime we seek to obey God diligently and serve Him with devotion, there will be obstacles. But God always paves a way for our path of discipleship. He doesn't ever make rebellion or laziness profitable in the end.

IN DEED   What level of diligence guides your life? Are you proactive about your choices— even the small ones— or are you herded like livestock through the fields of life, unwittingly pushed and pulled by those around you? Do you feel that God is firmly directing your steps? Or do you feel that you're just floating with the current and conforming to the expectations of this world?

God calls for diligence. Laziness and discipleship do not mix. He doesn't mean for us to obsess about every minor choice, but He expects us to draw a line in the sand and refuse to let the demands of the culture dictate our lives. We are to guard His plan for our lives with zeal. Don't get off the highway. Let Him be Lord of your choices.

Seeing His Face

When a king's face brightens, it means life; his favor is like a rain cloud in spring.   PROVERBS 16:15

IN WORD   Perhaps we don't enter the courts of kings as they did in the ancient world. Maybe we don't understand the implications of a king's expression when he sees us. But the king's acceptance once meant the difference between life and death, or at least the difference between blessing and misery. When his face lit up, his servants could rest easy. To their great relief, his good mood would result in the glory of his favor. It would bring joy to the heart.

So how is this relevant to us? Aren't we rarely privileged to enter the halls of national authority or the courts of sovereigns? No, the privilege has been granted to us. We are to come into the throne room of the Most High God—the ultimate authority in all of existence—and voice our concerns. We are allowed to serve in His fields. We are allowed to consult with the wisdom of eternity for our daily endeavors. And we are blessed to become partakers of His glory. He shares His kingdom with us! There is no greater joy.

But what do we see on His face? Is it brightened by our presence? Many are afraid not. Many see a rightfully angry God on the throne when they pray. Many feel the holy disappointment of our pure and perfect Father. Many believe that God could never love them as He loves a treasured child. Until we believe otherwise, we will not know His favor. Knowing His delight is contingent on our being absolutely convinced of His good will toward men. His favor falls on us when we know from whom it falls.

IN DEED   When God sees you, does He see Jesus? If you believe in the Savior, God will consider His life a substitute for yours. And as you serve the Savior, God will fill your life with His Spirit. Your life and the life of Jesus will become so intertwined, so connected, that in heaven there can be no distinction between the two. As a husband and wife are "one flesh," the Savior and His bride are "one Spirit." The two have become one, and that One is a delight to His King. Accept the King's delight with gratitude.

OCTOBER 20
*Proverbs 16:15;
Matthew 25:21*

Christianity is about acceptance, and if God accepts me as I am, then I had better do the same.

—Hugh Montefiore

293

The Pleasure of God

My soul will be satisfied as with the richest of foods; with singing lips my mouth will praise you. PSALM 63:5

We never better enjoy ourselves than when we most enjoy God.

—Benjamin Whichcote

IN WORD When we speak of learning God's wisdom and having the mind of Christ, it often sounds like we're sitting in a sterile classroom environment. We assume that we're being mentally trained in a new way of life. We are, but it's not in a cold, calculated transfer of information; it's a warm, wonderful learning experience, a hand-in-hand adventure with a loving Father who wants us to be like Him.

With God, familiarity does not breed contempt. It breeds passion and pleasure. We can dispense with the idea that we serve a cold, hard master. We can let go of the image of the ever-unsatisfied holiness of our Creator. He has satisfied His holy requirements Himself in the person of Jesus. What's left for us is an affectionate Father who laughs when we laugh and cries when we cry. The more we get to know Him, the more we come to love Him. It is, of course, a holy and respectful kind of love—He is entirely above us and worthy of our awe. But there is a warmth to Him that many people never feel. And we are called to feel it deeply.

IN DEED How would you characterize your relationship with God? Cold and sterile? Distant and frustrating? It need not be any of these. It can actually be—dare we suggest it?—*fun*.

Yes, the wisdom of God—His mind, His ways, His character—can be beautiful and charming. He is not the cruel killjoy we often make Him out to be. And that's the great tragedy of sin: It fails to understand the amazing implications of knowing Him. It turns Him into someone He's not.

Learning the wisdom of God is not just an intellectual pursuit. It is a heartfelt pleasure in His personality. The presence of the Almighty can be an emotionally satisfying affection. His character is lovely, His words winsome. Abandon the image of the stern, distant God. His wrath toward us, though entirely legitimate, was poured out on Jesus. It has been fully satisfied. Our only response is to be fully satisfied in Him.

Praying God's Mind

You may ask me for anything in my name, and I will do it.
JOHN 14:14

IN WORD One of the most emphatic promises from Jesus to His disciples is the promise that the Father will give them whatever they ask in His name. It is profoundly encouraging to believe that promise, but truly bewildering not to see it answered. We know the usual warnings given about such prayers: They must be according to His will, we must ask in faith, we must not harbor sin or bitterness in our hearts, we cannot pray selfishly, etc. Still, we wonder why we don't always receive what we've asked for, even when, as far as we can tell, we've met all the prior conditions.

James gives a prayer to pray that should come before all our other prayers. It is a prayer for wisdom (James 1:5). We can ask God to put His thoughts into our minds and His will into our hearts. We are not asking for Him simply to point the way; we are asking for Him to infuse His way into the very depths of our souls. We are asking for His Spirit to direct us from within. We are praying to receive His mind as our own.

Most assuredly, this is an answerable prayer. God waits with anticipation for us to ask it. He encourages it and appeals for it, calling us into it repeatedly. He doesn't just want to pass on His information to us; He wants to fill us with Himself. Then our desires become His, His plans are written into our dreams, and He lives the life of His Spirit in the body of our flesh. It's a powerful communion, amazing in its mercy.

IN DEED Do you pray with reservations, wondering if you are hitting or missing God's mark, holding your breath and crossing your fingers for His answer? It doesn't need to be that way. Ask for His wisdom. Pray for His thoughts. Look for a drastic revision to your character and your dreams, and then pray the desires of the new you. No, asking for His thoughts does not mean to grasp the next whim that enters your mind—He may not have put it there. But over time, you will see within yourself a blessed conformity to His purposes. Then you will know how to pray.

OCTOBER 22
John 14:14;
James 1:5-8

Prayer is none other but the revelation of the will or mind of God.

—John Saltmarsh

Perspective

When I consider your heavens, the work of your fingers . . .
PSALM 8:3

OCTOBER 23

Psalm 8

We seem to have lost the vision of the majesty of God.

—John Stott

IN WORD If there's anything our generation lacks in wisdom, it's perspective. Sin has always distorted our thoughts, making us larger than we ought to be and making God smaller than He is. As a result, our problems seem bigger than God, our plans seem better than His will, and our faulty logic makes more sense to us than His infallible Word.

What can correct us? What can bring us back into the right perspective? This psalm offers a good approach. All it takes is for us to consider the way things really are. Consider the vastness of God's work. Consider the frailty of our flesh. When we see ourselves relative to God, we, along with David in this psalm, are amazed that God is even mindful of us. Such a perspective reminds us constantly of grace: that we are made by grace, saved by grace, sustained by grace, and completely dependent on grace. The majesty of God's name and the glory and honor with which He has crowned His fallen creatures are mind-boggling. What a merciful condescension! The infinite, almighty, eternal God—the One who holds vast universes in the palm of His hand—has cared for pitifully small, broken human beings. He has even crowned us with honor. What a staggering contrast of proportions! A glimpse of it will deepen our perspective.

Understanding the vastness of God and the finiteness of humanity brings us back to sanity. Our problems become smaller than God, our plans bow to His will, and our faulty logic submits to His Word. Order is restored.

IN DEED Has your perspective become distorted? Do your problems seem huge and your God small? Do you prefer your plans over His will and His Word? Spend some time "considering." Contemplate His handiwork. Know your place in His creation. Observe the contrast between the majesty of the Almighty and the neediness of the weak. See the marvels of His grace. Let yourself be trained in such thoughts. Let God shape your perspective.

Pure Joy

*Consider it pure joy, my brothers, whenever you
face trials of many kinds.* JAMES 1:2

IN WORD What rational person would consider the trials of life pure joy? Only those who can see the surprising benefit in them. Through the lens of Scripture, we can see that benefit. We are told that our trials develop our character in ways that will produce eternal profit for us; and we are told that the God who allows them always has our welfare in mind. These are things that an unbelieving world cannot see, but they have been revealed to those who will believe.

The book of Acts is an amazing chronicle of the early church. In chapter 5, the apostles who were arrested for preaching Jesus left the court of the Sanhedrin "rejoicing because they had been counted worthy of suffering disgrace for the Name" (v. 41). In chapter 16, Paul and Silas sang praises to God from the depths of a filthy Philippian prison. What kind of mind reacts to trials this way? According to the world, an irrational one. But according to Scripture, only a mind grounded in the truths of the gospel can recognize the glorious realities behind our temporary problems.

Though James points to the benefit our trials have for our own character, we know that there is an even greater blessing in them. Jesus is revealed in us. His power is made manifest in our weakness (2 Corinthians 12:9-10), and participating in His sufferings lets us participate in His resurrection (Philippians 3:10). Not only is our character sharpened in painful processes, the resurrection of Jesus is displayed in the crosses we bear. Such trials are worth rejoicing about.

IN DEED Are you going through difficult times? Don't despair. Discouragement and depression are not the biblical responses, only the natural ones. But we live above the natural because the lens of Holy Scripture lets us see beyond the natural. We know the end result of our pain. Perseverance results in maturity, and problems give Jesus a stage to show His resurrection power. There is no greater blessing than that. Consider it pure joy.

OCTOBER 24
James 1:2-4

More crucifixion, more resurrection. The more we suffer, the more we are drawn to Christ and His power.

—A Persecuted Christian in Nepal

A Rogue Ruler

Everyone who wants to live a godly life in Christ Jesus will be persecuted. 2 TIMOTHY 3:12

OCTOBER 25

2 Timothy 3:10-15

The Christian life is not a playground; it is a battleground.

—Warren Wiersbe

IN WORD Satan rules a rogue nation in one small corner of God's cosmos. But to us, it's not a faraway corner; we were born in it. It is exceedingly relevant to our lives. It affects us every day, constraining our choices and influencing our personalities. We were born as its citizens, destined to die when it is overthrown. But we have found a way of escape: We can flee as refugees into the safe asylum of Jesus. His Kingdom will grant us protection.

Paul tells Timothy that everyone—no exceptions—who wants to live a godly life will face persecution. This is one of God's promises we rarely claim by faith, but it is certain anyway. It's a solid guarantee: We will be harassed within our born-again hearts and harassed on the outside by a campaign of misinformation and even physical threats. Temptations aim to dissuade us from our holy calling, and people try to convince us that we need to conform to their wishes and their corrupt world. The battle wasn't over the day we placed our faith in Jesus. It had only just begun.

Evil doesn't die without a fight, and sometimes the fight can be really nasty. Satan's tactics aren't fair; lawlessness is one of his core attributes. We might as well get used to his attempts to hit us below the belt. We cannot turn a blind eye to his tactics. The only sure way to resist them is to be aware of them. Our awareness will turn us to the refuge of Jesus at exactly the right times.

IN DEED Do you wonder why you struggle? Are you disheartened because you thought the Christian life was easier than this? Avoid such illusions. You're in a war. Maybe you didn't realize that when you joined the Kingdom, but you will have to realize it now.

The good news is that the only harm that can come to you in this battle is temporary, and the only victory Satan can win is psychological. Real victory, lasting victory, is certain. It is our inheritance. Do not be disheartened. Stand firm. The day of triumph is coming.

Wisdom through Prayer

Give me understanding according to your word.
PSALM 119:169

IN WORD We know that God offers us His mind as one of the many blessings of His salvation. And the promise of His mind is great: It includes His guidance, His counsel, His purposes and plans, and the intricacies of His ways. It is the great storehouse of all of life's mysteries and the key to all understanding. There is no greater place of knowledge.

But how do we get it? How does the mind of God become ours? How does His wisdom flow from His mind and into our small, distorted thoughts? There is a way, and the first step is prayer.

In an economy of grace, all things come by asking and believing. That is the foremost requirement: to forsake our dependence on all self-effort and ask. God is generous with all things. He has offered His salvation, bestowed His Spirit, and equipped us with His Word. The only thing left is to receive these blessings. And the way to receive—the only way in such a Kingdom—is to ask.

The petitioner who asks God for His wisdom acknowledges the deficiency of his own. There can be no confusion of providence and pride when the gift begins with a humble request. The one who prays that he or she might be saturated with the mind of God has admitted that the mind of a human being is not enough to make it in this world. It is finite and it is fallen. We need more.

IN DEED Have you sought God's guidance? His counsel? His plan? Do more than that. Seek His mind. Ask Him to integrate His thoughts into yours. He has been extravagantly generous with all things to those who approach Him in humility and love. He offers Himself because He made us in His image. We were built for His habitation. Let Him dwell where He wants to.

But be incredibly open to change; His thoughts are much higher than ours. He offers them only to those who want more than a road map. He offers them to those who want *Him*—and who will be bold enough to ask.

OCTOBER 26
Psalm 119:169-176

What is most necessary for understanding divine things is prayer.

—Origen of Alexandria

299

Wisdom through Meditation

My eyes stay open through the watches of the night, that
I may meditate on your promises. PSALM 119:148

OCTOBER 27
Psalm 119:145-152

Meditation is . . .
allowing the Holy
Spirit to take the
written word and
apply it as the
living word to
the inner being.

—Campbell McAlpine

IN WORD Our receiving God's wisdom begins with prayer, but it does not end there. He has a method in His transformation process, and it requires our full cooperation. We are not passive recipients of His mind; we are active in our pursuit. He offers it, but we must want it. And there is more to wanting than just asking.

We can learn the Word of God through study. But it does not become a part of us until we meditate on it. Lacking that step, we become knowledgeable without becoming wise. There is a profound difference between knowing about God's will and His ways and actually *knowing* God's will and His ways. One leads to an illusion that we're spiritual when we're not. The other leads to life.

Churches are full of people who hear the Word of God preached on Sunday and then have forgotten it on Monday. There are many tools to incorporate God's truths into our lives, but the first, after prayer, is to meditate on it. What does that mean? It means to chew on it, think of what God does with it and why it came from His mouth, how we've failed it in our past, and how it might be applied in our everyday lives. The Word of God is not given simply to be admired; it is given to be learned. It is not spoken to make us smart; it is spoken to change us and conform us to the bright image of the living God.

IN DEED At all costs, do not passively let the Word of God go in one ear and out the other. Do not read it so casually that it is forgotten the next day or the next hour. There's power in it! It is a gift that will craft us into the person God wants us to be, the person we were designed to be from the very beginning. That molding process is the greatest earthly fulfillment we can ever experience. And God first begins to answer our prayers for that when we meditate on His truth. Let it soak in, completely and deeply. Let it do its powerful work.

Wisdom through Recall

I have hidden your word in my heart that I might not sin against you. PSALM 119:11

IN WORD Some Christians carry a Bible with them constantly, but most do not. Even if we did, however, we would not always have immediate access to the right verse for the right occasion. Even in a day of electronic micro-Bibles, on-the-spot research does not always lead to the right word for the moment. We need something more than gadgets and resources. And we need something more than the pages of Scripture at our side. We need them in our hearts.

We have prayed for God to give us His wisdom. We have meditated on His Word. But we want to contemplate it more thoroughly, more constantly, more effectively. We want the wasted moments of our day to be redeemed for spiritual growth. The best way for the Word to be written on our hearts is to learn it—by heart.

Many people associate memorization with learning historical dates or geometric formulas in high school. That was an imposed pressure with a potentially ominous grade pending. The very idea of memorization suffers in that context. But God does not threaten us with an ominous grade, and He does not impose His Word on us against our will. He invites us into it so we will invite it into us. That's where real blessing is to be found; that's where we enter into His mind and His thoughts become ours. Memorizing God's Word is no boring task; it is a powerful tool that will guide us into His will.

IN DEED When you've memorized a variety of Scripture passages, you will find them deeper and more relevant than ever before. When you're in the midst of a crisis, the Spirit will bring the right word into your situation. When you are tempted, the sacred rebuttal will be on your tongue as it was with Jesus in His wilderness test. When a fellow believer has a deep need, the Spirit will bring up within you a deep word of counsel or hope. The Word of God becomes not part of your baggage but part of you. It is written on a tablet of flesh, and you are its handiwork.

OCTOBER 28
Psalm 119:9-16

I know of no other single practice in the Christian life more rewarding, practically speaking, than memorizing Scripture.

—Charles Swindoll

Wisdom through Words

With my lips I recount all the laws that come from your mouth.
PSALM 119:13

OCTOBER 29
Psalm 119:9-16

Words, those
precious cups
of meaning . . .

—St. Augustine

IN WORD   Experts in memory techniques tell us that if we use a new acquaintance's name in our conversation, we'll be more likely to remember it. Students who discuss the subject matter of a class with each other are going to integrate it into their thinking better. Those who have a hard time remembering good jokes are those who never tell them. There is something powerful about uttering newfound knowledge. Speech reinforces thinking.

The principle is written into God's Word as well. After we've prayed for His wisdom, meditated on His truths, and memorized some Scriptures, we may find that the process is furthered by our willingness to speak what we've learned. In contemporary Western cultures, the spoken word is a casual thing, a simple, verbal expression of sometimes meaningless thoughts. Not so in the Bible. There is power in the spoken word. When God created, He spoke. When He and His people blessed, they spoke. When people cursed, they spoke. What was said out loud could not be unsaid. It was concrete; its utterance made it so.

That truth should be enough to cause us all to examine our speech. Are we reinforcing negative thoughts and false suppositions when we open our mouths? Or are we reinforcing truth? Do our tongues practice righteousness and praise or discouragement and doubt? We think the mind has complete influence over the mouth, but it is often the other way around. Our own words can train us well.

IN DEED   When you have learned one of God's truths in your mind, try speaking it with your mouth. Repeat it out loud to yourself. Share it with someone else. Discuss its application with other believers. Let it become a sensory reality rather than an inaudible thought. The likelihood of its remaining a part of your thinking and a part of your character will increase dramatically. Your mouth and your ears will establish what's in your heart.

Wisdom through Practice

This has been my practice: I obey your precepts.
PSALM 119:56

IN WORD An old training program book shows novice swimmers how to swim. It shows pictures of the position of the body in the water, the proper technique for various strokes, the most efficient ways to breathe while maintaining speed, and everything else one would need to know to get in a pool and not drown. But no one ever learned how to swim by simply reading that book. Perhaps its readers obtained the necessary knowledge, but they did not really learn. Some things can only be grasped by experience.

God's wisdom is one of those things. If speech reinforces the truths He's given us, practice reinforces them even more. The best way to learn how to do something—really learn it—is to actually do it. Reading or hearing a lesson only involves one of our senses. Putting a lesson into practice involves them all. Obviously, the mind is better trained when it is fed by multiple senses.

James comes down hard on those who are hearers of the Word and not doers of the Word (James 1:22-25). It isn't just a matter of hypocrisy; it's a matter of training. It is easy to forget the things our minds have entertained. It is much more difficult to forget the things that our minds have entertained, *and* our mouths have spoken, *and* our hands have done. And we want to make forgetfulness difficult. When it comes to the wisdom of God in our hearts, retention is everything.

IN DEED The wisdom of God is not theoretical, it is intensely practical. It is not a matter of speculation for religious intellects, it's a matter of instruction and training for real-life situations. If we want God's wisdom, we must be honest with ourselves and determine that we want it for a purpose. Living it must be our priority.

Do you find a gap between the knowledge you've learned from God's Word and your lifestyle? Are His truths a matter of your mind and not a matter of your heart? Then put them into practice. They will be learned in ways that nothing else can teach us.

OCTOBER 30
Psalm 119:49-56

Do good with what you have, or it will do you no good.

—William Penn

Wisdom through Fellowship

I am a friend to all who fear you, to all who follow your precepts.
PSALM 119:63

OCTOBER 31
Psalm 119:57-64

Christians are not
lone rangers.

—Chuck Colson

IN WORD   We like to think of our relationship with God as a highly personal matter involving no one but ourselves and Him. But God will not work that way. He calls us into community. The learning that we do must be done in community. The wisdom we acquire is imparted partly through fellowship. The truths we speak are meant to edify others as well as ourselves. Receiving the mind of Christ requires living in the body of Christ.

As we become steeped in the wisdom of God, we will find ourselves in tune with others who are steeped in His wisdom. It is more than a common interest; it is a spiritual bond. To receive His mind is to receive His Spirit, and to receive His Spirit is to have fellowship with one another. Why? Because God has poured out His Spirit on many members of one body. He has distributed His gifts widely so that, if we want to know Him in fullness, we must depend on one another. The Three-in-One is communal, and His people must be people of community. There is no way to be well-rounded in His truths without fellowship.

But that's a problem for many. Sometimes it's hard to see Christ in the body of Christ. Seekers are often turned off from God because of the people who represent Him. Though He dwells in us, we often do not let Him dwell visibly. These clearly earthen vessels often hide their treasure within an opaque crust of sin. The mind of God is sometimes obscured.

IN DEED   Don't idealize the church. It is made of redeemed but flawed people in a process of transformation. But don't underestimate it, either. God really dwells there. His wisdom is too great to be completely absorbed by a solitary mind, so He has spread it among many. The body of Christ is the physical presence of Jesus in this world. Do you really want to learn the mind of God? Then we need each other. It is in His Word, written on our hearts, and cultivated in the fellowship of His people.

Jesus in This World

I no longer live, but Christ lives in me.
GALATIANS 2:20

IN WORD The enormity of this realization—that it is actually Jesus who is now our life—will never fully be understood. We just can't fathom it. It is deeper than our finite minds will go. But we can know one thing for sure: The God who gave His Son's life in exchange for ours has invested a priceless treasure in us. He does not want mediocre returns on His investment. And, when we really think about it, neither do we.

The life of Jesus in us will make us ill-adapted to live comfortably in the ways of the world. But the life of Jesus in us will make us entirely satisfied as misfits. We'll prefer His Kingdom over the corruption of a truth-impaired society. We'll dream His dreams, pursue His plans. We must not bury the treasure of His life within an exterior of common humanity. We must become uncommon—still fully human, still an earthen vessel, but one with a priceless, eternal life within. We must forsake the self-life for the life of Jesus in our hearts. We crave that life, and God craves it for us. He first came to dwell among us; now He comes to dwell within us.

IN DEED Do you honestly want the power of Jesus to live in you? Be careful how you answer: His life was ultimately joyful, but also deeply painful. We must choose it, though. Pray this prayer today, and tomorrow, and the next day—until it becomes as natural as your breathing:

"My Lord, You have mercifully exchanged Jesus for me. I now walk in His identity, His power, His will, His resurrection and life. May I live worthy of that calling, praying His prayers, seeking His possessions, desiring His desires, dreaming His dreams, doing His work. I'm a fellow heir of Your Kingdom, and I don't want to waste the privilege. Please give me Your wisdom. Please plant Your desires deep within me. Let me see Jesus' miracles, His power, His compassion. Yes, I know I will also feel His cross. But I gladly will, if I can only experience His life. Please let me live as Jesus in this world. Please. Amen."

NOVEMBER 1
Galatians 2:19-20

To be in Christ is the source of the Christian's life.

—Charles Hodge

Identity Gift

I no longer live, but Christ lives in me.
GALATIANS 2:20

Galatians 2:19-20

The very essence of Christ's deliverance is the substitution of Himself for us— His life for ours!

—Horatius Bonar

IN WORD We can scarcely understand the blessing of the life of Jesus within us. We were not holy, but we don't live anymore; He lives in us. We weren't able to produce any fruit, but we're dead branches; He's the Vine—the whole vine. We couldn't find a mountain in daylight, but we don't have to look anymore; He led us straight to God. He fulfilled the Law for us, He paid the price for us, He died our death for us. And now, He is raised to life for us—and in us.

Christ in us: It's like identity theft from the divine, but freely offered, not stolen. You've heard of criminals who steal ID numbers, write checks, and apply for credit cards using someone else's name. We're as illegitimate in our use of Jesus' name, except for one act of God: He took our place. We *are* in Him. We *have* His name. His ID number is the only one God recognizes, and He has given it to us. We're in His family. It's as if God said: "Here's my Son's identity. Use it. Live in it. You will never be prosecuted for it. It's a gift. Mercy says it's yours."

What a God. What a Savior. What a promise. We were bankrupt, and our credit with God was no good. We owed an unpayable debt to an infinite lender. And instead of making us work it off—which we could never have done—or punishing us for delinquency—which we could never have survived—He forgave it. Cancelled it. Just tore up the certificate, erased our names off of His books, and put the name of His Son in our place. You know that Son, the One with perfect credit and infinite resources. His identity is ours. Our checks will never bounce again, our charges will never be declined.

IN DEED Have you considered the implications of that? When you pray, you pray with the mouth of Jesus. When you learn, you learn with His mind. When you worship, you worship in His Spirit and in His truth. Consider your inadequacy dead and buried along with the rest of you. Jesus is our sufficiency. He is our life.

Just Like Jesus

Whoever claims to live in him must walk as Jesus did.

1 JOHN 2:6

IN WORD It seems obvious, but somehow we miss this truth. We who claim salvation by faith in Jesus—that we are filled with the Holy Spirit of God and worship our Father in spirit and in truth—are often remarkably unlike our Savior.

What causes such incongruity in our lives? Do we want only the benefits of salvation without its responsibilities? Do we grab the "free gift" of grace while forgetting the cross-carrying side of discipleship? Whatever our reason, we are not alone. Every religion has adherents who claim to follow its precepts but are noticeably indifferent to them. Christians are adept at such games as well. We fool ourselves into thinking that agreement with the gospel equals living it. But it doesn't.

Perhaps as John wrote this sentence he was recalling the sharp words of Jesus when He asked His disciples a penetrating question: "Why do you call me, 'Lord, Lord,' and do not do what I say?" (Luke 6:46). John had seen crowds surround the miracle-working Jesus with admiration and even worship, and he had also seen them walk away when the teaching got tough. Are we only miracle seekers as well? Do we seek a salvation that doesn't disrupt our lives? Do we claim to live in Him and yet not live like Him?

IN DEED First John was written to help believers know whether their faith was genuine or not. High on the list of indicators for authenticity is a consistent lifestyle. John tells us, in essence, that there is no such thing as an un-Christlike Christian. He acknowledges our imperfection and our need to confess, of course, but he never implies that we can claim saving faith without a serious regard for the way we live. We must be like Him. Students resemble their teachers. Servants resemble their masters. Children resemble their parents. And Christians resemble Christ. It's a given.

Devote all diligence to this truth. The watching world is skeptical of the faith because it has seen un-Christlike "Christians." God's Word calls His witnesses to be like Him.

NOVEMBER 3
1 John 2:3-6

A Christian's life should be nothing but a visible representation of Christ.

—Thomas Brooks

307

Authenticity

Each one should test his own actions.
GALATIANS 6:4

Galatians 6:1-5

Real holiness has a fragrance about it which is its own.

—Father Andrew

IN WORD   What is the measure of hypocrisy? Is it defined by acting contrary to your feelings? Is it pretending to be someone you're not? We know that acting holy while harboring sin is hypocrisy. Is a born-again child of God who acts contrary to the new nature also a hypocrite?

Christians easily get drawn off the course of authentic faith. On the one hand, we can quickly become pretenders, acting outwardly according to others' expectations—or even according to biblical standards—while cultivating corruption within. We appear sanctified, but we're not. On the other hand, we can become so open to our impulses and so transparent in our indulgences that we are authentic, but not very sanctified. It's a confusing balance, and we need to ask the questions: Is a holy life a hypocritical life? Is an authentic life an indulgent one?

We must find that balance. We must avoid hypocrisy but embrace the call to holiness. There's a difference between pretending to be who you're not and disciplining yourself to be who you ought to be. The hypocrite will feign holiness with no commitment to it. But the authentic, sanctified person will embrace God's call, seek to live it outwardly, and openly confess both the inward struggle to do so and the failures that will inevitably come. Purity does not have to imply pretense. In fact, if it's real, it never will.

IN DEED   Don't fall for the lie that if you act contrary to your feelings, you're a hypocrite. Truth isn't always about feelings. If you struggle with sinful thoughts, confess them openly to trustworthy people and let them help you through your struggles. But do not indulge those struggles in the name of avoiding hypocrisy.

At the other extreme, do not be so focused on your image that you become inauthentic. Don't pretend to be holier than you are. A truly consecrated life does not need to put on airs. Its transformation is more than skin-deep.

Authentic Worship

The LORD detests the sacrifice of the wicked, but the prayer of the upright pleases him.   PROVERBS 15:8

IN WORD   Several Bible passages tell us that the fear of God is where wisdom begins (Proverbs 9:10, for one example). If we are to be truly wise, we *must* understand who He is. All of creation was based on His character. His heart is written into the fabric of every part of this universe, even if sin obscures it. Those who find understanding will be those who can recognize the imprint of God in the depths and design of creation. They will be ardent observers of the way He deals with humanity. They will take their cues from Him.

The proverbs point out numerous such cues. This one in 15:8 tells us something profound about our Creator. He desires the essence of worship more than its demonstration. In Old Testament times, the sacrifice would have most often been an animal or a grain offering. Today, it comes from our finances at one level and our time and talents at others. In any case, it's not the gift that matters most. God already owns everything anyway. What really matters is the heart of the giver. Why? Because things do not honor God nearly as much as does a devoted, living being.

Why does God hate the sacrifice of the wicked? Because it is superficial. It is an attempt to brush Him off and get on with the self-life. It bears the appearance of devotion, but there is nothing of relationship in it—no love, no honor, no passion. That tells us volumes about the One who made us. He is no distant force, a cosmic "first cause" who observes us from afar. He is deeply, intensely personal.

IN DEED   Have you really considered the implications of that? It means that when you think He's far off, He isn't. It means that those deep longings in your heart—you know, the ones that leave agonizing, gaping holes when unfulfilled— are longings He wants to satisfy in the right way at the right time. It means that your soul is a place of warm communion, not cold solitude. It means that what you thought was too good to be true—His unconditional love and His enjoyment of your personality—is real.

NOVEMBER 5
Proverbs 15:8-11

I beg You to come into my heart, for by inspiring it to long for You, You make it ready to receive You.

—St. Augustine

Authentic Living

The LORD detests the way of the wicked but he loves those who pursue righteousness.   PROVERBS 15:9

NOVEMBER 6
Proverbs 15:8-11

Wisdom requires a surrender, verging on the mystical, of a person to the glory of existence.

—Gerhard Von Rad

IN WORD   God has put order and design into creation. He has woven His own character into it. The winds of the world blow according to His plan. The currents of the sea flow in ordered cycles. The river of life gushes in one direction, and the direction is toward Him. Order, purpose, a plan. Our God is a God of righteousness.

That's the problem with sin. It goes against the flow, drives against the wind, swims against the currents. It does not recognize the character of the Compassionate in the details of the cosmos. It corrupts and obscures the knowledge of the Holy in the heartbeat of the world. The pulse of mankind races and staggers at ungodly rates and rhythms. Rebellion has violated the very character of creation, contradicted the very logic of the Logos. It is an affront to the foundation of wisdom on which this earth was laid. God detests it.

Our treacherous, treasonous departure from the order of His handiwork has no remedy apart from a completely new creation. So God spoke Jesus into a virgin's womb and began a new order of things. The new creation was uncorruptible by sin and unconquerable by death. And the Spirit of the new creation is put into us by the simple act of believing it is true and of relying on its worth.

IN DEED   That's why God loves those who pursue righteousness. They are demonstrating a love for the rhyme and reason by which all things are established. We cannot truly have such a love unless He gives it, but the re-creation always does. God puts within us a mind for wisdom, a heart for passion, and a spirit for the purity of His Kingdom. Our newborn instincts drive us right along with the winds and the currents of His plan.

Do you struggle with stubborn disobedience? Let it go and flee into the heart of God. Go with His flow. Know Him and love Him. Let that knowledge and love shape you. God delights in such a pursuit. It fits Him perfectly.

Authentic Trust

*Stern discipline awaits him who leaves the path; he who
hates correction will die.* PROVERBS 15:10

IN WORD It is hard for human nature to accept correction. We like to think that we were born in a pristine natural state, corrupted only over time under the influence of a rotten society. We want to be able to say, "This is just the way I am," and consider it a good enough defense. But wisdom begins when we fear God and understand who He is. So wisdom begins when we acknowledge His intense interest in making things right in our lives.

That requires an immense amount of trust. When a word from heaven speaks against our natural tendencies, we need a lot of faith to follow it. And God will grant it. He knows that those who are redeemed out of the human rebellion will be a little disoriented. He knows we may get confused over right and wrong. He understands that it takes time for our eyes to adjust to light and for our senses to discern the direction of the wind. So He speaks. In numerous pages, in red letters and black, in many kinds of fellowships, in the intricacies of our hearts, He speaks. We are not children of a silent God.

What are we to do when His voice is stern? Reject it because it confronts us with ourselves? Or follow it because we know where it will lead? One choice leads to death, the other to life. The voice of the Father is firm but loving. Blessed are those who can accept its firmness while discerning its love.

IN DEED All cultures of all ages have hated God's correction. Ours is no exception. It takes a move of His Spirit to inspire genuine repentance anywhere in this world. But He has moved often. He does not leave us to our own devices unless we insist on them.

How much do you trust God's voice? When He calls for a radical life change, can you accept it? When He points out a sin, can you resist being defensive? When He pits you against your culture, can you stand firm? Trust in God's corrective Word is a powerful thing. It changes hearts and directs lives. It puts us on a straight path into His arms.

NOVEMBER 7
Proverbs 15:8-11

It is in mercy and in measure that God chastises His children.

—John Trapp

Authentic Thoughts

Death and Destruction lie open before the LORD—how much more the hearts of men! PROVERBS 15:11

NOVEMBER 8
Proverbs 15:8-11

He is nearer than our own soul, closer than our most secret thoughts.

—A. W. Tozer

IN WORD If we want to get to that place of fearing the Lord—you know, the place where wisdom begins—then all we have to do is consider this: He knows *everything!* All of those exceedingly embarrassing thoughts—hateful? lustful? twisted? all of the above?—are laid bare before Him. We are publicly stripped, the nakedness of our soul held right in front of His eyes—that burning, piercing, holy gaze. The bright spotlight of glory shines right on our most private places. Everything we were ever ashamed of is in His full view.

Our first reaction to that is shame. Just as Adam and Eve nervously covered themselves with fig leaves and hid from God's presence, we push thoughts of His judgment to the back of our minds. "Surely we're not that bad, are we? Everyone knows He's lenient, right? Doesn't grace give us a pretty big margin of error?" But all we've done is justify ourselves or compromise God in order to reconcile the two. Our fig leaves overestimate our righteousness or underestimate His holiness—or both. We just can't face up to our shame.

But the penetrating gaze of God is gracious. Yes, our shame is, in fact, legitimate. And no, He doesn't casually overlook our sins. We are entirely right to feel guilty. But we are invited to lay our guilt on Jesus, exchanging our rotten life for His perfect one. Oh, the mercy of the all-seeing God! He does not just look at us and shake His head in bewilderment. He deals with it all. He doesn't give us a margin for our errors, He crucified His righteousness to pay for them. Everything He sees is accounted for. *Everything!* Which is really important for us to know, because there is nothing He doesn't see.

IN DEED The one who understands God's perfect, merciful vision is the one who will live sober-minded and aware of the gravity of a life in His view. Wisdom thrives in that life. There is no pretense there, only gratitude. The authentic life will never be casual again. And though completely laid bare, it will never have cause to be ashamed.

The Real Thing

Love must be sincere.
ROMANS 12:9

IN WORD We are called by Jesus to love one another. Love is the defining characteristic of the Christian community; Jesus called it His "new command" and said it would distinguish us as His disciples (John 13:34-35). He did not lay it out for us as a good option; it was an order. Obedience requires that we love Him and that we love others.

Knowing that, we usually try to put on love—or at least the appearance of love. Even when we cultivate bitterness in our hearts toward another, we cultivate smiles and warmth on our faces. Our words and our inner feelings do not always match. We act loving because we know we are supposed to; but we do not *feel* loving. That's a problem.

Which is genuine love? When Paul tells us to love each other sincerely, does he really expect our feelings to fall in line with our obedience? Is it acceptable to *act* loving rather than to *be* loving? It's a start, but we can't be content with that. Our feelings change slowly, especially when we've been offended or slighted. In such cases, we can at least act as we know we are supposed to act. But we cannot stop there. We must guard our hearts diligently. That is where all actions will eventually flow from. At some point, obedience must include sincerity. Otherwise, it doesn't come close to the character of God.

Think about that. Does God love us reluctantly? Does He say: "You've sinned so much that I don't have strong feelings for you, but according to My promise I'll treat you lovingly"? Of course not. There is no internal contradiction in God's attitudes. He is not superficial in the least. His love is real—the most authentic, genuine love there is. So must ours be.

IN DEED How can we get there? Genuine love is so hard, especially when we're told to love our enemies! Fallen, sinful natures cannot fulfill that command. The answer must be supernatural.

Trust God to live His life in you. That's what our life in the Holy Spirit is all about. Ask Him not to reform your character by giving you love, but to replace your character by giving you His. His love is utterly sincere. Ours must be as well.

NOVEMBER 9
Romans 12:9-13

Has God commanded something? Then throw yourself back on God for the means to do what He has commanded.

—Watchman Nee

A New Culture

Hate what is evil; cling to what is good.
ROMANS 12:9

He that sees the beauty of holiness
. . . sees the greatest and most important thing in the world.

—Jonathan Edwards

IN WORD A man went to live in a foreign country. He loved it. He wanted to apply for citizenship, and having no real ties to his former country, he began to live "like the natives." He adopted the dress and habits of his new culture. He began to learn the language. He refused to eat food from his former diet and dined exclusively on the cuisine of his adopted homeland. He wanted no visual reminders of his past and embraced all the customs of his present and future. He established a new identity.

That's what God tells us to do. We have left the kingdom of darkness and been adopted into the Kingdom of light. We are to put off the clothing of the old nature and live in the Spirit of the new. We are conforming to a different culture and being shaped into a different nature. The old has passed away; all things have become new.

When Paul tells us to hate what is evil and cling to what is good, he is not giving us friendly advice. He is using graphic images to define our transition. We are to "turn in horror from wickedness" (v. 9, AMP), loathing any semblance of ungodliness. The deeds of darkness are no longer appropriate in our new Kingdom; they do not fit into this culture. And then we are to cling to what is good—embrace it, desperately grab hold of it, never let it go. It is to be our obsession, of a sort. We are to pursue godliness with unbridled zeal.

IN DEED Few Christians make such a dramatic transition, but those who do can testify to the rest of us that it's a greater blessing to make radical changes than to make slow, imperceptible ones. Sanctification is a lifelong process, but blessed are those who are on the fast track. They are quicker candidates for usefulness in the Kingdom, they are greater testimonies to the power of God, and they are less likely to fade away into the apostasy of lukewarmness. Real godliness is radical.

Are you in a spiritual rut? Hate what is evil and cling to what is good. Let sin horrify you, and embrace the culture of the Kingdom of blazing light. Total immersion is always the best way to fit in.

Brotherly Devotion

*Be devoted to one another in brotherly love. Honor one
another above yourselves.* ROMANS 12:10

IN WORD Paul exhorted the believers in Philippi: "Do
nothing out of selfish ambition or vain conceit, but in humility consider others better than yourselves" (Philippians 2:3).
There had been infighting, and Paul provides the antidote.
True Christian humility will cause us to subvert our own
interests for the well-being of others. It isn't natural, but it's
Christlike. Sacrifice is the way of the Cross.

Didn't Jesus tell His disciples that those who would
follow Him must take up their cross (Luke 9:23)? Not only
is cross-bearing an initial act of sacrifice; it is to be a daily
event. Those who cannot suffer for the sins of others, those
who cannot inconvenience themselves for another's needs,
those who will not lay down their life for their friends have
little in common with Jesus. Our agendas are more often
than not a matter of self. Jesus' agenda is always about
someone else.

Years ago on a Judean hill, Jesus' agenda was about us.
Had that not been the case, we would not be alive today, at
least not spiritually. We cannot call Him our example and
our Lord if we do not follow His path. The Christian heart
is to be filled with compassion—devotion toward brothers
and sisters in Christ and a desire to see others honored. It is
the way of the Kingdom, and the world is watching to see
if the Kingdom is worthwhile.

IN DEED We must show them a different way. The world
has lost hope for a utopian fellowship, and while Christians
are not perfect in this life, we can be perfected in love by the
Spirit of God. It is our holy calling. We are forever bound in
Christ with all other believers around the world. Our relationship with them will never be severed.

How devoted are you to the well-being of others? Do
you blow wind in the sails of your brothers and sisters in
Christ? Or are you always seeking your own advancement?
We cannot simply be happy with their honors; we must seek
to build them up. That's what Jesus did, and we are in Him.
The devoted God calls us into devoted relationships.

NOVEMBER 11
Romans 12:9-13

The measure of
a man is not how
many servants he
has but how many
men he serves.

—D. L. Moody

Spiritual Fervor

Never be lacking in zeal, but keep your spiritual fervor, serving the Lord. ROMANS 12:11

NOVEMBER 12

Romans 12:9-13

Catch on fire with enthusiasm and people will come for miles to watch you burn.

—John Wesley

IN WORD Jesus once rebuked a church for its lukewarmness. The Laodiceans were neither hot nor cold, and the language Jesus used to describe His reaction was graphic and blunt. It nauseated Him (Revelation 3:15-16). Spiritual apathy is far from the heart of God.

Several times in the Old Testament—Isaiah, in particular—it is said that God will accomplish His will with zeal. He is a zealous God, and there is nothing lukewarm about Him. He is violently opposed to sin. He is passionately loving toward those who trust Him. His holiness, His compassion, His mercy, His provision, His protection—all of His attributes are portrayed in the Bible as complete. He is not somewhat loving, partially holy, mostly omniscient, or sort of wise. Everything He is, He is in the extreme.

We are His children. It would not make sense for God to give His children a spirit different from His own. We cannot envision Him as passionate and zealous and remain apathetic ourselves. If He is fervent, we must be fervent. If He serves zealously, we must serve zealously. Jesus' love led Him to wash dirty feet and it took Him to the Cross. Will ours? The Holy Spirit sent Paul all around the Roman Empire against all kinds of opposition. Would He not give us that same drive? The early believers died in fires and coliseums for their faith. Would we?

IN DEED How would you characterize your level of zeal? Does it drive you to pursue God's Kingdom and His righteousness with a passion? If He dwells within you and your fellowship with Him is deep, it will. It is not possible to be powerfully filled with the Holy Spirit and yet to be lukewarm in our love or our service. His Spirit and our apathy cannot coexist in the same place; there is no fellowship between them. As we're fond of saying, the apple doesn't fall far from the tree. The extreme God *will* have extreme children.

A Prescription for Pain

Be joyful in hope, patient in affliction, faithful in prayer.
ROMANS 12:12

IN WORD   When clouds gather, we get discouraged. It's a natural reaction. Our eyes tell us to run for cover, to hang on for survival, or to prepare to die. And we believe our eyes. We put an awful lot of faith in what they tell us. We let their information sink into our hearts and thrive there—no matter how painful that is.

Paul gives us a prescription for our pain. He tells us how to have joy, patience, and faith. We are to place our hope not on what our eyes tell us—that is too often hopeless—and we are to place our faith in God. When the clouds gather, we are to gather to Him. When faced with a choice between letting the clouds obscure Him or letting Him obscure the clouds, we are to choose the latter. Not to do so is to overestimate our problems and to underestimate our God.

Our perspectives are distorted so easily. We are habitual twisters, making dark things our surest truth and God's light our most uncertain refuge. Such a distortion is a sure recipe for despair. Instead, we are to believe what the Word and the Spirit tell us, regardless of the witness of the clouds. God must always loom larger. Until we're trained in this perspective, our minds are not renewed.

IN DEED   So what are the details of the prescription? (1) We are to fix our eyes on hope and to be joyful about it. God has given us a glimpse of reality: His strength, His Kingdom's inevitability, His promise of intervention, His eternal rewards. Why would we let a few clouds undermine those certainties? (2) We are to be patient in affliction. Those realities are invisible for a time, but they will be clear soon enough. And, (3) we are to be faithful in prayer. Why? Not because prayer changes things, but because God changes things and we must communicate with Him. His intervention is not arbitrary; it is the result of the give-and-take of relationship, and prayer is the means to that relationship. When we've followed this prescription, we'll notice a remarkable change: Clouds don't seem to matter so much anymore.

NOVEMBER 13
Romans 12:9-13

Hope is the power of being cheerful in circumstances which we know to be desperate.

—G. K. Chesterton

A Reflection of Grace

Share with God's people who are in need. Practice hospitality.
ROMANS 12:13

NOVEMBER 14
Romans 12:9-13

A cheerful giver does not count the cost of what he gives. His heart is set on pleasing and cheering him to whom the gift is given.

—Julian of Norwich

IN WORD Our spiritual gospel has far-reaching, material implications. It commands us to focus on eternal realities rather than temporary provisions. It calls for an increasing detachment from the things that once gripped us. And one of the ways to cultivate such focus and detachment is by a radical and voluntary meeting of needs.

We are never given permission in the Bible to allow our material things to create division between our eternal brothers and sisters. And yet they do. Within the church are awkward class structures and rigid social strata. No, Jesus was not a socialist, and God's Word does not compel us to seek absolute equity between all who believe. But it does command us to share. We who have much are to notice those who have little. The implication is not that we will grudgingly give when confronted; the New Testament context implies that we will seek opportunities to give.

Why is this such an imperative in Christian fellowship? Because our fellowship is meant to reflect Jesus' kingdom. We are to be a taste of heaven on earth. We are to reflect God's glory, and His glory is displayed when He meets our needs. That means our reflection will involve meeting the needs of others. The generous God calls us to be generous. The hospitable God who will welcome us into heaven with open arms calls us to welcome others with the same spirit.

IN DEED Sometimes it is hard to see heaven on our earth. But the church is to make sure that the Kingdom of God is visible. It is our divine mission, given us by the One who called us to follow Him in every area of our lives. How did Jesus display heaven? He touched and healed, fed and watered, taught and cultivated, forgave and poured out His life. His followers can do no less, if we are in fact to be His followers. Share on earth as you will share in heaven. Let the hospitality of heaven define your hospitality here. Let His Kingdom be demonstrated in you.

Hardship Happens

Endure hardship as discipline; God is treating you as sons.

HEBREWS 12:7

IN WORD Trials come, and we plead for relief. Circumstances oppress, and we pray for deliverance. Health, relationships, work, and just about everything else in our lives grow difficult, and we ask God to straighten them out. We don't like the pressures of life, and we lift every anxious thought to God, as we should. But we forget a guiding principle: Hardship is part of the program. It grows us up into maturity. There are things that God wants to do with us that cannot be done in a perfect environment.

We view discipline as God's remedial recourse for a Christian who has gone far astray. But it is more universal than we like to think. It comes not only to those who have failed, but to those whom God is preparing for greater success. It's what a father does for his children, and it's what our Father does for us. Only those who are already perfect can avoid the trials that God allows—which means no one can. The trials will come, and God will let them stay for a while.

We don't like pain. We ask God to take away every reminder that we live in a broken world, but He won't do it. We will live out our days with some scars, or sometimes even with open wounds. We cannot become ministers of His grace otherwise. We can't even learn it for ourselves until He puts us in great need of it. If we are to represent our merciful Father in a broken world, we must actually live in that broken world. We must know the needs that require mercy, and we must know them from experience. There is no other way.

IN DEED Do you constantly ask God to clean up every messy area of your life? To brighten every dark corner and to dress up every shabby appearance? That's okay; our concerns are His concerns. But don't expect perfection. The perfect world we crave is for a future glory, not for now. Ease and comfort are not usually His prescription for us, because they will not prepare us for that future glory. No, God will leave us reminders of brokenness to serve as reminders of His grace. Endure those reminders well.

NOVEMBER 15
Hebrews 12:1-11

Out of suffering have emerged the strongest souls; the most massive characters are seared with scars.

—E. H. Chapin

Promised Safety

*The L*ORD *will rescue me from every evil attack and will bring me safely to his heavenly kingdom.* 2 TIMOTHY 4:18

NOVEMBER 16

2 Timothy 4:16-18

No soldiers of Christ are ever lost, missing, or left dead on the battlefield.

—J. C. Ryle

IN WORD   Are you a worrier? Join the club. Its membership includes the entire human race. Yes, there are those who will deny that they worry, and on the surface they seem carefree. But deep down inside, they fear something—tragedy, abandonment, certainly the day of their death. Human anxiety is universal. We were born in the insecurity of a fallen world and a sinful disposition.

God offers security. That is perhaps the most profoundly good element of the Good News. The gospel has comforted so many hearts because it touches the heart's deepest needs. Our need for companionship, for love, for provision, for purpose—all are part of our inheritance in Christ. And no need seems to bubble up quite so often as our need for security. We worry about failure, injury, loneliness, debts, and death. But we can claim with Paul: "The Lord will rescue me from every evil attack and will bring me safely to his heavenly kingdom."

Perhaps you thought this verse was for the superspiritual, apostle-like servants in God's Kingdom. Perhaps you assumed it is only for those who have been beaten or imprisoned for the sake of the gospel. There are many such servants in our world who are persecuted, and God's promise for them is sure. But it is meant for the rest of us as well. Evil attacks come to all who live for Jesus. That's a fact. And God promises to deliver all who live for Jesus. That's also a fact.

IN DEED   There is no limit to the fears our minds will entertain. Some worry about them more than others. If you are one of the worriers, rehearse this verse often. Memorize it. Say it to yourself daily. You are not psyching yourself up, you are training yourself to accept an absolute truth. This truth can go to the very depths of your soul and instill enormous confidence in your heart, because it is in the Word— and Jesus said the Word cannot be broken (John 10:35). Trust it. You are safe in Him.

Asa's Folly

The eyes of the LORD range throughout the earth to strengthen those whose hearts are fully committed to him.
2 CHRONICLES 16:9

IN WORD King Asa of Judah, the great-grandson of King Solomon, was a remarkably modern man. No, he didn't have the technology or the historical perspective that we have, but his approach to his problems fits the modern era easily. Though he had begun his reign with devotion to God and the heart of a spiritual reformer, he ended it with passive faithlessness. Though he had removed idols from the land, he had not replaced the idols in his own heart. He became secular.

In chapter 16, Asa twice made a foolish mistake. He trusted something other than God. When the king of Israel attacked, Asa made a pact with the Syrians for protection. The prophet Hanani came to him with the remarkable message of verse 9: God is actually searching for hearts devoted to Him in order to bless them. He *wants* to protect, to guide, and to provide. He is not reluctant—unless we're not devoted to Him.

Asa should have learned that lesson, but he didn't. He came down with a severe disease that led him not to God but to doctors. His secular mind sought out kings and physicians as his first resort and God as his last. He would fit into our culture well.

NOVEMBER 17
2 Chronicles 16

There is no other method of living piously and justly than that of depending upon God.

—John Calvin

IN DEED Where do you go when you're in trouble? Have you made the mistake of going to the doctor first and then praying to God only when medicine fails? Have you thought that our only hope for peace lies in political treaties and cooperative governments? Have you thought of God as a means to fill in the gaps around our science, technology, economics, business strategies, and other areas of secular competence?

Science, medicine, law, business, and every other aspect of modern know-how do not need to conflict with God. They aren't necessarily wrong. They just cannot be our hope. Avoid Asa's folly: God is always our first resort.

Ezra's Honor

*I was ashamed to ask the king for soldiers and horsemen
to protect us from enemies on the road.*   EZRA 8:22

NOVEMBER 18
Ezra 8:21-23

A firm faith in the
universal provi-
dence of God is
the solution to all
earthly problems.

—B. B. Warfield

IN WORD   Ezra did what Asa wouldn't do. He sought God in a time of peril. Unlike the king who sought alliances for protection and doctors for healing—faithless acts that put God last on the providence list—Ezra determined not to profane the name of the Lord. Having told Babylon's ruler of the favor and strength of God, he could not slander the reputation he had just proclaimed. He knew his actions would speak louder than words. So he prayed. He didn't pray *and* request an escort of warriors—that would have demonstrated a serious lack of faith. No, he just prayed, and God answered. Ezra demonstrates for us a dependence that God honors.

IN DEED   Do you trust God as Healer and then, as an afterthought, ask people to pray for your illness? Do you trust God as Provider and then, if you happen to think about it, pray for His supply? Do you trust God as Protector and then, just in case, invest in the best security systems money can buy? Are you an Asa or an Ezra?

Human effort in meeting our needs is not a sin. There's nothing biblically wrong with seeing a doctor, investing wisely, and locking your doors. The sin is in our hearts. Where do we place our hope? On what or whom do we depend? When we think of ministering in Jesus' name, do we shy away from dangerous places because we're just not sure God will protect? Do we avoid the expense because we're just not sure He'll provide? Has sin caused us to measure our well-being in terms of materials and strategies rather than in the God in whom we believe?

God is first. Human effort is second, if at all. In God we trust. In human effort we obey what God tells us to do. But we can't supplement our prayers with our own devices and then claim that we have faith. Faith actually trusts Him to do what He says He will do. Honor God with your faith, and He will honor your faith with Himself.

Anatomy of a Surrender: Idolatry

What fellowship can light have with darkness?

2 CORINTHIANS 6:14

IN WORD   Paul points out the obvious conflict between light and darkness to urge the Corinthians to disassociate from corrupting influences. The principle applies to our social relationships, but it also applies to the struggles within our hearts. If light and darkness do not mix within the church, which is the temple of God collectively, they do not mix within ourselves, who as individuals are the building blocks of that temple. We cannot entertain elements of the Kingdom of light and elements of the kingdom of darkness simultaneously and expect God to bear fruit in us. He wants purity.

NOVEMBER 19

2 Corinthians 6:14–7:1

Whatever a man seeks, honors, or exalts more than God, this is the god of idolatry.

—William Ullathorne

That's a problem for every human being who has ever lived. We aren't pure. Long after we've made that landmark decision to follow Jesus, we still have internal struggles with sin and obedience. The decision was right, but the follow-through proves difficult. And it's the follow-through that makes the difference between unusual blessing and mediocrity. We cannot be mature Christians until the initial decision to let Jesus be our Lord actually becomes a way of life. We cannot make a commitment to light while maintaining our grip on darkness. We must surrender ourselves.

Nearly every Christian has remnants of darkness that cloud his or her discipleship. We like to call them character flaws or weaknesses of the flesh. In reality, they are idols. They may range from the alarming addictions of temper, lusts, and obsessive greed to the relatively minor flaws of bad diets, time mismanagement, and mild obsessions with hobbies. Regardless of their severity, they are our battlegrounds. They are points of conflict between us and our Creator. They test us on whether we will, or will not, obey.

IN DEED   All Christians have had their struggles with idolatry. Many of those struggles rage today. Some of them rage within your heart. The issue is not whether they are big or little sins; the issue is whether we trust God enough to do what He tells us, even in the small things. Choosing our will over His, at any level, is idolatry.

Anatomy of a Surrender: Lies

What agreement is there between the temple of God and idols?

2 CORINTHIANS 6:16

NOVEMBER 20

2 Corinthians 6:14–7:1

Obedience means marching right on whether we feel like it or not.

—D. L. Moody

IN WORD We know the solution to our idolatry. We are to surrender it and trust ourselves to God. But knowledge isn't our problem. Knowing what to do and actually doing it are separate issues. One is intellectual, the other is a matter of the will. We let our desires influence our level of surrender. We *think* we want to obey God, but we don't really *want* to. At least not in those areas we zealously guard. You know what your weaknesses are. Everyone knows his or her besetting sins because everyone has them.

Everyone also knows the games we play to justify our idols. We make excuses for them. Maybe we can argue that they're physical addictions or emotional wounds, not spiritual issues. Maybe we can convince ourselves that our flaws can somehow be useful in ministering to others one day. Maybe we excuse ourselves from "borderline" sins because "we're only human," or we don't want to be "holier than thou," or we need to relate to "the real world." Or perhaps we simply take for granted the grace that is greater than all our sins.

What is behind this desperate attempt to hang on to our idols? Simmering underneath this struggle is a subtle suspicion that we will have to take care of our own needs because God won't. As much as we want to be obedient and submissive to God, we like our sins. They do something for us that we're afraid God won't do. We think we find "life" in them. We think we might be more fulfilled if we take a few small matters into our own hands. So we hang on, and we try to convince ourselves and our God that we're justified in doing so, or at least more justified than most people. But God is not convinced.

IN DEED We need to dispense with the lies and cut to the chase. Our flaws, addictions, hang-ups, and other issues are sin. Disobedience. Hindrances to the abundant life that God promises. The longer we try to convince ourselves otherwise, the longer we prolong the pain of surrender and postpone the amazing blessings of the surrendered life.

Anatomy of a Surrender: Death

Therefore come out from them and be separate, says the LORD.
2 CORINTHIANS 6:17

IN WORD There comes a time, when all the idols have proven false and when all the lies have proven empty, that we're ready to surrender. We quit hanging on to those things that we thought gave us life, because we found out that they didn't. In a sense, we're ready to die. We've believed in our minds for a long time that the promise of God is greater than the promise of sin, but now we're ready to put that belief to the test. We want to move from intellectual belief to biblical belief—the kind that acts. The time for putting our money where our mouth is has come. We can let go.

This surrender of our idols can be a painful process. We don't know what life will be like without them. Sometimes that ignorance will cause us to go back and forth on our surrender: We lay those false treasures down and then pick them up, over and over again. But that just adds to our guilt and deepens the difficulty. These idols have grown roots in our hearts, and those roots have run deep. They will require more than a gentle weed-pulling if we've had them for any significant time at all. The larger the tree and the deeper the roots, the more violent the uprooting. When our idols go, it will hurt. We have to expect that. It's part of that cross Jesus told us we would carry if we want to be His disciples. It will leave a big hole, and we pray that God will fill it.

IN DEED Have you died? Our body of sin was nailed to the cross when Jesus substituted Himself for us, of course. But in a practical sense, does your sinful flesh linger? The deeper Christian life, the abundant life we're promised, demands a death. This surrender of our false gods is akin to willingly sacrificing the things we've always trusted for our comfort. We forget how much pain that "comfort" has caused us, and how it has diverted our walk with God. We think we'll miss our sin and we'll feel as if a deep, dark night is descending. But the night is necessary. We must surrender, we must be emptied, and we must forsake our idols. We know it's what God calls us to do. We must die.

NOVEMBER 21

2 Corinthians 6:14–7:1

Holy obedience . . . mortifies our lower nature and makes it obey the Spirit.

—St. Francis of Assisi

Anatomy of a Surrender: Trust

I will be a Father to you, and you will be my sons and daughters, says the LORD Almighty.   2 CORINTHIANS 6:18

NOVEMBER 22

*2 Corinthians
6:14–7:1*

Obedience is the child of trust.

—John Climacus

IN WORD   We don't get to our point of surrender unless we have come to a place of trust. It may be a scary trust to forsake all those false comforts we've depended on in exchange for the invisible blessing of God. But it will require at least *some* trust. No one can loosen his grip on his counterfeit securities without first understanding this vital truth: God has promised His fatherhood to us, and we can count on His loving care. *Nothing* He has asked us to do will harm us. *Everything* He asks us to do will bring blessing.

Do you really believe that? If you have died the death of surrender and trusted that God's instructions are worthwhile, however painful, then you have begun to realize: Those things you clung to were worthless. They are like a plastic trinket that a child refuses to trade in for a diamond ring because he's grown attached to it. The absurdity of our idols begins to dawn on us. What we held on to for so long wasn't worth hanging on to. When we're dealing with God, a trust exercised always becomes a trust vindicated. We will not second-guess our sacrifices. Why? Because He gives us ample reason, at least in the long run, to be glad we made them. He never ends up owing us anything. The blessing that follows obedience is always well worth the cost that accompanies it.

IN DEED   Is trust an issue in your struggle with sin and idolatry? Do you cling to habits, possessions, security, or affections from a fear that God will ask you to give them up and not make the sacrifice worthwhile? That's always the lie of idols. The enemy convinced our first parents that God didn't have their best interests in mind, that He was withholding something valuable from them. Do not be deceived by such slander of our Father. Good fathers *always* want the best for their children, and our Father is always good. You can count on that. His blessings for obedience are incredible. He is far more trustworthy than our idols.

Anatomy of a Surrender: Faith

Since we have these promises, dear friends, let us purify ourselves from everything that contaminates body and spirit, perfecting holiness out of reverence for God.   2 CORINTHIANS 7:1

IN WORD   The flesh-life and the faith-life stand in stark contrast to one another. One sends us in search of the things we think will give us enjoyment, security, and love. The other sends us to God. Those two paths are so similar in their agenda that we get them confused often. Sometimes we even think God gave us our idols to comfort us. Maybe He did, but that was before we began to depend on them. Now they must go.

But those two paths are so different in direction that they cannot, under any circumstances, coexist. We will choose one or the other. As surely as we can't drive on two roads at once, we can't pursue God and our idolatry at the same time. To embrace one is to reject the other. We cannot worship God as an add-on to all the comforts, pleasures, securities, and emotional dependencies we've built our lives on. They must be dethroned and God must reign. It's only right.

Faith can grasp that and let go of everything but God. People, places, possessions, pastimes—they are wonderful gifts from our Father, but they are not our treasures. He is. Only He *can* be. No other treasure is appropriate, and no other treasure will fulfill. That's the conviction of biblical faith. God is worth *everything*.

IN DEED   Faith has the power to surrender all to Jesus, not just during the closing hymn at church but on Mondays at work or on Saturdays at home. Faith is wise enough to see through the idols we've constructed and to know how empty they are. Faith is discerning enough to understand: No matter how hard it seems, obedience is *always* the right choice, the way to receive God's blessing, and the thing that will satisfy us most. God has designed us that way. When we try to satisfy ourselves with other things, we are reaching in the wrong direction and falling for a lie. The faith-life experiences God's best—at all costs.

NOVEMBER 23

2 Corinthians 6:14–7:1

I do not want merely to possess faith; I want a faith that possesses me.

—Charles Kingsley

An Act of Gratitude

Give thanks to the LORD, call on his name; make known among the nations what he has done. PSALM 105:1

NOVEMBER 24
Psalm 105:1-7

Thanksgiving is good, but thanksliving is better.

—Matthew Henry

IN WORD We know both by way of Scripture and by the impulses of our hearts that God is to be thanked. There is no way to understand the profound implications of His grace and to remain thankless in our attitude. In fact, Paul links gratitude with a true knowledge of God and the desire to glorify Him (Romans 1:21). It's an inviolable scriptural principle: To know what God has done is to be thankful.

What does that mean for us? Is it simply an attitude of the heart? Though it begins there, we know there should be more. When we are truly grateful for another person, we want to do things for him or her. Do we have the same impulse with God? Does our gratitude result in an intense desire to offer some gift to Him as an act of devotion? If so, Psalm 105 gives us at least one natural response to His grace: We can make Him known.

God's grace is deeply personal, but it is not private. Scripture tells us repeatedly that God desires a reputation among our families and among the nations. From the hordes passing through the Red Sea to the recipients of Jesus' miracles, the natural response to God's mercy has always been a deep desire to tell about it. The glimpse that the Bible gives us of gratitude is a spontaneous proclamation of His goodness. If we have no urge to tell, perhaps we have no deep awareness of His works. His goodness is too good to keep to ourselves.

IN DEED Do you have that urge for others to know how good your God is? Then you understand: You have recognized His work within you and you are grateful for it. In all of the overflow that begins this psalm, there is a direct, vertical worship of God, and there is also a horizontal relationship with others that gives us ample opportunity to declare what we know of Him. We are to "tell of all his wonderful acts" (v. 2). The gifts of God are public domain. He is worthy of the highest reputation we can proclaim.

The Joy of Gratitude

Let the hearts of those who seek the LORD rejoice.
PSALM 105:3

IN WORD The hearts of those who seek the Lord are often tentative and fretful. Why do we approach God this way? We're not sure of how we'll be received. We know He is loving, but we also know He is holy. We know He is near, but we also know He is utterly transcendent, completely different from what we can imagine. We know that He is light, but we also know that "clouds and thick darkness surround him" (Psalm 97:2). Everyone who ever got a glimpse of Him really couldn't explain it to others very well. The mystery is too great. So we sometimes seek God with a little fear or a little pessimism. We're not sure what we'll find on the other side of the mystery.

Psalm 105 gives us other instructions. Yes, He is mysterious, shrouded in transcendence, incomprehensible in His holiness. But we can still approach Him with joy. We can rejoice because we know that everything He does is good. It may be hard and it may be confusing, but it will be good. God never spurns those who approach Him with an elementary understanding of who He is.

How does this help us? Our natural tendency, like Adam and Eve, is to hide from God. We don't necessarily sit behind the bushes hoping He won't discover us, but mentally we're not entirely open to Him. We dress up our prayers to sound right to His ears, we dress up our deeds to appear worthy before Him, and we dress up our worship to appeal to His glory.

IN DEED In doing so, we sometimes hide things. We don't come to Him boldly, as the writer of Hebrews encourages us to do (Hebrews 4:16). We're spiritual actors when we don't need to be. We underestimate His mercies. We're not quite sure who He is.

Gratitude reminds us never to underestimate Him. It reminds us of what He has done, what He has forgiven, and what He has promised. It acknowledges who He is. And it sends us into His presence with joy.

NOVEMBER 25
Psalm 105:1-7

The best way to show my gratitude to God is to accept everything, even my problems, with joy.

—Mother Teresa

329

Gratitude Believes

Look to the LORD and his strength; seek his face always.
PSALM 105:4

NOVEMBER 26
Psalm 105:1-7

Faith without
thankfulness
lacks strength
and fortitude.

—John Henry Jowett

IN WORD Faith without thankfulness is like a huge, unanswered question. It comes to God with possibilities, but has no assurance that He will address them well. It knows He *can* do good things, but it doesn't know that He *will*. Forgetting the God of the past, it tries in vain to figure out the God of the present and the future. It is weak.

Faith with thankfulness doesn't just look for the Lord, it looks *to* the Lord. It knows who He is. It remembers past mercies and bases today's needs on their proven source. It comes to God with possibilities, not knowing how He will address them, but knowing He will address them well. It is not a tentative question about God; it is a knowledgeable statement. It understands His grace.

We need no reminders to seek God; it is a natural impulse, especially when we're in trouble. No, our problem is remembering *how* to seek Him. Paul's letters are abundant in instructions to utter prayers filled with thankfulness. The faith that Jesus always applauded was a faith that acknowledged up front who He was. We may have lots of questions when we come to God, and we may be confused about many spiritual issues. But we have no reason to ever come to Him questioning His goodness. Our gratitude for what He has done in the past will prepare us to know what kinds of things He will do in the future. It will get us in sync with His heart.

IN DEED Are your prayers filled with fear and confusion? Do you wonder if God will be good to you? There is no need for such uncertainty. Scripture is filled with His goodness, and so is your life. Look between the hardships and the pain and see that He has granted life and redemption. There are always blessings to find—far more than we can count.

Gratitude makes faith strong. Thankful people understand the God who is strong. They see His face and are not afraid. They aren't just hoping for His goodness. They're expecting it.

Gratitude Remembers

*Remember the wonders he has done, his miracles, and
the judgments he pronounced.*   PSALM 105:5

IN WORD   Many people are waiting to be thankful until
they have something to be thankful for. It's a flaw of fallen
humanity. We are always looking forward to what we want
and always aware of what we don't have. For most of us,
the glass is always half empty—at least.

What is our remedy? It's given often in Scripture. We
are to be "rememberers." God urges us to rehearse His past
mercies intentionally and actively. Whenever we begin to
focus on what we are lacking, we're to redirect our focus
to what we've been given. The change in attitude that will
result is remarkable. Joy begins to resurface and faith gets
stronger.

That's what Psalm 105 is all about. It is a brief summary
of history from the call of Abraham to the victories of David.
It reminded Israel's worshipers that God began a great plan
with His people and would certainly continue it. It encouraged them to count the miracles He had done. It helped
them think of God as their Provider, Deliverer, Protector,
Strength, Warrior, and more—just in case they had forgotten, as fallen human beings are prone to do. It stirred up a
sense of destiny and a confidence in God's ability to bring
them through. It created the context for true worship.

IN DEED   Don't we need such reminders? We easily forget God's providence, salvation, and love. We fear that He
might not protect us this time, or that He might not hear our
prayer this time, or that He might abandon His plan for us.
An intentional memory of His works will help us dispense
with those lies. It will cultivate all the things we need to
believe in Him and worship Him again.

Try making a list of all the things you are thankful for.
Remember God's past mercies and write them down. Try
composing your own psalm of remembrance. Then read
over these things often. Set them to music if it helps. Let your
mind be saturated with the goodness of God, and you'll be
amazed at how the goodness of God becomes real.

NOVEMBER 27
Psalm 105:1-7

Gratitude is born
in hearts that take
time to count up
past mercies.

—Charles Edward
Jefferson

Understanding Life

Show me, O LORD, my life's end and the number of my days; let me know how fleeting is my life. PSALM 39:4

NOVEMBER 28
Psalm 39:4-6

It ought to be the business of every day to prepare for our last day.

—Matthew Henry

IN WORD How long do you have left to live? It's a sobering question for this sobering reason: We don't know the answer. We can't know, unless God has given us some peculiar revelation that most will never receive. Whether we've just been given a clean bill of health or diagnosed with a terminal disease, we still don't know how long we have in this world. The diagnoses of doctors are always subject to human error. Furthermore, a perfectly healthy person can be killed in a car accident. Only God knows the day of our passage out of these earthen vessels.

Many people would prefer not to consider such questions. They are too morbid, perhaps. But David *wants* to know; he asks God to show him, to remind him of how transient his life is. No, he isn't necessarily asking to know the date of his death. He wants the sense of urgency that reflects the reality of our short lives. He wants to make every moment count.

So should we. Far from being a morbid thought, understanding the brevity of our earthly life spans will bring us a sense of focus like nothing else will. We will begin to strive for what is important and forsake whatever isn't. We will get our priorities straight. Ask anyone who has been given only a short time to live. Understanding life's uncertainty can lead to a remarkable shift in values.

IN DEED Do you want that kind of focus? Don't wait for a doctor's diagnosis. Go ahead and choose a time. What length would give you a proper perspective and help you live with the right priorities? A year? Five years? Six months? You decide. Then go ahead and live as though you have only a year left, or however much time you've chosen. Assume, for example, that God will take you home one year from today. Watch your priorities change. Watch your relationship with God and with others transform. Begin living in the light of eternity, and understand the life God has given us.

The Easy Way

There is a way that seems right to a man, . . .
PROVERBS 14:12

IN WORD When given a choice between an easy option and a difficult one, which are we more likely to select? All other things being equal, the easy one. But all other things are not equal. Our choices have far-reaching ramifications, and God usually has a preference in them. And, not surprisingly to us, His will has little to do with what's easy.

The United States Declaration of Independence asserts our right to life, liberty, and the pursuit of happiness. That's ingrained in us. We are not often encouraged to do difficult things unless the rewards are great—and clear to our senses. No, more often we prefer the path of least resistance. We'll work for a self-serving cause, or even a selfless cause we feel passionately about. But we do not see God's benefits easily. We are unaware of His rewards, unfamiliar with His Kingdom's ways, and often unconcerned with the glory of His name. We are creatures of the easy way.

That's a natural tendency of a fallen humanity, and cultural ideals and elders who know better try to train us otherwise. But, like the Israelites in one terribly lawless period, everyone does as he or she sees fit (Judges 21:25). We forget that God never asked us to do what seems right in our own eyes; He asks us to do what is right in His eyes. Before the Holy Spirit lovingly invades our lives, we have no spiritual discernment and are guided by impure minds. At the time, that seems like a satisfying independence. But in truth, it's a scary way to live.

IN DEED Consider God's ways with those in the Bible. If difficulties indicated being out of God's will, Paul had most certainly gone astray. (His hardships are itemized in 2 Corinthians 6:4-10.) If obedience were always an easy decision, Abraham's willingness to sacrifice Isaac was pointless. No, our God calls us to hard things. We don't like that, but we need to get used to it. It's a temporary but certain component of the Kingdom of God: The way that seems right often isn't.

NOVEMBER 29
Proverbs 14:12;
Judges 21:25

I was not born to be free. I was born to adore and to obey.

—C. S. Lewis

God's Way

. . . but in the end it leads to death.
PROVERBS 14:12

NOVEMBER 30
Proverbs 14:12;
Deuteronomy 30:19

Carry the cross patiently and with perfect submission, and in the end it shall carry you.

—Thomas à Kempis

IN WORD The way of human ingenuity and discernment, according to the Bible, leads to death. This verse is often applied to salvation, but it is much farther-reaching than that. It applies to all of our choices. We are confronted with constant decisions between self-will and God's will. And the choices may be much more subtle than that: the easy way vs. the hard way, small compromises vs. absolute truth, or any other such confusing fork in the road. We don't realize the gravity of our direction. Man's way leads to death, while God's way leads to . . . well, death.

Have you considered that? If we serve ourselves and cling to our false values, we will die. If we submit to Jesus, we *must* die. But the outcome is not as uniform as it seems. This world offers us "life" and then death—forever. God offers us "death" and then life—forever. Fools choose the "life" of this world, the "life" of the party, the "life" of freedom from all responsibility. The wise choose God. Yes, that means a cross now—a daily cross, a painful cross, a difficult path of aversion to our own wills and submission to God's. But in the end, it leads to life.

IN DEED God is constantly calling us into His will. We're afraid of Him. We've been convinced by a hostile world and a lying enemy that God's will involves untold sacrifice and pain without a corresponding benefit. We think it's all pain, no gain—or a lot of pain with a very uncertain gain. We just can't see the blessing beyond the cross.

But do you think you have a real alternative? That cross we carry may be painful and sacrificial—it is not the easy way. But it's the only way. The alternative is to live outside the will of God, which equals a thousand deaths, each a thousand times worse than the blessed life of submission to the compassionate Lord. What "life" are we embracing when we opt for self-will? A momentary sense of satisfaction, perhaps. But that won't last. God's Kingdom will. It's where life will live forever.

Purpose in Planning

The plans of the diligent lead to profit as surely as haste leads to poverty. PROVERBS 21:5

IN WORD "Haste makes waste." It's a proverb many of us grew up with, and it's a reflection of biblical truth. Those who are diligent and want to accomplish much cannot approach life haphazardly. Diligence implies a plan, and haste is an enemy of planning.

We who are remade in God's image can take our cues from God. The Bible frequently refers to His plans, and we often refer to the plan of salvation, the plan for the end times, and all sorts of other designs from His hand. We can be reasonably sure that God didn't figure out what to do on the second day of creation after He got through with the first. His wisdom had a purpose in mind when He began. And His plans have been long and thorough. God does not make it up on the run. Neither should we.

God is certainly not an enemy of spontaneity, but He is an enemy of carelessness. Philip was responding spontaneously when God put him on the Gaza road; Peter was flexible when God told him to go to Cornelius; and Paul was able to turn from Asia to Macedonia when God redirected him. Those of us who make plans and will not diverge from them under any circumstances have deified the plans. We must always hold God above them, not them above God. But given His authority, we are urged to live wisely in this world. And wisdom calls for the intentional pursuit of a godly purpose.

IN DEED Consider the stewardship of your time. Is it spent efficiently? Don't think that God wants us working as machines and suppressing individuality. And don't think that He discourages us from being flexible and available when He directs us. But also don't assume that He advocates a random approach to our lives. The God with a purpose bears children with a purpose. And the God who has a plan to accomplish His purposes bears children who will also plan to accomplish His purposes. Without a goal, we are aimless—even when we're incredibly busy. God calls us to aim high and to know how to get there.

DECEMBER 1
Proverbs 21:5;
Isaiah 25:1

Purpose is what gives life a meaning. . . . A drifting boat always drifts downstream.

—Charles H. Parkhurst

Never Be Bought

Do not crave his delicacies, for that food is deceptive.
PROVERBS 23:3

DECEMBER 2
Proverbs 23:1-3

A man's god is that for which he lives, for which he is prepared to give his time, his energy, his money, that which stimulates and rouses him.

—Martyn Lloyd-Jones

IN WORD Greek mythology tells us of half-human creatures called sirens who would sing melodies so beautiful and seductive that passing sailors would be drawn to their island. Though the appeal was irresistible, the outcome was severe. It would always end in disaster for the sailors as they were dashed on dangerous rocks.

This world offers us numerous delights. Ascetic religion tells us to avoid all of them, but Scripture says that God has given us good things to enjoy (1 Timothy 6:17; James 1:17). But human nature takes us quickly past enjoyment and into slavery. There is a fine line between enjoying a pleasure as God's gift and seeking it as a sinful indulgence. The danger is that whether we are sitting at the table of an earthly king or at the table of "the prince of this world" (John 14:30; 16:11), we are easily bought. We develop tastes that will keep us from following the full will of God.

How can we know the difference between the gifts God has given and temptations the enemy uses to enslave us? It takes sharp discernment to walk through this world. Some gifts appear good and acceptable on the surface, and yet they will quickly master us if we let them. Jesus said that when we sin we become slaves of our sin (John 8:34), and Paul reiterated the point in Romans 7. He found the dividing line between what is good and what is not: "All things are lawful for me, but I will not be mastered by anything" (1 Corinthians 6:12, NASB). Rules aren't the point; allegiance is.

IN DEED That is the key to discernment: Never let anything or anyone but God be your master. Worldly wealth and rulers will seek to buy our affections, and dark, unearthly princes will seek to enslave us. The goal of all such temptation is to compromise our love for God and our service in His kingdom. Ignore the song of the siren, and hear God's more beautiful melodies. He has bought us already—with a heavy, heavy price. Never be bought by anything else.

Proud Weakness, Humble Strength

*The LORD tears down the proud man's house but he keeps
the widow's boundaries intact.* PROVERBS 15:25

IN WORD The self-improvement section is almost always the hottest corner of the bookstore. Why? Because it is human nature to build ourselves up. We want more security, more education, better skills, more income, stable mental health, stronger relationships, deeper passions, more adventure, and a higher standard of living. And God has even put those basic impulses into our hearts.

We might be surprised then to find out that God always opposes our most natural strategy for growth. We're into self-improvement, with an emphasis on the "self." We want to be stronger, better, smarter, and richer—ourselves. And we always try to attain our status with personal strategies and hard work. Does God oppose strategy and work? Hardly. He just hates the pride that those things foster.

There is a remarkable contrast in this proverb. The proud man has a house. It's likely gorgeous, or at least very sturdy. The walls are thick, the decor is stylish, and the construction is solid. How do we know? Because he is proud; proud people don't settle for second best. The widow, on the other hand, may not have much of a house. She may not have walls around her property. There's no security system, no guards, nothing to stop anyone from taking what little she has. The proud man is insulated, but the widow is completely vulnerable. He is the epitome of strength, and she is the epitome of weakness. So which one is more secure? According to the proverb, she is. The proud man's thick walls will be torn down by God Himself. The widow's naked boundaries will be guarded by God Himself. Yes, God chooses sides.

IN DEED Why, when we're guaranteed such divine strength in our vulnerability, do we almost always opt for more of our own "strength"? Are we just too proud to be dependent? We can have either our self-sufficiency or God's sufficiency. Having both is not an option. This is not a difficult question: Which would you prefer?

DECEMBER 3
Proverbs 3:34; 15:25

Pride alienates man from heaven; humility leads to heaven.

—Bridget of Sweden

Necessary Trust

I trust in you, O LORD; I say, "You are my God."
My times are in your hands. PSALM 31:14-15

He rides at ease
whom the grace
of God carries.

—Thomas à Kempis

IN WORD David was stressed. Enemies hounded him. People lied about him. Onlookers looked on with contempt. When everything seemed bleak, when he felt ashamed and beaten down, David was able to turn to God. Somewhere between the despair of this psalm's opening verses and the strength of its closing lines, David took heart in the nature of God. Desperate prayer turned to confident worship. He realized that the refuge he sought was a thoroughly reliable refuge. It sank into the depths of his being: God is good.

We can relate. We get stressed. We feel as if we live in a besieged city (v. 21)—physically, spiritually, financially, socially, mentally. We may go through illness, anger, poverty, or any other evidence of our fallen world, and we begin to feel it will never end. The psychology of being "under siege" begins to affect every area of our lives. We seek God as our refuge, but it is a weak faith at first. We must be reminded constantly of who He is. We must read psalms like this one and hear the witness of others who have been through similar circumstances and have seen His faithfulness. Somewhere in the process—usually when we have no choice but to just give up—God's power and faithfulness become real. We get a glimpse of who He is. Trust turns our despair into worship.

IN DEED Sooner or later, circumstances will overwhelm you. God will let it happen—even ordain it—to force you into a necessary choice. Will you trust Him or not? There is no way to mature as a disciple without having to make that self-surrendering choice in the fires of trial; having once declared your trust is not enough. God will let it be tested, and the only way some of us are able to come to that place of rest in God is first to be absolutely overwhelmed.

Our helplessness will intensify until we realize: We can trust Him, and we must. We have no other reasonable option. We can let go and believe that all of our circumstances are His. We can relax, take a deep breath, and let it sink in that God is utterly trustworthy.

Productivity and Purpose

Whatever you do, work at it with all your heart. . . . It is the Lord Christ you are serving. COLOSSIANS 3:23-24

IN WORD Surveys indicate that more than half of employees are dissatisfied with their work situation. Much of that is human nature: In our eyes, the grass is always greener somewhere else. But the issue goes deeper than a general, natural discontentment. We want to know that our work matters, and many people come to the conclusion that theirs does not.

It is easier to find meaning in some jobs than others, but nearly all have an apparent pointlessness in one or more areas. Whether our work is as predictable as an assembly line, as impressive as a political or economic power trip, or simply as profound as raising children and managing a family, we often have a deep-seated desire to be more, to do more, to see more results. Deep down, we want to be important.

Paul sometimes worked as a tentmaker. What do we remember about his tent production? The design? The quality? The quantity? No, we know nothing of it. The work of his hands left no legacy in this world. But we know a lot about the way he conducted business and related to others. The legacy is astounding. We're studying it even today.

Zacchaeus, the wee little man who forsook his deceitful tax-collecting practices when Jesus showed him a better way, is not remembered for his business. The empire that he fed is long gone. The records that he kept do not exist. The projects that his collections funded are now rubble. But the manner in which he did his business after he met Jesus—that's an eternal testimony in the Word of God.

IN DEED Don't get confused. It's not your productivity that matters most. It won't last. What's important to God is the way in which you do your work. That can have an eternal impact. We too easily base our sense of fulfillment on the work of our hands. But that job is only the platform that supports us as we live the work of our lives. The gospel is what matters. Live it with all your heart—even at work.

DECEMBER 5
Colossians 3:23-25

Work becomes worship when done for the Lord.

—Anonymous

Who You Are

You are the salt of the earth. . . . You are the light of the world.
MATTHEW 5:13-14

DECEMBER 6
Matthew 5:13-16

According to the New Testament, God wills that the church be a people who show what God is like.

—Stanley J. Grenz

IN WORD Jesus has gathered an odd collection of disciples and other listeners to a place on a hillside. His opening words to them are perhaps a little surprising. The way to blessedness, He has told them, is through poverty, grief, meekness, hunger and thirst, mercy, purity, pacifism, and persecution. These aren't the standards human beings are prone to strive for. Nevertheless, they are the divine prescription for a fallen character.

His next statements are a little more promising, however. "You are the salt of the earth," He tells them; and not only that, they are "the light of the world." That's a little more affirming, a positive statement that is sure to stroke the self-importance of the listeners. But Jesus' statements about our identity are more than positive affirmation; they are an indication of our responsibility. Those who follow Him have taken on the weight of influencing the grave situation that this world finds itself in.

The principle is that God's people are key to the Kingdom of God in this world. That Kingdom is coming, but not apart from the work of its ambassadors. Those who hear Jesus, who have ears to hear truth and act on it, are the vehicle of God's activity in this world. They are salt and light, preserving, seasoning, illuminating, and pointing to the one true Light. There is something profound and humbling about a God who does His work through a ragtag collection of redeemed throwaways. The scavenger God has gathered a remnant for an amazing re-genesis through the coming of His Son.

IN DEED Our lives are largely shaped by our perceptions of ourselves. Perhaps that's why Satan has targeted our sense of identity from Eden until now. So Jesus begins His great sermon with words designed to bring our self-perception in line with His truth. We can never come to grips with reality—God's reality—until we understand His assessment of ourselves and begin to live accordingly: We are called to be His salt and His light in a decaying, dark world.

Where You Are

God raised us up with Christ and seated us with him
in the heavenly realms. EPHESIANS 2:6

IN WORD Paul is eloquent in Ephesians 1 about the power of God in raising Jesus from the dead. This strong God, high above every authority and every name in every realm—spiritual, physical, or otherwise—has demonstrated His glory in the fullness of the risen, exalted Jesus. The splendor of such descriptions is unimaginable. Words cannot do it justice.

But Paul writes of Jesus' exaltation not only for us to admire it, but also for us to understand our role in it. We aren't just passive observers of the divine drama. We've been drawn into the drama itself. Not only is Jesus seated in the heavenly places above all rule and dominion, *so are we!*

Think of that. The first verses of Ephesians 2 are almost insulting in their description of our natural condition. We were dead. Disobedient. Objects of wrath. There is no lower place to be in the created order of beings than our fallen, sinful state. And yet the rest of the passage is mind-boggling in its promise: God, who is rich in mercy, raised us and seated us where He is—high above all other powers. Why? For a divine demonstration of grace. For any observers of this drama, there can be no more astounding demonstration. The ultimate in mercy has already been done.

IN DEED Self-perception deceives us. We get discouraged, think negatively, become pessimists, and wonder if our faith is worth the trouble. The darkness of the world, the distortions of our flesh, and the schemes of the evil one combine to create illusions of despair. Resist them all. God's truth is remarkably contrary to what our souls perceive.

Remember that principle in your days of discouragement. We don't fully understand the implications of being seated with Christ, but we know this: It's an amazing place to be. We are organically united with the ultimate authority in all the universe. We're not just His friends and not just His servants. We're grafted into *Him*!

DECEMBER 7
Ephesians 2:1-10

A Christian has a union with Christ more noble, intimate, and perfect than the members of a human body have with their head.

—John Eudes

Whose You Are

You are all sons of God through faith in Christ Jesus.
GALATIANS 3:26

DECEMBER 8
Galatians 3:26–4:7

God His own doth tend and nourish; in His holy courts they flourish.

—Caroline Sandell-Berg

IN WORD   Perhaps we take our identity as God's children a little too casually. After all, the world uses the term "God's children" for everyone He created. The Bible affirms that God created everyone and everything; but it reserves the status of a child for those who have been born of His Spirit. We are His children because He has fathered us Himself.

That's different from being His servant, His disciple, or His follower. Children should obey their fathers, but they aren't defined by their obedience. Children should accept their father's values, but they aren't defined by their behavior. So how are children different? Children are defined by parental genes, and those genes will cause them to resemble their father. They are children because of whom they are born to, not because of whom they can make themselves out to be.

That should be a relaxing thought for those who have in fact been born again. All of our striving for Christlikeness, while admirable and important, doesn't define us. Neither do our failures. No, we are defined by the Spirit who raised us up and called us God's own children. Even the faith that completed the transaction was a gift (Ephesians 2:8). We are not self-made Christians. We are God-made children.

IN DEED   In a culture that defines us by what we do or how we think, it's easy to fall into the identity trap of believing that we are shaped by our past. But you are not shaped by your history, contrary to what the psychiatrists have preached. You are shaped by your destiny. You are a child of God with an eternal inheritance.

What does that mean in practical terms? It means that we need not strive after false comforts; every meaningful resource of heaven and earth is part of our future inheritance. It means that we need not fill our lives with meaning apart from God; we have all the meaning a person could ever need. And it means that we need not suffer from low self-esteem. Is there any higher esteem than being a child of the highest Being there is?

What You Are

You are God's field, God's building.
1 CORINTHIANS 3:9

IN WORD It's hard to grasp the illustrations God uses to describe His children. Ephesians 2:10 says we are His workmanship. Jesus told us in John 15 that we are branches on the Vine, drawing our life and bearing our fruit through the life He gives. In 1 Corinthians, the analogies are even more mind-boggling: In 3:9, we are God's building; 6:19 tells us that He's not only the architect, but also the inhabitant; and that at an even more personal level, we're not just His functional building, but His living body (12:27).

We could spend eternity trying to understand all the implications of our identity—we probably will, in fact—but there's at least one thing we can sure of now: God has bound Himself inextricably to those who are born of His Spirit by faith in His Son. He is not a detached observer of our affairs; He is not a commander pulling our strings for His purposes; and He is not just waiting for us to fail so He can discipline us. He is more than just someone we relate to, and we are more than His servants or friends. We are born of His own self. For some amazing reason, He has invested Himself in His creation to a degree we can hardly understand. He is united to us in intimate detail.

IN DEED If you've ever doubted God's commitment to your welfare, let these truths erase your suspicions. He is as committed to your welfare as He is to His own. And if you're a believer who has been born of His Spirit and still felt distant from Him at times, you can know that your feelings are lying to you. The experience of fellowship may be weak at times, but our spiritual union with Him is constant. It doesn't change, because God doesn't change.

Try to think about yourself from God's perspective, if you can. Imagine having created someone and then literally going to great pains to redeem that person. Imagine giving this person your name, your authority, and your promise. Now, how committed to this person would you be?

Consider your answer well; that's how much God is committed to you.

DECEMBER 9
1 Corinthians 3:5-9

The person you are now, the person you have been, the person you will be—this person God has chosen as beloved.

—William Countryman

343

Disciplines of the Mind

A simple man believes anything, but a prudent man gives thought to his steps. PROVERBS 14:15

DECEMBER 10
Proverbs 14:15;
Colossians 3:1-2

Untilled ground, however rich, will bring forth thistles and thorns; so also the mind of man.

—Teresa of Avila

IN WORD A surface reading of this proverb will tell us to think through our actions, to avoid rash behavior, and not to be gullible in the directions we pursue. And we need such reminders; the call for spiritual discernment is frequent in Scripture. But there's more to this proverb than what we find on the surface. If we really think it through, we'll realize that it has everything to do with the way we discipline our minds to see God, ourselves, and our world. The call for discernment is rarely an *ad hoc* proposition in which we seek God's guidance situation by situation. God wants an overhaul in the way we see things. He wants us to have thoughtful lives that will naturally produce prudent steps.

Simple people—those who have little spiritual depth and do not care much about living for God and eternity—will act on whims. They will go with the flow of any current that seems appealing, and they end up tossed around on the waves of passing styles, questionable doctrine, selfish interests, and empty ideologies. They are easily deceived. As the proverb says, they believe anything.

The serious Christian will find his or her thought life to be a critical battlefront, where faith, hope, love, and all their rivals are cultivated. Those of us who want to live for God and eternity can't just change our steps—we'll have to change our thinking. Unless we want a constant battle between obedience and our heart's inclinations, we will seek a fundamental change within. We will train our minds; our thought patterns will be matters of intense concern. We don't just want to act differently; we want to *be* different.

IN DEED If you try to walk in discipleship with Jesus as a matter of behavior rather than inner transformation, you will find it an arduous, impossible walk. Discipleship begins deep inside, and it is not a quick magic trick. It requires training. Are you able to correct your faulty thinking when God points it out? Do you consciously discipline your mind to think truth? That's where faithfulness begins.

Disciplines of the Mind: Fear

I heard you in the garden, and I was afraid.
GENESIS 3:10

IN WORD Ever since one dismal day in the Garden, humanity has lived in fear. Some of us seem to fear it all: We are full of hang-ups, anxious about every next day and every pending disaster. Others of us seem to fear nothing, but boldness and arrogance are usually masks for deeper insecurities. Deep down, all of us are now, or were once, afraid.

What do we do with our fear? Where can we take it? It is so universal that it has ordered much of the world we live in. Most religions are built on it. Most proposed political and social remedies attempt to relieve it. Our economics are founded on it. We stock up wealth because we fear the future. We create huge governments because we fear chaos. We worship idols because we're afraid there might be no one to take care of us. We don't want to be some anomaly of life spinning on some random planet with no meaning to it all. Chance scares us. Ever since we severed ourselves from God's fellowship, we've been very, very afraid.

Perhaps our initial fear, this angst that plagues every human who thinks realistically about his or her existence, was entirely legitimate. After all, our sin has offended the one true Sovereign, the Lord of all there is. No wonder Adam was afraid. Where can we relieve our fear when the universe's greatest power is the One we're afraid of?

IN DEED But God tells us not to be afraid if we've come to Him in repentance and faith. Having accepted His salvation, we can rely on this unalterable truth: All our fears are based on lies. Think about that. Our insecurity? He has made us secure. Our future? He has ordained it with blessing. Our enemies? They are weaker than He is. Our chaos? He is a God of order. What is it within us that contradicts these truths? Faith must convince us of them. Discipline your mind to dwell on truth. Replace your fear with faith.

DECEMBER 11
Genesis 3:8-10;
Proverbs 1:33

All fear is bondage.

—Anonymous

Disciplines of the Mind: Faith

Don't be afraid; just believe.

MARK 5:36

Faith tells us of things we have never seen, and cannot come to know by our natural senses.

—John of the Cross

IN WORD Do we really believe that our fears are based on lies? We must. We have to realize that every threat that comes against us is under God's watchful eye. We must understand that every concern of our lives is easily within His ability to relieve. While our sinful flesh and an aggressive enemy want to keep us preoccupied—even obsessed—with our security and status, God wants us preoccupied—even obsessed—with Him. If we would invest all of our emotions and thoughts into Him, He would manage our lives. We have such a hard time with that. We try to manage ourselves and give Him what's left over. But nothing is ever left over. We're completely spent on other things long before we turn to Him.

Why? Because we believe the threats are real. We believe the future may be dreadful. We believe that the economy may collapse, that the terrorists may win, and that the culture may grow inhospitable. Closer to our hearts, we believe that we may get sick, that we may not be able to pay the phone bill this month, or that our relationships may be easily broken. And as long as we think about these things, we cannot have faith. No one ever gets mountain-moving faith by obsessing about the mountains. We get it by focusing on God.

IN DEED This takes discipline. It requires an active management of the thought life that perhaps we've never tried. It means that when a bill comes that is too large to pay, we must think about the God who is larger. We cannot lie awake at night wondering how we will pay it. It means that when there is crime in the neighborhood or terror in the world, we cannot obsess about the possible threats. We must think about the God who is Sovereign—our Protector, our Refuge, and our Strength.

We think that we are victims of our fear, but we are wrong. We actually cultivate it. We think about the threats to our well-being, never realizing that the threats are lies and our God is true. Will we suffer harm? Perhaps—but not ultimately, not out of His time, and not without a greater purpose. Faith knows that, and it isn't afraid.

Disciplines of the Mind:
Regret

I will repay you for the years the locusts have eaten.
JOEL 2:25

IN WORD The attitude that is perhaps most subtle in corrupting our perspective is the sense of regret we feel over
missed opportunities and past failures. We play a devastating mind game that wonders what life would have been
like "if"—if we hadn't fallen, if so-and-so hadn't hurt us,
if we had turned right instead of left, if, if, if. That game
will destroy us, always turning our gaze backward, never
forward and never upward. Though the locusts have consumed our past, we extend an open invitation for them to
consume our present and eventually our future. We live in
our regrets far too easily.

What is the point of that? Are we trying to change the
past? Are we telling the Sovereign God that He missed a
chance to make things better for us? We are as nearsighted
looking backward as we are looking forward. We forget that
the God who exalted Joseph to the political apex of Egypt
first allowed his brothers to betray him and a prison to hold
him captive. We forget that the God who put David on the
throne let him hide out in caves for years. We forget that
the God who raised Jesus from the dead sent Him to die in
the first place. The deliverer Moses was first an exiled stut-
terer. The apostle Paul was first a rebel Saul. The powerful-
preaching Peter was first a spineless self-preservationist.
All of these could have lived with an obsession about the
locusts. None of them did, and God did amazing things
through them.

IN DEED Do you have regrets? Do not be gentle with
them. Get over them. You have trained yourself in paraly-
sis. You are committing a slow, painful suicide, dying past
deaths over and over again until you've run out of life.
You're living in a dismal fantasy.

How is that a fantasy? Think about it: God has removed
your past from you, separating you from your sins as far as
the east is from the west and comforting you more deeply
than anyone has grieved you. That's truth, and to the extent
you dwell on those past events, you're out of touch with
reality. Base your life on truth. It's calling you forward.

DECEMBER 13
Joel 2:21-27

In Christ we can
move out of our
past into a mean-
ingful present and a
breathtaking future.

—Erwin Lutzer

Disciplines of the Mind: Hope

Set your hope fully on the grace to be given you when Jesus Christ is revealed. 1 PETER 1:13

DECEMBER 14

1 Peter 1:13-21

The future belongs to those who belong to God. This is hope.

—W. T. Purkiser

IN WORD The kind of hope that is natural to the fallen human mind is based on wishful thinking. It is a dream that things will one day work out well, that desires will be met, that somehow things will get better. It is the pot of gold at the end of the rainbow or the fairy tale of true love. It has a great imagination but no confidence. We always wake up from that dream.

But biblical hope is not wishful thinking. It looks forward to the fulfillment of certain promises, and it even brings those promises into the present. The faulty, human hopes we dream about are vestiges from before the Fall, reminders that we were built for an eternal Kingdom of peace and perfection. Biblical hope brings those dreams back to reality and lines us up with the God who created us to dream big. It is not held captive by today's circumstances, it cannot be squelched by anything this world brings against it, and it cannot die. Hope is not a figment of our imagination, it is a life based on truth.

But we cannot have hope unless we've disciplined our minds to accept it. We're too used to our fantasies proving false, and we're afraid the Kingdom of God will end up as just another fantasy. The natural mind always makes God's promises seem unrealistic and hopelessly out of reach. But it lies, and we must redirect our thoughts. Much of discipleship is simply understanding and believing reality. We must turn from false thinking.

IN DEED Hope knows who God is. The mountains we encounter in life are irrelevant, because the Rock is a greater reality. A mind trained in biblical hope can apply God's ultimate promises to current situations. It can base our present reality on our future grace.

Don't let hopelessness influence your life. It is based on lies and it will paralyze you. We hope in our God because He has told us the truth and His promises are certain.

Disciplines of the Mind:
Bitterness

See to it that no one misses the grace of God and that no bitter root grows up to cause trouble and defile many.
HEBREWS 12:15

IN WORD You can't believe how you've been treated. Somewhere in your past, someone has done you wrong. You've been betrayed, lied about, cheated, or deceived. And it just eats at you, doesn't it? The fact that there are people less worthy than you who seem to be enjoying life more—earning more and playing more—drives you crazy. It just isn't right when the wicked prosper. Especially when you don't.

Everyone has been there; our offendedness can run awfully deep. And sometimes—usually, in fact—it is quite legitimate. It isn't just a matter of perception; people *do* step on our toes and treat us badly. Sometimes it's intentional, and sometimes it's just carelessness. Either way, many people lack integrity, and their lack affects us. We live in a world in which arrogance, meanness, deception, and pettiness abound. We can hardly avoid such things.

Are we wrong to be offended? No, but we are wrong to hold on to that offense. It is pointless, even harmful, to wallow in our hurt and to count all the ways things could be better otherwise. It doesn't harm the person who angered us; it only harms us—and the people around us who have to live with our bitterness. We cultivate a destructive, cancerous disease when we lament how we have been wronged. We ignore the grace of God for ourselves and for others when we dwell there. God never calls us to that place of lament.

IN DEED Imagine winning a billion-dollar lottery and then getting all steamed up about a ten-cent shortchange at the convenience store. That's a monetary image of our spiritual outrage. God has given us all things and promised us all things. He has pledged Himself and His bounty as our never-ending supply. He has guaranteed that we will never lack anything we truly need. Why then do we obsess about the wrongs we've faced? God can make up the difference, and He can deal with the offenders in His time. Is there any grievance worth harboring in that arrangement?

DECEMBER 15
Hebrews 12:14-15

There is no torment like the inner torment of an unforgiving spirit.

—Charles Swindoll

Disciplines of the Mind: Love

*Love does no harm to its neighbor. Therefore love is
the fulfillment of the law.* ROMANS 13:10

Romans 13:8-10

Love is the only
spiritual power that
can overcome the
self-centeredness
that is inherent
in being alive.

—Arnold J. Toynbee

IN WORD Retraining the mind requires extraordinary
focus at first. Not only must we learn not to think in all of
those negative patterns of thinking, holding on to bitterness,
fear, regrets, and our weaknesses as we do. We must also
embrace the character of God: His faithfulness, His power
and might, His grace and mercy, His love. Just as redirecting
a river from its centuries-old path is a monumental task of
engineering, so is redirecting those streams of thought that
have long flooded our souls. We cannot do it without God's
Spirit. Only He has the power. And every power He exerts
in us will eventually lead to one thing: love.

In the past, our streams of thought have always carved
valleys that pointed in the direction of self. Even our seemingly selfless acts are often done for selfish purposes. That
has to change. The natural mind has no God-centeredness in
it, and the renewed mind that the Spirit forms in us has nothing else. This is more than a slight rearrangement of water
flow; it is a radical reversal. The landscape of our minds
must be tilted in an entirely different direction. All anger,
bitterness, competition, jealousy, and selfishness are foreign
to the heart of God, and if He has given us His heart, they
are foreign to us as well.

How can we take every thought captive to Christ? We
must learn to recognize selfish thinking. Whenever we find it
hard to applaud another's talent, encourage another's spiritual gift, or give for another's welfare, we must be acutely
aware of it. Whenever we hold on to envy, competitiveness,
or a distaste for another's personality, we must be grieved.
That does not mean we must instinctively like everything
and everyone. It does mean we must treat everyone as a
priceless child of God—or at least a *potential* priceless child
of God.

IN DEED Selfless love goes against our sinful nature.
But so does God's Spirit. Living in His Spirit and His love
requires a conscious discipline of thinking. If we live for
Him, we live for His people.

Disciplines of the Mind:
Weakness

I love you, O LORD, *my strength.*
PSALM 18:1

IN WORD The most frustrating feeling we can have when our circumstances are overwhelming is our sense of powerlessness. We cannot pull enough strings to control hurtful people, to heal an illness or a broken relationship, or to ensure our own security in times of trouble. But often we try. We attempt strength, believing that enough willpower, self-effort, or money and power will make things right. Or we go in the other extreme, declaring our efforts futile and resigning ourselves to unpleasant situations. The balance between being passively weak and overassertive is hard to find.

Our identity is the issue. God tells us how He hates pride, so we don't want to take things into our own hands and manipulate circumstances for our own purposes. Neither do we want to sit idly by while evil runs rampant. We don't know who we are. Are we weak or are we strong? Are we David against Goliath or David on the run from Saul? Are we Elijah embarrassing 450 priests of Baal, or are we Elijah fleeing from Jezebel? Are Christians to roar like lions or be eaten by them? It's hard to know. God's Word gives us both pictures.

IN DEED The reason we're confused is that both pictures are accurate. We are weak. But we are strong. We have no power in ourselves, but we are not in ourselves, we are in Christ. Like Paul, we can do all things in Christ who strengthens us (Philippians 4:13). But like Paul, we delight in weakness (2 Corinthians 12:10). We have great strength, but not ours. We have amazing status, but we didn't earn it. We can be incredibly influential in matters of eternity, but only by the Spirit who works within us.

The mind must be disciplined to know two extremes: our utter poverty of power and our indestructible position in Christ. When we focus on the former, we become helpless and impotent. When we focus on the latter, we become proud. But the balance will keep us humble, and it will change our lives dramatically. Our weakness is God's opportunity to be strong.

DECEMBER 17
Psalm 18

All God's giants have been weak men who did great things for God because they reckoned on His being with them.

—Hudson Taylor

Disciplines of the Mind: Power

It is God who arms me with strength and makes my way perfect.
PSALM 18:32

DECEMBER 18
Psalm 18

The same power that brought Christ back from the dead is operative within those who are Christ's.

—Leon Morris

IN WORD When we believe that we are powerless to change anything, we believe a lie from the enemy. When we think we are victims of circumstances or of people, we are wrong. We don't have an accurate picture of who we are in Jesus. We are dwelling on the very real human frailty that resulted from the Fall, and we are forgetting the heights to which we've been raised in Christ. Yes, we were sinful, impotent, broken, and beaten down, and in and of ourselves we still are. But the Bible declares us seated with Christ in the heavenly places at God's right hand—the right hand of power. It tells us that the power of the Resurrection lives within us. It tells us that God is exceedingly capable of doing more than we can even comprehend, *and that we have access to Him*! How irrational it is to behave as victims who have no recourse. What folly to resign ourselves to the circumstances at hand.

The Bible is full of tentative people who did not think they could accomplish anything important. Moses told God He had the wrong guy. Gideon argued that God had picked the weakest tribe and the least of its families. They knew their frailty well, but they needed to learn the truth about God.

IN DEED Do you want to think straight? Do you want to have a firm grip on reality? Then meditate on the blessings of God in Christ. Read through your New Testament with the assurance that God's promises are true. The statements about our salvation, though unbelievably extravagant, must be believed anyway. God doesn't lie. When we accept an impotent prayer life, an unfruitful position, or a joyless, defeated Christianity, we are tacitly implying that He does lie. We are slandering our powerful Creator who arms us with His strength. Confidence is His gift. Rest confidently in Him.

Disciplining the Mind

*We demolish arguments and every pretension that sets itself up
against the knowledge of God, and we take captive every thought
to make it obedient to Christ.*   2 CORINTHIANS 10:5

IN WORD   Paul made this assertion to a church that was
struggling with false doctrine and fleshly disobedience. It
was attacked from without by philosophies contradicting
the gospel, and it was attacked from within by internal divisions and petty arguments. And though he was speaking
primarily of church life, all of the dynamics the Corinthians
were facing in their fellowship are also dynamics we face
in our own minds. We struggle with disobedience, we stir
up mental discord with others, and we wrestle with false
ideas about God and about life. Paul would heartily agree
to applying this verse to our minds as well as our fellowships.

What we learn from this concept of taking every thought
captive is that God wants us to think correctly. He wants us
to know Him in truth. He wants us to treat others according to who they are in Christ, or at least who they can be in
Christ. He wants us to forsake the thoughts that are built on
lies—the ones that say, "God won't protect me or provide
for me; my future is in doubt; my enemies might get the
upper hand; I'll have to take matters into my own hands."
And He wants us to embrace truth: "God is my Father and
He holds me securely in His hand; His people are my people
and I will fellowship with them forever; His Kingdom is my
only citizenship, and eternity shapes my present." The mind
must be retrained to accept these truths. We must eat, drink,
and breathe them.

IN DEED   How can we do that? There are four imperatives: (1) We must ask God to make us aware of our faulty
thinking; (2) we must ask His Spirit to conform us to His
image; (3) we must consciously deny the wrong things we
think; and (4) we must consciously replace those wrong
thoughts with truth. The Word of God must shape us, the
Spirit of God must fill us, and the purposes of God must
become ours. Our minds must be renewed.

DECEMBER 19
2 Corinthians 10:4-5

There is no salva-
tion save in truth,
and the royal
road of truth is
by the mind.

—Martin Cyril D'Arcy

Celebrate Good Times

When times are good, be happy.
ECCLESIASTES 7:14

DECEMBER 20
Ecclesiastes 7:13-14

Christians are the only people in the world who have anything to be happy about.

—Billy Graham

IN WORD Some Christians feel guilty when they are happy. With a personal history of sin, a world of grief, and so much to be done before Jesus returns, how can times be good? They look at the heart of God and see only sadness and stress. They reason that a good God could not be happy with what He sees and, therefore, neither can we.

But God has not created us for futility. This is perhaps a surprising message from the sad book of Ecclesiastes, but we read about this God of joy in other books of the Bible, too. Fruitfulness, prosperity, blessedness, contentment, and inner peace are all gifts from above. And it's never wrong to enjoy His gifts.

Is that hard to do? Some people have too easy a time of it, but historically some of our denominations and theological perspectives have discouraged happiness. They meant to discourage meaningless and profane frivolity, not true joy. The Christian life is to be a joyful life; the Bible makes that clear. Rather than always seeing what's wrong in our lives, what's wrong in the world, and what God wants to do to fill in the gaps, we are to frequently look at what God has given us, how He has blessed His gifts, and what He has already done to fill in the gaps. Spiritually speaking, we often barely notice that our glass is filling up; we focus on its remaining emptiness. In truth, we're allowed and even urged to notice that the glass is often half empty on this planet. But we are to dwell on the fact that it's half full. Thankfulness is to dominate over discontentment in our thinking.

IN DEED How can we do this? Like soldiers in combat, we can be altogether serious about our jobs while still enjoying a rest and a laugh in between the battles. Like athletes in training, we can enjoy the competition now and can already look forward to the victory celebration. If we think being serious about the Kingdom of God means deferring gratification until heaven, we're wrong. God and His gifts are to be enjoyed. Now. When times are good—and if you look hard enough, they usually are—be happy.

Dedicate Bad Times

*But when times are bad, consider: God has made the
one as well as the other.*   ECCLESIASTES 7:14

IN WORD   Some Christians feel guilty when they find it
hard to be joyful in the face of painful trials. The weeping of
prophets and priests, the book of Lamentations, and many
other grief-filled passages in the Bible make it clear to us: It's
okay to mourn. We do not have to have our happy faces on
all the time. We are to be authentic people, and sometimes
we're authentically sad. That's expected.

But we do need to realize a profound truth in the midst
of our sadness: *God is in it.* We may find that hard to believe.
How could a loving God allow this disaster to strike us?
How could disease and death serve His purposes? How can
He say He cares while He lets these kinds of trials go on?

These are hard questions that brief devotionals can't
answer. But the witness of the Word, nevertheless, is that
God is sovereign and He is intimately involved in our pain.
He was with Joseph in his brothers' treachery and his long
imprisonment; He was with Joshua in every battle for the
Promised Land; He was with Jeremiah in the destruction
of Jerusalem; and He was actually *in* Jesus on the Cross.
His hand had a purpose in every one of these traumatic
events. He did not frantically come up with plans B, C, or
D because of an unforeseen failure in His plan A. He had
already counted on the trials to come. They were part of His
foreknowledge and His design from the beginning.

IN DEED   Isn't that comforting? Maybe not as comforting as a quick resolution to your problem would be, but
God has His purposes, and His purposes have their proper
time. Meanwhile, you hurt. You don't have to deny that.
But try to recognize that God is deeply involved in your
critical moments, even when He seems critically absent. Just
because life seems difficult doesn't mean God has missed
something. He knows all about "difficult." He didn't promise easy, pain-free lives. He promised redemption. Dedicate
your trial to His glory. It is part of His plan.

DECEMBER 21
Ecclesiastes 7:14

He who knows
how to suffer will
enjoy much peace.

—Thomas à Kempis

God's Remedy

The Word became flesh and made his dwelling among us.

JOHN 1:14

DECEMBER 22

John 1:1-14

Christ became what we are that He might make us what He is.

—Athanasius of Alexandria

IN WORD What was in the mind of God when He sent His Son to live with us? Was it frustration over all of His failed attempts to get people to behave correctly? Was it because the Law did not do what it was supposed to do? Was the spoken Word so lacking that, in a last-ditch effort, God tried turning the spoken Word into the living Word?

We know, of course, that the Incarnation was not a last-ditch effort. It was the plan from the beginning. All of the prior judgments—of Noah's contemporaries, of Sodom and Gomorrah, of degenerate Canaanite tribes—were foundational to this incarnation. All of the prior promises—to Abraham and his descendants, to the newly freed Israelites at Sinai, to the prophets of restoration and hope—were wrapped up in this plan. The righteousness of God first had to be established, then the depravity of man. Then the plan would work. The wisdom of God, the "logos" and logic of the universe, the Spirit of the Eternal could clothe Himself in humanity and have it actually mean something.

What does it mean to you? When you read your Bible, does it make a difference that the Word is not just telling you what to do, but offering to re-create the fundamental nature of your spirit? When you worship God, is it better to do so with a transformed heart than with a slavish obedience to an unknown deity? Does it matter to you that instead of simply being religious as best you can, you relate to a Person—a Person who lived in the same kind of body you have and yet is still powerful and wise enough to be your God? Are you glad your faith is this . . . well, personal?

IN DEED Some people are not. They would prefer a distant God who will leave them alone until requested to show up. The God who became flesh has so much better in store for us. Yes, sometimes it feels a little too personal—there's sin and obedience to deal with. But ultimately, we appreciate it. We're flesh and we need to relate to flesh. The Word knew that, so Jesus came to dwell.

God's Timing

When the time had fully come, God sent his Son.

GALATIANS 4:4

IN WORD   Good plans require patience; they cannot be done hastily. When it comes to our salvation and God's will for our lives, we would like to push the Eternal to act a little more quickly. We may wonder why He waited millennia before the Messiah came. We may also wonder why He waits years before saving us from a difficult situation or even saving our souls from eternal death. The answer in every case of God's timing is the same: preparation.

We don't know exactly why centuries of dry judgment prevailed before grace rained freely on all. We don't know why some cultures remain in nearly complete darkness today. We don't know why the chosen people's history required such long periods of obedience, apostasy, and then judgment. And we don't know why God doesn't solve every problem the moment we pray, or why our Savior waits with veiled grace sometimes before opening our eyes to it. Perhaps the human race needed to exhaust its resources before God's offer of providence became meaningful. Perhaps the world had to be subjected to utter frustration before it could even accept a Savior. Perhaps so do we.

What we *do* know, however, is that God is thorough. His plans are lengthy but well conceived. His artistry is slow, but His colors are rich, His layers of meaning are many, and His purposes are completely pure. We can trust His timing.

IN DEED   The patience of the eternal God and the temperament of impulsive human beings often stand in stark contrast. A thousand years are as a day to the Lord, but not to us. We're much too impatient for that. We think God's plan for future generations might unnecessarily leave current generations shortchanged. We think a full revelation of His gospel was essential the first day after Eden.

But in His plan, a nation was cultivated, a law was given, human nature was exposed, prophets spoke, and creation waited. Then the Savior came. We were prepared for salvation, and we now celebrate the fullness of time.

DECEMBER 23
Galatians 4:4-7

The coming of Jesus into the world is the most stupendous event in human history.

—Malcolm Muggeridge

God's Ruler

He will stand and shepherd his flock in the strength of the LORD.
MICAH 5:4

DECEMBER 24
Micah 5:1-4

The fact of Jesus' coming is the final and unanswerable proof that God cares.

—William Barclay

IN WORD   What kind of Savior do you know? Many suppose that He is nothing but gentle, always overlooking sin and letting His sheep roam as freely as they want to. Others suppose that His fences are confining and His rod is ready for action. In the context of the Incarnation, neither image makes sense. Why would God send Jesus into this world to be either one of those saviors?

No, if Jesus had come only to enforce the Law, there would be no point in His coming. Others were already enforcing it. They had a distorted interpretation of it, but they did not lack for discipline. There was no shortage of attempted lawkeepers in Jesus' day.

And there also would have been no point in Jesus coming only to declare the Law irrelevant. If it were irrelevant, Israel had it wrong and the rest of the world had it right. Most cultures today would still have it right; in modern civilization, moral lawlessness rules. Many societies today are aware of no need for salvation, only for "enlightenment." They are not looking for any kind of savior, much less a shepherd.

We need a shepherd. God has known that from the foundation of the world, and many of us come to that conclusion after years of futility. But what kind? The harsh, whip-carrying shepherd? Or the passive, anything-goes shepherd? One readies his rod with vigilance; the other plays his flute under the distant tree. Neither knows much about sheep.

IN DEED   Do you know Jesus as a harsh master? A permissive pushover? Know why the Shepherd came into this world? He came because there were stray sheep in a land of fierce predators. He came to rule *and* to forgive. The shepherd of religious imaginations does one or the other. That shepherd will do us no good, while the Shepherd God sent us will do us no wrong. We need Him. We need both His rod *and* His staff, His guidance *and* His mercy. Get to know this good Shepherd well. He brings us to God.

God's Purpose

For what the law was powerless to do . . . God did by sending his
own Son in the likeness of sinful man to be a sin offering.
ROMANS 8:3

IN WORD Have you ever really pondered the meaning of Christmas? Was it just God's attempt to give us a good example to show us the way to live? Was it simply the birth of a great teacher? Did that innocent little bundle of flesh and blood in the feeding trough really hold the answer for us all?

We can never fully understand the depths of all of God's mysteries, but we can understand a lot. He has revealed His purposes to us, so we know why Jesus was sent to this broken planet. As much as our proud society hates the idea of an atoning sacrifice, Jesus was sent into this world to die. Like the cattle around Him, the baby of Bethlehem was born for slaughter. He bore the brunt of a fallen world so we could escape its tragic direction. He descended deep so we could ascend high. He gave us a way out of the horrible implications of our rebellion.

God demonstrated for centuries that the human condition could not be fixed by humans. It could not even be repaired by an external work of God. No, there had to be a sacrifice to pay the price; there had to be a person to live the life; and it had to be perfect on both counts. Only God could do that. He clothed Himself in flesh to die, He was raised to live, and He put His Spirit within us. He doesn't just give us life; He *is* our life.

IN DEED Long ago, we were created in the image of God. We didn't know exactly what that meant; the image shattered and we weren't able to see clearly. But in Jesus, we now see the Spirit of God dwelling in the image of God, and we know: We were made for glory. The glory we see in Jesus is offered to us freely—in Him. The earthen vessels that once walked with God in the Garden are now filled with the very God who made them.

Christmas is our assurance: Jesus came in our likeness to die our death, and He came in God's likeness to live our life. In Him, the image of God and the image of man meet. And now He lets them meet in us.

Christmas is the day that holds all time together.

—Fulton John Sheen

God's Wisdom

. . . Christ the power of God and the wisdom of God.

1 CORINTHIANS 1:24

DECEMBER 26

1 Corinthians
1:18-25

His wisdom's
vast, and knows
no bounds, a
deep where all
our thoughts
are drowned.

—Isaac Watts

IN WORD Contemplating the Incarnation can teach us much about the wisdom of God. In the plan of the ages, the plan that cultivated a nation and sent a Messiah into its culture, God demonstrated His patience, His thoroughness, His righteousness, His mercy, and His love. He did not opt for expediency. He was not rash. His anger was pure and His holiness relentless. There were no depths to which He would not go for His love. There were no limits to His grace. There were no enemies that could thwart His intentions or sway His heart. He let us know what He is like.

The biblical purpose of God's wisdom is never simply to display it. Though it is beautiful and awe inspiring, it is not just a show for His glory. It is to be emulated. We are to become wise like Him, drinking our fill of His plan and knowing intimately His ways. If He is patient, we are to be patient. If His anger is pure, our anger is to be pure. If His holiness is relentless, so must ours be. In His righteousness, His mercy, His love, His peace and calm, His passions and purposes, and His thorough approach to separating and conforming a people to Himself, we are to find our calling. The wisdom of God is not just for our admiration; it is for us. We are to internalize it.

IN DEED Do you appreciate the wisdom of God? There is always a need to contemplate it more deeply. It is unsearchable, yet we must continue to search it. We will never exhaust its lessons, but we have to try. The wisdom of God created us, had mercy on us, and redeemed us. The wisdom of God built the universe we live in. It is not just an extra benefit to knowing Him; it is the Architect's plan that preceded our world and our lives.

We try to get wisdom by reading and asking God to speak to us. Let His wisdom speak more deeply. Consider the Incarnation. Meditate on His ways and contemplate His eternal plan. You will find yourself beginning to think like Him. There is no greater source of wisdom than that.

A Zealous Voice

*His head and hair were white like wool, as white as snow,
and his eyes were like blazing fire. His feet were like
bronze glowing in a furnace, and his voice was like the
sound of rushing waters.*   REVELATION 1:14-15

IN WORD   What was Jesus like? Many envision Him as a guru of peace who never said a harsh word. Others envision Him as a mellow mystic who could not relate to our humanity. There is no shortage of opinions, but few are entirely consistent with Scripture.

The misty-eyed, airy-voiced, peace-marching Jesus of modern films, wishful imaginations, and popular theology never existed. He has been crafted by those who have either never read the four Gospels or have never really believed them. The real Jesus was the Incarnation of the Jealous God (Exodus 34:14), the Warrior God (Exodus 15:3), the One who dwells in mystery and majesty. There was fire in His eyes and passion in His voice. And according to Revelation 1, there still is.

Jesus still speaks. Is the Hollywood Jesus the one you expect to hear? Don't be swayed by false characterizations. Read the Gospels and see the anger at hypocrisy and the anguish of the Cross. Hear the violence in His prayers and the divisiveness of His words. Know that His coming was a crisis event, the turning point for the whole human race.

IN DEED   The fiery, zealous Jesus may speak to us with a still, small voice, but do not rule out the roaring voice of thunder and lightning. He doesn't always nudge us; sometimes He jolts us. The Jesus who offered comfort, healing, and peace to the troubled and outcast also blasted the legalists and the proud. The Jesus who drew calmly in the sand and urged the meek to persist in their meekness also made a scene at the Temple with His violent outburst. The Man of Sorrows is also a man of action. The Lamb of God is also the Lion of Judah. Make no assumptions about His voice. Just be open to it. Have ears that hear. When He speaks, it will be powerful enough to change your life.

DECEMBER 27
Revelation 1:9-18

The voice of God, having once fully penetrated the heart, becomes strong as the tempest and loud as the thunder.

—Ignatius of Loyola

The Intimidation of Unbelief

The fool says in his heart, "There is no God."
PSALM 14:1

All unbelief is the
belief of a lie.

—Horatius Bonar

IN WORD   It's easy to be intimidated by a secular culture. Many of our most highly educated elites are skeptics. They look with condescension at those who maintain faith in divine revelations. Their skepticism has permeated our society, and many of the people we run into daily have swallowed their unbelief. Their hyperrationalism inhibits the sharing of our supernatural faith.

We are often accused of being ignorant of all of mankind's amazing scientific, philosophical, and ideological discoveries. But have you considered the atheist and agnostic's self limitations? They have embraced a broader ignorance than have the people of faith. They have said, in effect, that anything beyond our observation is unknowable. They accept only the knowledge that unreliable senses, variable consciences, and finite little brains can learn. That's a pretty narrow view of reality.

We know our limitations. That's why we depend on a revelation from above. We don't accept it naively, and we use our brains to interpret it and apply it. But we must be humble enough to realize we didn't come up with it. God's Word is an act of God. We would not have known Him in any coherent detail unless He had revealed Himself. And what a revelation! It makes marvelous sense to those who embrace it by faith.

IN DEED   Don't be intimidated by your agnostic friends. The biblical witness is clear: Unbelieving minds are usually masks that hide a desire to disobey God. They are an easy excuse for immorality and rebellion. But they are foolishness. They turn their back on divine mysteries in order to cling to a feeble and faulty human wisdom. There is nothing reliable or eternal about their frame of reference. It will end in disaster.

Rather than be intimidated, live your life of faith in front of your agnostic friends. The fruit of the Spirit has a way of refuting hostile beliefs. It is clearly from above. Let your life always point in that direction.

An Intellectual Assault

There is no wisdom, no insight, no plan that can succeed against the LORD. PROVERBS 21:30

IN WORD Intellectual pride has been dressed up and presented charmingly throughout all generations. From the philosophies of ancient Greece to the sophistry of modern academics, men and women have speculated about who God ought to be. There is a fine line between making honest, intellectual inquiry and raising human reasoning to be infallible, and we have crossed it often. We tag our intellectual eras with names like "The Age of Reason," "The Enlightenment," and other such misnomers. All the while, we forget how limited are our senses and how unreliable are our thoughts.

The assumption underlying much religious philosophy is that revelation is a myth, and if we are to know anything at all, it must be from our own investigation. That approach resigns the human race to a long, twisted path to truth that may lead us there on some occasions but will lead us far away on others. In short, it gives up on the knowable God.

The sophisticates of our age seem to think they are an intellectual match for God, challenging—even rejecting—His wisdom at nearly every point. Biblical morality? Outdated and irrelevant. The nature of God? Unbalanced and far too harsk. The identity of the church? A gross overestimation. These are the biases that have been thoroughly integrated into our culture, influencing our media and dominating our universities.

IN DEED Do you want to be wise? Take everything you hear with a grain of salt and cling to divine revelation. The human mind is given by its Creator to learn from Him, not to overthrow Him. Surely we must know deep within that we are ill equipped to discover truth. But the Word of God— there's the living Truth. It is powerful and exalting. Breathe it, eat it, drink it, sleep on it, hold it tight. There is nothing deeper, nothing more reliable to be found.

DECEMBER 29
Proverbs 21:30;
Romans 9:20

Human salvation demands the divine disclosure of truths surpassing reason.

—Thomas Aquinas

Majestic Wisdom

How precious to me are your thoughts, O God! How vast is the sum of them!   PSALM 139:17

DECEMBER 30
Psalm 139

The whole science of the saints consists in finding out and following God's will.

—Isidore of Seville

IN WORD   We're amazed at the planning put into a successful event or a work of art. We can't comprehend the talent required to write or perform a musical masterpiece or to dazzle spectators with precise acrobatic leaps. We're mystified by scientific insights and the human ingenuity that has gotten us far out of our own atmosphere. We're legitimately but easily impressed.

Yet we rarely appreciate our Creator as much as we appreciate human accomplishment. Perhaps we're caught up in some lie about a universe of randomness. Or maybe we're just too overwhelmed to begin to comprehend the Creation. But dwell on the complexity of our world. Think about the amazingly intricate relationships between plant and animal, cell and atom, or galaxy and space. The complex symbiosis between all the elements in our universe is utterly staggering. The development of even one human brain—much less billions—is beyond our understanding. The mathematical regularities of creation are inexplicable to human reasoning. The codings of our DNA, our Scriptures, and our cultures all point to a dazzling, brilliant, unfathomable Intelligence. God is a Master of design.

Think about that. Our God is the Creator both of macro-majesties and micro-marvels. Scientists tell us that all matter in the known universe at one time was pressed into one tiny ball of unimaginable density. The Bible tells us that God spoke, and that matter was formed and distributed by His word. It's more than we can ever take in.

IN DEED   But there's more to the Creator's purposes than this sense of awe we feel. This marvelous master Craftsman wove us together and ordained our days. He didn't just throw this world into being; He breathed His creativity into us. Every one of us. Individually.

Knowing that, doesn't His every thought become our holy passion? Don't we need to treasure His ways? Could there ever be any greater pursuit than the wisdom of God?

In Pursuit of Truth

Buy the truth and do not sell it; get wisdom, discipline and understanding. PROVERBS 23:23

IN WORD The world is full of counsel. People offer advice openly, sometimes solicited, sometimes not. Firms pay thousands—even millions, in some cases—for consultations with experts in their particular field. And it is all about predicting the future. Some circles call it "risk management." We want to base our decisions on what is likely to happen next. Whether we are seeking a greater income, a different work, a new relationship, or any other future endeavor, we plan to succeed. We want to hedge our bets and set ourselves in security.

The problem with our plans is that they rarely get us very far. The vagaries of human reasoning will not always set us on the right path. Why? Because when it comes down to it, none of us knows what will happen in the future. We may plan and save according to all conventional counsel and yet fall flat on our faces in the end. We do not hold the future in our hands. We do not hold the will of God in our hearts. And we do not hold His wisdom in our minds. At least not at first.

That's why we must live our lives by feeding on God's daily bread. His Word must come to us regularly, frequently, and repeatedly. It must be driven into our minds and embraced by our hearts. At all costs, at any sacrifice, we must "buy the truth" and not sell it. The counsel of Solomon is on target. There is nothing more valuable than being able to make decisions based on the knowledge of the Omniscient.

IN DEED Many a movie or TV show has featured someone who got a glimpse of a future newspaper, a prophecy, or a vision. The usual plot is of thwarting disaster or becoming wealthy with such knowledge. But God does not usually reveal to us our tomorrows. He only reveals to us what we need to know to live them well.

We can't know the future, but we can have the wisdom of the One who does. That's just as good. It requires faith, not sight, to walk in such wisdom, but that's the whole point. We are drawn into a living, daily relationship with the only wise God. Buy His truth, and never let it go.

DECEMBER 31
Proverbs 23:22-25

What is offered to man's apprehension . . . is not truth concerning God, but the living God Himself.

—William Temple

TOPICAL INDEX

Absolutes.........................March 1

Acceptance .... May 13, October 20, October 21

Accountability................ February 24

Action ....April 29, June 9, October 30

Adversity.................. July 29, July 31, September 16

Advice.............. June 27, September 5

Anxiety.........June 4, June 14, August 28

Appearances ....July 25–26

Applying God's Word........... January 15

Approval .... February 7

Authenticity ....November 4–8

Beatitudes ....August 13–20

Bible .... February 1, May 17, July 1–3, December 29

Bitterness .... December 15

Body of Christ................... April 22, September 30, October 17

Boldness .... October 8–9

Caution .... January 16–17, May 10

Change .... July 5, July 26

Choices .... January 29, October 19, November 29–30

Christlikeness .... August 8, August 12, November 1–3

Church....................... October 17

Community......June 26–27, September 30, October 17, October 31

Comparison....................... July 9

Compassion.............. April 9, June 11, July 18, August 9

Conflict .... August 26

Conformity .... February 7, October 9

Conscience....................... July 19

Consequences .... April 2

Consistency.................... March 7

Contentment.......... January 24, May 25, September 4, September 12, September 22

Control .... August 1, August 4

Counsel.................... September 5

Creation.................... December 30

Crisis....................... August 3–5

Death....... November 28, November 30

Debt......................... January 31

Delighting in God............. July 20–21

Depending on God .. February 14, March 16, July 12, July 28, November 17

Desires.......... May 1, July 22, August 16

Direction............... March 14, June 28

Discernment .... April 4, September 20

Discipline ...... February 20, March 19–20, October 4, December 10–19

Discouragement .... November 13

Dreams .... May 11

Dying to self .... November 21

Dying with Christ............. February 18

Emotions............. January 16, May 26

Encouragement................... May 20

End times .... September 29

Endurance...................... May 16

Enemies....................... April 6

Envy .... April 11, September 28

Eternal perspective .... January 12–13, February 26, March 4, March 12, March 29, April 30, May 2, July 10, August 11, September 29

Evangelism .... April 7

Fairness.......... April 21, June 13, July 29

Faith ....January 28, April 25, May 26–30, June 1, June 9, July 23–24, July 30, November 18, December 12

Faithfulness............ March 27, June 22,
 September 13
Fear............... January 12, October 1,
 December 11
Fearing God .... January 1, April 13,
 October 10
Fellowship.................... October 31
Flexibility .... April 3
Following God................. January 18
Fruit of the Spirit .... February 12,
 June 15–24
Fruitfulness.................. February 12
Generosity............... April 5, April 19
Gentleness....................... June 23
Giving................. March 18, June 10
Glorifying God .... January 21
God's care .... March 8
God's character .... March 30
God's eternal nature .... May 7
God's faithfulness .... January 26,
 July 15, September 21
God's glory .... July 14, August 5
God's love .... January 22, October 21
God's power.................... October 7
God's provision .... January 27, June 10,
 October 12
God's sovereignty ...... February 8, May 13,
 May 23, August 2
God's strength.................... July 28
God's timing .... July 6–9, September 19,
 October 3
God's will .... August 25, September 19,
 October 22
Godliness..................... January 26
Goodness....................... June 21
Grace.......... February 11, February 13,
 February 15, June 13,
 September 7
Gratitude............... November 24–27
Grief .... August 14, December 21
Guidance.......... January 4–5, January 7,
 February 9, August 29–30
Guilt .... July 19
Happiness .... December 20
Health .... March 16
Heart................ March 11, May 10,
 July 25, October 14
Heaven .... April 19
Holiness................ May 5–6, May 15,
 June 2–3, September 18
Honesty.............. January 9, May 13

Hope .... April 30, October 7,
 November 13, December 14
Hospitality .... November 14
Humility .... February 21, March 21–23,
 May 31, June 5, June 30,
 August 6, August 13,
 October 18, December 3
Hypocrisy .... November 4
Identity .... June 25, December 6–9
Idolatry .... November 19–23
Image of God...................... May 3
Incarnation . . December 22, December 24–26
Instruction ....August 7
Integrity ....March 25, July 26
Intentions ....April 28–29
Jesus .... December 27
Joy ....June 17, September 6, October 24
Judgment.................... February 24
Justice .... April 21, June 12
Kindness .... June 20
Knowing God ....April 3
Law .... February 11
Lies ....November 20
Living in the Spirit .....February 13, April 2,
 June 15
Lordship ....February 3, February 28
Love........ March 11, March 24, June 16,
 November 9, November 11,
 December 16
Loving God ....March 28
Materialism................... January 13
Meditation.................... October 27
Meekness......................August 15
Memorization .... October 28
Mercy .... January 25, April 21, June 11,
 August 7, September 23,
 September 25
Mind of Christ ..... January 3, March 21–23
Money..... January 31, March 3, March 17,
 May 2, August 23, August 31, September 1
Motives ....April 28–29, August 24
Mourning .... December 21
Need ....April 5
Negativity................... January 24
New self....... February 6, February 16–17,
 July 11, November 10
Obedience ....January 8, March 1,
 May 30, September 20, October 5,
 October 10, November 29
Occult .... May 28
Patience........January 10, April 1, June 19

Peace . . . . April 10, June 18, August 19, October 6

Permanence. . . . . September 26

Persecution . . . . August 20, October 25

Perseverance . . . . March 6, May 16

Perspective . . . . . . October 23, November 28

Persuasion. . . . . .March 26

Pessimism . . . . January 24

Planning . . . . December 1

Poverty . . . . April 9, July 18, August 22

Power . . . . December 18

Prayer . . January 10, January 25, February 2, March 26, June 29, July 17, August 21–22, August 25, October 22, October 26

Preparation . . . . December 23

Pride . . . March 26, April 12, June 5, June 30, August 6, December 3

Priorities . . . . . March 3–4, March 17, July 16

Prophecy . . . . October 4

Purification .March 5

Purity . . . . . .March 2, August 18, August 21

Purpose . . . May 3, December 1, December 5

Reason. . . . . May 27

Rebuke. February 20

Redemption . . . . .September 2

Refuge . . . . . . April 24, May 18, September 3

Regret . . . . May 23, October 6, December 13

Renewal. . . . . January 11

Repentance . . . . .April 23

Reputation. . . . . March 12

Resisting the devil. . . . . .March 31

Rest . . . . .September 9

Resurrected living. . . . . February 16–18

Rewards. . . . . .April 8

Righteousness . . . . . January 29, February 10, April 7, July 20, November 6

Rivalry .September 28

Sacrifice. . . . . January 14

Safety. . . . . September 10–11, October 2

Satan . . . . July 13–14, September 14, October 25

Security. . . . . May 21

Self-centeredness. . . . . March 15, June 6

Self-control . . . . June 24, September 7

Selfishness. . . . . February 5

Self-reliance. . . . . March 15, October 12

Separateness . . . . .September 14

Service. . . . . January 14, November 11

Shepherd . . . . . . September 25, December 24

Sin. . . . . February 15, April 20, May 5–9, August 21, August 27, September 24

Sovereignty .August 2

Spiritual gifts . . . . June 26

Spiritual growth . . . . . . .January 15, March 7, July 20, July 26

Spiritual warfare. . . . . .February 22, March 9, March 31, July 13, September 15

Submission . . . . January 5

Success . . . . January 30

Suffering . . . . March 8, April 22, May 16

Surrender . . . . .January 6, February 28

Temptation . . . . April 26–28, December 2

Testing. . . . . .March 5, July 29

Thankfulness. . . . . February 23, April 25

Thought life. . . . . April 4, November 8, December 19

Tongue. . . . .January 19, March 2, May 19–20

Transformation . . . . February 6

Trials . . . . . May 22, May 24, July 29, July 31, September 8, October 24, November 15

Trust . . . . February 8, February 19, March 13–14, May 12, May 18, May 21–22, June 10, September 11, October 1, October 5, October 11, November 7, November 17, November 22, December 4

Truth . . . . October 13–14

Unbelief. . . . . December 28

Unity. June 26, July 4

Victory. . . . . .February 22, September 15, September 17

Vindication . . . . October 11

Voice of God . . . . October 8

Waiting . . . . .April 1, June 28, July 27, September 19, October 3

Weakness. . . . . .February 14, July 28, September 17, December 17

Wisdom . . . . January 1, January 3, January 7–8, February 9, February 25–27, March 13, March 28, May 4, May 14, June 27, October 15, October 26–31, December 26, December 28–31

Wisdom from the cross . . . . .April 14–18

Words . . . . January 19, March 2, May 19–20, June 7–8, August 10, October 29

Work . . . . .February 3–4, September 27, December 5

World . . . . September 12–13, October 16

Worry . . . . .March 10, November 16

Worship. . . . . January 2, January 20, January 23, July 15, November 5

Zeal . . . . .November 12

SCRIPTURE INDEX

OLD TESTAMENT

Genesis 1:26-28 . . . . *May 3*
Genesis 3:1-7 . . . . *April 26–28*
Genesis 3:8-10 . . . . *December 11*
Genesis 50:20. . . . . *August 30*
Leviticus 26:14-17. . . . . *July 19*
Numbers 9:15-23. . . . . *April 3*
Numbers 24:10-14. . . . . *August 25*
Deuteronomy 30:19 . . . . *October 19,*
November 30
Joshua 3:9-17 . . . . *July 24*
Joshua 7:1-26 . . . . *September 18*
Joshua 23:6-11 . . . . *February 22*
Judges 3:1-4 . . . . *September 16*
Judges 7 . . . . *September 17*
Judges 21:25. . . . . *November 29*
1 Samuel 12:19-25. . . . . *June 29*
1 Samuel 13:5-15. . . . . *July 27*
1 Samuel 16:1-13. . . . . *July 25*
1 Samuel 26 . . . . *September 19*
2 Samuel 12:1-13. . . . . *April 23*
1 Kings 13:7-26 . . . . *September 20*
1 Kings 17:7-16 . . . . *June 10*
1 Kings 19:1-18 . . . . *July 12*
1 Chronicles 29:14-19 . . . . *July 26*
2 Chronicles 16 . . . . *November 17*
2 Chronicles 36:15-16 . . . . *October 4*
Ezra 8:21-23 . . . . *November 18*
Nehemiah 8:1-12. . . . . *June 17*
Job 1 . . . . *July 29*
Job 1:6-12 . . . . *July 13–14*
Job 1:13-22 . . . . *July 15–16*
Job 2:7-10 . . . . *February 8*
Job 13:13-19 . . . . *July 30*
Job 23:1-12 . . . . *March 5*
Job 31:24-28 . . . . *May 21*
Job 37 . . . . *July 31*
Job 38:1-21 . . . . *August 1*
Job 41:1-11 . . . . *June 13*

Job 42:1-6 . . . . *August 2*
Psalm 1. . . . . *February 11–12*
Psalm 3. . . . . *January 28*
Psalm 5:12 . . . . *January 26, June 6*
Psalm 7. . . . . *January 27*
Psalm 8. . . . . *October 23*
Psalm 9. . . . . *August 20*
Psalm 9:1-10 . . . . *May 12*
Psalm 14. . . . . *December 28*
Psalm 16. . . . . *September 3–6*
Psalm 18. . . . . *December 17–18*
Psalm 19. . . . . *March 2*
Psalm 23. . . . . *June 21*
Psalm 27. . . . . *October 1–3*
Psalm 31. . . . . *December 4*
Psalm 37:1-11. . . . . *August 15*
Psalm 37:30-40 . . . . *August 19*
Psalm 37:39-40 . . . . *April 24*
Psalm 38. . . . . *August 14*
Psalm 39:4-6 . . . . *November 28*
Psalm 40:1 . . . . *January 10*
Psalm 40:1-5 . . . . *February 19*
Psalm 41:1-3 . . . . *June 11*
Psalm 42. . . . . *August 16*
Psalm 49. . . . . *August 31, September 1–2*
Psalm 50. . . . . *April 25*
Psalm 51. . . . . *August 13, August 18*
Psalm 51:3-6 . . . . *March 25*
Psalm 55:4-8, 16-18. . . . . *May 16*
Psalm 55:16-23 . . . . *March 8–10*
Psalm 57. . . . . *January 20*
Psalm 62:5-10 . . . . *July 4*
Psalm 63:1-8 . . . . *October 21*
Psalm 65. . . . . *April 5*
Psalm 69:13-18 . . . . *January 25*
Psalm 71:1-3 . . . . *May 18*
Psalm 74. . . . . *August 3–5*
Psalm 78:9-16 . . . . *September 21*
Psalm 78:17-31 . . . . *September 22*

Psalm 78:32-39 . . . . *September 23*
Psalm 78:56-64 . . . . *September 24*
Psalm 78:65-72 . . . . *September 25*
Psalm 81:11-16. . . . . *January 5*
Psalm 82:3-4 . . . . *August 22*
Psalm 86. . . . . *May 15*
Psalm 89:1-8 . . . . *June 22*
Psalm 89:14-18 . . . . *January 23–24*
Psalm 90. *August 11*
Psalm 90:8 . . . . *August 27*
Psalm 91. . . . . *September 9–10*
Psalm 92:12-15 . . . . *September 11*
Psalm 96. . . . . *January 21*
Psalm 100. . . . . *February 23*
Psalm 105:1-7 . . . . *November 24–27*
Psalm 106:1-23 . . . . *June 28*
Psalm 107. . . . . *January 22*
Psalm 112. . . . . *July 20–22*
Psalm 119:9-16. . . . . . . *July 1, October 28–29*
Psalm 119:41-48. . . . . *July 3*
Psalm 119:49-56. . . . . *October 30*
Psalm 119:57-64. . . . . *October 31*
Psalm 119:97-104. . . . . *July 2*
Psalm 119:145-152. . . . . *October 27*
Psalm 119:169-176. . . . . *October 26*
Psalm 128:1-2 . . . . *April 13*
Psalm 139. . . . . *December 30*
Psalm 139:1-17 . . . . *May 13*
Psalm 139:23-24 . . . . *August 24*
Proverbs 1:20-33 . . . . *February 20*
Proverbs 1:33. . . . . *December 11*
Proverbs 2:6. . . . . *March 26*
Proverbs 3:1-12 . . . . *March 11–20*
Proverbs 3:13-18 . . . . *March 3*
Proverbs 3:34. . . . . *December 3*
Proverbs 4:1-9 . . . . *February 25–27*
Proverbs 4:20-27 . . . . *January 15–19, May 10*
Proverbs 5:21. . . . . *February 24*
Proverbs 6:20-29 . . . . *March 27*
Proverbs 7:2. . . . . *March 28*
Proverbs 8 . . . . *May 5–9*
Proverbs 9 . . . . *May 4*
Proverbs 9:10-12 . . . . *January 1*
Proverbs 9:17. . . . . *August 27*
Proverbs 10:3. . . . . *February 10*
Proverbs 10:19. . . . . *August 10*
Proverbs 10:29. . . . . *May 14*
Proverbs 11:2. . . . . *August 6*
Proverbs 11:6. . . . . *January 29*
Proverbs 11:17. . . . . *June 20*
Proverbs 12:2. . . . . *June 6*

Proverbs 12:11. . . . . *May 11*
Proverbs 12:15; 15:22 . . . . *June 27*
Proverbs 12:21. . . . . *May 22*
Proverbs 12:22. . . . . *January 9*
Proverbs 12:25. . . . . *June 14*
Proverbs 14:2. . . . . *March 1*
Proverbs 14:12. . . . . *November 29–30*
Proverbs 14:14. . . . . *April 8*
Proverbs 14:15. . . . . *December 10*
Proverbs 14:30. . . . . *April 10–11*
Proverbs 14:31. . . . . *April 9*
Proverbs 14:32. . . . . *May 18*
Proverbs 15:3. . . . . *May 13*
Proverbs 15:8-11 . . . . *November 5–8*
Proverbs 15:19. . . . . *October 19*
Proverbs 15:22. . . . . *June 27*
Proverbs 15:25. . . . . *December 3*
Proverbs 15:29. . . . . *August 21*
Proverbs 15:32. . . . . *October 4*
Proverbs 16:2. . . . . *August 24*
Proverbs 16:3. . . . . *January 30*
Proverbs 16:5. . . . . *April 12*
Proverbs 16:7. . . . . *February 1*
Proverbs 16:9. . . . . *August 29–30*
Proverbs 16:15. . . . . *October 20*
Proverbs 16:20. . . . . *August 7*
Proverbs 16:24. . . . . *June 7–8*
Proverbs 16:25. . . . . *April 26–28*
Proverbs 17:14. . . . . *August 26*
Proverbs 19:3. . . . . *February 5*
Proverbs 19:11. . . . . *June 19*
Proverbs 20:6. . . . . *March 7*
Proverbs 21:5. . . . . *December 1*
Proverbs 21:13. . . . . *August 22*
Proverbs 21:30. . . . . *December 29*
Proverbs 22:7. . . . . *January 31*
Proverbs 23:1-3 . . . . *December 2*
Proverbs 23:22-25 . . . . *December 31*
Proverbs 24:10. . . . . *July 28*
Proverbs 25:21-22 . . . . *April 6*
Proverbs 25:28. . . . . *June 24*
Proverbs 27:20. . . . . *May 25*
Proverbs 28:1. . . . . *July 19*
Proverbs 28:9. . . . . *February 2*
Proverbs 29:25. . . . . *February 7*
Proverbs 29:26. . . . . *June 12*
Proverbs 30:5. . . . . *May 17*
Ecclesiastes 1:1-11 . . . . *April 30, May 1*
Ecclesiastes 2:1-11 . . . . *May 2*
Ecclesiastes 3:1-8. . . . . *July 5–8*
Ecclesiastes 3:11 . . . . *July 9*

Ecclesiastes 3:12-13. . . . . *September 27*
Ecclesiastes 3:14 . . . . *September 26*
Ecclesiastes 4:1-3. . . . . *July 18*
Ecclesiastes 4:4 . . . . *September 28*
Ecclesiastes 4:9-12. . . . . *September 30*
Ecclesiastes 5:1-3. . . . . *July 17*
Ecclesiastes 6:7 . . . . *May 25*
Ecclesiastes 7:8-9. . . . . *June 19*
Ecclesiastes 7:13-14. . . . . *December 20*
Ecclesiastes 7:14 . . . . *December 21*
Ecclesiastes 7:20 . . . . *April 20*
Ecclesiastes 11:5-6. . . . . *March 30*
Song of Songs 2:1-4 . . . . *June 16*
Song of Songs 6:3 . . . . *March 24*
Isaiah 25:1 . . . . *December 1*
Isaiah 26:7-11. . . . . *May 24*
Isaiah 30:15-18. . . . . *February 21*
Isaiah 30:18 . . . . *June 12*
Isaiah 48:17-19. . . . . *October 5–6*
Isaiah 50:1-3. . . . . *October 7*
Isaiah 50:4-9. . . . . *October 8*
Isaiah 51:7-8. . . . . *October 9*
Isaiah 51:12-16. . . . . *October 10*
Isaiah 54:15-17. . . . . *October 11*
Isaiah 55:1-7. . . . . *October 12*
Isaiah 59:2 . . . . *February 2*
Jeremiah 6:13-15 . . . . *October 13*
Jeremiah 17:5-13 . . . . *October 14*
Lamentations 3:26 . . . . *April 1*
Daniel 2:19-23 . . . . *February 9*
Daniel 4:28-37 . . . . *May 31*
Daniel 12:1-4 . . . . *April 7*
Joel 2:21-27. . . . . *December 13*
Jonah 3:1–4:11 . . . . *August 17*
Micah 5:1-4 . . . . *December 24*

NEW TESTAMENT

Matthew 5:13-16 . . . . *December 6*
Matthew 7:24-27 . . . . *October 15*
Matthew 12:36. . . . . *August 10*
Matthew 16:24-27 . . . . *March 29*
Matthew 21:28-32 . . . . *May 11*
Matthew 24:36-51 . . . . *September 29*
Matthew 25:21. . . . . *October 20*
Mark 5:35-43 . . . . *December 12*
Mark 10:42-45 . . . . *January 14*
Luke 10:25-37 . . . . *August 9*
Luke 12:13-21 . . . . *January 13*
Luke 16:10-15 . . . . *August 23*
John 1:1-14. . . . . *December 22*
John 12:31 . . . . *September 15*
John 14:1-6. . . . . *August 12*

John 14:8-14. . . . . *August 8*
John 14:14 . . . . *October 22*
John 14:30 . . . . *September 15*
Acts 14:19-22 . . . . *September 8*
Acts 24:24-26 . . . . *September 7*
Romans 3:10-18. . . . . *April 20*
Romans 3:21-31. . . . . *August 28*
Romans 6:1-14. . . . . *February 15–17*
Romans 6:11 . . . . *February 18*
Romans 8:1-4. . . . . *December 25*
Romans 8:18 . . . . *July 9*
Romans 8:28-30. . . . . *June 25*
Romans 9:20 . . . . *December 29*
Romans 12:1-2. . . . . . . *January 2, January 11*
Romans 12:9-13. . . . . *November 9–14*
Romans 13:8 . . . . *January 31*
Romans 13:8-10. . . . . *December 16*
1 Corinthians 1:18-25 . . . . *December 26*
1 Corinthians 1:18-31 . . . . *April 14–16*
1 Corinthians 2:1-16 . . . . *April 17–18*
1 Corinthians 2:6-16 . . . . *January 3*
1 Corinthians 3:5-9 . . . . *December 9*
1 Corinthians 6:18-20 . . . . *January 6*
1 Corinthians 12:1-20 . . . . *June 26*
1 Corinthians 15:32. . . . . *March 4*
2 Corinthians 2:5-11 . . . . *March 31*
2 Corinthians 3:18. . . . . *August 7*
2 Corinthians 5:1-4 . . . . *April 19*
2 Corinthians 5:1-7 . . . . *May 26–30*
2 Corinthians 6:14–7:1 . . . . . *November 19–23*
2 Corinthians 10:4-5 . . . . *December 19*
2 Corinthians 12:7-10 . . . . *February 14*
2 Corinthians 12:9-10 . . . . *July 28*
Galatians 2:19-20. . . . . *November 1–2*
Galatians 3:1-5. . . . . *February 13*
Galatians 3:22-29. . . . . *June 1*
Galatians 3:26–4:7. . . . . *December 8*
Galatians 4:4-7. . . . . *December 23*
Galatians 5:16-26. . . . . *June 15*
Galatians 5:16-26; 6:7-8 . . . . *April 2*
Galatians 6:1-5. . . . . *November 4*
Ephesians 2:1-10 . . . . *December 7*
Ephesians 4:17-24 . . . . *February 6*
Philippians 1:6 . . . . *September 26*
Philippians 2:1-11 . . . . *March 21–23*
Philippians 2:3 . . . . *September 28*
Philippians 3:12-14. . . . . *May 23*
Philippians 4:4-5. . . . . *June 23*
Philippians 4:4-7. . . . . *June 4*
Philippians 4:6 . . . . *June 14*
Philippians 4:8-9. . . . . *April 4*

Colossians 3:1-2 . . . . *December 10*
Colossians 3:1-10 . . . . *July 10–11*
Colossians 3:12 . . . . *June 20*
Colossians 3:15-17 . . . . *June 18*
Colossians 3:16 . . . . *May 17,*
October 17
Colossians 3:23-25 . . . . *February 3–4,*
December 5
Colossians 4:6 . . . . *June 7–8*
2 Timothy 1:7. . . . . *June 24*
2 Timothy 2:23-24. . . . . *August 26*
2 Timothy 3:10-15. . . . . *October 25*
2 Timothy 3:12. . . . . *February 1*
2 Timothy 4:16-18. . . . . *November 16*
Hebrews 11:1, 6. . . . . *July 23*
Hebrews 11:8-10 . . . . *January 12*
Hebrews 12:1-11 . . . . *November 15*
Hebrews 12:14-15. . . . . *December 15*
Hebrews 13:1-3. . . . . *April 22*
James 1:2-4. . . . . *October 24*
James 1:2-7. . . . . *January 7–8*
James 1:5-8. . . . . *October 22*

James 1:9-11. . . . . *June 30*
James 1:22-25. . . . . *June 9*
James 2:8-13. . . . . *April 21*
James 2:14-17. . . . . *April 29*
James 3:1-12. . . . . *May 19–20*
James 3:13-18. . . . . *June 5*
James 4:4-6. . . . . *September 13*
James 4:13-17. . . . . *August 29*
James 5:7-11. . . . . *March 6*
James 5:16 . . . . *August 21*
1 Peter 1:13-16. . . . . *June 2–3*
1 Peter 1:13-21. . . . . *December 14*
1 Peter 3:15-16. . . . . *February 28*
1 Peter 5:5 . . . . *August 6*
1 Peter 5:5-6. . . . . *April 12*
1 Peter 5:5-7. . . . . *October 18*
1 John 2:3-6 . . . . *November 3*
1 John 2:15-17 . . . . *September 12*
1 John 3:11-16 . . . . *October 16*
1 John 5:18-20 . . . . *September 14*
Jude 1:17-21. . . . . *January 4*
Revelation 1:9-18 . . . . *December 27*

Begin a Daily
Habit That Will
Change Your Life

Reading the *Daily Walk Bible* will...

> Help you read the entire Bible in 365 days
> Lead you to wisdom
> Lift your burdens
> Guide your steps
> Bring you joy and peace
> Help you understand God's plan for His people
> Bring you back to God!

The *Daily Walk Bible* makes reading the Bible easy, enjoyable, and insightful. Through masterful tools interspersed throughout the Scripture you will discover a new level of understanding and intimacy with God. The chapter overviews, "insight" sections, charts, devotionals, and weekly recaps will help you read and live the Word like never before—and it will change your life!

SPECIAL PRICING!
20% off per copy OR
40% off per case

Use the *Daily Walk Bible* for personal reading, family devotionals, character studies, and as a small group discussion guide. Makes a perfect gift! Help others begin a new habit that will change their life!

Available in NIV and NLT Translations (Hard or Soft Cover)

www.walkthru.org • 1-800-361-6131

WALK
THRU THE
BIBLE
TAKE A WALK. CHANGE THE WORLD.

CP0108